Ruby for Rails

Ruby for Rails

RUBY TECHNIQUES FOR RAILS DEVELOPERS

DAVID A. BLACK

MANNING

Greenwich
(74° w. long.)

For online information and ordering of this and other Manning books, please visit
www.manning.com. The publisher offers discounts on this book when ordered in
quantity. For more information, please contact:

Special Sales Department
Manning Publications Co.
209 Bruce Park Avenue   Fax:(203) 661-9018
Greenwich, CT 06830   email: manning@manning.com

 Manning Publications Co.   Copyeditor: Liz Welch
209 Bruce Park Avenue   Typesetter: Gordan Salinovic
Greenwich, CT 06830   Cover designer: Leslie Haimes

ISBN 1932394699

Printed in the United States of America
1 2 3 4 5 6 7 8 9 10 – VHG – 10 09 08 07 06

```
for n in nephews + nieces
```

which is to say: Annie, David, Elizabeth, Rebecca, and Robert,
with all my love. You're all absolutely amazing, and I adore you.

brief contents

contents

ix

foreword

I can't learn a language for the sake of it. I need to have a concrete desire to do something with it—to solve a problem or a task, to create something of value... That's how I got into Ruby around the summer of 2003. I wanted to build a Web application and decided this was the perfect opportunity to learn Ruby. That Web application was Basecamp, which eventually served as the point of extraction for Rails.

Coming from PHP and Java, I remember how many of Ruby's most wonderful features seemed odd at first. "What is it exactly that makes blocks so special?" I thought. "They're just convenience for writing a line of code at the beginning and the end." Little did I know... As I started using Ruby and extracting Rails, I quickly wised up. Ruby is such an incredibly rich and expressive language that it's hard to appreciate its beauty by simply relating it to past experiences with other languages.

To create Basecamp, I needed to live and breathe Ruby. And when I did, I kept finding aspects of the language that were exactly what I needed for the situation at hand. Tasks that would have made my eyes roll in PHP or Java made my smile light up as Ruby time and time again showed that programming could be simple, fun, and outright beautiful.

As I was learning the language, I often consulted the ruby-talk mailing list. One voice in particular seemed to know Ruby well and appeared to have the ambition as well as the ability to help others understand it more fully. That voice belonged to David A. Black, the author of this book.

David clearly has an encyclopedic knowledge of Ruby. Not only does he understand how to use it, but he can also explain why things are the way they are. He connects the dots and allows you to see the bigger picture, providing the missing piece that turns puzzle into picture. I couldn't imagine a better person to write *Ruby for Rails*. It's a great honor to have the man who taught me so much about Ruby now help others understand the language for use with my framework.

This is the book that everyone coming from another language to Rails should have. To fully realize the potential of Rails, it's crucial that you take the time to fully understand Ruby—and with *Ruby for Rails* David has provided just what you need to help you achieve that goal.

DAVID HEINEMEIER HANSSON
Creator of Ruby on Rails
Partner at 37signals

preface

When the editors at Manning asked me whether I thought the time was ripe for a new Ruby book, and if so, what it should be about and who should write it, I answered:

"Yes.... A Ruby language book purpose-written for Rails practitioners.... Me."
They agreed.

I warmly welcomed the opportunity. I'd been thinking along "Ruby for Rails" lines since I started using the Ruby on Rails framework in the Fall of 2004 (which, by the way, makes me an almost-early adopter). Rails had been first released that summer, and I learned about it from the presentation by David Heinemeier Hansson, the creator of Rails, at the 2004 International Ruby Conference.

Ruby for Rails sounds like it might mean "...as opposed to regular Ruby," a tool for dividing Ruby users into Rails and non-Rails camps. I saw it as the opposite: real Ruby, regular Ruby, on its own terms, but studied primarily because of what it can do for Rails developers. I was in a good position to understand the potential of this approach: I'd been programming in Ruby for almost four years before I started using Rails; and when I did start using it, I quickly gained a view of how a deeper knowledge of Ruby could help Rails programmers achieve their goals.

An alarm went off in my head, therefore, when I saw how many budding Rails developers were asking themselves whether it was necessary to learn Ruby in order to use Rails. The fact that this question was the subject of disagreement and debate surprised me. And it suggested a couple of points.

First, there was clearly room for education about the basics: that Rails is written in Ruby, and Rails applications are written in Ruby, so if you're writing Rails applications, you've *already decided* to use Ruby. Second, I could see the beginnings of an inadvertent, self-imposed quarantine on the part of these Rails developers (who were perfectly well-intentioned, but not in possession of the full picture) and I saw that something could and should be done about it. People were talking themselves into living under a glass ceiling, where they could get Rails applications to run and do some reasonably adroit things with Rails techniques and idioms, but where they were denying themselves the chance to deploy the full power of Ruby—the language which they were in fact already using. That needed to be addressed.

I also noticed a large number of questions in various forums (and various forms) along the lines of "I know I'm supposed to write `belongs_to :customer`, but what *is* that?" A number of Rails users told me that they were able to get applications up and running by imitating and adapting lines of code from other applications, but they were finding it unsatisfying because they didn't feel they knew what was going on. The fact that people were having trouble understanding Rails code in Ruby terms meant that they were not in a position to go to the next level: using the full power of Ruby to enhance and extend the functionality of their Rails applications.

It occurred to me that a Rails-centric Ruby language tutorial could serve the dual roles of, first, explaining to Rails developers who didn't yet see that Ruby and Rails don't reside in separate silos but, rather, enjoy a parent/child technology relationship with extremely open lines of communication; and, second, smashing the glass ceiling that separated Rails people from using Ruby more effectively.

As the book project got under way, my goal became to explain that the learning of Ruby by a "Rails person" is an entirely additive, win-win proposition. It doesn't mean Rails has some deficiency that has to be compensated for by knowing a foreign technology. Rather, Rails has a tremendous strength—the strength of having been written in an elegant, concise, very approachable programming language—the implications of which for day-to-day Rails programming are important and are a pleasure to explore.

Thus *Ruby for Rails*: a reaffirmation and explanation of the way things stand, and have always stood, between the language and the framework, and an invitation to shatter that glass ceiling.

acknowledgments

This book has benefited from support of many kinds from many quarters.

At Manning Publications, assistant acquisitions editor Megan Yockey and publisher's assistant Blaise Bace saw me ably and enthusiastically through the proposal and contract phases of the project. I worked initially, and productively, with development editor Doug Bennett; subsequently, for reasons of scheduling and logistics, my project was reassigned to development editor Lianna Wlasiuk, who worked with me in an intense, sustained way through the writing of the book, coupling a marvelous collegiality with a gentle but firm refusal to settle for anything other than a strong, polished product.

Review editor Karen Tegtmeyer sought, and found, specialists from both the Ruby and Rails spheres to review the manuscript at the various prescribed phases of partial completion—a process I like to think I became less surly about, the more evidence I saw of how materially helpful it could be. Book designer Dottie Marsico worked with me on the illustrations; I have Dottie to thank for my newfound OpenOffice Draw skills as well as for her encouragement and quick responsiveness to questions and concerns.

As the book moved through the latter stages of preparation and into the production stages, I had the indispensable support and help of production director Mary Piergies, who coordinated the geographically far-flung process in a way that brought it unity and momentum. To copy editor Tiffany Taylor I can pay no greater tribute than to say that I quickly got into the habit of telling OpenOffice to hide the history of changes in the document and only show me the text as it appeared after Tiffany had worked on it. I have no doubt, moreover, that several trees owe their lives to Tiffany's ability to trim away excess verbiage.

Technical proofreader Bruce Williams made numerous suggestions and corrections which, I can assure readers, have measurably improved the readability of the code samples as well as the text. There's nothing like a keen second set of eyes, and a second tester, to convince one, once and for all, that one *really* must not make little changes to code after cutting-and-pasting it in….

I worked with three proofreaders. Elizabeth R. Martin, who kindly stepped in to tide the project over during a scheduling gap, brought a sharp eye to bear on the book's first chapters. The balance of the manuscript was proofread by Elizabeth Welch, on whom I have relied not only for error-catching but for constant consultation in discretionary matters of typographical consistency and style. Barbara Mirecki gave the manuscript a close, skillful final read. Katie Tennant brought a professional's skill and care to bear on my well-intentioned, but inevitably imperfect, indexing efforts. Typesetter Gordan Salinovic has worked diligently and responsively with us to ensure a consistent, reader-friendly look.

Manning webmaster Iain Shigeoka worked behind the scenes to keep the information flow going among the various members of the production team and me, and quickly stepped up to help on the few occasions when glitches cropped up.

On the marketing side, Manning's sales and marketing chief Ron Tomich and marketing director Helen Trimes have kept the book before the Ruby/Rails public eye and have sought my input and collaboration throughout the process. As much as the popularity of Ruby and Rails can help, there's no such thing as a book that promotes itself, and Helen and Ron have been anything but complacent in getting the word out.

Last but by no means least among the members of the Manning team to whom I offer my thanks is publisher Marjan Bace, who saw the viability of this project quickly, supported it unreservedly, and piloted it skillfully through many ups and a sprinkling of downs. Both the book and I benefited from Marjan's availability, attentiveness, and mastery of the contours of the publication landscape.

I'd like to thank the reviewers of the original book proposal and all of the outside readers who participated in the various partial-manuscript review cycles. Many of the comments and criticisms of the latter group had more of an impact on the book than they themselves might have anticipated. Thanks go to Anjan Bacchu, Christopher Bailey, Jamis Buck, Stuart Caborn, Tom Copeland, Ryan Cox, Jeff Cunningham, Pat Dennis, Mark Eagle, Sasa Ebach, Shaun Fanning, Hal Fulton, Benjamin Gorlick, Erik Hatcher, David Heinemeier Hansson, Jack Herrington, Bob Hutchison, Duane Johnson, Albert Koscielny, Robert McGovern, Andrew

Oswald, George Peter, Michael Schubert, Nicholas Seckar, Jon Skeet, Dave Steinberg, Mike Stok, Jon Tirsen, Wayne Vucenic, Doug Warren, Mark Watson, and two anonymous reviewers.

I owe a lot to the subscribers to the Manning Early Access Program (MEAP) version of the book, who spotted and reported a nontrivial number of nontrivial errors while the text was still fluid enough to take corrections. I won't name them here (their reports are posted at the Author Online Forum at http://www.manning.com/black) but my thanks go to each and every one of them.

I have been using Ruby for more than five years and Rails since a few months after its first release. I have many, many friends and colleagues in the collective Ruby/Rails sphere, a number of whom have helped in one way or another with bringing this project to fruition. My friend and Ruby Central co-director Chad Fowler, a constant presence in my Ruby world (and my AIM window), has supported me with advice, encouragement, a sympathetic ear, and a critical eye, throughout the book's evolution. I first learned the rudiments of Rails in a surreptitious private IRC chat with David Heinemeier Hansson during a conference presentation we were both ostensibly listening to (and maybe David was); as I've worked on *Ruby for Rails*, David has been a strong supporter of the project as well as a gracious adviser on technical matters. He has also kindly provided the book with its foreword.

I've also benefited from help and expressions of interest from many participants on mailing lists and IRC channels, as well as fellow Rubyists I've met at conferences and user group meetings—too many people to list, as the cliché goes, but I must mention Marcel Molina and Wayne Vucenic; the members of the New York Ruby Users Group, especially Sebastian Delmont, Conor Hunt, Francis Hwang, Gianni Jacklone, Matt Pelletier, and Zed Shaw; the members of both the London and Denver Ruby Users Groups, who invited me to speak about my work in progress; and the denizens of the #ruby-lang channel on irc.freenode.net, with whom I have had a (mostly) delightful nonstop five-year conversation. If anyone feels unjustly left out of this undoubtedly partial list, please hit me up for a drink at the next conference.

My family has been enthusiastic and supportive from day one of the project, following its progress in depth in spite of the book's remoteness from any of their areas of interest. Thanks and love go to Barbara Aronstein Black, Gavin Black, Robin Black, Richard Goldberg, Laurie Schafer, and the book's dedicatees.

I've received help, feedback, input, and guidance throughout the book-writing process. Nonetheless, any factual or technical errors, or misjudgments of style, are my responsibility alone.

about this book

Welcome to *Ruby for Rails*. This book is an introduction to the Ruby programming language, purpose-written for people whose main reason for wanting to know Ruby is that they're working with, or are interested in working with, the Ruby on Rails framework and want to do Rails knowledgeably and right.

Ruby is a general-purpose, object-oriented, interpreted programming language designed and written by Yukihiro Matsumoto (known widely as "Matz"). Introduced in 1994, Ruby rose rapidly in popularity among Japanese programmers. By the early 2000s, more than twenty Japanese-language books on Ruby had been published. The first English-language book on Ruby, *Programming Ruby* by Dave Thomas and Andy Hunt, appeared in late 2000 and ushered in a wave of Ruby enthusiasm outside of Japan. Ruby's popularity in the West has grown steadily since the appearance of the "Pickaxe book" (the nickname of the Thomas-Hunt work, derived from its cover illustration).

But 2004 saw a second massive surge of interest, with the introduction of the Ruby on Rails Web application framework by David Heinemeier Hansson. Built on a cluster of separate component libraries, the Rails framework handles database storage and retrieval, HTML templating, and all the middle-layer work necessary to connect the underlying data to the Web pages and input forms that display and update it.

Rails has grown very rapidly in popularity, gaining a solid, wide reputation as a tremendously powerful development tool. Partly cause, partly effect, Ruby has also drawn favorable attention and interest from more and more programmers in a variety of fields.

Do you have to learn Ruby to use Rails?

Although the Ruby on Rails framework is written in Ruby, it feels in some respects like a programming language unto itself. There are Rails idioms and conventions, just as there are Ruby idioms and conventions. The process of writing Rails applications has a characteristic rhythm and feel that aren't the same as the rhythm and feel of other Ruby-based environments. (Those are nice, too. They're just different.)

Nonetheless, Ruby is the underlying, parent technology of Rails. When you're working on a Rails program, you are, by definition, working on a Ruby program. It follows logically that the more you know about Ruby, the better you will be—the better you *can* be—at developing applications with Rails.

Even if you know little or no Ruby, you can probably get a Rails application up and running just by copying what others have done. But you won't really understand it, and you certainly won't be in a position to solve problems when they arise, nor to keep up knowledgeably with changes and updates in the Rails framework.

To do those things, you need a Ruby foundation. That's what this book—written specifically for you, the Rails enthusiast who wants to do it right—will give you. *Ruby for Rails* is a Ruby how-to book, more than a Rails how-to book. That doesn't mean you shouldn't read Rails how-to books too. But if you're serious about Rails, you should learn at least as much Ruby as this book contains.

How Ruby can help you, in more detail

A solid grounding in Ruby can serve you, as a Rails developer, in four ways:

- By helping you know what the code in your application (including Rails boilerplate code) is doing
- By helping you do more in, and with, your Rails applications than you can if you limit yourself to the readily available Rails idioms and techniques (as powerful as those are)
- By allowing you to familiarize yourself with the Rails source code, which in turn enables you to participate in discussions about Rails and perhaps even submit bug reports and code patches
- By giving you a powerful tool for administrative and organization tasks (for example, legacy code conversion) connected with your application

The last item on this list gets the least attention in this book. The third item, familiarizing yourself with the Rails source code, gets occasional mention and then a whole chapter (chapter 17, the last in the book) to itself.

It's the first two items—knowing what your code does, and knowing how to do more—that drive the book. Virtually everything you'll see here is designed to contribute to one or both of those goals. They may not always be on the front burner, as we dig into some of the details and subtleties of Ruby syntax or puzzle over fine points of domain modeling. But the Ruby syntax, and the code that arises from the domain modeling, and all the rest of it—it's all in the book to help you know what you're doing and learn how to do more, as a Rails practitioner, through a deeper knowledge of the Ruby language.

How this book is organized

Ruby for Rails consists of 17 chapters and is divided into four parts. Parts 2 and 3 are closely linked, so there are really three "super-parts":

- Part 1, "The Ruby/Rails landscape"
- Part 2, "Ruby building-blocks" and part 3, "Built-in classes and modules"
- Part 4, "Rails through Ruby, Ruby through Rails"

The book takes a breadth-first approach to its topic(s). Part 1 provides an overview of the programming environment of Ruby and Rails. This part includes a medium level of detail, but it's detailed enough to include the creation of a working Rails application as well as a considerable amount of introductory Ruby material. Parts 2 and 3 perform two functions. First, they do the lion's share of the book's nuts-and-bolts teaching of Ruby; the chapters in these parts are where you'll find a real Ruby tutorial. Second, while this tutorial is going on, the chapters in parts 2 and 3 keep in close contact with Rails. Examples are drawn from Rails applications, both real and (where it makes more sense) hypothetical, as well as from the Rails source code. In addition to giving you a "for Rails" perspective on Ruby in the process of learning Ruby, this infusion of Rails awareness into the Ruby tutorial looks ahead to part 4. In the final part, the book returns to the sample application developed in part 1, revising and augmenting it by deploying Ruby techniques mastered in the tutorial sections in the middle of the book.

As the book proceeds, the center of gravity shifts back and forth between the Ruby language and the Rails framework. But wherever the center of gravity lies in a particular chapter or part of the book, both components of the landscape—Ruby and Rails—are present to some degree.

Who should read this book

Rails application development is attracting a growing population—a rather motley crew, consisting not only of career programmers but also of system administrators, project managers, Web designers, database experts, and other computer practitioners.

This book is of potential interest to all of them. You don't have to be a programmer by trade to benefit from this book, although you do need a grasp of the basic concept of writing and running a computer program. You also need an understanding of some common underlying concepts of computer and Internet systems, many of which will be referred to without detailed explanation. You need to know, for example, what a server is, what a client is; what HTML is; the concept of a shell and a command line; about files and directory layouts; the basics of how Web clients and servers talk to each other, including the basics of CGI-based form processing; and the function and purpose of a database.

Finally, you need to know at least something about the Rails framework. You don't have to be a grizzled Rails veteran; you can use this book as part of your growth as a Rails developer. But you should have a sense of the realm in which Rails operates—or, if you're really new to Rails, be willing to combine this book with other sources of information to get the combined picture by working on several fronts.

If you meet all of these requirements, the material in this book should be accessible and the learning curve comfortable. In short: If you think of yourself as a Rails person and would also like to bring out your inner Ruby person, this book is for you. You'll be rewarded not only with a dramatically greater understanding of Rails but also with the beginnings of expertise in a very attractive, adaptable, and popular programming language.

What this book doesn't include

This book is largely tutorial and explanatory. It is neither a complete Ruby reference work nor a complete Rails reference work. Decisions have been made as to what does and does not need to be included in a book whose purpose is to make the power of Ruby more easily accessible to Rails practitioners. This isn't to say that you'll never find, say, Ruby threads or a benchmark library or the Tk API useful. They're just not on the "A-list" of goals for this book; and the A-list will give you a full book's worth of material to learn, think about, and try out.

The book includes the development of a working Rails application (actually, two versions of it, tailored for different points in the book) as well as a lot of Ruby code. It does not, however, take you through everything you can and should do in the course of developing a real-world application. The biggest task in that category is probably *testing*. Please don't interpret the absence of information about code testing in this book as a position statement against testing: You should learn how to test code, and you should test code.

Code conventions

In the text, names of Ruby variables and constants are in `monospace`. Names of classes and modules are in `monospace` where they represent direct references to existing class or module objects; for example, "Next, we'll reopen the class definition block for `Composer`." Where the name of a class or module is used in a more high-level narrative sense, the name appears in regular type; for example, "The domain will include a Composer class." In all cases, you'll be able to tell from the context that a class, module, or other Ruby entity is under discussion.

Names of directories and files are in `monospace`. Names of programs, such as `ruby` and `rails`, are in monospace where reference is made directly to the program executable or to command-line usage; otherwise, they appear in regular type.

Names of relational database tables and fields appear in *italics*.

Technical terms, on first mention, appear in *italics*. Italics are used for wildcard expressions, such as *entity*`_controller.rb`, which indicates a file name with an "entity" component plus an underscore and the remaining text. A matching filename would be, for example, `composer_controller.rb`.

Code examples

The standalone code samples in the book can be run either by placing them in a text file and running the `ruby` command on them, or by typing them into the interactive Ruby interpreter irb. (Both of these techniques are explained in chapter 1.) Toward the beginning of the book, you'll be walked through the process of creating and naming program files and saving code samples in them. As the book progresses, it will assume that you can do this on your own. Only if it really matters—including, of course, in connection with the actual Rails applications you'll develop—will specific filenames for examples be suggested after the first few.

A considerable number of examples in the book, particularly in part 3 (Ruby built-ins), are presented in the form of irb (Interactive Ruby) sessions. What you'll see on the page are cut-and-pasted lines from a live interactive session, where the code was entered into irb and irb responded by running the code. You'll be alerted the first few times this format is used and when it reappears after a hiatus. You'll also come to recognize it easily (especially if you start using irb). This mode of presentation is particularly suitable for short code snippets and expressions; and because irb always prints out the results of executing whatever you type in (rather like a calculator), it lets you see results while economizing on explicit print commands.

In other cases, the output from code samples is printed separately after the samples, printed alongside the code (and clearly labeled as "output"), or embedded in the discussion following the appearance of the code.

Some examples are accompanied by numbered cueballs that appear to the side of the code. These cueballs are linked to specific points in the ensuing discussion and give you a way to refer quickly to the line to which the discussion refers.

Command-line program invocations are shown with a dollar-sign ($) prompt, in the general style of shell prompts in UNIX-like environments. The commands will work on Windows, even though the prompt may be different. (In all environments, the availability of the commands depends, as always, on the setting of the relevant path environment variable.)

Code downloads

The complete source code for both versions of the music store Rails application is available for download from the publisher's Web site at http://www.manning.com/black. These downloads include SQL command files with which you can initialize the database tables for the applications and populate those database with some sample data. Also available for download are some of the longer code samples from the book that are not connected with the music store application.

Author Online

Purchase of *Ruby for Rails* includes free access to a private Web forum run by Manning Publications where you can make comments about the book, ask technical questions, and receive help from the authors and from other users. To access the forum and subscribe to it, point your Web browser to http://www.manning.com/black. This page provides information on how to get on the forum once you are registered, what kind of help is available, and the rules of conduct on the forum.

Manning's commitment to our readers is to provide a venue where a meaningful dialogue between individual readers and between readers and the author can take place. It is not a commitment to any specific amount of participation on the part of the author, whose contribution to the book's forum remains voluntary (and unpaid). We suggest you try asking the author some challenging questions, lest his interest stray!

The Author Online forum and the archives of previous discussions will be accessible from the publisher's Web site as long as the book is in print.

about the cover illustration

The figure on the cover of *Ruby for Rails* is an "Officer of the Grand Signoir," or an officer in the army of the Ottoman Sultan. The illustration is taken from a collection of costumes of the Ottoman Empire published on January 1, 1802, by William Miller of Old Bond Street, London. The title page is missing from the collection and we have been unable to track it down to date. The book's table of contents identifies the figures in both English and French, and each illustration bears the names of two artists who worked on it, both of whom would no doubt be surprised to find their art gracing the front cover of a computer programming book...two hundred years later.

The collection was purchased by a Manning editor at an antiquarian flea market in the "Garage" on West 26th Street in Manhattan. The seller was an American based in Ankara, Turkey, and the transaction took place just as he was packing up his stand for the day. The Manning editor did not have on his person the substantial amount of cash that was required for the purchase and a credit card and check were both politely turned down. With the seller flying back to Ankara that evening the situation was getting hopeless. What was the solution? It turned out to be nothing more than an old-fashioned verbal agreement sealed with a handshake. The seller simply proposed that the money be transferred to him by wire and the editor walked out with the bank information on a piece of paper and the portfolio of images under his arm. Needless to say, we transferred the funds the next day, and we remain grateful and impressed by this unknown person's trust in one of us. It recalls something that might have happened a long time ago.

The pictures from the Ottoman collection, like the other illustrations that appear on our covers, bring to life the richness and variety of dress customs of two centuries ago. They recall the sense of isolation and distance of that period-and of every other historic period except our own hyperkinetic present.

Dress codes have changed since then and the diversity by region, so rich at the time, has faded away. It is now often hard to tell the inhabitant of one continent from another. Perhaps, trying to view it optimistically, we have traded a cultural and visual diversity for a more varied personal life. Or a more varied and interesting intellectual and technical life.

We at Manning celebrate the inventiveness, the initiative, and, yes, the fun of the computer business with book covers based on the rich diversity of regional life of two centuries ago, brought back to life by the pictures from this collection.

Part 1

The Ruby/Rails landscape

This book is about the Ruby programming language, viewed chiefly from the perspective of interest in the Ruby on Rails framework. The goal of this first part of the book is to familiarize you with the landscape of both Ruby and Rails: what's there, and why, and how it all connects.

This part contains three chapters:

Chapter 1, "How Ruby works," is about the Ruby programming environment: how to write and execute a Ruby program; where the files associated with Ruby are located; and what tools Ruby gives you (in addition to the Ruby interpreter itself) to help you write and maintain programs.

Chapter 2, "How Rails works," gives you a guided tour of the basic structure of the Ruby on Rails framework: its components and how they interact; how the Rails framework fits together with Ruby; and the relation between and among Ruby, Rails, and a given Rails application. It also includes the first version of the book's major sample Rails application, the R4RMusic online sheet-music store. (The second version of R4RMusic will be developed in part 4 of the book.)

Chapter 3, "Ruby-informed Rails development," is a plunge into the process of understanding in specific terms the ways that knowing Ruby well can help you as a Rails developer. This chapter is thus a first fulfillment of the book's overall goal—and, at the same time, an anchor for the detailed exploration of the Ruby language to come in the next two parts.

After reading these chapters, you'll have your bearings in the landscape. You'll know how the Ruby programming language, the Rails application development framework, and your specific applications all fit together, in considerable technical detail. You will have walked through the process of writing and running everything from a small, proof-of-concept Ruby program, to a working Rails application. Along the way, you'll pick up a number of useful and important Ruby programming techniques.

Most importantly, you'll have started to understand and to experience the effect of Ruby expertise on Rails development power.

How Ruby works

This chapter covers

- A Ruby literacy bootstrap guide
- An overview of the Ruby programming environment
- Walk-throughs of sample Ruby programs

This book will give you a foundation in Ruby, and this chapter will give your foundation a foundation.

We're going to look at how Ruby works: what you do when you write a program, how you get Ruby to run your program, and how you split a program into more than one file. You'll learn several variations on the process of running the Ruby *interpreter* (the program with the actual name ruby, to which you feed your program files for execution) as well how to use some important auxiliary tools designed to make your life as a Ruby programmer—a *Rubyist*, to use the prevalent term—easier and more productive.

This first view of Ruby is from a middle distance; more detail is yet to come. Still, you'll learn several very specific, real, and useful Ruby techniques in this chapter. After all, in order to jump-start the process of writing and running real programs, you need to write and run real programs. They'll be kept simple—but in Ruby, some of the simplest things are among the most often used and most powerful. When you see Ruby code in this chapter, it's real Ruby.

1.1 *The mechanics of writing a Ruby program*

The goal of this section is to take you through the actual process of writing and running a Ruby program. Don't worry if some of what you see appears to be a bit of a black box for the moment. The breadth-first approach we're taking will help to bootstrap you into the programming cycle from beginning to end. This, in turn, will give you your bearings for the rest of the chapter and the detailed discussion of the Ruby language that lies ahead in parts 2 and 3.

NOTE   Ruby, ruby, and ... RUBY?! Ruby is a programming language. We talk about things like "learning Ruby," and we ask questions like, "Do you know Ruby?" The lowercase version, ruby, is a computer program; specifically, it's the Ruby *interpreter*, the program that reads *your* programs and runs them. You'll see this name used in sentences like, "I ran ruby on my file, but nothing happened," or "What's the full path to your ruby executable?" Finally, there's RUBY—or, more precisely, there isn't. Ruby isn't an acronym, and it's never correct to spell it in all capital letters. People do this, as they do (also wrongly) with Perl, perhaps because they're used to seeing language names like BASIC and FORTRAN. Ruby is not such a language. It's Ruby for the language, ruby for the interpreter.

1.1.1 Getting the preliminaries in place

At this point you need to have Ruby installed on your computer. The process of installing Ruby is discussed in the appendix. Before proceeding with this chapter, you should read the appendix and make sure that Ruby is installed and working.

You also need a text editor and a directory (*folder* to some of you) in which to store your Ruby program files. You can use any text editor you like. You can even use a word-processing program, as long as you can save files in plain-text format (not, for example, Microsoft Word format, RTF, or anything else fancy) and as long as you can give them filenames that end with the extension .rb (signifying a Ruby program file).

Meet Interactive Ruby (irb), your new best friend

Some advice for the impatient, as they say—and for everyone, in this case: A wonderful command-line tool called irb (Interactive Ruby) comes with Ruby. You type Ruby commands and expressions into irb, and it executes them on the spot. Written by Keiju Ishitsuka, irb is indispensable to Ruby programmers, and just using it to experiment and play with Ruby will speed up your learning and your comfort with Ruby tremendously.

Because irb is really a kind of alternative Ruby interpreter, it's not discussed in detail until section 1.2.2. Feel free to jump to that section and have a look. You can start using irb right away. Having an open irb session means you can test Ruby snippets any time and in any quantity.

Meanwhile, we'll bootstrap your Ruby literacy so we have a shared ground on which to continuing building and exploring.

1.1.2 A Ruby literacy bootstrap guide

As part of the bootstrap process, it's worth taking a little time to learn some of the most common elements of Ruby syntax. Even if the code you're looking at has some black-box qualities, you can get a lot of mileage out of an awareness of the meanings of a small number of elements.

The examples in this chapter use the techniques set forth in table 1.1. In the interest of making the Ruby bootstrapping process as comfortable as possible, they're summarized here for you to peruse in advance and easily reference later. A couple of very fundamental aspects of Ruby and Ruby syntax, however, are too involved for summary in a table. You need at least a preliminary sense of what an *object* is in Ruby and what a *method call* looks like. We'll take a first, brief look at both of those features next. (Like the items in the table, they'll also be explored at greater length later in the book.)

Table 1.1   Synopsis of key elements of Ruby syntax for Ruby literacy bootstrapping purposes

Operation	Example(s)	Comments
Arithmetic	2 + 3 *(addition)* 2 - 3 *(subtraction)* 2 * 3 *(multiplication)* 2 / 3 *(division)*	The examples show integers. You can also use floating-point numbers (2.0).
Putting a value into a variable	x = 1 string = "Hello"	This is called variable *assignment*.
Printing something to the screen	puts "Hello" print "Hello" x = "Hello" puts x x = "Hello" print x x = "Hello" p x	puts adds a newline to the string it outputs, if there isn't one at the end already. print prints exactly what it's told to and leaves the cursor at the end. (Note: on some platforms, an extra newline is automatically added at the end of a program.) p outputs an *inspect* string, which may contain extra information about what it's printing.
Getting a line of keyboard input	gets string = gets	You can assign the input line directly to a variable (the variable string in the second example).
Turning a string into a number	x = "100".to_i s = "100" x = s.to_i	To perform arithmetic, you have to make sure you have numbers rather than strings of characters. to_i performs string-to-integer conversion.
Comparing two values	x == y	Note the two equal signs (not just one, as in assignment).

Conditional execution	if x == y
	    # execute this code
	else
	    # execute this code
	end
		Conditional statements always end with the word end.

Putting comments in code files	# This is a comment line.
	X = 1 # Comment to end of line
		Comments are ignored by the interpreter.

1.1.3 *A brief introduction to method calls and Ruby objects*

A lot of what you'll see and write in Ruby programs are *method calls*. Method calls sometimes consist simply of the name of a method, in bareword form, possibly followed by one or more arguments to the method. For example, this code calls the method `puts` with one argument:

```
puts "Hello."
```

Other method calls use a special syntax: a *dot* operator, which establishes a relationship between a value or expression to its left and a method name to its right. In this example from table 1.1

```
x = "100".to_i
```

the dot means that the *message* "to_i" is being *sent* to the string "100", or that the method `to_i` is being called on the string "100". The string "100" is called the *receiver* of the message.

Here's a method call that uses the full dot notation and also takes an argument. This is a way to generate a decimal integer equivalent to the base-nine number 100:

```
x = "100".to_i(9)
```

x is now equal to 81 decimal.

This example also shows the use of parentheses around method arguments. These parentheses are usually optional, but in more complex cases they may be required to clear up what might otherwise be ambiguities in the syntax. Many programmers use parentheses in most or all method calls, just to be safe (and for visual clarity).

In these examples, the string "100" functions as the receiver of the message "to_i". Basically, you're addressing the string with the request *Convert yourself to an integer.* The string itself is an *object*. The whole universe of a Ruby program consists of messages being sent to objects. An object might be a string (as in the last example). It might be an integer—perhaps an integer you want to convert *to* a string:

```
100.to_s
```

When you write a Ruby program, you spend most of your time either telling Ruby what you want objects to be able to do—what messages you want them to be able to understand—or sending messages to objects. Nor are you limited in your object universe to things that Ruby already knows about, like strings and integers. If you're writing a Rails application in which one of your entity models is, say,

Customer, then when you write the code that causes things to happen—a customer logging into a site, updating a customer's phone number, adding an item to a customer's shopping cart—in all likelihood you'll be sending messages to customer objects.

We'll explore all of this in much greater depth later in the book. Again, this brief sketch is just for Ruby literacy bootstrapping purposes. When you see a dot in what would otherwise be an inexplicable position, you should interpret it as a message (on the right) being sent to an object (on the left).

1.1.4   *Writing and saving a sample program*

Armed with some Ruby literacy (and a summary to refer back to when in doubt), let's walk through the steps involved in running a program. It's highly recommended that you create a separate directory for examples from this book. Something like this should be suitable:

```
$ cd
$ mkdir ruby4rails
$ cd ruby4rails
```

From this point on, the book will assume that all sample programs are kept in this directory. In some cases it won't matter, but in others it will (especially when you start writing programs that take up more than one file, and the multiple files must be able to find each other easily).

Now you'll create a program file. The program will be a Celsius-to-Fahrenheit temperature converter. We'll walk this example through several stages, adding to it and modifying it as we go. The first version is very simple, because the focus is on the file-creation and program-running processes.

Creating a first program file

You can use any text editor (vi, Emacs, Notepad, and so on) to create this and future Ruby program files; none of the instructions or explanations in this book are editor-specific. Remember that if you use a word-processing program, you have to save your file as plain text.

Type the code from listing 1.1 into a text file, and save it under the filename `c2f.rb` in your `ruby4rails` directory.

> **Listing 1.1   Simple, limited-purpose Celsius-to-Fahrenheit converter (`c2f.rb`)**

```
c = 100
f = (c * 9 / 5) + 32
puts "The result is: "
```

```
puts f
puts "."
```

You now have a complete (albeit tiny) Ruby program on your disk, and you can run it.

> **NOTE** RUNNING RUBY PROGRAMS STANDALONE Depending on your operating system, you may be able to run Ruby program files *standalone*—that is, with just the filename, or with a short name (like c2f) and no file extension. Keep in mind, though, that the .rb filename extension is mandatory in some cases, mainly involving programs that occupy more than one file (which you'll learn about in detail later) and that need a mechanism for the files to find each other. In this book, all Ruby program filenames end in .rb to ensure that the examples work on as many platforms as possible.

1.1.5 *Feeding the program to Ruby*

The process of writing and running Ruby programs revolves around passing your program source files to the Ruby interpreter, which is called ruby. You'll do that now... sort of. You'll feed the program to ruby; but instead of asking Ruby to run the program, you'll ask it to *check* the program code (the lines of Ruby in the file) for *syntax errors*.

Checking for syntax errors

If you accidentally type a space in the middle of the method-call print in c2f.rb (pr int), that constitutes a syntax error. If you forget to type the # character before a comment line, you'll almost certainly introduce a syntax error (unless the comment you expose is written in perfect Ruby!).

Conveniently, the Ruby interpreter can check programs for syntax errors without running the programs. It reads through the file and tells you whether the syntax is OK. To run a syntax check on your file, do this:

```
$ ruby -cw c2f.rb
```

The -c flag means *check*—that is, check for syntax errors. The -w flag activates a higher level of warning; Ruby will fuss at you if you've done things that are legal Ruby but are questionable for one reason or another.

Assuming you've typed the file correctly, you should see the message

```
Syntax OK
```

printed on your screen.

Running the program

To run the program, you pass the file once more to the interpreter, but this time without the -c and -w flags:

```
$ ruby c2f.rb
```

If all goes well, you'll see the output of the calculation:

```
The result is
212
.
```

Trouble in paradise

The result of the calculation is correct, but the output, spread as it is over three lines, looks bad. You want it all on one line.

Fixing your first Ruby error

The problem can be traced to the difference between the puts command and the print command. puts adds a newline to the end of the string it prints out, if the string doesn't end with one already. print, on the other hand, prints out the string you ask it to and then stops; it doesn't automatically jump to the next line.

To fix the problem, you can change the first two puts commands to print:

```
print "The result is "
print f
puts "."
```

(Note the blank space after is, which ensures that there will be a space between is and the number.) Now the output is as follows:

```
The result is 212.
```

puts is short for *put [i.e., print] string*. Although *put* may not intuitively invoke the notion of skipping down to the next line, that's what puts does: Like print, it prints what you tell it to, but then it also automatically goes to the next line. If you ask puts to print a line that already ends with a newline, it doesn't bother adding one.

If you're used to print facilities in languages that don't automatically add a newline (such as Perl's print function), you may find yourself writing code like this in Ruby when you want to print a value followed by a newline:

```
print f, "\n"
```

puts, of course, does this for you. You'll pick up the puts habit, along with other Ruby idioms and conventions, as you go along.

WARNING EXTRA NEWLINES WHEN YOU MAY NOT WANT THEM   On some platforms (Windows in particular), an extra newline character is printed out at the end of the run of a program. This means a `print` that should really be a `puts` will be hard to detect, because it will act like a `puts`. Being aware of the difference between the two, and using the one you want based on the usual behavior, should be sufficient to ensure you get the desired results.

On the other side of the equation is the matter of data *input*. Not every program comes bundled with all the data it needs hard-coded into itself, as the examples have so far. Data comes from many sources. In the typical Rails application, it comes from a database. In Ruby usage generally, program data often comes from the keyboard and/or one or more files. We'll look next at how Ruby handles these forms of input.

1.1.6 Keyboard and file input

Ruby offers lots of techniques for reading and writing data during the course of program execution. As a Rails developer, you may find yourself using relatively few of these facilities, because Rails does the data-fetching for you; and your users, when they input from the keyboard, will generally be typing on a Web form.

Nonetheless, it's a very good idea to learn at least the basic Ruby keyboard and file I/O operations. You'll find uses for them, if not in the course of writing every Rails application, then almost certainly while writing Ruby code to maintain, convert, housekeep, or otherwise manipulate the environment in which you work.

Keyboard input

A program that tells you over and over again that 100° Celsius is 212° Fahrenheit has limited value. A more valuable program lets you specify a Celsius temperature and tells you the Fahrenheit equivalent.

Modifying the program to allow for this functionality involves adding a couple of steps and using two methods (one of which you're familiar with already):

- `gets` (*get string*) suspends the program and waits for one line of input from the keyboard. (The "newline" character created when you hit the enter key is included as the last character in the input line.)
- `to_i` (*to integer*) converts a string to an integer. You need this method so that the string you enter will play nicely with the other numbers when you calculate the Fahrenheit result.

Because this is a new program, not just a correction, put the version from listing 1.2 in a new file (`c2fi.rb`; *i* stands for *interactive*):

Listing 1.2   Interactive temperature converter (`c2fi.rb`)

```
print "Hello. Please enter a Celsius value: "
c = gets
f = (c.to_i * 9 / 5) + 32
print "The Fahrenheit equivalent is "
print f
puts "."
```

(Note the use of print versus puts to control when the output drops to a new line and when it doesn't.)

A couple of sample runs demonstrate the new program in action:

```
$ ruby c2fi.rb
Hello. Please enter a Celsius value: 100
The Fahrenheit equivalent is 212.
$ ruby c2fi.rb
Hello. Please enter a Celsius value: 23
The Fahrenheit equivalent is 73.
```

NOTE   SHORTENING THE CODE   You can shorten the program considerably by consolidating the operations of input, calculation, and output. A compressed rewrite looks like this:

```
print "Hello. Please enter a Celsius value: "
print "The Fahrenheit equivalent is ", gets.to_i * 9 / 5 + 32,
".\n"
```

This version economizes on variables—there aren't any!—but requires anyone reading it to follow a somewhat denser (although shorter) set of expressions. Any given program usually has several or many spots where you have to decide between longer (but maybe clearer) and shorter (but maybe a bit cryptic). And sometimes, shorter can be clearer. It's all part of developing a Ruby coding style.

Example with file input

Reading a file from a Ruby program isn't much more difficult than reading a line of keyboard input. You'll dip your toes in it here: You'll read one number from a file and convert it from Celsius to Fahrenheit. (Reading data in from a file does get more elaborate than this, at times, but this example will show you the basic operation.)

First, create a new file called temp.dat (temperature data), containing just one line with one number on it:

```
100
```

Now, create a third program file, called c2fin.rb (*in* for *[file] input*), as shown in listing 1.3.

Listing 1.3   Temperature converter using file input (c2fin.rb)

```
puts "Reading Celsius temperature value from data file..."
num = File.read("temp.dat")
c = num.to_i
f = (c * 9 / 5) + 32
puts "The number is " + num
print "Result: "
puts f
```

This time, the sample run and its output look like this:

```
$ ruby c2fin.rb
Reading Celsius temperature value from data file...
The number is 100
Result: 212
```

Naturally, if you change the number in the file, the result will be different.

For the sake of symmetry—and for practical reasons, because you're likely to want to do this at some point—let's look at what's involved in writing a variant of the program that saves the result *to* a file.

Example with file output

The simplest file-writing operation is a little more elaborate than the simplest file-reading operation (but not much more). If you're scrutinizing the code, you can see that the main extra item specified when you open a file for writing is the file *mode*—in this case, w (for *write*).

Save the version of the program from listing 1.4 to c2fout.rb, and run it.

Listing 1.4   Temperature converter with file output (c2fout.rb)

```
print "Hello. Please enter a Celsius value: "
c = gets.to_i
f = (c * 9 / 5) + 32
puts "Saving result to output file 'temp.out'"
fh = File.new("temp.out", "w")
fh.puts f
fh.close
```

(The variable fh is named for *file handle*. Note that you use puts—actually fh.puts, where the reference to the filehandle (fh) steers the output to the file stream rather than to the screen—to output a line to the file represented by the file handle.)

If you inspect the file `temp.out`, you should see that it contains the Fahrenheit equivalent of whatever number you typed in.

An exercise for the reader

Based on the previous examples, can you write a Ruby program that reads a number from a file and writes the Fahrenheit conversion to a different file?

1.1.7 One program, multiple files

Up to this point, we've approached the writing and execution of a Ruby program as involving two entities: a program file and the Ruby interpreter. As you start to write longer programs—and when you look at longer and more complex applications, including Rails applications and Rails itself—you'll quickly discover that very few programs occupy only one file. Unless you're writing something really compact, like a Celsius converter, your program will probably extend over two, three, or in some cases dozens of files.

Believe it or not, that's good news.

True, having a program in a single file lets you see it all in one place. But this starts to be a liability rather than an asset when you've got hundreds or thousands—or hundreds *of* thousands—of lines of code. Breaking your program into separate files then starts to make lots of sense.

"require"-ing a file

When your program is spread across multiple files, the technique you'll use most often to run it as one program is the `require` command (the `require` method, more accurately), which pulls in a second file from a file that's already running.

To demonstrate the use of `require`, you'll need (no surprise) a program written across two files. The first file, `reqdemo.rb`, should contain the following Ruby code:

```
puts "This is the first (master) program file."
require 'requiree.rb'
puts "And back again to the first file."
```

When it encounters the `require` method call, Ruby reads in the second file. That file, `requiree.rb`, should look like this:

```
puts "> This is the second file, which was 'require'd by the first."
```

Now, run Ruby on `reqdemo.rb`, and see the results:

```
$ ruby reqdemo.rb
This is the first (master) program file.
> This is the second file, which was 'require'd by the first.
And back again to the first file.
```

This program doesn't do much—it's just a proof-of-concept demonstration of the process of using more than one program file—but you can see from the messages that the second file, `requiree.rb`, was executed at the point where you put the `require` statement in the first file.

Essentially, `require` goes and looks for another file and (assuming it finds it) executes it. If it doesn't find it, your program will terminate with a fatal error.

"load"-ing a file

A close relative of `require` is `load`. The main difference is that if you do this

```
require "requiree.rb"
require "requiree.rb"
```

nothing happens the second time; whereas if you do this

```
load "requiree.rb"
load "requiree.rb"
```

Ruby reads in the file twice.

Doing it twice in a row in the same file is almost certainly pointless, but in some cases this kind of multiple loading is useful. Rails uses `load` in preference to `require`, for example, in development mode—which means that if you're trying your application in a browser and making changes to the code at the same time, your changes are reloaded, overriding any caching behavior on the part of the Web server. Multiple `require` calls in the same place don't have the same effect if the application has already read the file in once.

The facilities for getting multiple files to work together loom very, very large in Ruby programming generally and certainly in the Rails framework. You'll see examples of multifile interaction in part 4 of the book, especially in chapter 17, where we dig into the Rails source code. File-to-file connections make both Ruby and Rails cohere, separately and together.

Meanwhile, let's return to the basic Ruby procedural scenario.

1.2 Techniques of interpreter invocation

You've roughed out the lifecycle of a Ruby program. Now you're in a position to back-and-fill a bit.

As already noted, when you run a Ruby program, you're really running a program called ruby and feeding *your* program to that program. Here, we'll look at further options available to you in the course of doing this. These options include *command-line switches* (of which you've seen an example in the -cw syntax-checking flag), techniques for directing your program to the Ruby interpreter without having to invoke ruby on the command line, and details of how to run the irb interpreter.

1.2.1 Command-line switches

When you start the Ruby interpreter from the command line, you can provide not only the name of a program file but also one or more command-line switches. The switches you choose instruct the interpreter to behave in particular ways and/or take particular actions.

Ruby has more than 20 command-line switches. Some of them are used rarely; others are used every day by many Ruby programmers. Here we'll look at several more of the most commonly used ones. (You've already seen two of them, -c and -w, used in combination with each other.) These common switches are summarized in table 1.2 and then explained separately.

Table 1.2   Summary of commonly used Ruby command-line switches

Switch	Description	Example of usage
-c	**C**heck the syntax of a program file without executing the program	`ruby -c c2f.rb`
-w	Give **w**arning messages during program execution	`ruby -w c2f.rb`
-e	**E**xecute the code provided in quotation marks on the command line	`ruby -e 'puts "Code demo!"'`
-v	Show Ruby **v**ersion information, and execute the program in **v**erbose mode	`ruby -v`
-l	**L**ine mode: print a newline after every line, if not otherwise present	`ruby -l -e 'print "Will jump down!"'`
-rname	Load the named extension (**r**equire it)	`ruby -rprofile`
--version	Show Ruby **v**ersion information	`ruby --version`

Check syntax (-c)

The -c switch tells Ruby to check the code in one or more files for syntactical accuracy without executing the code. It's usually used in conjunction with the -w flag.

Turn on warnings (-w)

Running your program with -w causes the interpreter to run in warning mode. This means you'll see more warnings than you otherwise would printed to the screen, drawing your attention to places in your program which, although not syntax errors, are stylistically or logically suspect. It's Ruby's way of saying, "What you've done is syntactically correct, but it's weird. Are you sure you meant to do that?" (Even without this switch, Ruby issues certain warnings, but fewer than it does in full warning mode.)

Execute literal script (-e)

The -e switch tells the interpreter that the command line includes Ruby code, in quotation marks, and that it should execute that actual code rather than executing the code contained in a file. This can be handy for quick scripting jobs where entering your code into a file and running ruby on the file may not be worth the trouble.

For example, let's say you want to see your name backward. Here's how you can do this quickly, in one command-line command, using the execute switch:

```
$ ruby -e 'puts "David A. Black".reverse'
kcalB .A divaD
```

What lies inside the single quotation marks is an entire (although short) Ruby program. If you want to feed a program with more than one line to the -e switch, you can use literal linebreaks inside the mini-program:

```
$ ruby -e 'print "Enter a name: "
puts gets.reverse'
Enter a name: David A. Black

kcalB .A divaD
```

Or, you can separate the lines with semicolons:

```
$ ruby -e 'print "Enter a name: "; print gets.reverse'
```

> **NOTE** NEWLINES IN REVERSED STRINGS Why is there a blank line between the program code and the output in the two-line reverse examples? Because the line you enter on the keyboard ends with a *newline character*—so when you reverse the input, the new string *starts* with a newline! Ruby, as always, takes you literally when you ask it to manipulate and print data.

Run in line mode (-l)

If you look back at the result of executing the first version of the Celsius conversion program, the output from Ruby—the number 212—runs together on the screen with the prompt from the shell (the $ character). The reason, as you saw, was that you used `print` rather than `puts`, so no newline character followed the number.

The `-l` switch gives you blanket coverage on putting lines of output on separate lines. It's sometimes convenient to do this when you're not sure whether the lines you plan to print end with newlines. In most cases, you can use `puts`, but the `-l` switch helps you in cases where you don't have control over the code.

Let's say someone else writes a program that goes through a file of names and prints out the first names. For whatever reason, the original programmer uses `print` rather than `puts`, which means that a run of the program on a typical file produces output like this:

```
$ ruby firstnames.rb
AdaBarbaraClaraDoris
```

Now, let's say you want to use the program, but you want each name on a separate line. You can tell Ruby to operate in line mode, and you'll get what you need:

```
$ ruby -l firstnames.rb
Ada
Barbara
Clara
Doris
```

You won't see the `-l` flag as often as you'll see programs that use `puts` to ensure similar behavior. But it can be useful, and you'll want to be able to recognize it.

Require named file or extension (-rname)

The `-r` switch lets you specify files to require on the command line. As you'll see, `require` also has the broader purpose of activating *extensions* (add-on programming facilities). You can use the `-r` flag for that flavor of require, too.

Run in verbose mode (-v)

Running with `-v` does two things: It prints out information about the version of Ruby you're using, and then it turns on the same warning mechanism as the `-w` flag. The most common use of `-v` is to find out the Ruby version number:

```
$ ruby -v
ruby 1.8.2 (2004-12-25) [i686-linux]
```

(In this case, we're using Ruby 1.8.2, released on Christmas Day, 2004, and compiled for an i686-based machine running Linux.) Because there's no program or code to run, Ruby exits as soon as it has printed the version number.

Print Ruby version (–version)

Not surprisingly, this flag is like -v except that *all* --version does is to print the Ruby version information. It doesn't proceed to execute any code, even if you provide code or a filename. It just prints the version information and exits. You'll see ruby -v much more often than ruby --version.

Combining switches

It's not uncommon to combine one or more command-line switches in a single invocation of Ruby.

You've already seen the cw combination, which checks the syntax of the file without executing it, while also giving you warnings:

```
$ ruby -cw filename
```

Another combination of switches you'll often see is -v and -e, which shows you the version of Ruby you're running and then runs the code provided in quotation marks. You'll see this combination a lot in discussions of Ruby, on mailing lists and elsewhere; people use it to demonstrate how the same code might work differently in different versions of Ruby. For example, if you want to show clearly that an operation called lstrip (strip all whitespace from the left-hand side of a string) was not present in Ruby 1.6.8 but is present in Ruby 1.8.2, you can run a sample program using first one version of Ruby, then the other:

```
$ ruby-1.6.8 -ve 'puts "  abc".lstrip'
ruby 1.6.8 (2002-12-24) [i686-linux]
-e:1: undefined method `lstrip' for "  abc":String (NameError)

$ ruby -ve 'puts "  abc".lstrip'
ruby 1.8.2 (2004-12-25) [i686-linux]
abc
```

The undefined method 'lstrip' message on the first run (the one using version 1.6.8) means that you've tried to perform a nonexistent named operation. When you run the same Ruby snipped using Ruby 1.8.2, however, it works: Ruby prints abc (with no leading blanks). This is a convenient way to share information and formulate questions about changes in Ruby's behavior from one release to another.

At this point, we're going to go back and look more closely at the interactive Ruby interpreter, irb. You may have looked at this section already, when it was alluded to near the beginning of the chapter. If not, you can take this opportunity to learn more about this exceptionally useful Ruby tool.

1.2.2 A closer look at interactive Ruby interpretation with irb

One of the great pleasures of using Ruby is using irb. irb is an interactive interpreter—which means that instead of processing a file, it processes what you type
in during a session. irb is a great tool for testing Ruby code, and a great tool for
learning Ruby.

To start an irb session, you use the command `irb`. irb will print out its prompt:

```
$ irb
irb(main):001:0>
```

Now, you can enter Ruby commands. You can even run a one-shot version of the
Celcius-to-Fahrenheit conversion program. As you'll see in this example, irb
behaves like a pocket calculator: It evaluates whatever you type in and prints the
result. You don't have to use a `print` or `puts` command:

```
irb(main):001:0> 100 * 9 / 5 + 32
=> 212
```

To find out how many minutes there are in a year (if you don't have a CD of the hit
song from the musical *Rent* handy), type in the relevant multiplication expression:

```
irb(main):001:0> 365 * 24 * 60
=> 525600
```

irb will also, of course, process any Ruby instructions you enter. For example, if
you want to assign the day, hour, and minute counts to variables, and then multiply those variables, you can do that in irb:

```
irb(main):001:0> days = 365
=> 365
irb(main):002:0> hours = 24
=> 24
irb(main):003:0> minutes = 60
=> 60
irb(main):004:0> days * hours * minutes
=> 525600
```

The last calculation is what you'd expect. But look at the first three lines of entry.
When you type `days = 365`, irb responds by printing `365`. Why?

The expression `days = 365` is an assignment expression: You're assigning the
value 365 to a variable called `days`. The main business of an assignment expression is to assign, so that you can use the variable later. But assignment expressions
themselves—the whole `days = 365` line—have a value. The value of an assignment
expression is its right-hand side. When irb sees *any* expression, it prints out the
value of that expression. So, when irb sees `days = 365`, it prints out 365. This may

seem like overzealous printing, but it comes with the territory; it's the same behavior that lets you type 2 + 2 into irb and see the result without having to use an explicit print statement.

Once you get the hang of irb's approach to printing out the value of *everything*, you'll find it an immensely useful tool (and toy).

> **TIP** EXITING FROM IRB (INTENTIONALLY OR OTHERWISE)   If you get stuck in a loop or frozen situation in irb, press Ctrl-c. To exit, press Ctrl-d or type exit. Occasionally, irb may blow up on you (that is, hit a fatal error and terminate itself). Most of the time, though, it will catch its own errors and let you continue.

Next on our tour of the Ruby landscape are Ruby extensions and libraries. Looking at these facilities will give you a sense of how the core language interacts with the add-ons that are either bundled in the Ruby distribution or distributed separately by third-party programmers interested in enriching the Ruby programming environment.

1.3 Ruby extensions and programming libraries

Earlier, you saw a simple example of the use of require to pull in one file from another during program execution. require is the foundation of a huge amount of Ruby's power and richness as a programming language. Specifically, this mechanism gives you access to the many *extensions* and *programming libraries* bundled with the Ruby programming language—as well as an even larger number of extensions and libraries written independently by other programmers and made available for use with Ruby.

The full range of Ruby's standard library is outside of the scope of this book. This section provides guidelines and pointers about what Ruby offers and how to use libraries in your own programs.

1.3.1 Using standard extensions and libraries

When you install Ruby on your system, you really install several layers. First is the *core Ruby language:* the basic operations and programming techniques available when you run the Ruby interpreter.

Second are a large number of *extensions* and *programming libraries* bundled with Ruby—add-ons that help you write programs in different areas of specialization. These are usually referred to collectively as the *standard library*. Ruby comes with extensions for a wide variety of projects and tasks: database management, networking, specialized mathematics, XML processing, and many more.

To use a Ruby extension, you `require` it:

```
require 'cgi'
require 'REXML/Document'
```

Extensions are basically just program files (or clusters of related program files that `require` each other) containing specialized code, dedicated to a particular area of programming. When you use, say, the CGI extension, as in the previous example, you immediately have access to a wide variety of programming commands and techniques designed to help you write CGI programs. (Ruby on Rails does this; you'll see the line `require 'cgi'` in a number of the program files that make up the Rails package.) The purpose, as with any extension, is to save everyone a lot of trouble. Because all those CGI programming techniques are already available through a simple `require` command, everyone can use them. The alternative would be for everyone to write the code required to support those techniques, which would be difficult and a waste of time.

Note that you say `require 'cgi'`, not `require 'cgi.rb'`. Aside from looking nicer, this bareword way of referring to the extension is necessary because not all extensions use files ending in `.rb`. Specifically, extensions written in C (more in the next section) are stored in files ending with `.so` or `.dll`. To keep the process transparent—that is, to save you the trouble of knowing whether the extension you want uses a `.rb` file or not—Ruby accepts a bareword and then does some automatic file-searching and trying out of possible filenames until it finds the file corresponding to the extension you have requested.

> **NOTE** *EXTENSION* OR *LIBRARY*? The broadest term for a collection of programming commands and techniques that you can pull into your own program via a `require` statement is *library*. The term *extension* is usually reserved for libraries that are distributed with Ruby, as opposed to those written by third-party programmers and made available to others for use in their applications. One exception is extensions to Ruby written in the C programming language—both those provided with Ruby and those written as add-ons—which are frequently referred to as *extensions*.

1.3.2 *Using C extensions*

Some of the extensions that come with Ruby are written in Ruby. They use the techniques available in the core language to conjure up more layers of functionality and language features. Some extensions, however, are written in C. C extensions in the Ruby distribution include a socket-programming library (for network applications), a syslog (system logging) programming facility, and several libraries devoted to database handling.

Some of these C extensions could have been written in Ruby. There are a couple of reasons for writing them in C. The main reason is speed—execution speed, that is. Some C extensions have to be in C; their goal is to provide a bridge between Ruby and what's already available to C programmers. They can't be written in Ruby because they're bringing these features *to* Ruby.

The Ruby interpreter handles extensions in such a way that when you use one, you don't have to worry about whether it was written in Ruby or C. You just `require` it

```
require 'gdbm'
```

and Ruby finds the files it needs to load, whether they are Ruby files or binary files produced during the compile process from C source files.

1.3.3 *Writing extensions and libraries*

Many extensions and add-on libraries are bundled with the official distribution of the Ruby programming language and are installed on your system when you install Ruby. But anyone can write an extension or library. When you write Ruby code that lets you and other programmers do something new and valuable with Ruby, you've written an extension. Your code may not make it into the collection of extensions that comes with the Ruby language. But you can still make it available to other programmers, thereby adding value to the Ruby programming environment.

The difference between writing a library and breaking your program into multiple files lies in what happens to your code. Do you use it in more than one program? Do other people use it? If so, then it's reasonable to call it a library.

The Rails framework is a library (really a bundle of interrelated libraries). As a Rails developer, you may or may not write Ruby libraries. But you *can* do so, and it's not uncommon for Ruby programmers involved in diverse projects to release parts of what they're working on as libraries and extensions useable by other programmers.

> **TIP**   VISIT THE RUBY APPLICATION ARCHIVE AND RUBYFORGE   If you're interested in seeing the kinds of Ruby projects that other Rubyists have made available, including applications as well as programming libraries and extensions, the best places to look are the Ruby Application Archive (RAA; http://raa.ruby-lang.org) and RubyForge (http://www.rubyforge.net).

We'll conclude this chapter with an examination of the Ruby programming environment: what comes with Ruby (including the source code for Ruby); where Ruby installs itself on your system; and what kinds of applications and programming facilities Ruby provides you.

1.4 *Anatomy of the Ruby programming environment*

Installing Ruby on your system means installing numerous components of the language, possibly including the source code for the language, and definitely including a number of disk directories' worth of Ruby-language libraries and support files. You won't necessarily use everything in this section every time you write something in Ruby, but it's good to know what's there. Also, quite a few of the programming libraries that come bundled with Ruby are written *in* Ruby—so knowing your way around the Ruby installation will enable you to look at some well-written Ruby code and (we hope) absorb some good habits.

   We'll start with the Ruby source code.

1.4.1 *The layout of the Ruby source code*

The Ruby source code directory (tree) contains the files that house the program code for the Ruby interpreter as well as a number of bundled add-ons. The core Ruby language is written in C, so in order to read and fully understand the files, you need to know C. But even if you don't know C, you can learn a lot from perusing the comments and documentation contained in the source files.

> **TIP**   MAKE SURE YOUR PACKAGE MANAGER GIVES YOU ALL OF RUBY   If you install Ruby via a remote package manager, you may not end up with the Ruby source on your machine. If that happens, and you want the source, check for a package named "ruby-source" or something similar. If there's no such package, you can download the source from ruby-lang.org and un-tar it. See the book's appendix for more information about installing Ruby and pointers on how to get platform-specific information.

If you examine a directory listing of the top-level directory of the Ruby source tree, you'll see the following:

- Several subdirectories, including ext/ and lib/ (both discussed shortly)
- Informational, legal, and license-related files (such as COPYING, GPL, and README)
- Files pertaining to the process of building and installing Ruby (all the config* files, Makefile.in, install-sh, and so on)
- C program and header files (*.c and *.h)

Some of these files are only needed during the building of Ruby. Some of them are copied over directly when Ruby is installed. And, of course, the building process generates a number of new files (including `ruby`, the interpreter) that make their way onto your system permanently when you install Ruby.

1.4.2 Navigating the Ruby installation

We'll look at several of the subdirectories of the main Ruby installation to give you a general sense of what's in them. This is just an overview. The best way—really, the only way—to get to know the Ruby installation layout and become comfortable with it is to navigate around it and see what's there.

Before you can either navigate generally or pinpoint files specifically, you need to know where Ruby is installed on your system. The best way to find out is to ask Ruby.

How to get Ruby to tell you where it's installed

Ruby is installed to directories with different names on different platforms and/or by different packaging systems. You can find out where the installation is on your system by using irb. First, start up irb with the `-r` flag, requiring the extension named `rbconfig`:

```
$ irb -rrbconfig
```

This command causes irb to preload some configuration information for your particular installation, including information about where various components of Ruby have been installed.

To get the information, enter an expression like this into irb:

```
irb(main):001:0> Config::CONFIG["bindir"]
```

This request shows you the directory where the Ruby executable files (including `ruby` and `irb`) have been installed; that's the `bindir`. To get other information, you need to replace `bindir` in the irb command with other terms. But each time, you'll use the same basic formula: `Config::CONFIG["term"]`.

In each of the following sections, *the section subtitle includes the term you need.* Just plug that term into the irb command, and you'll be shown the name of the directory.

The extensions and libraries subdirectory (rubylibdir)

Inside the `rubylibdir` (whatever that directory may be called on your system), you'll find program files written in Ruby. These files provide standard library facilities, which you can require from your own programs if you need the functionality they provide.

Here's a sampling of the files you'll find in this directory:

- `cgi.rb`—Tools to facilitate CGI programming
- `fileutils.rb`—Utilities for manipulating files easily from Ruby programs
- `tempfile.rb`—A mechanism for automating the creation of temporary files
- `tk.rb`—A programming interface to the Tk graphics library

Some of the standard extensions, such as the Tk graphics library (the last item on the previous list), span more than one file; you'll see a large number of files with names beginning with *tk*, as well as a whole `tk` subdirectory, all of which are part of the Ruby Tk library.

Browsing your `rubylibdir` will give you a good (although possibly overwhelming, but in a good way) sense of the many tasks for which Ruby provides programming facilities. Most programmers use only a subset of these capabilities, but even a subset of such a large collection of programming libraries makes a huge difference.

The C extensions directory (archdir)

Usually located one level down from the `rubylibdir`, the `archdir` contains architecture-specific extensions and libraries. The files in this directory generally have names ending in `.so` or `.dll` (depending on your platform). These files are C-language extensions to Ruby; or, more precisely, they are the binary, runtime-loadable files generated from Ruby's C-language extension code, compiled into binary form as part of the Ruby installation process.

Like the Ruby-language program files in the `rubylibdir`, the files in the `archdir` contain standard library components that you can require into your own programs. (Among others, you'll see the file for the `rbconfig` extension—the extension you're using with irb to uncover the directory names.) These files are not human-readable, but the Ruby interpreter knows how to load them when asked to do so. From the perspective of the Ruby programmer, all standard libraries are equally useable, whether written in Ruby or written in C and compiled to binary format.

The site_ruby directory (sitedir) and its subdirectories (sitelibdir, sitearchdir)

Your Ruby installation includes a subdirectory called `site_ruby`. As its name suggests (albeit telegraphically), `site_ruby` is where you and/or your system administrator store third-party extensions and libraries. Some of these may be code you yourself write; others are tools you download from other people's sites and archives of Ruby libraries.

The `site_ruby` directory parallels the main Ruby installation directory, in the sense that it has its own subdirectories for Ruby-language and C-language extensions (`sitelibdir` and `sitearchdir`, respectively, in `Config` terms). When you require an extension, the Ruby interpreter checks for it in these subdirectories of `site_ruby` as well as in both the main `rubylibdir` and the main `archdir`.

The gems directory

This directory is a little different; it isn't part of Ruby's internal configuration information because it's for something that gets installed separately: the Ruby-Gems packaging system. But you'll probably see it on any system with Rails installed, for the simple reason that the Rails framework is usually distributed and installed using the RubyGems system.

The `gems` directory is usually at the same level as `site_ruby`; so, if you've found `site_ruby`, look at what else is installed next to it. Inside the `gems` directory are one or more subdirectories; and if you explore these, you'll find (possibly among other things) the source code for the Rails framework.

We'll stop here, because the Rails source is a topic for later in the book (particularly for the last chapter, chapter 17). But you have a sense for where Ruby puts files and directories. We'll finish this section with a look at some applications and other programming facilities that come bundled with Ruby.

1.4.3 *Important standard Ruby tools and applications*

We'll round out our overview of the Ruby programming environment by examining some of the most important tools Ruby provides for programmers. (irb belongs on this list, but it was discussed already and therefore isn't reintroduced here.)

The debugger

Debugging—fixing errors—is part of programming. There are many techniques for debugging programs, ranging from rigorous testing to asking for advice on a chat channel.

The Ruby debugging facility (found in the library file `debug.rb`) helps you debug a program by letting you run the program one instruction at a time, with pauses in between. During the pauses, you're presented with a prompt; at this prompt, you can examine the values of variables, see where you are in a nested series of commands, and resume execution. You can also set *breakpoints*—places in your program where the debugger stops execution and presents you with the prompt.

Here's a run of `c2fi.rb`—the version of the Celsius converter that takes keyboard input—through the debugger. Note the use of the `step` command; it tells the debugger to run the next instruction. Note too that the debugger's prompt gets run in with the output of the `print` command—which, as you'll recall, doesn't automatically add a newline character to its output. You use the `v l` command along the way to examine the values of the local variables `c` and `t`. This example runs Ruby with the `debug` extension loaded:

```
$ ruby -rdebug c2fi.rb #1
Debug.rb
Emacs support available.

c2fi.rb:3:print "Please enter a Celsius temperature: "
(rdb:1) step
Please enter a Celsius temperature: c2fi.rb:4:c = gets.to_i
(rdb:1) step
25
c2fi.rb:5:f = (c * 9 / 5) + 32
(rdb:1) step
c2fi.rb:5:f = (c * 9 / 5) + 32
(rdb:1) step
c2fi.rb:6:puts f
(rdb:1) v l
  c => 25
  f => 77
(rdb:1) step
77
```

Some programmers are more at home in the debugger than others. Running a program this way differs a great deal from a normal run, and some people prefer to debug a program by inserting instructions in the program itself to display information on the screen during a program run. That approach to debugging can be messy, because you have to go back into your program file and disable or remove the lines that do the displaying. On the other hand, you have to go back into the file anyway to fix the bug.

Whatever your personal work habits in the realm of debugging, it's useful to know that the Ruby debugging facility is available.

Profiling

In programming terms, *profiling* means measuring how much use is made of system resources—time, principally—by different parts of your program. This starts to matter with longer programs, particularly programs that involve looping through instructions many times (for example, a program that reads in a long file and examines or modifies the contents of each line as it's read in).

None of the examples up to this point require profiling, because they're short and simple. However, if you want to see the kind of information that the profiler gives you—and if you can regard it stoically without worrying, because much of it will be hard to decipher, at this stage—try running the following command:

```
$ ruby -r profile c2fi.rb
```

Stand back to make room for the output.

Profiling pinpoints the spots in a program that are using lots of system resources and therefore potentially slowing the program. The information provided by the profiler may lead you to tweak part of a program to make it run more efficiently; or, if there's no relatively easy way around the resource bottleneck, it may lead you to rewrite part of the program in C, to make it run faster.

ri and RDoc

ri (Ruby Index) and RDoc (Ruby Documentation) are a closely related pair of tools for providing documentation about Ruby programs. ri is a command-line tool; the RDoc system includes the command-line tool rdoc. ri and rdoc are stand-alone programs; you run them from the command line. You can also use the facilities they provide from within your Ruby programs.

RDoc is a documentation system. If you put comments in your program files (Ruby or C) in the prescribed RDoc format, rdoc scans your files, extracts the comments, organizes them intelligently (indexed according to what they comment on), and creates nicely formatted documentation from them. You can see RDoc markup in many of the C files in the Ruby source tree and many of the Ruby files in the Ruby installation.

ri dovetails with RDoc: It gives you a way to view the information that RDoc has extracted and organized. Specifically (although not exclusively, if you customize it), ri is configured to display the RDoc information from the Ruby source files. Thus on any system that has Ruby fully installed, you can get detailed information about Ruby with a simple command-line invocation of ri. For example, if you want the full, official description of what require does, you can type

```
$ ri require
```

(You'll get more than you want or need, right now—but exactly the right amount once you've learned about the roots and branches of the require mechanism.)

ri and RDoc are the work of Dave Thomas.

ERb

Last but not least (not by a long shot, in connection with Rails), Ruby provides you with a program called ERb (Embedded Ruby), written by Seki Masatoshi. ERb allows you to put Ruby code inside an HTML file. Or is it putting HTML in a program file?

It's really both: You get to embed (hence the name) Ruby inside non-Ruby, and ERb interprets the whole thing as program input.

ERb reads a file—an ERb *document*—and prints it out again. Except you're allowed to insert Ruby programming instructions in the document (using a special syntax, described in a moment). When ERb hits the Ruby instructions, it executes them. Depending on what you've asked for, it either moves on or prints out the results of executing the instructions.

ERb reads along, word for word, and then at a certain point (when it sees the Ruby code embedded in the document) it sees that it has to fill in a blank, which it does by executing the Ruby code.

You need to know only two things to prepare an ERb document:

- If you want some Ruby code executed, enclose it between <% and %>.

- If you want the *result* of the code execution to be printed out, as part of the output, enclose the code between <%= and %>.

ERb will figure out what to do when it hits <% or <%=.

Here's an example. Save the code from listing 1.5 in your `ruby4rails` directory as `erbdemo.rb`:

Listing 1.5   Demonstration of ERb (erbdemo.rb)

```
<% page_title = "Demonstration of ERb" %>
<% salutation = "Dear programmer," %>
<html>
<head>
<title><%= page_title %></title>
</head>
<body>
<p><%= salutation %></p>
<p>This is a brief demonstration of how ERb fills out a template.</p>
</body>
</html>
```

Now, run the program using the command-line utility erb instead of ruby:

```
$ erb erbdemo.rb

<html>
<head>
<title>Demonstration of ERb</title> #5
</head>
<body>
<p>Dear programmer,</p>
```

```
<p>This is a brief demonstration of how ERb fills out a template.</p>
</body>
</html>
```

The output of the program run is just what you'd expect, given the rules for how ERb reads and interprets its input. The first two lines of the program are interpreted as Ruby instructions (that is, the parts inside the `<%...%>` markers; the markers themselves are ignored). Once those two lines have been read, you have two variables to work with: `page_title` and `salutation`. The HTML markup instruction `<html>` is read in literally and printed out literally, with no change. That's the first line of output (except for two blank lines; erb gave you a blank line for each of those `<%...%>` lines). The `<head>` tag also comes through in the output just as it appeared in the input.

In the `<title>` tag, you see some Ruby code inside a `<%= ... %>` delimiter pair. These are the delimiters you use when you want the result of evaluating the code to be inserted into the ERb output. The Ruby code, in this case, is the single variable `page_title`, and the value of that variable is the string "Demonstration of ERb". (You know this because you assigned that value to the title variable on the first line.) So, at this point in the output, ERb fills in the perceived blank with "Demonstration of ERb".

ERb looms very large in the Ruby on Rails framework. Essentially, what you see on the screen when you connect to a Rails application is, in many cases, the output from an ERb document. That's a major part of how Rails works: It sets up values for variables based on the database it's working with (and various formulas and manipulations you specify), and then, based on the values of those variables, it renders a screen's worth of HTML, courtesy of asking ERb to insert the values into the document at the appropriate places. Getting a conceptual handle on ERb at this stage will serve you well in the course of your use of Rails.

1.5 Summary

In this chapter, we've walked through some important foundational Ruby material and facilities. You've learned some important terminology, including the difference between Ruby (the programming language overall) and ruby (the name of the Ruby interpreter program). You've completed (in miniature, but still from start to finish) the process of writing a Ruby program, saving it in a file, checking it for syntax errors, and running it. You've gotten a taste of how to do keyboard input in Ruby as well as file input and output. You've also learned how to pull in one program file from another with `require` and `load`.

Section 1.2 introduced some of the details of interpreter invocation, in particular Ruby's command-line switches (not all of them, but a selection of the most common and useful) and the use of the interactive Ruby interpreter, irb, for testing, learning, and playing with Ruby.

We then looked at Ruby extensions and libraries, including some specific example but focusing mainly on the mechanism for calling up extensions in your code (with `require`). This overview also included discussion of C extensions, which are often used for speed or for easy interaction with existing C libraries written outside of Ruby.

The last section in this chapter took you on a guided tour of the Ruby programming environment. We took stock of the source tree for Ruby—a fount of information and detail—as well as the Ruby installation. The programming environment also includes useful applications and program development facilities, such as ERb, RDoc, `ri`, and the debugging and profiling libraries bundled with Ruby.

You now have a good blueprint of how Ruby works and what tools the Ruby programming environment provides. In the next chapter, we'll present a similar introduction to the Rails development environment, but we'll go a lot further in the direction of writing actual code. As you'll see, the Ruby and Rails environments interact very effectively.

How Rails works

2

This chapter covers

- Overview of the Rails framework
- Details of how Rails handles incoming requests
- Domain modeling and database creation
- A complete sample Rails application

In this chapter, we'll look at the anatomy of both the Rails framework overall and the typical Rails application. In the spirit of chapter 1, this exploration will include both a medium-level overview and an introduction to some important concepts. In the spirit of Rails—the spirit, that is, of easy, rapid development of Web applications—it will also include the creation of a working application.

The Ruby on Rails *framework*—the programs and programming libraries that you get when you install Rails on your system—exists for the purpose of allowing you to write individual Rails *applications*. A Rails application is the program that takes control when someone connects to a Rails-driven Web site. It may be an online shopping service, a survey site, a library catalog, a collaborative authorship site, or any of many other things. The nature and purpose of Rails applications vary widely. But the overall shape of one Rails application is much like that of another; and the framework holds steady. We'll be looking closely at how both the framework and a typical application work.

2.1 *Inside the Rails framework*

A framework is a program, set of programs, and/or code library that writes most of your application for you. When you use a framework, your job is to write the parts of the application that make it do the specific things you want.

> **NOTE** GETTING RAILS AND RAILS INFORMATION   This book's appendix contains information about installing Rails and pointers on where to get more information. You may be working on a system with Rails installed already; but if not, or if you want to make sure you have your finger on the pulse of the major sources of Rails information, look at the appendix.

The term *framework* comes from the field of building construction, where it refers to a partially built house or building. Once a house reaches the framework stage, much of the work of building is done—but the house looks exactly like any other house in the same style at the same stage. It's only after the framework is in place that the builders and designers start to do things that make the house distinct from other houses.

Unlike scaffolding, which gets removed once the house is built, the framework is part of the house. That's true in the case of Ruby on Rails, too. When you run your application, the Rails framework—the code installed in the various Rails directories on your computer—is part of it. You didn't write that code, but it's still part of your application; it still gets executed when your application runs.

A computer application framework like Rails and a house framework are different in one important respect: The computer framework is reusable. Install Rails once, and it serves as the framework for any number of applications. What it provides, it keeps providing; you *never* have to write the parts of your application that are pre-written as part of Rails.

The difference between what you can do with Rails and what you would have to do if you wrote the equivalent of a Rails application from scratch is considerable. If you're developing a shopping cart site with Rails, you have to decide things like whether shipping charges will be shown before checkout, or whether to slap up links to products similar to those in the customer's cart. But you *don't* have to design a translator that automatically maps database table names to Ruby method names, or write a comprehensive library of helper routines that automate the generation of HTML form elements, or engineer a system that layers automatic method calls in a particular order based on a simple list. These tasks (and many more) have been programmed already, and they're available to every Rails application.

The Rails framework exists to be used, and it's designed for use. The best way to understand both the "what" and the "why" of its design, and its relation to the language in which it's written, is to first grasp what you're supposed to do when you use it.

2.1.1 *A framework user's–eye view of application development*

When you set out to write a Rails application—leaving aside configuration and other housekeeping chores—you have to perform three primary tasks:

1 *Describe and model your application's domain.* The domain is the universe of your application. The domain may be music store, university, dating service, address book, or hardware inventory. Whatever it is, you have to figure out what's in it—what entities exist in this universe—and how the items in it relate to each other. The domain description you come up with will guide the design of your database (which you'll need to create and initialize using the administrative tools provided by the database system) as well as some of the particulars of the Rails application.

2 *Specify what can happen in this domain.* The domain model is static; it's just things. Now you have to get dynamic. Addresses can be added to an address book. Musical scores can be purchased from music stores. Users can log in to a dating service. Students can register for classes at a university. You need to identify all the possible scenarios or actions that the elements of your domain can participate in.

3   *Choose and design the publicly available views of the domain.* At this point, you can start thinking in Web-browser terms. Once you've decided that your domain has students, and that they can register for classes, you can envision a welcome page, a registration page, and a confirmation page. Customers shopping for shoes may have access to a style selector, a shopping cart, and a checkout page. Each of these pages, or *views*, shows the user how things stand at a certain point along the way in one of your domain's scenarios. You have to decide which views will exist.

Just about everything you do when you develop a Rails application falls into one of these three categories. In some respects, the categories are related; in particular, scripting the specific actions that take place in your domain (category 2) and deciding what views of the domain you'll provide (category 3) go hand in hand. But the layers of development are also separate. That separation isn't a flaw or a fault line, but a strength. Keeping the distinct phases of development separate, while ensuring that they interoperate smoothly, is precisely what a framework should do.

Even frameworks have frameworks; there are different *types* of framework. In the case of Ruby on Rails, we're dealing with a *Model/View/Controller* (MVC) framework.

2.1.2   *Introducing the MVC framework concept*

MVC is the family of frameworks to which Rails belongs, and getting to know about the family traits will help you understand Rails.

The MVC principle divides the work of an application into three separate but closely cooperative subsystems. Although the correct term is MVC, for the sake of matching the framework with the three tasks listed in section 2.1.1, we'll flip it temporarily to MCV (arguably a more sensible order anyway). Model, controller, and view, in the general case of any framework of this type, can be described as follows:

- *Model*—The parts of the application that define the entities that play a role in the universe of the application (books, hammers, shopping carts, students, and so on)

- *Controller*—The facility within the application that directs traffic, on the one hand querying the models for specific data, and on the other hand organizing that data (searching, sorting, massaging it) into a form that fits the needs of a given view

- *View*—A presentation of data in a particular format, triggered by a controller's decision to present the data

Three things happen in an MVC application: You get information; you store and manipulate that information; and you present that information. On its own, that's not remarkable; most computer programs perform operations on data and give you the results. The MVC principle, however, isn't just a description of what happens to the data. It's also the governing principle behind how you, the developer, work on a program.

When you're writing program code to handle one of these areas or *layers* of your application (the models, the controller actions, the views), you are *only* writing code for that layer. If you wake up one day and decide to write all the entity-modeling code for an address-book application, *all* you have to do is make decisions about how you think the address-book universe should be broken down into entities. You don't have to worry about how many fields you'll have to fill in on the screen to add a new entry, or whether to use a Confirm button when you delete someone, or anything else practical or visual. All you have to do is model the domain of the address book. After you've done that, you can start thinking about what you want to be able to *do*, and what kinds of data presentations you want access to (one person at a time, everyone who lives in a particular state, all the G's or B's or T's grouped together, and so on).

This clear-headed division of labor—*your* labor, as well as the application's—makes the MVC approach attractive. You'll get a lot of mileage out of sticking to this three-part worldview when it comes to Rails. Whether you're getting a handle on Rails' theoretical underpinnings, bearing down on the details of writing a real-life Rails application (we'll do both in this chapter), or navigating the directory structure of your application, you'll find that you're always in this three-part structure: a universe populated with entities that are manipulated and controlled through actions that culminate in publicly available views.

2.1.3 *Meet MVC in the (virtual) flesh*

To see MVC close up, if you haven't already—and even if you have (you'll need to perform this next step anyway, for later)—run the following command from a directory in which you'd like to place the sample Rails application directory:

```
$ rails r4rmusic1
```

The program `rails`, which is installed with the Rails framework, performs the task of creating an application directory—in this case, a directory called `r4rmusic1`. (Any name will do for this example; but that particular name and directory will come in handy when we write the sample application.) Inside the application directory, Rails creates a set of standard subdirectories, populating them with files necessary for the development and running of a Rails application. If you look inside the app subdirectory, you'll see (among other things) subdirectories called models, controllers, and views. The relevant model and controller program files and view templates will reside in these subdirectories. The MVC principle guides the layout of the application and the way the work of programming is organized.

NOTE RAILS APPLICATION NAMES Unlike a domain name, which everyone who wants to connect to your site must know, the internal name of your Rails application (for example, r4rmusic1, or myrailsapp) is only the business of whoever's writing and/or maintaining the application. It's just a directory name; it doesn't even have to be publicized. If you plan to distribute or sell your Rails application, then you have to start worrying about "branding" the application with a unique name. But that kind of branding is independent of what the application and its directory are called internally on the system that hosts them.

You've now seen that three phases or layers of activity are associated with writing a Rails application, and that they correspond to the three elements of the MVC framework concept. Let's turn to a closer look at how the Rails framework operates as an MVC implementation.

2.2 Analyzing Rails' implementation of MVC

The MVC concept is all about dividing the work of programming and the functioning of a program into three layers: model, view, and controller. In accordance with its MVC foundations, Rails is made up largely of three separate programming libraries—separate in the sense that each has its own name and you can, if you need to, use them separately from each other.

The three libraries forming the bulk of the Rails framework are listed in table 2.1. You can see these three libraries installed on your computer. They usually reside in the gems area of a Ruby installation. (See the book's appendix for information about RubyGems.) Assuming a standard, default installation, you can find them like this:

```
$ cd /usr/local/lib/ruby/gems/1.8/gems
$ ls
```

Table 2.1 Overview of how Rails implements the MVC framework design

MVC phase	Rails sublibrary	Purpose
Model	ActiveRecord	Provides an interface and binding between the tables in a relational database and the Ruby program code that manipulates database records. Ruby method names are automatically generated from the field names of database tables, and so on.
View	ActionView	An Embedded Ruby (ERb) based system for defining presentation templates for data presentation. Every Web connection to a Rails application results in the displaying of a view.
Controller	ActionController	A data broker sitting between ActiveRecord (the database interface) and ActionView (the presentation engine). ActionController provides facilities for manipulating and organizing data from the database and/or from Web form input, which it then hands off to ActionView for template insertion and display.

You'll see subdirectories including (but not limited to) the following:

- `actionpack-1.11.2`
- `activerecord-1.13.2`
- `rails-1.0.0`

NOTE YOUR VERSION NUMBERS MAY VARY   The version numbers you see on the right sides of the directory names may differ from those in this example. And on some systems, more than one version of each package may be installed. If that's the case, look for the versions with the highest numbers, which will give you the most recent version of each library installed on the system.

ActionView and ActionController are bundled together under ActionPack. To see them separately, do this:

```
$ ls actionpack-1.11.2/lib
```

You'll see subdirectories for each of them.

Looking at these directory listings gives you a concrete sense of the fact that Rails is made up of component packages and that these packages, collectively, constitute an implementation of the MVC structure.

NOTE THE CONTENTS OF ACTIONPACK   ActionView and ActionController are bundled together as ActionPack because in the MVC structure, V and C (view and controller) tend to be closely intertwined. For example, the template files that ActionView processes must use the same names for variables that the controller code, based on ActionController, uses. That means you can't design a view without knowing fairly specifically what's going on in the controller files. Although they are separate libraries in a sense, ActionView and ActionController can also be seen as two parts of a single suite.

Rails: the ties that bind

If these three MVC-friendly, separate libraries are the components of Rails, what exactly is Rails?

The Rails framework is to a large extent *the simultaneous deployment* of all three of these component packages or libraries. ActiveRecord provides a range of programming techniques and shortcuts for manipulating data from an SQL database. ActionController and ActionView (ActionPack, collectively) provide facilities for manipulating and displaying that data. Rails ties it all together.

Figure 2.1 gives you a schematic view of how Ruby and Rails fit together, along with the database system that stores your Rails data and the Web server that exports your finalized HTML pages. Arrows indicate close collaboration between system components.

Subdirectories in your Rails installation correspond to the support libraries mentioned in figure 2.1. We won't discuss these libraries in as much detail as the "Big Three" (those that correspond directly to the MVC framework concept), but these other libraries provide important support and auxiliary functionality outside the strict MVC division and are often used in more than one of the phases.

Having gotten as far as connecting the dots, so to speak, between the components of Rails and the components of the MVC framework structure, and situating the bundle in the context of the relationship between Rails and Ruby, we'll now embark on writing a Rails application. It will be small; the purpose is to do a breadth-first walk-through of the process. We'll revisit and extend this example to in part 4 of the book. For now, we'll get a foot in the Rails door with a modest—but working—application.

The application we'll develop is an online classical sheet-music store. We'll name the mythical store in honor of this book: R4RMusic. If you haven't already done so, issue the `rails r4rmusic1` command to create the directory for the application. (The `1` at the end signals that this is the first version of the application.)

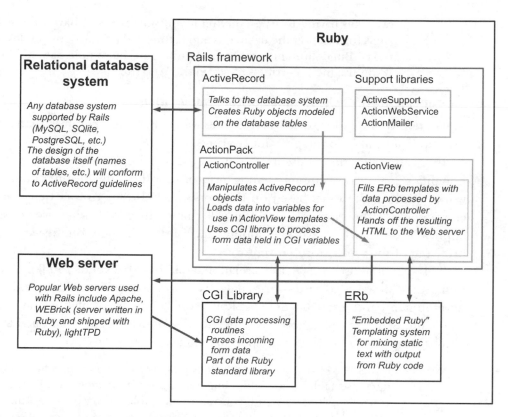

Figure 2.1   Schematic view of Ruby and the Rails framework

2.3   *A Rails application walk-through*

The steps we'll follow in writing the R4RMusic application are, in essence, the three steps outlined at the beginning of this chapter and echoed in the MVC concept—or, in keeping with how we'll proceed initially, the MCV concept: modeling the domain, programming the possible actions, and designing the available views. The goal at the moment is to have something in place that we can add to incrementally. That's often the way Rails applications evolve.

NOTE   DOWNLOADING THE MUSIC STORE CODE AND SQL FROM THE BOOK'S WEB SITE   You can download the complete application code for R4RMusic (both the version developed in this chapter and the revised version developed in part 4), along with files containing the SQL commands for creating the tables and adding some sample data to them, from the *Ruby for Rails* Web site (http://www.manning.com/books/black). Doing so will save you having to type everything yourself. You still have to follow the steps for creating the databases and setting the permissions (as described next). But defining the tables and pulling in the sample data will be easy if you use the pre-written file from the Web site.

2.3.1 *Introducing R4RMusic, the music-store application*

The details of the music store will unfold as we go. But a few comments and directives up front will help you get your bearings.

In this first iteration of the music store, we'll only implement a couple of functionalities, mainly pertaining to letting a visitor view the online listings of available works. We'll create views based on the works and also let visitors view works by composer. For the moment—and this will change in part 4, when we revisit the application—we won't have any shopping facilities. We'll focus on the viewing and browsing of the music store's inventory.

This example uses MySQL as its relational database backend. You'll create and initialize a MySQL database—three databases, to correspond to the production, development, and test databases that Rails expects to have available. You can also adapt the SQL examples here for other Rails-supported relational database systems. (PostgreSQL and SQLite are popular alternatives to MySQL.)

> **NOTE** RAILS MIGRATIONS Rails provides a facility for generating and updating database tables and fields semi-automatically: *migrations*. Migrations let you specify the structure you want your tables to have using Ruby code, rather than SQL; the migrations engine takes care of the SQL creation. Migrations also allow for tracking of changes to a database design and even the reversing of design changes. In the long run, using migrations instead of writing SQL by hand can make a lengthy, complex development process easier. At the same time, migrations introduce complexities of their own. We're not using them in this book, both because of some of their complexities and because spelling out the SQL better serves the purpose of keeping the layers of the Rails application universe in clear view. But you should investigate migrations for yourself, in connection with your Rails work.

The databases will be named *r4rmusic1_production*, *r4rmusic1_development*, and *r4rmusic1_test*. Assuming that you called the application r4rmusic1 when you asked Rails to create the directory for it, these database names will appear automatically in the application's database configuration file (the file database.yml in the application's config subdirectory). What you have to do to create the databases will depend on the database system you're using. (Some further details, especially for MySQL, are included in the next section.)

2.3.2 *Modeling the first iteration of the music-store domain*

The first phase of development is to model the domain. *Model*, taken broadly, means not only defining and describing the entities in the universe of our application, but also designing and creating the databases that the application will use. On the Rails side, it also means putting in place the files and program code that the ActiveRecord subsystem—the library concerned with the database records and their manipulation through Ruby code—can use.

In the spirit of creating something simple but operational, we'll model three entities:

- WORK (that is, musical composition; *work* is a conveniently short word)
- COMPOSER
- EDITION

It would be even simpler (or at least smaller) to model only WORK rather than both WORK and EDITION. But a little reflection reveals that splitting the work from its editions makes sense. A symphony doesn't have a publisher or price; those things pertain to specific published editions. Keeping the work separate from the edition also means that the database design can be expanded later to include CDs and other formats, in addition to sheet music.

Diagraming the domain

Much of the work of modeling a domain comes down to this fact: A domain consists of *entities* (things), and an entity consists of a combination of *properties* (text-strings and numbers; simple, flat, scalar values, like the title of a composition or a year of publication) and *other entities*.

There are lots of ways to represent domain models visually. One of the simplest, and one that you can use regardless of whether you have graphics software, is to list the entities in your domain and, under each entity, to list that entity's properties. In some cases, a property of one entity is another entity; for example, a musical work has a *composer* property, and a composer is an entity in its own right. We'll indicate this by using uppercase for all entities, whether they appear at the top level of the diagram or are embedded under another entity as one of that other entity's properties.

Rendered this way, the domain looks like this:

```
WORK
   COMPOSER
   EDITION(S)
   title

COMPOSER
   WORKS(S)
   first name
   last name

EDITION
   WORK
   description
   publisher
   year
   price
```

(The *description* property of the EDITION entity will contain strings, like "Second" for a second edition, or "Facsimile" for a facsimile edition.)

Figure 2.2 shows a graphical representation of the same domain.

Notice that the entity relations are circular: A WORK has one or more EDITIONS, and each EDITION has a WORK. To translate these relationships into Rails terms, we need to make a subtle but important distinction between two shades of meaning of *has*. When you see a one-to-many relationship like this, you're really seeing a relationship where Thing X *has* one or more Thing Ys, and Thing Y *belongs to* a Thing X.

Translating that into WORK/EDITION terms, a WORK *has* one or more EDITIONS (zero or more, but that's logically impossible); and an EDITION *belongs to* a WORK. Similarly, each WORK *belongs to* a COMPOSER, and each COMPOSER *has* one or more WORKS.

That way of looking at it will see you through the rest of the database creation and entity modeling processes.

Figure 2.2   Graphic sketching out of the R4RMusic entities and their properties

Initializing the databases

To create the database for the application, you need to initialize a database on your system. How you do this will depend on which database backend you're using. In these examples, the database system is MySQL. (Instructions for, and discussion of, using other database systems, including MySQL, PostgreSQL, and SQLite, abound on the various Ruby on Rails Web sites and discussion groups.)

In keeping with Rails practice, we'll initialize three databases: one for development, one for production, and one for testing. In keeping with default Rails terminology, because we called the application r4rmusic1, we'll call the databases *r4rmusic1_development*, *r4rmusic1_production*, and *r4rmusic1_test*. You should initialize all three of them and create a user and password on them with full read and write privileges.

> **WARNING** MAKE UP YOUR OWN PASSWORDS Where you see the password *railzrulez* in these examples, you should choose a password of your own. Otherwise, everyone who sees this book will know your database password.

In MySQL, a console session in which you do this looks something like this:

```
mysql> create database r4rmusic1_development;
Query OK, 1 row affected (0.01 sec)

mysql> grant all privileges on r4rmusic1_development.*
to 'r4r'@'localhost' identified by 'railzrulez';
Query OK, 0 rows affected (0.00 sec)
```

You then do the same thing for two more databases: *r4rmusic1_production* and *r4rmusic1_test*.

At this point, you need to let Rails in on the user name and password for the databases. You do this in the file database.yml, in the config subdirectory. This file has live configuration sections for MySQL databases and sample sections for other database systems. In each of the sections you use (the three MySQL sections, if you're using MySQL as per the examples here), you need to change the username and password lines to reflect the permissions on the databases you've created:

```
username: r4r
password: railzrulez
```

The names of the databases should correspond to the ones you've created. (If they don't, you've probably mistyped either the database names when you created them or the application name when you created the application. You'll need to fix these before you proceed.)

Designing and creating the database tables

We have three modeled entities in our domain, and we want three database tables. With more complex domains—even the music store domain, in more complex form—the correspondence isn't always one to one. Sometimes there are extra tables that store information about relationships between entities rather than information about specific entities. For the moment, though, our domain model yields a one-to-one relationship between entities and tables.

Translating a domain model into SQL is generally straightforward, as long as you remember that you have to write Rails-friendly SQL. Down the road, Rails will work with the database—not just pluck records from it, but also look at the design of the tables and use that design as a point of departure for providing you with a lot of programming functionality. Your end of the bargain is to set things up in such a way that all of Rails' techniques for interpreting table structure will work.

In practical terms (and to the extent it relates to our three tables), that means that you have to follow certain rules:

- Each entity (such as EDITION) gets a table in the database named after it, but in the plural (*editions*).

- Each such entity-matching table has a field called *id*, which contains a unique integer for each record inserted into the table.

- Given entity x and entity y, if entity y belongs to entity x, then table *y* has a field called *x_id*.

- The bulk of the fields in any table store the values for that entity's simple properties (anything that's a number or a string).

The third rule is slightly opaque. In this case, it means that the *editions* table has a field called *work_id*. This corresponds to the concept that each edition belongs to a particular work. When an edition record is inserted into the table, its *work_id* field will be given the same value as the *id* field of the work to which it belongs. That way, each edition record is labeled with a kind of property tag, identifying it as the property of a particular work. (Because *id* values are unique—they serve as *primary keys*—a single integer is enough to identify an edition unambiguously with the correct work.)

You can also flip this explanation and say that each work has one or more editions. The *have* and *belongs to* relationships are the same thing, just expressed from a different perspective. And what's true of the work/edition relationship is also true of the composer/work relationship in this domain model.

The domain diagram and the requirements and constraints pertaining to the SQL result in the SQL commands shown in listing 2.1.

Listing 2.1   SQL commands for creating the basic music store database tables

```
USE r4rmusic1_development;
DROP TABLE IF EXISTS works;
DROP TABLE IF EXISTS editions;
DROP TABLE IF EXISTS composers;

CREATE TABLE works (
   id INT(11) NOT NULL AUTO_INCREMENT,
   composer_id INT(11),
   title VARCHAR(100),
   PRIMARY KEY (id)
);

CREATE TABLE editions (
   id INT(11) NOT NULL AUTO_INCREMENT,
   work_id INT(11) NOT NULL,
   description VARCHAR(30),
   publisher VARCHAR(60),
   year INT(4),
   price FLOAT,
   PRIMARY KEY  (id)
);

CREATE TABLE composers (
   id INT(11) NOT NULL AUTO_INCREMENT,
   first_name VARCHAR(25),
   last_name VARCHAR(25),
   PRIMARY KEY (id)
);
```

You can create the tables in the database by saving these SQL commands to a file or, even better, using the file r4rmusic1.sql, which you can download as part of the complete R4RMusic application package from the *Ruby for Rails* Web site (http://www.manning.com/books/black). Feed the SQL file to MySQL like this (entering the password when prompted):

```
$ mysql -u r4r -p < r4rmusic1.sql
```

The *r4rmusic1_development* database now contains tables; and if you used the prewritten file from the book's Web site, it also contains sample data. Now, let's work on some Rails application code to match the database.

Writing the Rails model files

It's time to work on the Rails application code—specifically, the two model files `work.rb` and `edition.rb`. First, we have to create those models. Rails does this semi-automatically. From the top level of the application directory, issue the following commands:

```
$ ruby script/generate model work
$ ruby script/generate model edition
$ ruby script/generate model composer
```

You'll find the three files you need in the `app/models` directory. `work.rb` looks like this:

```
class Work < ActionRecord::Base
end
```

`composer.rb` and `edition.rb` look similar. What you see (and don't worry if there's a bit of black-box syndrome at this stage) are empty definitions of Ruby classes. (They're not as empty as they look; they have facilities for setting and retrieving all the entity properties: *title, composer, publisher,* and so on. Rails endows them with those facilities automatically, courtesy of examining the field-names in the database tables.) You need to add directives that tell Rails about the *associations* between entities—that is, the details of the *has* and *belongs to* relationships.

Associations is both a descriptive and a technical term. Associations are part of the ActiveRecord database-handling library. They're a kind of inter-entity modeling subsystem, in which you tell Rails what you consider the relationships between entities to be and, assuming the table and field names you've chosen mesh with what you've asserted, Rails responds by handing you a set of programming features that let you manipulate those relationships easily.

To set up this functionality, you need to tell Rails what relationships you want to establish within the data system. To do so, modify `work.rb` to look like this:

```
class Work < ActionRecord::Base
  belongs_to :composer
  has_many :editions
end
```

Modify `edition.rb` to look like this:

```
class Edition < ActionRecord::Base
  belongs_to :work
end
```

Composers get similar treatment; `composer.rb` should look like this:

```
class Composer < ActionRecord::Base
  has_many :works
end
```

Because we've followed the rules in naming the id-related fields in the database, Rails cooperates by making it easy to add new editions to those belonging to a particular work or even to change which work an edition belongs to (an unlikely scenario, but possible).

Adding records to the database

There are numerous ways to add data to your database, including through Web forms. Here, we'll do it the clunky way: with SQL. This expedient will let us get into the middle of the stream—doing something *with* the data—as quickly as possible.

The SQL commands in listing 2.2, issued to the *music store_development* database, create a small number of records on which we can practice. You are free to add as many records as you like, for any works (real or imagined) you wish.

Listing 2.2   SQL commands for sample music store inventory data

```
INSERT INTO composers
  VALUES (1,"Johannes","Brahms");
INSERT INTO composers VALUES
  VALUES (2,"Claude","Debussy");

INSERT INTO works
  VALUES (1,1,"Sonata for Cello and Piano in F Major");
INSERT INTO works
  VALUES (2,2,"String Quartet");

INSERT INTO editions
  VALUES (1,1,"Facsimile","D. Black Music House", 1998, 21.95);
INSERT INTO editions
  VALUES (2,1,"Urtext","RubyTunes, Inc.", 1977, 23.50);
INSERT INTO editions
  VALUES (3,1,"ed. Y.Matsumoto","RubyTunes, Inc.", 2001, 22.95);
INSERT INTO editions
  VALUES (4,2,"","D. Black Music House", 1995, 39.95);
INSERT INTO editions
  VALUES (5,2,"Reprint of 1894 ed.", "RubyTunes, Inc.", 2003, 35.95);
```

NOTE   GETTING SQL DATA FROM THIS BOOK'S WEB SITE   You can download some sample or *seed* data from the *Ruby for Rails* Web site (http://www.manning.com/books/black), along with the source code for the application.

Note that the second field of each edition record matches the first field—the *id* field—of a particular work. Thus the first two editions are both editions of the Brahms Sonata, whereas the third edition is an edition of the Debussy String Quartet.

We've now completed the domain-modeling phase (and then some) and can move on to defining actions.

2.3.3 *Identifying and programming the actions*

Now we need to think about the scenarios we want to see happen in our domain. The possibilities are endless, depending on your application. In this particular iteration of this particular application, the possibilities are relatively few, but they are more than enough to take us successfully through this phase and onward to the next.

We'll define the following actions:

- Welcome the visitor with a list of all composers whose music is in stock.
- Allow the visitor to click any composer's name and be shown all works by that composer.
- Allow the visitor to click the name of composition and be shown all editions of that composition.
- Allow the visitor to click any edition and be shown details of that edition.

For each of these scenarios, we need to identify (and create, because they don't exist yet) an appropriate *controller*, and in the corresponding controller file, we need to define the appropriate *action*. For each controller/action pair, we also need to design a *view*; this will come in the next section.

Welcoming the visitor

The majority of controllers correspond directly to an entity model: If there's a "work" controller, then there's probably a "work" model. We'll start, however, with a slightly different type of controller. The action of welcoming someone to a site isn't logically connected to an entity. It wouldn't make sense, therefore (although it would be technically possible) to define *welcoming* as an action performed by a work controller or an edition controller. Instead, we'll create another, disembodied controller—a controller that performs actions for us but that isn't specific to one entity—and define the `welcome` action as an action of that controller. We'll call this controller `main`.

The process for creating a controller is always the same, and it's similar to the process we've already used for creating a model. The exact command syntax, however, is a bit different:

```
$ ruby script/generate controller main welcome
```

This command accomplishes several tasks, of which the following are relevant here:

- It creates a file called (including path) app/controllers/main_controller.rb.
- It inserts an empty method definition for the welcome action into that file.
- It creates a file called app/views/main/welcome.rhtml, which will be the file in which you place the ERb template code for this view.

The welcome action

If you look at main_controller.rb, you'll see this:

```
class MainController < ApplicationController

def welcome
  end
end
```

This is a controller file, with one action defined—although the definition is empty. The next step in the process is to decide what, if anything, to put in the definition.

It pays to bend a little on the separation of programming layers and start thinking about the view—not in detail, but in terms of data exchange. The purpose of an action is to stuff data into Ruby variables that the ERb code in the view file can unstuff and display. So, we need to anticipate what data the view will need.

The welcome screen will include a list of all the composers whose works we stock. It turns out that this is easy to accomplish by adding one line to the welcome action:

```
def welcome
  @composers = Composer.find(:all)
end
```

This code asks the *Composer* entity model (not any particular composer, but the model itself—the presiding genius of the model, so to speak) to hand back a list of all known composers. We should do some sorting, so the list looks as nice as possible, so let's change the method as follows:

```
def welcome
  @composers = Composer.find(:all).sort_by {|c| [c.last_name, c.first_name] }
end
```

(You'll learn about sorting collections of objects in chapter 11. For now, note that this call to the sort_by method sorts on the composers' last names and then on their first names in case of a tie.)

Showing a work, edition, or composer

We need controller files for edition, work, and composer, all equipped with a show action. To create them, issue the following commands:

```
$ ruby script/generate controller work show
$ ruby script/generate controller edition show
$ ruby script/generate controller composer show
```

You'll find three new controller files in the app/controllers subdirectory, named for composer, edition, and work. Because we gave the show argument when generating the controllers, an empty show method definition appears in each of the three controller files. You now need to add code to those empty methods.

Both the work show action and the edition show action will utilize a common Rails idiom: grabbing the value of the CGI variable id and using it as an index to find the correct instance of the relevant entity. In other words, if you're in the work controller, performing the show action, and the value of the CGI variable id is 2, then you want to show the work that's indexed as 2. Exactly what *indexed* means (how the number translates into which work is produced) is up to the model. But in the typical case, 2 will be treated as the value of the *id* field in the appropriate database table.

Here's how this idiom looks, in the appropriate place in work_controller.rb:

```
def show
  @work = Work.find(params[:id])
end
```

It looks this way in edition_controller.rb:

```
def show
  @edition = Edition.find(params[:id])
end
```

And, following the same pattern, it looks like this in composer_controller.rb:

```
def show
  @composer = Composer.find(params[:id])
end
```

The composer controller stashes a particular composer into a variable called @composer (and does the same for the edition and work). The values contained in these variables are available to the ERb code in the respective views—as you'll now see.

2.3.4 *Designing the views*

A *view* is an ERb program that shares data with controllers through mutually accessible variables. This differs from the ERb examples in chapter 1, where you put everything—variable assignments and HTML template information—into one file, and feed the file to ERb. (You *can* put controller-style code, such as calculations and data-sifting operations, in your view files, but doing so is consider lopsided. You should perform the calculations in the controller and then let the view use the results.)

If you look in the app/views directory of the music store application, you'll see one subdirectory for each of the controllers we've created: main, composer, edition, and work. Each of these subdirectories was created automatically when the same-named controller was created with the generate script. (You'll also see a layouts subdirectory. We'll create a default layout in the next subsection.)

For every *action* that was specified at the time of the creation of the controller files—the welcome method in the main controller file and the three show methods in the other controller files—you'll find an ERb template file with a matching name. For example, the app/views/work directory contains a file called show.rhtml. This file is the template that will be rendered when the application receives a request for the show action of the work controller.

Controller actions and view template files are connected through naming conventions: An incoming request for the main/welcome action triggers execution of the welcome method in the main controller, followed by rendering of the main/welcome.rhtml file in the views area. You can override the default behavior: You can instruct an action to render a differently named template, and you can piece together views from more than one partial template file, so there's no longer a one-to-one correspondence between the actions and the template files. (We'll use partial templates for the second iteration of the music store application, in part 4 of the book.) But in the basic case, the controller preps the data and stores it in variables, and those variables are used in the ERb file corresponding to that action.

> **NOTE**   ERB ALTERNATIVES ERb provides one mechanism for producing HTML from the data + template formula—but not the only such mechanism. An alternative approach called Builder was developed and contributed to the Rails framework by Jim Weirich. We'll stick to ERb examples here, but you should be aware that there's at least one alternative way to handle this phase of the work of a Rails application.

We've defined four possible controller actions, and we have four views to design: a welcome screen, and one show screen for each of the composer, edition, and work models. We'll now design those views. First, however, we'll design a default layout. This layout will encapsulate everything that we want displayed for *every* view. We'll then proceed to the four views.

Designing a default layout

Layouts are like meta-templates. They contain general template code that surrounds the specific template code of one or more views. A typical default layout might include a menu bar, a copyright notice, and other site-wide elements that it would be a nuisance to have to insert individually into every template file.

The layout uses a special, "magic" variable, `@content_for_layout`, at the point where you want the specific view inserted. The base layout for the music store, shown in listing 2.3, displays a banner above the view and a copyright notice at the bottom of the page. The base layout also contains appropriate XML declarations—again, saving you the trouble of putting them in every template file.

Listing 2.3   Base layout for R4RMusic

```
<!DOCTYPE html PUBLIC "-//W3C//DTD XHTML 1.0 Strict//EN"
"http://www.w3.org/TR/xhtml1/DTD/xhtml1-strict.dtd">
<html xmlns="http://www.w3.org/1999/xhtml" xml:lang="en" lang="en">
<head>
  <title><%= @page_title %></title>
</head>
<body>
<h1 class="banner">The R4R Music Store</h1>
<%= @content_for_layout %>          ⟵——— Interpolate value of magic
<hr/>                                      @content_for_layout variable
<p>Copyright &copy; 2006, R4RMusic</p>
</body>
</html>
```

To use this view as the default, put it in a file with a reasonable name (such as `base.rhtml`) in the `app/views/layouts` directory, and add the following line to the file `app/controllers/application.rb`:

```
class ApplicationController < ActionController::Base
  layout "base"
end
```

`application.rb` is an umbrella controller file; anything you put in here governs not just what happens in connection with a particular controller (such as the composer controller) but all actions, application-wide. Thus specifying a default layout in this file causes all your views to be wrapped appropriately.

> **TIP**   A DEFAULT-DEFAULT LAYOUT NAME   If you call your default layout application.rhtml, you don't even have to specify it in application.rb. (It's good to know how to do the specifying, though.)

The main/welcome view

The welcome view takes advantage of the information in the variable @works to generate a list of works. Each item in the list is a hyperlink pointing to the show action for that work.

Listing 2.4 shows the main/welcome view, which goes in app/views/main/welcome.rhtml. (If you find any automatically generated placeholder lines in this or any other template file, delete them before you enter the template code.)

Listing 2.4   main/welcome.rhtml, **the view for the** main/welcome **action**

```
<p>Click on a composer's name
to see all of that composer's works.</p>
<ul>
  <% @composers.each do |composer| %>        ❶ each
                                                method
  <li><%= link_to "#{composer.first_name} #{composer.last_name}",
                :controller => "composer",
                :action     => "show",
                :id         => composer.id %>
  </li>
  <% end %>
</ul>
```

The main action here is a loop, which goes through the list of works one at a time (that's the gist of the each method ❶). Each time through the loop, a list item is created, complete with a hyperlink generated by the built-in Rails helper method link_to. The advantage of automating the creation of the list of links in this manner is that it scales: Once you've written this template, together with the controller that populates the @composers variable in the first place (which takes all of two lines of code), you never have to change it, whether your database has 3 composers or 300. (With 300 composers, you may want to present them differently—a list of letters, perhaps, each linked to a second-level action and template that displays all the composers whose last names start with that letter. But once you've written the templates you want, they deal with whatever data is thrown at them.)

The show views

We have three entities—*WORK, EDITION*, and *COMPOSER*—and for each of them, we'll define a scenario called show. Each show will be slightly different, in keeping with the fact that each of these three entities consists of different properties:

- Showing a work means showing a list of all available editions of that work.

- Showing an edition means displaying its publisher, date of publication, and price.

- Showing a composer means displaying a list of all works by that composer.

We'll make these showings as mutually hyperlinked as we can.

Each show scenario requires a view file. Hence we'll need three of these:

- app/views/work/show.rhtml

- app/views/edition/show.rhtml

- app/views/composer/show.rhtml

These three template files are shown in listings 2.5, 2.6, and 2.7, respectively.

Listing 2.5 `work/show.rhtml`, **the view for the** `work/show` **action**

```
<p>Available editions of
 <%= @work.title %> by
 <%= "#{@work.composer.first_name} #{@work.composer.last_name}" %>
</p>

<table>
  <tr>
    <th>Edition</th>
    <th>Publisher</th>
  </tr>
  <% @work.editions.each do |ed| %>     ◁————————❶ @work.editions
  <tr>                                              method
    <td><%= link_to ed.description || "(no descr.)",
            :controller => "edition",
            :action     => "show",
            :id         => ed.id %></td>
    <td><%= ed.publisher %></td>
  </tr>
  <% end %>
</table>
```

In the `work/show.rhtml` template, as in the `main/welcome` template, an `each` instruction performs a loop through a list—this time, a list accessed through the method call `@work.editions` ❶. Note that nowhere in any file have we defined a method called `editions`. Rails provides this method automatically, because we have stated that a work *has many* editions.

```
<% @page_title =
   "#{@edition.work.title} (#{@edition.description})" %>
<p>Details of <%= @edition.work.title %>
(<%= @edition.description %>),
by
<%= "#{@edition.work.composer.first_name}
   #{@edition.work.composer.last_name}" %></p>
<table border="1">
  <tr>
    <th>Publisher</th>
    <th>Year</th>
    <th>Price</th>
  </tr>
  <tr>
    <td><%= @edition.publisher %></td>
    <td><%= @edition.year %></td>
    <td>$<%= @edition.price %></td>
  </tr>
</table>
```

In the `edition/show.rhtml` template, notice that a number of method calls to the object `@edition`—and double-barreled method calls, like `@edition.work.title`—are used to extract the information necessary to complete the view. Again, none of these methods had to be defined manually. Some of them exist as a result of directives in the model file—specifically, the directive `belongs_to :work` in the file `edition.rb`. Some, such as `year` and `price`, exist because the *editions* table in the database has fields with those names. The methods spring into being, courtesy of ActiveRecord, so that you can pass information back and forth between the database records and your program using simple Ruby method-call syntax.

```
<% @page_title =
   "Works by #{@composer.first_name} #{@composer.last_name}" %>
<p>Click on any work to see all available editions of that work.</p>
<ul>
  <% @composer.works.each do |work| %>
    <li><%= link_to work.title,
                :controller => "work",
                :action     => "show",
```

```
                    :id          => work.id %>
    </li>
  <% end %>
</ul>
```

The `composer/show.rhtml` template presents a flat list of all the works by the relevant composer. Each item in the list is a link to the `show` view of that work. Admittedly, this list could become long for composers whose works we stock many of. If it ever gets too long, it will be relatively easy to split into several pages. One of the advantages of the MVC layering of program responsibility is that you can make changes at the view level without having to alter the data structures.

At this point, we have everything we need to start the application and connect to it. We have a database that reflects the current state of our domain model and contains a little data. We have ActiveRecord model files containing association directives (`belongs_to`, `has_many`) that will prompt Rails to engineer the relationships among entities that you need. The view templates are ready to be filled in, and the controller files are ready to provide them with the data they need.

Now, we'll connect to the application.

2.3.5 *Connecting to the application*

We'll serve the application by using WEBrick, a Web server bundled with Ruby. (You can also use Apache or another server, but WEBrick is easier to demonstrate because it doesn't require a lot of configuration up front—and everyone who has Ruby installed also has WEBrick installed.) Before doing that, let's add a finishing touch: setting the default page for the application to be the welcome page.

Specifying a default top-level page with a route

We need to define a *route*: a translation rule, which is applied to the URL of the incoming request to a Rails application. In this case, we want to translate an empty URL (that is, a domain) into a call to the `welcome` action of the `main` controller.

Routes are defined in the file `config/routes.rb`. Add the following line, which must be the first `map.connect` line in the file:

```
map.connect '', :controller => "main", :action => "welcome"
```

This line establishes the rule that will perform the appropriate translation of an empty URL.

To get this default page working correctly, you also have to remove the *default* default page—namely, the file `public/index.html`. You can either delete this file or rename it to something else (such as `index.html.hidden`) so that it won't compete for top-level-page status with the `main/welcome` action.

Starting WEBrick and connecting to the application

Start the WEBrick server with the following command (issued, like the others, from the top level of your application directory):

```
$ ruby ./script/server [-b domainname] [-p port]
```

The `-b` and `-p` flags are optional (as indicated by their placement in square brackets). You can use them to specify values if the server doesn't start up correctly.

Now, point your browser at `http://localhost:3000` (or whatever values you gave, if you used the optional flags). You should see the welcome screen—and, if all went well, the list of works.

> **NOTE** CHECKING THE DEVELOPMENT LOG FILE   If all did not go well, and if you can't tell what's wrong, look in the `log/development.log` file. Here you'll see error messages that tell you about syntax and other errors that may have been encountered. Fix anything that's misnamed or mistyped, and try again. If a syntax error occurred, you can try connecting again during the same server session. If it's a problem affecting the database connection, you may need to stop the server (with Ctrl-C or a `kill` command) and restart it. (If in doubt, there's no harm in doing this.)

We've completed the circuit: The application is running. Play with the site as you wish. You can add new database records, move elements around in the views—whatever you wish. Save a copy of the pristine application, because you'll be using it as a point of reference and a starting point for further development later in the book. But there's no reason not to also use it as a scratchpad for learning your way around, if you wish.

Now that we've reached the plateau of a working application, we'll take the opportunity to examine more deeply what's happening during a successful Rails session.

2.4 *Tracing the lifecycle of a Rails run*

You've seen the way a framework helps organize an application, and you've seen the way Rails implements the MVC concept. You've also walked through the process of writing and running a Rails application—a modest one, but one that involves the three major steps.

To round off this annotated tour of how Rails works, we'll look in detail at what happens when a request comes in from a Web client to a Rails application. The players in the game include the Web server and several auxiliary scripts and programs automatically made available to the Rails application. Although we're using WEBrick for the working example, we'll examine the basics of what's involved with setting up Apache to serve a Rails application. This process is more complicated—which is why you aren't doing it in the working example, and why it contains useful lessons about how the whole request-handling process operates.

The process of listening to and responding to a request coming in to a Rails application can be broken into several stages: the Web server talking to the dispatcher (which is a Ruby program); the dispatcher awakening the appropriate controller and asking that controller (which is also a Ruby program) to perform a particular action; the performance of that action; and the filling out of the view, based on the calculations and data manipulations carried out in the controller action. We'll look at each of these stages in turn.

As you read, you may want to refer to figure 2.3, which gives a graphical overview of the Rails request-handling process.

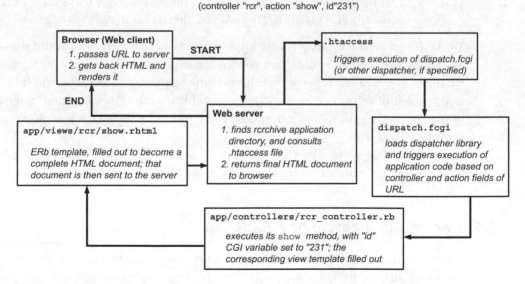

Figure 2.3   Flow of steps involved in Rails' typical handling of an incoming request

Figure 2.3 uses a URL sent to the RCRchive (Ruby Change Request) site as an example; the URL triggers the display in the client's browser of RCR #231. Note that this figure is schematic; the arrows leading from one step to another give you an indication of the sequence, rather than a technical characterization of how information is handed around. Still, as a visual anchor for understanding the basic steps in the process, the figure can help you as you proceed through the rest of this section.

2.4.1 Stage 1: server to dispatcher

The Web server—Apache, lightTPD, or whatever it may be on a given system— receives the request from the browser. The server configuration causes the server to pass the request along to what will turn out to be a Rails application. The server doesn't know what Rails is; it just does whatever redirecting or deflecting of the incoming request it's set up to do.

For example, to steer the Apache server to the directory of your Rails application, you put something like this in the Apache configuration file:

```
<VirtualHost www.r4rmusic.com>
ServerName www.r4rmusic.com
ServerAlias r4rmusic.com
DocumentRoot "/usr/local/share/railsapps/r4rmusic/public/"
</VirtualHost>
```

(Of course, you need to register the r4rmusic.com domain and point it to your site.) Now, when someone contacts this server with a URL that looks like this

```
http://www.r4rmusic.com/
```

or like this typical Rails-style URL

```
http://www.r4rmusic.com/work/show/2
```

Apache will treat the directory /usr/local/share/railsapps/r4rmusic/public as the directory for this request. Different Web servers handle this process slightly differently, but we'll stick with Apache for the sake of illustration.

When the Apache server is pointed to a directory, it looks in that directory for a file called .htaccess. Such a file is found in the public directory of any Rails application. The job of this file is to trigger the execution of the *dispatcher*: a small program that is responsible for getting the Rails application to do something.

You can see the dispatcher (actually, several dispatchers; the one your application uses can be configured) in the public subdirectory of r4rmusic:

```
$ cd public
$ ls dispatch.*
dispatch.cgi    dispatch.fcgi    dispatch.rb
```

Which dispatcher is called doesn't matter for purposes of this overview. The salient point is that one of these three dispatcher programs gets called.

2.4.2 *Stage 2: dispatcher to controller*

The dispatcher's job is to dispatch the request—that is, to send it to the appropriate controller. Controllers are the subprograms in a Rails application that perform tasks. They reach back into the database and get data, they search and sort, they test for password matches, and so forth. Typically, a Rails application has several controllers, and each controller is capable of multiple *actions*. For example, you may have a *customer* controller that can perform *login*, *logout*, *edit* (edit profile), and other actions.

How does the dispatcher know which controller to summon, and which action to request from that controller? It knows by analyzing the incoming URL. More precisely, it gleans the correct controller and action from the URL after the URL has passed along an internal conveyor built of transformations and translations. The URL with which the user connected contains the directives necessary to trigger the correct response from the application, but those directives may need to be interpreted first. This all happens automatically (although you have to set up the URL interpretation rules manually if they're complex).

The upshot of all this rewriting and interpreting of the URL is that the Rails dispatcher is armed with three pieces of information, two of which are required and one of which is optional:

- The name of a controller
- The name of an action
- A value for the request's id

At the point where these values have been established, the automatic processing of the incoming request meets what you've done as the application developer. Once the dispatcher passes control onward, what happens is as follows.

2.4.3 *Stage 3: performance of a controller action*

When the appropriate action, inside the appropriate controller, is executed, it has automatic access to the following:

- CGI data, including data from a submitted form (via the built-in `params` method)
- The controller's session information (via the built-in session method)

CGI variables and their values are available through the built-in Rails `params` method. For example, to dig out the value of the email input field of a form, you call `params` as follows:

```
params[:email]
```

Or, if the values are stored in a more deeply nested structure, you call `params` this way:

```
params[:user][:email]
```

(`params` returns a *hash*: a data structure organized as a collection of values coupled with keys through which you can access those values. Some of the values in `params` may be inner or nested hashes, like `params[:user]`. The details of how these hash data structures work will be explained in chapter 11, when we talk about collections and container objects.)

The CGI data made available to the controller in this manner includes an *id* entry. The value of this entry is automatically set to the third of the elements in the canonical Rails URL. For example, suppose the incoming URL looks like this (or translates to this, based on whatever rewriting and routing rules are in operation):

```
http://www.r4rmusic.com/work/show/12
```

As you saw in section 2.3.3, the `show` action uses the expression `params[:id]` to grab the value of the CGI *id* variable. Thanks to the presence of "12" in the appropriate field in the URL, the value of that variable will be automatically set to "12". The `show` action then uses this value to determine which work to display, namely the work whose *id* number is 12.

The `controller` action also has access to its own session information. Rails applications can cache information from one invocation to another. This can be handy, for instance, for enabling customers to navigate a site without having to log in every time they go to a different part of the site. The login status is maintained in the session cache and checked for validity. The action can set session values:

```
session['user'] = user.id
```

It can also retrieve values (if any) set by previous actions:

```
if session['admin']
  # administrator is logged in
else
  not an administrative session; don't allow special privileges
end
```

What you call your session data, and whether you use the session facility, is up to you. The session method gives you a kind of cubbyhole where one action can leave notes for the other actions, if and when that kind of cross-action communication is necessary.

> **NOTE**   THE @params AND @session VARIABLES The information available through the params and session methods is also available through the special predefined variables @params and @session. (These are *instance variables*, a special-purpose kind of variable you'll learn more about in part 2.) You may see @params and @session in Rails applications; however, using the methods, rather than the variables, has come to be considered better practice.

Controller actions, then, are sequences of Ruby code that correspond directly to the tasks this application can be asked to do: log in a user, add a recipe to a cookbook, display thumbnails of the first 10 photographs in an online album, and so forth. A Rails action (the lines of code that define an action in a controller file) maps closely to what users can do with the application.

Having looked at both models and controllers, let's see how they relate to each other.

Controllers and models

Entity models lie close to the database. Controllers don't; they manipulate database records through instances of the models. Here, user is a specific case or *instance* of the User model:

```
user.email = params[:email]
user.update
```

In this example, the controller asks the user instance to set its email address equal to the email address entered on a form and then update itself. The controller doesn't know what becomes of that request. But the user instance knows how to handle the request; it creates an SQL command something like the following:

```
UPDATE users SET email = 'dblack@wobblini.net' WHERE id = 33;
```

(This example assumes, arbitrarily, that this user's record has the value 33 in its *id* field.) The controller is protected from having to deal directly with the database.

So are you. When you write Rails application code, you always write code that manipulates data through nicely named, neatly ordered variables. The code you write triggers a cascade of database operations. But you don't have to address the database directly. You have to design the database, and you have to know what the database tables and fields are called (because that knowledge has a direct bearing on what your model can do). But then you manipulate the database at an abstract level.

TIP   LEARN SQL, EVEN IF IT'S NOT YOUR MAIN FOCUS   As a Rails programmer, you generally don't have to write SQL statements; Rails provides short-cuts and automated querying facilities to handle most of that for you. But it's likely that you'll need to write a little SQL now and then—and if you're working with a database system that speaks SQL, you'll probably have occasion to interact with the database outside of Rails (for instance, in an interactive monitor). Picking up the rudiments of SQL is highly recommended for all Rails developers.

2.4.4 Stage 4: the fulfillment of the view

You're now on the downslope of the process. The rest of the controller's job is to pass the data to the view. The view fills in its template, resulting in an HTML document that is then handed to the Web server and from there back to the original Web client.

The basic process is as follows: An incoming HTTP request is deflected from the server's default document location to the home directory of the Rails application, where a dispatcher program is executed. That dispatcher program dispatches the request to the appropriate controller/action combination, which it figures out from the URL (applying interpretive rules as needed). The controller then takes over. On the one hand, the controller has access to the universe of the models, through which it can manipulate data; and on the other hand, it has the ability to share data with the view template. The view template gets expanded into HTML, complete with interpolated data, and the Web server hands it back to the client.

2.5 Summary

In this chapter, we've surveyed the engineering of the Ruby on Rails framework. You've read about the MVC framework architecture and the Rails implementation of it through ActiveRecord (which models entities based on database design), ActionView (which provides templating facilities based on ERb), and ActionController (which runs interference between the data manipulation and its presentation). You've also gone through the process of creating and running a working Rails application—an application that you'll be able to enhance in part 4 of the book, thanks to your study of the Ruby language in the intervening chapters. We've taken a close look at the stages involved in the processing of an incoming request to Rails application: the server awakening the Rails dispatcher; the dispatcher contacting the appropriate controller; the controller executing the requested action; and the view template being filled out and handed back, in the form of an HTML document, to the server.

At this point, you have a grasp of how both Ruby and Rails work. Next, we'll finish part 1 with a chapter that takes an initial look at the ways in which they operate together.

Ruby-informed
Rails development

This chapter represents something of a pivot point. There's a lot of material coming up later: two parts of the book devoted to a Ruby language tutorial, and a final part that brings the threads together in a Ruby-aware second pass at R4RMusic, the Rails application we created in chapter 2. Still, we've already completed one complete cycle of the breadth-first examination of Ruby and Rails, and you're in a position to see more closely and more clearly how the study of Ruby can pay off for a Rails developer.

The focus in this chapter is on that *how*, and on the *why*. The full benefits of immersing yourself in Ruby can't, and won't, all present themselves in this chapter; much more will emerge during parts 2 and 3—the heart of the book's Ruby tutorial material—as well as during the further development of the music store application in part 4. But we're far enough along that you can clearly see by example, and not just take on faith, the kinds of advantages that a Rails developer can reap from a thorough Ruby grounding.

The introductory "About this book" section listed four ways in which knowing Ruby well can serve you as a Rails developer:

- By helping you know what the code in your application—including Rails boilerplate code—is doing

- By helping you do more in, and with, your Rails applications than you can if you limit yourself to the readily available Rails idioms and techniques (as powerful as those are)

- By allowing you to familiarize yourself with the Rails source code, which in turn enables you to participate in discussions about Rails and perhaps submit bug reports and code patches

- By giving you a powerful tool for administrative and organizational tasks (for example, legacy code conversion) connected with your application

As stated back in that section, the first two of these four items are the most central to this book. The main goal of this chapter is to demonstrate to you how much more meaningful and concrete those first two items *already* are, now that you've read the first two chapters. There's much more to learn and do in the chapters that lie beyond this—we're still mapping out the Ruby/Rails landscape at a fairly high level—but we're well underway.

In the interest of the "knowing what your code is doing" goal, we'll look at the relation between certain typical Rails coding conventions and the bigger Ruby-language context out of which they have emerged. By way of helping you do more, we'll carry out a few representative enhancements, via customized Ruby code, of Rails application model, helper, and controller files. The purpose is to give you a collective preview of some of what will come later in the book.

Finally, this chapter serves as the first and only home for the fourth item on the list, accomplishing application-related tasks. This area of Ruby use lies, for the most part, outside the *Ruby for Rails* landscape. But it's worth noting that Ruby's usefulness to you as a Rails developer isn't limited to the lines of Ruby code you write in your Rails applications; and we'll pursue that point by looking at some issues connected with the process of converting legacy data for use in a Rails application. While we're on the topic of Ruby helping you in a general way, we'll get slightly more specific and look at how you can run Interactive Ruby (irb) preloaded with the specifics of the universe of your Rails application.

This chapter will complete the foundation work for the more detailed Ruby and Ruby-informed Rails exploration to come.

3.1 A first crack at knowing what your code does

It's hard to imagine that a case needs to be made for understanding your own code, but it's worth a few words.

Specific code examples designed to train you in knowing what your Rails code is doing will be plentiful as we talk about Ruby and circle back to Rails later in the book. In this section, we'll look at some points and premises about knowing what you're doing—specifically, points about the relationship between Ruby and Rails.

The Rails framework does two things (among others) very well: It makes you feel like you're using not just Ruby but a *domain-specific language* (DSL) written in Ruby; and it makes you feel like you're not really programming but mainly writing configuration files. Both of these characteristics testify to the power of Ruby (Ruby is good as a host language for DSLs) and to its skillful deployment in the Rails framework.

But even when Rails coding feels like configuration—or feels like coding, but in a language unto itself—it is still, nonetheless, Ruby. That means you're well advised to keep an eye on how the layers fit together: that is, on how Ruby and Rails relate to each other and, contradictory as it may sound, what role Ruby plays in the process of making Rails sometimes feel like a separate language from Ruby.

In this section, we'll use the *Rails feels like configuration* idea and the *Rails feels like a programming language of its own* idea to examine the relationship between Ruby and Rails—which is to say, the idea that *Rails programming is in fact Ruby programming*. This will give you an informative look at an important aspect of knowing what your Rails code is doing.

3.1.1 *Seeing Rails as a domain-specific language*

One important effect of the configuration look-and-feel of Rails (along with the repertoire of Rails instructions and techniques available to you) is that using Rails often feels like using a domain-specific language. A DSL is a language designed to be used for a specific task or set of tasks in a particular field or domain, rather than for general-purpose programming. The instruction set in a DSL is relatively narrow. For example, an imaginary DSL for simulating a poker game might look like this:

```
with 4 Players:
  deal down: 2
  deal up: 1
  bet
  until Dealer.has(6)
    deal up: 1
    bet
  end
  # etc.
```

The instruction set of the language is limited to poker-related terms, and there are (presumably) built-in facilities for calculating winning hands, odds of making certain hands, and so forth.

Like any programming language or tool, a DSL must be designed and written by someone before it can be used by programmers. If you're writing a DSL, you write it in some other programming language.

It turns out that one of Ruby's strengths is its ability to serve as host language for DSLs: Ruby is a general-purpose programming language in which it's easy to write special-purpose programming languages. There are a couple of reasons for this. First, Ruby's relatively uncomplicated syntax makes it (relatively) easy for people who aren't principally programmers to learn a useful subset of language constructs. If you package such a subset as a little computer language of its own, you're well on the way to a DSL. Second, Ruby lets you do a great deal of redefining of language constructs, which means you have a lot of control over what elements of the language mean.

Here's a (still imaginary) Ruby version of the poker DSL snippet:

```
Game.start(:players => 4) do
  deal :down => 2
  deal :up   => 1
  bet
  until dealer.hand == 6
    deal :up => 1
    bet
  end
  # etc.
```

This is just a fragment; before writing this, you'd have to write the code that defines what Game is, and so forth. But people *using* this little DSL don't need to know how that was done. Someone could easily learn a rule like "The deal command is followed by :down and :up values" and could also learn the syntax for those rules without having to know what the code means in Ruby terms.

In some respects, Rails is likewise a domain-specific language written in Ruby. It's true that Rails applications span a wide range of use and usefulness; and looking at the whole spectrum of Rails applications, from shopping sites to bulletin boards to bug-trackers, there may not seem to be anything specific about the Rails domain. But that's just a reflection of the wide range of Web sites. Looking at it from the programming angle, Rails does have a specific domain: Web applications, particularly interactive, database-driven Web applications. And in a number of respects, Rails provides you with a domain-specific programming language.

It's important to develop a sense of how the specificity of Rails is engineered and how it relates to Ruby. Rails, especially to someone who hasn't seen much Ruby code outside of Rails, exhibits specificity at two levels: in the syntax, and in the terminology. We'll look at these two levels separately.

Domain specificity in relation to syntax

A common Rails idiom we've already seen, and that you may have seen before, is this:

```
has_many :editions
```

The syntax used here, with a verb-based directive on the left and what looks like a configuration spec on the right, seems like it could have been created specifically for a system like the Rails framework. In fact, it's a simple Ruby method call. The name of the method is has_many, and the argument is a Ruby symbol object.

Every time anyone uses this method, it will look essentially the same. You'll almost certainly never see this

```
send("has_many", "editions".intern)
```

which is equivalent to the previous example (send is a do-it-yourself way to send a message to an object; intern converts a string object to a symbol object). This send-based version is, admittedly, far-fetched enough not to be a close call. But you'll probably never even see this much more slight variation on the original:

```
has_many(:editions)
```

Many Ruby programmers like to put parentheses around method arguments, even when the parentheses are optional. But when writing Rails applications, even these programmers (and I'm one of them) don't use the parentheses—not because of Ruby (Ruby doesn't care), but because leaving the parentheses off is a standard Rails convention.

The common idioms you use in Rails aren't alternatives to Ruby; they're alternatives *within* Ruby. Long before Rails came along, it was possible to call a method with a `symbol` argument:

```
method_from_ten_years_ago :symbol
```

And when Rails did come along, it—that is, its creator, core developers, and developer community—settled on this style of calling such a method. Ruby, meanwhile, is happy; this method-call style is a mainstream, idiomatic Ruby technique.

Part of learning Ruby as a Rails practitioner is recognizing what's going on in your code, and the first lesson is that what's happening is always Ruby. If there's less variety in coding style from one Rails application to another than there *could* be—that is, if you see thousands of

```
has_many :editions
```

and never see

```
send("has_many", "editions".intern)
```

or even

```
has_many(:editions)
```

it's not because Rails has special syntax or rules. It's because the Rails community has had the sense to rally around a relatively small number of coding conventions, gaining visual uniformity and a de facto language specificity for Rails development.

Terminology and domain specificity

The other side of the domain-specific coin is the matter of the terminology: for example, the matter of having a term like `has_many`, considered separately from the matter of whether you use parentheses with the term.

The full domain specificity of Rails emerges in the terminology and semantics. The methods available for the manipulation of database records; the presence of the terms *model, view,* and *controller* in directory and file names; the names of the underlying libraries and data structures (ActionView and so on)—all of these contribute to the sense that when you're working on a Rails application, you're working in a particular context, a particular shop, with its own lingo and its own specific rules and procedures.

This idea meshes nicely with the fact that Rails coding practice is so uniform. The consensus about syntax keeps the scenery uniform and familiar, while the semantics of the method, data, and file names give the landscape its specific character.

At the same time, the Rails environment *isn't* a self-contained, self-sustaining, hermetically sealed world of its own. It's a Ruby environment that has managed to define its own boundaries elegantly while still functioning as a full-featured Ruby environment.

This means that if you're writing a Rails application and you decide you need to write a new method (because no methods available by default do what you need), you'll probably make calls to your new method that look like this

```
new_method :argument
```

or like some other common Rails idiom. The Rails environment *allows* for unlimited and unrestricted expansion, courtesy of Ruby, and it *encourages* programmers to carry out those expansions in accordance with stylistic conventions. The conventions, in turn, are generally chosen from among the visually most clean and uncluttered of the alternatives made available by Ruby.

Thus the language supports the domain specificity of the framework, and the framework supports the participation of the language.

Discussions of Rails coding style always come back to the frequent use of symbol objects (such as :editions) as method arguments and/or hash keys in Rails applications. We've already looked at some aspects of this topic, and next we'll return to symbols and head in a slightly different direction: ways in which Rails programming looks and feels less like programming and more like configuration. This subtopic, like domain specificity, flows into the stream of knowing what your Rails code is doing.

3.1.2 *Writing program code with a configuration flavor*

One of the attractions of Rails is that when you're writing Rails applications, it often feels like you're not so much writing a program as configuring a system—even though you're writing Ruby code. Not that there's anything wrong with feeling like you're writing a program. But configuring a system almost inevitably feels easier. When you type

```
has_one :composer
has_many :editions
```

in a file called app/models/work.rb, it doesn't feel so much like you're writing a roadmap of events as that you're informing the system of some of the conditions under which it's going to operate.

Rails often makes programming look like configuration. Exactly what *configuration* means depends on what you're configuring. For the sake of simplicity, it's reasonable to say that a configuration file generally contains declarative assignments:

```
something = some value
```

Examples abound. The Linux kernel configuration file looks like this, where everything is a comment (#) or an assignment:

```
#
# Block devices
#
CONFIG_BLK_DEV_FD=y
CONFIG_BLK_DEV_XD=m
CONFIG_PARIDE=m
CONFIG_PARIDE_PARPORT=m
```

Apache-style authorization files look like this, with the colon (:) serving as the association or assignment operator between the names and the encrypted passwords:

```
dblack:rtiU4FXvUmCYs
matz:b8P1eIatd3l1U
```

Configuration files can be more elaborate than this, but often they aren't. And this kind of simple assignment-style configuration has a well-deserved reputation for being easy to type and maintain. (It's even easier when you have a utility program to do it for you.)

Part of the Rails strategy for presenting a quickly understandable, relatively simple domain-specific language for Web application development is that a lot of what you do in Rails (definitely not all, but a lot) has a configuration-file look and feel. This fact manifests itself in a couple of ways. We've already looked at some of the ramifications of the frequent use of symbol objects as method arguments. In many cases, usually with longer argument lists, symbols end up serving not as lone arguments but as the equivalent of the left-hand side of what looks like a language for specifying item/value pairs in a configuration file:

```
<%= link_to "A hyperlink in a view template",
            :controller => "main",
            :action     => "welcome" %>
```

In this example, each symbol is associated with a value: the symbol :controller with the string "main", the symbol :action with the string "welcome". (The two symbols are *hash keys*, and the two strings are the corresponding hash *values*. The entire hash is the second argument to the method; the first argument is the first string: "A hyperlink...".) This syntax is standard Ruby; and although it's not identical to the classic `item:value` configuration-file syntax, it has some of the same simplicity and visual balance.

It's also worth noting that the tendency of Rails developers to adhere to certain stylistic conventions becomes more important as the code gets more complex. The configuration-style pairing of symbols and strings in the previous example would go by the wayside if people started using some of the alternatives, like this:

```
<%= link_to("A hyperlink in a view template",
        Hash[:controller, "main", :action, "welcome"]) %>
```

The adherence to convention scales upward nicely.

Program code can thus look like an excerpt from a configuration file, which can have advantages with respect to clarity, easy grasping of the logic of what's going on, and communication among developers. At the same time, oddly enough, configuration files—while also looking like configuration files—can be program code (of a particular sort). We'll look next at this phenomenon as it pertains to Rails.

3.1.3 *YAML and configuration that's actually programming*

The key case in point when it comes to configuration data that's program code is the file `config/database.yml`, which is where the details of the database backend are specified. This file isn't written in Ruby, but it's written in a format that can be directly read into and written out from Ruby objects: YAML.

YAML (which, tradition has it, originally stood for Yet Another Markup Language, but now stands for YAML Ain't Markup Language) is, depending on your view, either a markup language or a serialization format. Either way, YAML provides you with a way to store Ruby objects, including nested data structures, as text strings—and to thaw those strings back into life as Ruby objects. Here's a simple example, in which a nested array structure is turned into its YAML representation and then back into an array:

```
require 'yaml'
array = [1, 2, 3, [4, "five", :six]]
puts "Original array:"
puts array.inspect    <——— 1
yarray = array.to_yaml
puts "YAML representation of array: "
puts yarray
thawed = YAML.load(yarray)
puts "Array re-loaded from YAML string: "
p thawed    <——— 2
```

(Smuggled into this example are the `inspect` method ❶, which produces a detailed string representation of an object, and the `p` method ❷, which is equivalent to running `puts` on the result of `inspect`.)

The output from running this script is as follows:

```
Original array:
[1, 2, 3, [4, "five", :six]]
YAML representation of array:
- 1
- 2
- 3
- - 4
  - five
  - :six
Array re-loaded from YAML string:
[1, 2, 3, [4, "five", :six]]
```

Note that YAML not only remembers the nesting of the arrays, but also remembers that "`five`" was a string and `:six` was a symbol. Rails uses YAML in several contexts. In `database.yml`, you've seen blocks that look like this:

```
development:
  adapter: mysql
  database: r4rmusic1_development
  username: r4r
  password: railzrulez
  socket: /tmp/mysql.sock
```

Watch what happens when you run that through the `YAML.load` method. Put those lines in a file by themselves (say, `sample.yml`), and run the following command, which reads the file back, converts it from a YAML string to a Ruby object, and then prints out a representation of that object (with p):

```
ruby -ryaml -e 'p YAML.load(File.read("sample.yml"))'
```

The output, massaged here to look less run-together than it appears onscreen, is as follows:

```
{"development" => {"socket"=>"/tmp/mysql.sock",
                   "username"=>"r4r",
                   "adapter"=>"mysql",
                   "password"=>"railzrulez",
                   "database"=>"r4rmusic1_development"
                   }
}
```

You're seeing a printout of a Ruby hash, a data structure consisting of pairs made up of one key and one value. Actually, you're seeing two hashes. The first has the single key `development`; the value of that key is another hash. That second hash has keys called `socket`, `username`, and so forth. The values are, in every case, on the right-hand side of the `=>` separator.

Rails is storing its configuration data as potential Ruby data, easily brought to life with a YAML operation. Here, again, the worlds of programming and configuration melt into one another, thanks to the facilities and tools available in and for Ruby.

There's more to the matter of knowing what's happening when you use Rails conventions and idioms. The goal here hasn't been to cover it all but to encourage you to become curious about how even the most common Rails techniques work. No doubt this entails a certain loss of Rails innocence; you cease to be able to view Rails code as a world unto itself. But keep in mind that Ruby is good at supporting the kind of domain-specific language, or dialect, that Rails exemplifies. There are reasons that Rails was written in Ruby.

Meanwhile, in addition to knowing what Rails idioms mean (and this is an ongoing process, not one that's limited to the examples you've already seen), there's the important matter of learning Ruby so that you can add value and power to your Rails applications by writing custom code that supplements and enhances the techniques Rails makes available by default.

3.2 *Starting to use Ruby to do more in your code*

You want to know Ruby techniques so that you can add to what your application can do and increase the ease with which you get the application to do it. This doesn't mean everything you do will be spectacular. It means that you'll be able to do more, and do it easily.

Rails is your partner in this process. When you leverage your Ruby skills to enhance your Rails application, you aren't out-smarting Rails. You're doing what you're expected to do: work within the Rails framework to achieve the best results you can.

Nor is this a platitude. It's a characterization of how the Rails framework is engineered. The details of what you do on every Rails project—not just the code, but also the specifics of the setup and configuration—fall into three categories that cover a wide spectrum of constraint and freedom:

- Things you do a particular way because the rules of Rails say they have to be done that way
- Customizations you're likely to want to do and for which Rails provides an infrastructure (while leaving you a lot of freedom as to specifics)

- Open-ended enhancements and extensions of your program, along whatever lines you want, using any Ruby-language techniques you wish

The first category includes bedrock-level application characteristics like the file layout and the need to specify what database your application uses. It also includes tasks you won't always perform but that you're expected to do a particular way, like declaring associations between entities (`has_one :composer`, and so on), using `layout` to specify layouts, and so forth. These expectations come with the territory of being a framework.

The second category is important and interesting. It includes, for example, the `app/helpers` directory, the purpose of which is to house program files containing routines for use in your templates. You're in charge of naming and writing the methods, but Rails provides an infrastructure that rationalizes and pre-systematizes the code for you.

Another example of the second "support and encouragement" category (we might also call it "structured freedom") are the *method hooks* available to you in your model definition files. A method hook is a method that you may, but aren't obliged to, write; and if you do write it, it's automatically called at a predefined point during program execution. For example, if you write a method called `before_create` in one of your model files, then that method will be called automatically every time a database record corresponding to an instance of that model is created. This allows you to gatekeep the data in an orderly fashion and to manage your database at a low level while still writing everything in Ruby.

The third category from the earlier list—open-ended freedom—encompasses the fact that you're always writing Ruby code. Rails endows your objects with certain capabilities: some are inborn, some are based on your database's organization and naming scheme. You can endow those objects with any further capabilities you want. In many cases, you don't have to do much, if any, of this: The default Rails universe is very rich, providing a great deal of object functionality. But it can't provide every tweak for every imaginable application. What it doesn't provide, *you* provide.

In what follows, examples and discussion will include a sampling of all three levels at which you, the developer/programmer, operate when you're writing a Rails application. We'll start in the "structured freedom" category, with a look at examples of controller programming.

3.2.1 *Adding functionality to a controller*

The controllers are the traffic cops of a Rails application. They gather data from the database (generally through the friendly programmatic interface provided by the ActiveRecord models), manipulate and organize the data as required, and hand it off to bc inserted into the view templates.

In the "manipulate and organize" part, the code you write in your controller files can scale up in power and flexibility. Here's an example from the Ruby Change Request site, RCRchive (http://www.rcrchive.net). The purpose of this site is to let people submit suggestions for changes and enhancements to Ruby and browse through the changes that have been proposed. (You can also comment on and vote on the various RCRs.)

The first view you see includes a list of all the pending RCRs followed by lists of accepted, rejected, superseded, and withdrawn RCRs. This initial view is preorganized for you according to the status of the various RCRs.

However, a link takes you to a view of *all* the RCRs in the archive. (You can also get there directly by connecting to http://www.rcrchive.net/rcr/all.) By default, this list is sorted by RCR number, in descending order, so the most recent RCRs are listed first. By clicking the appropriate column heading, you can see the list sorted different ways:

- By title
- By author
- By status (pending, accepted, rejected)

When you click, say, the Title heading, you trigger another call to the same action—the `all` action in the `rcr` controller file—but with the CGI parameter `order` set to the value "title". The `all` method takes the hint and puts all the RCRs in a variable (`@rcrs`) sorted in the requested order. This sorted list of RCRs is then handed off to the view.

The logic of the sorting in the controller is as follows:

1 If the sort field is *author*, sort by author's name, then by RCR number (descending).

2 If the sort field is *status* or *title*, sort on whichever it is, then by RCR number (descending).

3 If the sort field is *number*, sort by RCR number (descending).

The Ruby method that does this—the `rcr/all` action, in `rcr_controller.rb`—is as follows:

```
def all
  @order = params[:order] || "number"       <———①
  sort_proc = case @order   <———②
    when "author"  then lambda {|r| [r.user.name.downcase, r.number] }
    when "status",
         "title"   then lambda {|r| [r.send(@order).downcase, r.number]}
    when "number"  then lambda {|r| -r.number }
  end
  @rcrs = Rcr.find(:all).sort_by &sort_proc     <———③
end
```

The variable `@order` (an *instance variable*) is set to the value of the CGI variable order ①, defaulting to the string "number" if that CGI variable isn't set. At that point, the variable `sort_proc` (sorting procedure) is set to one of three possible *lambda* expressions (anonymous functions). Which lambda is chosen depends on the value of `@order`; the selection is performed through a `case` statement ②.

Once the correct lambda has been chosen, all of the existing RCRs are sorted according to the logic of that lambda ③, using the ActiveRecord `find` method to grab all the RCRs and Ruby's `sort_by` method to filter the list through whichever lambda is stashed in `sort_proc`.

If you know Ruby, this isn't a difficult method to write. But you do have to know Ruby! Specifically, you have to know the following:

- The `case` statement
- The `lambda` keyword, with which you create an anonymous function
- The `send` method (notice how *status* and *title* can be handled together)
- The `sort_by` method, to which you hand a lambda

This code does nothing earth-shatteringly spectacular. You could write it (more lengthily) without some of the techniques it uses. What *is* spectacular is how much you gain in the way of adaptability and ease of development when you know those Ruby techniques.

Rails knows that it's a good idea to give the programmer freedom. You get several assists in exercising that freedom. An important one, to which we'll now turn, is the provision of the helper files.

3.2.2 *Deploying the Rails helper files*

The most common idioms and techniques—"common" meaning that many applications have them in common—are provided by Rails. But Rails also provides ways to address specific needs.

The helper files, located in `app/helpers`, are a good example and an important resource. They're also prime examples of the second category from the list in the introduction to section 3.2: Rails facilities that you don't *have* to use, but that you may well *want* to use, to customize and enhance your application.

A helper file is created automatically for every controller you create. Inside the helper files, you can write arbitrarily many Ruby methods; these methods are automatically accessible in your view template code.

The advantage of this arrangement is that it saves you repetition. If you're using a construct several times in one or more of your templates, you can write a method that generates the construct, and then call the method from the template.

Here's an example drawn from the list-sorting RCRchive code. Each of the column headings in the all view of the RCRs is hyperlinked to the `rcr/all` action. The links differ from each other in only one respect: the value of the `order` parameter ("author", "title", "number", or "status"). That means all four of these links use almost identical code. To save repetition, a helper method generates an appropriate link automatically. All you have to do is pass it an `order` argument.

The helper method, defined in the file `rcr_helper.rb`, looks like this:

```
def link_to_order(order)
  link_to(order.capitalize,
          :controller => "rcr",
          :action     => "all",
          :params     => { "order" => order })
end
```

As you can see, it piggybacks on the Rails method `link_to`. It uses `link_to` to write the appropriate HTML for a link to the correct action—with the `order` parameter set to the value of the variable `order`, which was passed in as an argument to the method.

Inside the view (`app/views/rcr/all.rhtml`), the following four lines create the table headers:

```
<th class="rcr"><%= link_to_order("number") %></th>
<th class="rcr"><%= link_to_order("title") %></th>
<th class="rcr"><%= link_to_order("status") %></th>
<th class="rcr"><%= link_to_order("author") %></th>
```

Each of these lines puts in a call to the custom-written link generator method `link_to_order`. The resulting HTML looks like this:

```
<th class="rcr"><a href="/rcr/all?order=number">Number</a></th>
<th class="rcr"><a href="/rcr/all?order=title">Title</a></th>
<th class="rcr"><a href="/rcr/all?order=status">Status</a></th>
<th class="rcr"><a href="/rcr/all?order=author">Author</a></th>
```

Why not type those four HTML lines into the view file in the first place? Because using a helper method is more encapsulated. Let's say I decide to put the column headings in pure uppercase, instead of capitalized format as they are currently—in other words, *NUMBER* instead of *Number*, *TITLE* instead of *Title*, and so on. Thanks to the fact that the headings are all processed via the same helper method, I can achieve this by making one change to that method: I change `order.capitalize` to `order.upcase`, and the new format is propagated automatically to all the headings. If the HTML lines are hard-coded into the template file, I have to dig around in the file and make the changes one at a time by hand, which is both troublesome and error-prone.

Helper methods figure in Rails in two distinct related ways. Rails provides you with the `apps/helpers` directory and file bank to encourage you to write methods that encapsulate functionality and to keep the view templates organized. But Rails also supplies you a large number of predefined helper methods. `link_to` is a perfect example: It's a built-in Rails helper method that gives you a programmatic interface (a way to get the job done through a method call, rather than by writing everything by hand) to the creation of the HTML you need.

When you write helper methods, you're adding to the stockpile of such methods that Rails has already given you. Rails *expects* you to build upward and outward: according to a particular structure, yes, but in an open-ended way.

Speaking of open-ended, we're now going to plunge into the wide-open area of enhancing the functionality of ActiveRecord models.

3.2.3 *Adding functionality to models*

ActiveRecord models are the Ruby incarnation of the same domain universe that governs your database design. You have an *editions* table; you have an `Edition` model. You then have an arbitrary number of `edition` objects. Those objects can perform certain actions, thanks to the methods built into the ActiveRecord library—and they can perform any action, if you write the code for it.

In part 4 of the book, when we come back to the music store application, we'll be writing custom model code. Here, in keeping with the spirit of this chapter, we'll see enough to make a case for the importance of the concept.

You can perform two levels of model enhancement: writing a method whose name corresponds to a predefined callback, or hook; and writing a method from scratch. The first of these resides in the second of our three freedom categories, as mapped out at the beginning of section 3.2: the category of structured freedom, facilitated but not mandatory enhancement. The second, writing methods from scratch, belongs in the third category: open-ended programming freedom. We'll look at an example of each.

Implementing predefined callback methods

The introduction to section 3.2 mentioned the existence of a `before_create` hook: If you write a method call `before_create` in an ActiveRecord model file, that method will be executed before the database record is created for each instance of that model.

You can see this in action by making a small and harmless change to the file `app/models/edition.rb` in the r4rmusic application. Every edition has a description—basically, a free-form text field for storing descriptive information like "revised" or the name of an editor. If you don't specify a string to fill this field, then by default the field is set to nil (no value).

It might be more graceful to have a default string value for the *description* field. If no description exists for the edition at the time the database record is first created, let's have it default to "standard".

To bring this about, insert the following method definition into `edition.rb` (just prior to the `end` that ends the file):

```
def before_create
  self.description = "standard" unless description
end
```

This code basically says: if *description* is nil, set it to "standard". The code is executed just before a new edition is saved to the database. Thus any edition without a description gets one.

(You can try this by changing one of the editions description fields in the `records` file created in chapter 2 to NULL [the SQL equivalent of Ruby's nil] and reinitializing the database and the records from the files. The "standard" designation should then show up when you look at that edition in your browser.)

Rails predefines quite a few callback and filter-methods like `before_create`, anticipating that you may want to perform programming actions in your application but not dictating what those actions should be. These filters are analogous to the helper-file facility: They're a halfway measure that makes it easy for you to add the finishing touches.

You can also write methods from scratch for your models. This is one of the most powerful and useful areas of Rails for the exercising of Ruby skills.

Free-form programmatic model enhancement

Let's say you have a Rails application in which you store people's names—perhaps the names of customers in a database. You have a table called (say) *customers*, and fields in that table called *title*, *first_name*, *middle_initial*, and *last_name*. On the Ruby side, you have a `customer.rb` model file. Thanks to the database table field names, you can easily retrieve the title and name components of a given customer.

For example, in a view template, given a customer object in the variable `@customer`, you can display the person's name like this:

```
<p>Hello, <%= @customer.title + " " + @customer.first_name + " " +
            @customer.middle_initial + ". " +
            @customer.last_name" %></p>
```

You'd want to finesse cases where someone doesn't have a middle initial, but the basic idea is that to display a name, you string together its parts.

However, this code is awfully wordy for a template. Besides, you may want to display the name more than once. It would be nice to have a method that could do this. You could write a helper method, as we did in the case of `link_to_order`. But you may want to access the nice version of the name somewhere else in the application (maybe when emailing the customer), not just in the views.

The most logical approach is to have the customer object generate the nice name. To do this, you write a method in the model file. The output of this method is a string with the components of the name pieced together. (We'll even take the precaution of interpolating an empty string if this customer has no middle initial.) Here's what your `customer.rb` file looks like:

```
class Customer < ActiveRecord::Base
  def nice_name
    title + " " + first_name + " " +
      (if middle_initial then middle_initial + ". " else "" end) +
      last_name
  end
end
```

If you're designing a view where you want the person's name displayed in this format, and your controller has stashed the relevant instance of `Customer` in the variable `@customer`, you can write the following, and `@customer` will know what to do:

```
<p>Good morning, <%= @customer.nice_name %>.</p>
```

In this example, the knowledge that Ruby lets you chain strings together with the plus sign enables you to add an enhancement to all customer objects. Conditional logic (the `if/else` handling of the middle initial) ensures that you don't end up with stray dots and spaces. Overall, a bit of Ruby skill lets you endow the `Customer` model with a new facility—the nice version of its name—and lets you do it well.

The more Ruby you know, the more of this kind of functionality you can create, and the more quickly and accurately you can do so. Rails and Ruby operate together as one system, and writing Ruby code is part of your role in that system.

3.3 Accomplishing application-related skills and tasks

As stated in the introduction to this chapter, administrative and organizational tasks won't figure prominently in the rest of this book, but this area definitely merits one section's worth of attention. I hope you'll find opportunities to use Ruby in and around your Rails work in a variety of ways, and this section is designed to encourage you to look for such opportunities.

We'll use a common case as our main example: converting legacy data to a Rails-usable format. This is an area where Ruby can help you a great deal—not only because the target format is ActiveRecord, but because Ruby is good at manipulating data in many formats and forms.

This section also includes an introduction to the irb-based application console, which is basically an irb session into which your model files have been preloaded. You can use this session interactively to examine and change database records and run any methods that have been defined for the use of your models. As a subtopic, the application console is an imperfect fit for this section; but because it's irb based, and irb is part of the general Ruby environment, we'll count it among the facilities Ruby gives you to enhance your work environment. (If you end up feeling that the application console is an integral Rails development tool, so much the better!)

3.3.1 Converting legacy data to ActiveRecord

When it comes to converting data, a lot depends on what you start with. You may be dealing with an old relational database and have to convert it to Rails-friendly SQL. Or you may need to turn information stored in flat text files into database records. There's no single scenario when it comes to the process of dealing with legacy data. But Ruby skills can help you bootstrap that data into Rails-accessible form in virtually any case.

We'll look at an extended example here, based on a real-life case (that's probably similar to many real-life cases) involving data from a discussion board stored in small text files. We get a lucky break because these text files are YAML files. That gives us a foot in the door when it comes to getting Ruby and, subsequently, Rails to understand what's in them.

Each file has a number of fields:

```
number: 251
username: dblack
date: 10-3-2005
previous: 244
title: I've got something to say about that
body: "This is a sample comment, which in practice could go on
for a long time and have all sorts of markup in it."
```

The software you've been using threads everything together based on message numbers and tracking responses. Now, you want to convert this to a Rails site.

First, design and create the new database. Based on the previous example, an appropriate set of tables might look like this:

```
CREATE TABLE messages (
    id INT(4) NOT NULL AUTO_INCREMENT,
    user_id INT(4),
    previous_id INT(4),
    number int(6),
    title VARCHAR(50),
    body TEXT,
    date CHAR(10),
    PRIMARY KEY(id)
);

CREATE TABLE users (
    id INT(4) NOT NULL AUTO_INCREMENT,
    name VARCHAR(20),
    PRIMARY KEY(id)
);
```

Now, create the Rails application:

```
$ rails board
$ cd board
$ ruby script/generate model user
$ ruby script/generate model message
```

In app/models/user.rb, add the following:

```
class User < ActiveRecord::Base
  has_many :messages
end
```

And put this code in app/models/message.rb:

```
class Message < ActiveRecord::Base
  belongs_to :user
  belongs_to :previous, :class_name => "Message",
                        :foreign_key =>"previous_id"
end
```

Then, set up `config/database.yml`.

Now you've got to filter the old data into the new Rails environment. The way we'll do this is as follows:

1   For each message file, read the file in via YAML.

2   Retrieve the user corresponding to the message's username from the database (or create a new user if no such user exists).

3   Set the new message's `user` property to the user just retrieved (or created).

4   Create a new `Message` object, and set its `date`, `number`, `title`, and `body` properties from the old values.

5   If this message has a previous field (used for threading), then set this message's `previous` property to the `id` for that message.

Listing 3.1 shows a Ruby script that will perform all these steps. It includes a few black-box techniques; but the commentary will help you see what it's doing and how it maps to the algorithm just prescribed. The script is engineered to be run from the root directory of the (imaginary) new Rails application; from there, it can easily find and load the `config/environment.rb` file, which gives it access to the necessary databases and other application-specific information.

Listing 3.1   Conversion script to load legacy YAML data into a Rails application database

```
require 'config/environment.rb'

mnums = {}     <——————❶
files = Dir["../file*"].sort

files.each do |file|   <———————❷
  m = YAML.load(File.read(file))      ┐❸
  num  = m['number']                  │
  prev = m['previous']                ┘

  user = User.find_by_name(m['username'])   ┐
  unless user                               │❹
    user = User.new                         │
    user.name = m['username']               │
    user.save                               │
  end                                       ┘

  message = Message.new      ┐❺
  message.save               │
  mnums[num] = message.id    ┘

  message.user   = user      ┐❻
  message.number = num       ▽
```

```
    message.body    = m['body']
    message.title   = m['title']                    6
    message.date    = m['date']

    if prev                                                    7
      message.previous = Message.find(mnums[prev])
    end

    message.save    ◁        8
  end
```

The script initializes an empty *hash* (key/value collection) called mnums, which will store message numbers in cases where one message is a response to another message ❶. Also, all of the names of the relevant legacy files are gathered, sorted alphabetically, into the array files. The script now cycles through the original, legacy data files one at a time, using each❷. (Make sure that the files are named in such a way that an alphabetical sort of their names will put them in order by date of message; for example, you could call them file000, file001, etc.)

For each file, the script creates a Ruby object based on a YAML reading of the file's contents ❸. (Remember that YAML serializes Ruby data to string form and then can load it back from the string—stored in a file, in this case—to in-memory data at runtime.) The variables prev and num store the values in the *previous* and *number* fields of this message. There will always be a value for *number*, but there will be a value for *previous* only if this message was a response to another message. (We'll need to know this later.)

 The script next searches for a user in the database matching the username from the file. If it doesn't find one, it creates a new user ❹. This ensures that each message will have a valid user associated with it.

The rest of the script handles the message . A new message object is created to store the message that's being parsed from the file ❺. The *id* field of the new message is stored in the mnums hash, keyed to the number of the *legacy* message. This provides a mapping between the old message numbering sequence and the sequence of id values in the new message database.

Various fields of the new message object are initialized to the corresponding values from the file: *user, number, body, title,* and *date* ❻. If a previous message exists to which this one was a response (which we'll know based on whether the variable prev has a value), that existing message is used to set the *previous* field of the new message ❼. Finally, the new message, with its properties set to reflect who wrote it and the message to which it was a response (if any), is saved to the database ❽.

The idea is to translate the data from the terms of one universe to the terms of another. Ruby can do it all for you: read the old data (easy in this case, because it's in YAML, but not difficult even if it's in other text-based or database formats), test the values and make decisions about what should be done, and create ActiveRecord objects whose properties match those in the original dataset. Not only Rails is open-ended: Ruby itself is equal to all sorts of tasks, including conversions like this that aren't part of a Rails application but that may make development of an application possible in the first place.

3.3.2 *The irb-based Rails application console*

Our last subtopic in this chapter could belong anywhere. It's an application-related skill, so it fits in this section. And it's something you'll find extremely useful: the Rails application console.

You've already started using irb to test Ruby code snippets and to do quick calculations. Rails applications come complete with an irb-based console—basically, an irb session preloaded with the components of your application.

To run the console, give this command (from the top level of the application directory):

```
$ ruby script/console
```

At this point, you're in an irb session (with the simple prompt option; the prompt is >>). During this session, you can examine data, create new data instances, and so forth. Listing 3.2 shows a session that creates a new Edition object and fills in its properties (except for description, which is filled in automatically when the object is saved, thanks to the before_create hook we wrote in section 3.2.3).

Listing 3.2 irb session that that creates an Edition object and fills in its properties

```
$ ruby script/console
Loading development environment.
>> e = Edition.new
=> #<Edition:0x40a0ed3c @new_record=true, @attributes={"price"=>nil,
   "publisher"=>nil, "description"=>nil, "year"=>nil, "work_id"=>0}>
>> e.work = Work.find(1)        <———❶
=> #<Work:0x40a04cec @attributes={"title"=>"Sonata for Cello and Piano in
   F\nMajor", "composer_id"=>"1", "id"=>"1"}>
>> e.price = 22.50
=> 22.5
>> e.publisher = "Ruby F. Rails, Inc."    <———❷
=> "Ruby F. Rails, Inc."
>> e.year = 2006    <———❷
=> 2006
```

```
>> e.save
=> true    <———— ❸
>> e.description
=> "standard"    <———— ❹
```

The console session makes changes to the database (the development database, by default). Here, we create an `Edition` object, assign something to its `work` property ❶ (so that it's an edition *of* something) as well as its `publisher` and `year` ❷, and save it to the database. The `save` operation returns `true` ❸, which means it has succeeded. The new edition's `description` property is set automatically to "standard" ❹, as we arranged.

You can make changes directly in your application's program files while the session is in progress. If you do, you must reload the files you've changed. You can do this using the `load` command (which, unlike `require`, loads a file even if it has already loaded the file once). For example, if you make a change to `edition.rb`, you type the following in the console session:

```
>> load 'edition.rb'
```

Rails knows how to find the file and reads it in again.

Don't forget that the application console is also a regular irb session. If, like many Ruby programmers, you become an irb devotee, you can save yourself the trouble of starting up an extra session if the application console is running already and you need to do a quick irb calculation or code test.

3.4   Summary

Chapter 3 has given you a grounding in a number of the many ways that knowing Ruby can help you as a Rails developer. It's a pivot chapter: not as detailed or extensive in terms of Ruby or Rails applicability as what is to come later in the book, but more detailed than anything that would have made sense before the first two chapters.

You've seen examples of what it means to gain knowledge of what your Rails code is doing, mainly in connection with the interplay between what looks like configuration syntax and what is programming code. (That's not the only area in which it pays to understand the Ruby/Rails relationship, but it's a good one to get a handle on.) You've also seen some initial examples of how to deploy your own code, both in cases where Rails provides you with an infrastructure for doing so (helper methods and predefined hooks) and in cases where you're writing methods from scratch for a certain purpose. As suggested in section 3.2, Rails is designed to provide you with different levels of choice and freedom; and you've seen examples of everything from prescribed, unchangeable application features (such as the layout and naming of the directories) to open-ended programming opportunities (such as adding methods to model files, which allows you to bring just about any Ruby technique to bear on your Rails application's behavior).

We also looked—for the first and pretty much the last time in the book—at the power of Ruby to help you with tasks related to, but not necessarily part of, a given Rails application. The legacy-data conversion example in section 3.3.1 points the way to a large number of similar tasks; and I hope you'll turn to Ruby productively in the future to help you accomplish them. Also in the "how Ruby helps you with Rails development" category, we covered the irb-based application console—a very useful tool in its own right, as well as a good example of the interflow between the Ruby programming environment and the Rails development process.

Now we'll turn to the systematic exploration of the Ruby programming language. Rails won't be lost to view, but the center of gravity of the next two parts of the book will be on Ruby. You now have a good overview of the kinds of tasks that a greater knowledge of Ruby can help perform do in Rails; and the return on time invested only gets greater as you go along.

Part 2

Ruby building blocks

This is the first of two parts of this book devoted to the exploration and study of the details of the Ruby programming language. This part comprises five chapters, over the course of which you'll learn about the major building blocks of Ruby: the essential constructs and techniques that drive Ruby programs and hold them together. This discussion includes an introductory situating of Ruby as an object-oriented language. From there, we'll move on to look at a series of topics concerned with how Ruby programs are constructed and how Ruby represents and manipulates data.

The focus in this part of the book, as well as in part 3, is on learning the Ruby language. But it's still Ruby for Rails, and Rails won't fade from view. Where possible, Rails-related examples serve the double purpose of illustrating Ruby features and also showing you Rails techniques or idioms, or nuggets of Rails information. You'll also find subsections that discuss in more depth the implications of particular Ruby constructs for the Rails framework.

We'll start part 2 with a close look at Ruby objects (the most basic building block) and variables. From there, we'll segue to an exploration of how you can organize and automate objects using the aggregation techniques made available by Ruby's class and module mechanisms. That will take us through chapter 6. Chapter 7 examines matters of scope in Ruby: where you are in the overall map of your program at a given point during execution, and how to tell. Finally, chapter 8 introduces Ruby's control-flow techniques: conditional execution `if` structures, looping, and other related programming facilities.

In short, part 2 will take you through a considerable amount of both the what and the how.

Objects and variables

4

In this chapter, we'll begin exploring the details of the Ruby programming language. We'll look first and foremost at the concept of the *object*, around which almost every line of Ruby code you write (for Rails applications or otherwise) will revolve. Toward the end of the chapter, we'll get deeper technically than we have so far into the nature and behavior of variables in Ruby.

Aside from giving you a technical basis for understanding the rest of Ruby, the study of objects also ties in directly to using a programming language to represent or *model* aspects of entities and processes. This kind of modeling of entities is also part of the design of a relational database, which in turn serves as the blueprint for the structure of your Rails application. In other words, a lot of modeling is going on at the programming-language, database-design, and application-design levels. A thorough and disciplined understanding of Ruby's object system is essential to seeing how these systems interoperate in Rails.

Ruby objects are often (perhaps most often) handled via variables that represent them; and in this chapter you'll learn about variables as well as objects. And what you do *with* objects, broadly speaking, is send them messages; accordingly, we'll also look at some details of message sending—the mechanics of calling methods on objects.

4.1 From "things" to objects

When you use Ruby—even when you're not writing applications, like Rails applications, that operate in close parallel with a database—you're always, to one degree or another, dealing with the matter of mapping "things" to the universe of your computer program.

In the case of Rails applications, this kind of mapping is front and center: You design a database with tables and fields, and your program derives filenames, variable names, and much of its programming logic from that database. But apart from Rails, Ruby *itself*, as a programming language, is designed such that much of what you do when you plan and write Ruby programs is to model domains, examine relations between entities or "things" (like composers and works, or teachers and students, or shirts and buttons), and find ways to embed those relations in the structure and terminology of your program.

When you write a computer program, you're creating a kind of symbolic universe whose components you manipulate using the syntax and semantics of your programming language. Some programming languages, however, encourage you further along this road than others.

Ruby is one of those.

In any Ruby program, the bulk of the design, logic, and action revolve around *objects*. When you write Ruby programs, you primarily *create objects* and *ask those objects to perform actions*. Objects are your handle on the universe of your program. When you want something done—a calculation, an output operation, a data comparison—you ask an object to do it. Rather than ask in the abstract whether *a* equals *b*, you *ask a whether it considers itself equal to b*. If you want to know whether a given *student* is taking a class from a given *teacher*, you ask the student: *Do you have this teacher?* Writing a Ruby program is largely a matter of engineering your objects so that they behave in a manner consistent with the domain or domains you want your program to emulate.

You'll learn in the following sections how to create an object, and what it looks like when you ask an object to do something. The main point, as we enter the world of objects, is that domain modeling (or real-world emulation) crops up not only when you're designing databases but also when you're designing Ruby programs. Once you get in the domain-modeling mindset, it will see you through the entire process.

4.1.1 *Introducing object-oriented programming*

Ruby comes to the idea of manipulating data through objects via a program-language design principle called *object orientation*. Many extremely popular programming languages are object-oriented (such as Java, C++, Python, as well as Ruby), and some languages that aren't fully object-oriented have facilities for writing object-oriented code (for example, Perl, as described in *Object-Oriented Perl* by Damian Conway, from Manning Publications). In object-oriented programming (OOP), you perform your calculations, data manipulation, and input/output operations by creating objects and then requesting information and actions from those objects.

Different objects have different capabilities. You wouldn't ask a `Book` object (that is, an object designed around the characteristics of a book) how many liters of liquid it could hold. But you might ask it who its author is—and save the liquid questions for a `Bottle` object. (It's possible to create nonsensical, badly named objects; but that's a practice to be avoided rather than cultivated.)

NOTE THE REAL WORLD The term *real-world* gets thrown around a lot in discussions of programming. There's room for debate (and there is debate) as to whether this or that programming language, or even this or that *kind* of programming language, corresponds more closely than others to the shape of the real world. A lot depends on how you perceive the world. Do you perceive it as peopled with things, each of which has tasks to do and waits for someone to request the task? If so, you may be into object orientation. Do you see life as a series of to-do items on a checklist, to be gone through in order? If so, you may want a more *procedural* language. In short, there's no one answer to the question of what the real world is—so there's no answer to the question of what it means for a programming language to model the real world.

Designing object-oriented software is largely a matter of figuring out what you want your objects to be: what they should do, how they interact with each other, how many of each there can be (only one music store; many musical works), and other such questions. As you'll see, Ruby provides a complete set of tools for naming, creating, addressing, and manipulating objects—and, through the manipulation of those objects, the data they operate on.

4.1.2 *I, object!*

At first, the concept of object-oriented computer programming tends to come across as both simple (you write programs that have `Books` and `Bottles` and `Cars` and `Houses`, and you hold a kind of conversation with those things) and abstract (*Object? What does that mean? What do I actually type into my program file to create a* `House` *object?*). It does have a component of simplicity; it lets you draw on objects, entities, roles, and behaviors as a source for how you design your program, and that can be a help. At the same time, to create and use objects in your programs, you have to learn how it's done in a given language.

   Seeing this explanation concretely can make the abstract parts easier to grasp. We'll therefore proceed to some Ruby code. We'll create a new object. It won't be an edition of music, a composer, or anything elaborate; it will be a generic object. We'll ask Ruby to create the object and assign it to a variable so that we can manipulate it further:

```
obj = Object.new
```

Now we have an object, stored in the variable `obj`.

The role(s) of the object

Objects are your agents, your proxies, in the universe of your program. You ask them for information. You assign them tasks to accomplish. You tell them to perform calculations and report back to you. You hand them to each other and get them to work together.

   What can our freshly minted, generic object do?

All Ruby objects are created with certain innate abilities. Those abilities, though important, aren't exciting, so we'll keep them to the side for the moment. More exciting is what happens when you teach your object how to do the things you want it to do.

Defining an object's behavior

Let's say you've created an object and you want it to do something interesting: You want it to talk. To get it to talk, you have to ask it to talk. But before you ask it to talk, you have to teach it *how* to talk.

Specifically, and more technically, you have to *define a method* for your object. You do this using a special term—a *keyword*—namely, the keyword `def`.

Here's how you define the method `talk` for the object `obj`:

```
def obj.talk
  puts "I am an object."
  puts "(Do you object?)"
end
```

Figure 4.1 shows an analysis of that chunk of code.

When you execute the code—that method definition—`obj` won't talk. Rather, `obj` will learn *how to talk*. You can now ask it to talk.

Sending messages to objects

To get your object to talk, you use a construct, a bit of syntax that is probably the most common and important construct you'll see in Ruby programs: the *message-sending* or *method-calling* syntax:

```
object.message
```

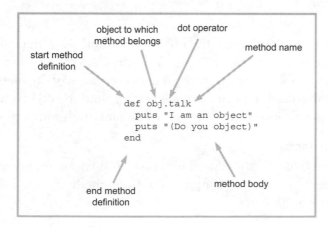

Figure 4.1
Anatomy of a method definition

In the context of this construct:

- `object` can be, and often is, a variable that stands in for an object. It may also be a *literal* object construct—for example, a string in quotation marks.

- The dot (`.`) is the message-sending operator. The `message` on the right is sent to the `object` on the left.

- `message` is the message that gets sent to `object`. In practice, `message` is almost always the name of a method (like `talk`, the method defined earlier). In any case, `object` always thinks `message` is the name of a method. If there's no method by that name, error-handling measures are taken. But the general idea is that every message you send to an object corresponds to a method the object can call.

> **NOTE**   CALLING METHODS VS. SENDING MESSAGES   You'll hear people talk more about "calling a method on an object" than about "sending a message to an object." It's fine to fall into that terminology, because that's what's happening most of the time. But it's important to understand that what's *really* happening is a two-phase process: You send a message to an object; and the object executes the method with the name that corresponds to your message. Understanding this will help you understand the possible outcomes of sending an object a message that does *not* correspond to the names of any of its methods.

Using this syntax, you can ask your object to talk:

```
obj.talk
```

And it talks:

```
I am an object.
(Do you object?)
```

An object is said to *respond to* a message if the object has a method defined whose name corresponds to the message. For example, the object `obj` responds to `talk`. The object to which you send a message is referred to as the *receiver* of the message.

The semantics of method calls let you go much further than the relatively one-dimensional `talk` case, particularly when you start calling methods with *arguments*.

Methods that take arguments

Methods in Ruby are much like mathematical functions: Input goes in, the wheels turn, and a result comes out. To feed input to a Ruby method, you call the method with one or more arguments.

In a method definition, you indicate the *required* and/or *optional arguments* by means of a list of variables in (sometimes optional) parentheses after the method. When you call the method, you provide values corresponding to these variables in your method call.

Let's say we want our object to function as a Celsius-to-Fahrenheit converter. We can teach it how to do the conversion by defining a method, which we'll call c2f:

```
def obj.c2f(c)
  c * 9 / 5 + 32
end
```

Notice the variable c, which is the name of the only argument to this method. When we call the method, we'll use a similar syntax (parentheses), and we'll insert a number where c appears in the method definition. Let's use the converter method to convert 100:

```
puts obj.c2f(100)
```

(We need the puts, or the method does the calculation but we never see the result.)

The result is printed, as requested:

```
212
```

> **WARNING** METHOD INPUT VS. KEYBOARD OR FILE INPUT Input to a function or method means the values you send as arguments—not keyboard input. Similarly, a method's output is the result it returns, not what it prints to the screen. It's more common to speak of the *return value* of a method—what it returns as a result of being executed. We can say that c2f *returns* the Fahrenheit equivalent of its argument.

The item in parentheses is an argument. Our c2f method takes one argument. As you see, there's a direct correspondence here between the way we define the method and the way we call the method.

The parentheses are optional in most cases. (In cases where the syntax is more complex or you call more than one method in a row, you may need the parentheses to make it clear to Ruby what you mean.) Most people use parentheses for method calls, but you'll see method calls with no parentheses—including, typically, in most Rails applications, for reasons we'll examine a little later.

At the other end of the process, every method call hands back—*returns*—a value.

The return value of a method

Ruby code is made up of expressions, each of which evaluates to a particular value. Table 4.1 shows some examples of expressions and their values (along with explanatory comments).

Table 4.1   Examples of Ruby expressions and the values to which they evaluate

Expression	Value	Comments
`2 + 2`	`4`	Arithmetic expressions evaluate to their results.
`"Hello"`	`"Hello"`	A simple, literal string (in quotation marks) evaluates to itself.
`"Hello" + " there"`	`"Hello there"`	Strings can be "added" to each other (concatenated) with the plus sign.
`c = 100`	`100`	When you assign to a variable, the whole assignment evaluates to the value you've assigned.
`c * 9 / 5 + 32`	`212`	The usual rules of precedence apply: Multiplication and division bind more tightly than addition and are performed first.

A method call is an expression. When you call a method, the method call evaluates to something. This result of calling a method is the method's *return value*.

Methods can be lengthy; but there's a universal rule for determining a method's return value: The return value of any method is the value of the last expression evaluated during execution of the method. In the case of the temperature-conversion method, the last expression evaluated is the only line of the method body:

```
c * 9 / 5 + 32
```

That means the whole value of the method—the return value—is the result of that calculation.

Ruby gives you a keyword for making this explicit: `return`. The use of this keyword is optional, but many programmers like to use it because it makes explicit what is otherwise implicit:

```
def obj.c2f(c)
  return c * 9 / 5 + 32
end
```

This is equivalent to the earlier version of the method, but it's more expressive about what it's doing. On the other hand, it's wordier. You have to decide, as a matter of your own style, whether you want to use `return`.

At this point, our object is doing what we need it to do: listening to our messages and acting on them. That's a good illustration of how Ruby works, but it's a bit scrappy. We started with a generic object and taught it to talk and to convert temperatures. That shows you the mechanics of defining and calling methods, but it's not an impressive example of objects modeling real-world entities. Let's get a little more real.

4.1.3 *Modeling objects more closely: the behavior of a ticket*

As we broaden our real-world modeling horizons, for variety's sake we'll model something other than an online sheet-music store. We'll model a *ticket to an event*—not a ticket-selling agency, but the ticket itself. We'll create it, we'll endow it with ticket-like properties, and then we'll follow its lead through an extended set of examples and techniques.

But first, let's take a high-level view at what we expect a `ticket` object to do and to know about itself.

The ticket object, behavior-first

We'll set our sights on a ticket object that can provide data about itself. We want to be able to ask a ticket, in programming terms, for information about the event it's for: when, where, name of event; performer; which seat; how much it costs.

When asked, the ticket will provide the following information:

```
01/02/03
Town Hall
Author's reading
Mark Twain
Second Balcony, row J, seat 12
$5.50
```

The goal is to create an object from which we can easily get all this information. Emphasis on *easily*: The point of object-oriented programming is that the programming language is your partner in designing programs that embody entities (real-world things) in a form that lets you store and retrieve information easily.

Creating the ticket object

First, we'll create our `ticket` object. We assign it to the variable `ticket`:

```
ticket = Object.new
```

Now, let's endow the object—the `ticket`—with properties and data. We do this by defining a series of methods, each of which has a return value matching the value we want the ticket to have for that item:

```
def ticket.venue
  "Town Hall"
```

```
end

def ticket.performer
  "Mark Twain"
end

def ticket.event
  "Author's reading"
end

def ticket.price      ◁━━━━━❶
  5.50
end

def ticket.seat
  "Second Balcony, row J, seat 12"
end

def ticket.date
  "01/02/03"
end
```

Let's pause for a moment and make some observations. The majority of the methods defined here return *string* values. You can see this at a glance: They hand back a value inside quotation marks.

The `price` method ❶ returns a *floating-point decimal number*: 5.50. Floating-point numbers have more complexity and quirkiness than you may think. Some day you'll probably come across something peculiar-looking, like this frequently cited example:

```
puts 0.5 - 0.4 - 0.1
-2.77555756156289e-17    ◁━━━━━ Not zero!
```

The problem—or, more accurately, the inevitable consequence of the laws of mathematics and computers—is that decimal floating-point numbers of arbitrary length can't be stored and operated on in binary form with complete accuracy. So, don't be surprised if you see this sort of code.

> **NOTE**   NOT ALL OBJECTS HAVE TO BE CREATED INDIVIDUALLY   A little further on, you'll learn how to create objects on a *factory* basis, without have to call `Object.new` and manually add methods for every object. Ruby gives you plenty of shortcuts; in practice, you rarely end up creating handcrafted, one-at-a-time objects. We're doing it here to give you a solid understanding of objects and methods. That, in turn, will help you understand the shortcuts when you encounter them.

Querying the ticket object

Now that our `ticket` object knows a little about itself, let's ask it to share the information. Rather than produce a raw list of items, let's make it look nicer. We'll use the built-in Ruby methods `print` and `puts` (which you encountered in chapter 1) to get the information in more or less narrative form:

```
print "This ticket is for: "
print ticket.event + ", at "
print ticket.venue + ", on "
puts ticket.date + "."
print "The performer is "
puts ticket.performer + "."
print "The seat is "
print ticket.seat + ", "
print "and it costs $"
puts "%.2f." % ticket.price      ◁——— Print floating-point number
                                       to two decimal places
```

Save all the code, starting with `ticket = Object.new`, to a file called `ticket.rb`, and run it. You'll see the following:

```
This ticket is for: Author's reading, at Town Hall, on 01/02/03.
The performer is Mark Twain.
The seat is Second Balcony, row J, seat 12, and it costs $5.50.
```

The code for this example consists of a series of calls to the methods defined earlier: `ticket.event`, `ticket.venue`, and so forth. We've embedded those calls—in other words, embedded the return values of those methods ("Author's reading", "Town Hall", and so on)—in a succession of `print` commands; and we've added connectors (", at", ", on", and so forth) to make the text read well and look nice.

It's a simple example, but it encompasses important Ruby procedures and principles. The knowledge of the program resides in the object: the `ticket`. We get at that information by asking for it via method calls. Each method, upon being called, hands back a value. Nothing is more central to Ruby than that process.

Our code works well, but it's wordy. Ruby has a reputation as a powerful, high-level language. You're supposed to be able to get a *lot* done with relatively *little* code.

This example takes ten lines of printing code to generate three lines of output. Sometimes a ratio like that may be inevitable, but this isn't one of them. We can definitely tighten up this code; so let's do that, while we're still on the simple ticket question-and-answer exercise.

Shortening the code via string interpolation

The goal of shortening the output of our little program gives us an excuse to dip into one of the most useful programming techniques available in Ruby: *string interpolation.* The *string interpolation operator* gives you a way to drop variables, method return values, or anything else, into a string. This can save you a lot of back-and-forth between print and puts.

Here's how the printing code looks, using string interpolation to drop the values we need into place:

```
puts "This ticket is for: #{ticket.event}, at #{ticket.venue}."
puts "The perform is #{ticket.performer}."
puts "The seat is #{ticket.seat}, "
puts "and it costs $#{"%.2f." % ticket.price}"
```

Whatever's inside the interpolation operator #{...} gets calculated separately, and the results of the calculation are pasted automatically into the string. When you run these lines, you don't see the #{...} operator on your screen; instead, you see the *results* of calculating or *evaluating* what was inside that operator.

We just eliminated six of ten lines of code. We also made the code look a lot more like the eventual format of the output, rather than something that works but doesn't convey much visual information.

Ticket availability: expressing Boolean state in a method

Some things we want to query a ticket about can be expressed as strings and numbers. Others are *true/false*—Boolean—values. And some may go either way.

Consider the matter of whether a ticket has been sold or is still available. One way to endow a ticket with knowledge of its own availability status is this:

```
def ticket.availability_status
  "sold"
end
```

Another way is to ask the ticket whether it is available and have it report back true or false:

```
def ticket.available?
  false
end
```

false is a special term in Ruby, as is the term true. true and false are objects. The reason for their existence is to provide a way to express truth and falsehood—which is helpful when you're writing conditional statements (if-based things) or methods where all you need to know is whether something is true (as opposed to methods where you need a number, string, or other object).

You may have noticed that the method name available? ends with a question mark. Ruby lets you do this so you can write methods that evaluate to true or false and make the method calls look like questions:

```
if ticket.available?
  puts "You're in luck!"
else
  puts "Sorry--that seat has been sold."
end
```

Every expression in Ruby evaluates to an object; and every object in Ruby has a truth-value. The truth-value of almost every object in Ruby is true. The only objects whose truth-value (or Boolean value) is false are the objects false and the special non-entity object nil. (You'll see Booleans and nil in more detail in chapter 9. For the moment, you can think of both false and nil as functionally equivalent indicators of a negative test outcome.)

You can play around with if expressions in irb, and you'll see this in operation:

```
>> if "abc"
>> puts "Strings are 'true' in Ruby!"
>> end
Strings are 'true' in Ruby!
=> nil
>> if 123
>> puts "So are numbers!"
>> end
So are numbers!
=> nil
>> if 0
>> puts "Even 0 is true, which it isn't in some languages."
>> end
Even 0 is true, which it isn't in some languages.
=> nil
>> if 1 == 2
>> puts "One doesn't equal two, so this won't appear."
>> end
=> nil
```

Notice how irb not only obeys the puts method-calls (when conditions are right) but also, on its own initiative, outputs the value of the entire expression. In the cases where the puts happens, the whole expression evaluates to nil—because the return values of puts is always nil. In the last case, where the string isn't printed (because the condition fails), the value of the expression is also nil—because an if statement that fails (and has no else branch to salvage it) also evaluates to nil.

Remembering that nil has a Boolean value of false, you can, if you wish, get into some amusing Boolean acrobatics with irb. A call to puts returns nil and is therefore false, *even though the string gets printed*. If you put puts in an if clause, the clause will be false. But it will still be evaluated. So...

```
>> if puts "You'll see this"; puts "but not this"; end
You'll see this
=> nil
```

The first `puts` is executed, but the value it returns, namely `nil`, is not true in the Boolean sense—so the second one isn't executed.

This is, to use the popular phrase, a contrived example. But it's a good idea to get used to the fact that everything in Ruby has a Boolean value, and sometimes it's not what you may expect. As is often the case, irb can be a great help in getting a handle on this concept.

We've now manually given our `ticket` object some behaviors; having done that, we're going to turn next to the matter of what behaviors every object in Ruby is already endowed with at its creation.

4.2 *The innate behaviors of an object*

Even a newly created object isn't a blank slate. As soon as an object comes into existence, it already responds to a number of messages. Every object is "born" with certain innate abilities.

To see a list of innate methods, you can call the `methods` method (and throw in a `sort` operation, to make it easier to browse visually):

```
p Object.new.methods.sort
```

The result is a list of all the messages (methods) this newly minted object comes bundled with. (Warning: the output looks cluttered. This is how Ruby displays *arrays*—and the `methods` method gives you an array of method names. If you want a list of the methods one per line, use `puts` instead of `p` in the command.)

```
["==", "===", "=~", "__id__", "__send__", "class",
"clone", "display", "dup", "eql?", "equal?", "extend",
"freeze", "frozen?", "hash", "id", "inspect",
"instance_eval", "instance_of?", "instance_variable_get",
"instance_variable_set", "instance_variables", "is_a?",
"kind_of?", "method", "methods", "nil?", "object_id",
"private_methods", "protected_methods", "public_methods",
"respond_to?", "send", "singleton_methods", "taint",
"tainted?", "to_a", "to_s", "type", "untaint"]
```

Don't worry if most of these methods make no sense to you right now. You can try them in irb, if you're curious to see what they do (and if you're not afraid of getting some error messages).

But a few of these innate methods are common enough—and helpful enough, even in the early phases of acquaintance with Ruby—that we'll look at them in detail here. The following methods fit this description:

- `object_id`
- `respond_to?`
- `send`

Adding these to your Ruby toolbox won't be amiss, on account of what they do and because they serve as examples of innate methods.

4.2.1 Identifying objects uniquely with the object_id method

Every object in Ruby has a unique id number associated with it. You can see an object's id by asking the object to show you its `object_id`:

```
obj = Object.new
puts "The id of obj is #{obj.object_id}."
str = "Strings are objects too, and this is a string!"
puts "The id of the string object str is #{str.object_id}."
puts "And the id of the integer 100 is #{100.object_id}."
```

Having a unique id number for every object can come in handy when you're trying to determine whether two objects are the same as each other. How can two objects be the same? Well, 100 is the same as 100. And here's another case:

```
a = Object.new
b = a
puts "a's id is #{a.object_id} and b's id is #{b.object_id}."
```

Even though the variables a and b are different, the object they both refer to is the same. (We'll be looking in depth at how object *references* work in section 4.4.)

Yet another scenario: Sometimes you think two objects are the same, but they're not. This happens a lot with strings. Consider the following example:

```
string_1 = "Hello"
string_2 = "Hello"

puts "string_1's id is #{string_1.object_id}."
puts "string_2's id is #{string_2.object_id}."
```

Even though these two strings contain the same text, they aren't, technically, the same object. If you printed them out, you'd see the same result both times ("Hello"). But the string objects *themselves* are different. It's like having two copies of the same book: They contain the same text, but they aren't the same thing as each other. You could destroy one, and the other would survive.

WARNING   THE (POSSIBLY) CONFUSING HISTORY OF THE `object_id` METHOD   The `object_id` method was introduced into Ruby fairly recently. Previously, the same method was known as `id`. The problem was that `id` is a common name: Lots of programs, including Rails applications, have methods called `id`. That meant the default `id` method (the one that gives a unique number) was inadvertently being replaced in a lot of programs. A method called `__id__` was introduced; the underscores make it less likely that anyone would choose this name for a method in their own program, so it's safer. The problem with underscores is that they're ugly. Matz decided to add a new method, without underscores (except the word separator): `object_id`. That's now the standard way to obtain an object's id number.

Although the Ruby `object_id` method and the ActiveRecord `id` method both return numbers, they're not the same thing. `object_id` gives you Ruby's internal id number for an object; ActiveRecord's `id` method gives you the value of the *id* field in the database table for the model you're dealing with, if there is such a field.

Id numbers and equality of objects

As in the case of human institutions, one of the points of giving objects id numbers in Ruby is to be able to make unique identifications—and, in particular, to be able to determine when two objects are the same object.

Ruby provides a variety of ways to compare objects for different types of equality. If you have two strings, you can test to see whether they contain the same characters. You can also test to see whether they are the same object (which, as we've just seen, isn't necessarily the case, even if they contain the same characters). The same holds true, with slight variations, for other objects and other types of objects.

Comparing id numbers for equality is just one way of measuring object equality. We'll get into further detail about more of these comparisons a little later. Right now, we're going to turn to the next innate method on our list: `respond_to?`.

4.2.2 Querying an object's abilities with the respond_to? method

Ruby objects respond to messages. At different times during a program run, depending on the object and what sorts of methods have been defined for it, an object may or may not respond to a given message. For example, the following code results in an error:

```
obj = Object.new
obj.talk
```

Ruby is only too glad to notify you:

```
undefined method 'talk' for #<Object:0x401aa18c> (NoMethodError)
```

You can determine in advance (before you ask the object to do something) whether the object knows how to handle the message you want to send it, by using the respond_to? method. This method exists for all objects; you can ask any object whether it responds to any message.

respond_to? usually appears in connection with conditional (if) logic. We haven't covered this yet, but its use in this example is easy to follow:

```
obj = Object.new
if obj.respond_to?("talk")
  obj.talk
else
  puts "Sorry, the object doesn't understand the 'talk' message."
end
```

respond_to? is an example of *introspection* or *reflection*, two terms that refer to examining the state of a program while it's running. Ruby offers a number of facilities for introspection. Examining an object's methods (with the methods method, as we did a little while ago) is another introspective or reflective technique.

4.2.3 *Sending messages to objects with the send method*

You've learned about the dot operator (.), which is used for sending messages to objects. But what if you don't know which message you want to send?

How could *that* happen? Suppose you want to let a user—someone at the keyboard—get information from the ticket object. The way you do this (and yes, there are slicker ways, but bear with me) is to let the user type in the appropriate word ("venue", "performer", and so on) and then display the corresponding value.

Let's start with the keyboard input part. Having created the ticket object and written the methods for it, you'd add this to the program to incorporate keyboard input:

```
print "Information desired: "
request = gets.chomp
```

The code gets a line of keyboard input and chomps off the trailing newline character.

At this point, you *could* proceed as follows, testing the input for one value after another (using the double equal-sign comparison operator (==) and calling the method it matches:

```
if request == "venue"
  puts ticket.venue
elsif request == "performer"
  puts ticket.performer
...
```

You'd continue through the whole list of ticket properties.

Or, you can *send* the word directly to the `ticket` object. Instead of the previous code, you do the following:

```
if ticket.respond_to?(request)    ◁———❶
  puts ticket.send(request)
else
  puts "No such information available"
end
```

This version uses the `send` method as an all-purpose way of getting a message to the `ticket` object. It relieves you of having to march through the whole list of possible requests. Instead, having checked that the `ticket` object will know what to do ❶, you hand the `ticket` the message and let it do its thing.

> **TIP** USING __send__ INSTEAD OF send *Sending* is a broad concept: Email is sent, data gets sent to I/O sockets, and so forth. It's not uncommon for programs to define a method called send that conflicts with Ruby's built-in send method. Therefore, Ruby gives you an alternative way to call send: __send__. By convention, no one ever writes a method with that name, so the built-in Ruby version is always available and never comes into conflict with newly written methods. It looks strange, but it's safer than the plain send version from the point of view of method-name clashes.

Most of the time, you'll use the dot operator to send messages to objects. However, the `send` alternative can be useful and powerful.

4.3 Required, optional, and default-valued arguments

Methods you write in Ruby can take more than one argument, or none at all. They can also allow a variable number of arguments. We'll look at a number of permutations here. These are summarized in table 4.2 at the end of this section.

4.3.1 Required and optional arguments

When you call a Ruby method, you have to supply the correct number of arguments. If you don't, Ruby tells you there's a problem. For example,

```
def obj.one_arg(x)
end

obj.one_arg(1,2,3)
```

results in:

```
ArgumentError: wrong number of arguments (3 for 1)
```

It's possible to write a method that allows a variable number of arguments. To do this, you put a star (an asterisk: *) in front of a single argument name:

```
def obj.multi_args(*x)
end
```

The *x notation means that when you call the method, you can supply any number of arguments (including none). In this case, the variable x is assigned an array of values corresponding to whatever arguments were sent. You can then examine the values one at a time by traversing the array. (We'll look more closely at arrays in chapter 11.)

You can fine-tune the number of arguments by mixing required and optional arguments:

```
def two_or_more(a,b,*c)
```

In this example, a and b are required arguments. The final *c will sponge up any other arguments that you may send and put them in an array in the variable c.

4.3.2 *Default values for arguments*

You can also make an argument optional by giving it a default value. The result will be that if that argument isn't supplied, the variable corresponding to the argument will receive the default value.

Here's an example:

```
def default_args(a,b,c=1)
  puts "Values of variables: ",a,b,c
end
```

If you make a call like this

```
default_args(3,2)
```

you'll see this result:

```
Values of variables:
3
2
1
```

You didn't supply a value for c, so c was set to the default value provided for it in the argument list: 1. If you do supply a third argument, that value overrides the default assignment of 1. The following call

```
default_args(4,5,6)
```

produces this result:

```
Values of variables:
4
5
6
```

4.3.3 *Order of arguments*

The order in which you provide the arguments must correspond to the order in which they're listed. That's always true, but it's particularly important to keep in mind when you're using optional and/or default arguments—either calling methods that take such arguments or writing such methods in the first place.

If you want to include optional arguments (*x), they have to come after any non-optional arguments:

```
def opt_args(a,b,*x)   # right
def opt_args(a,*x,b)   # wrong
```

You'll never get as far as calling that second version of the method, because Ruby won't let you write it. In order to understand why not, consider what would happen if you did call it:

```
opt_args(1,2,3,4)
```

Obviously, you want to assign 1 to a. But what about the rest? Do you want 2 and 3 to be put into an array and stored in x? Or do you want 2, 3, and 4 to be put in x? But then, what value does b get? b is a required variable, so something has to go into it. But that conflicts with the presence of the sponge expression *x to b's left.

There is logic to the constraints placed on you in the matter of the order of arguments, but the syntax allows for any permutations you need. Table 4.2 shows a number of argument-list permutations with sample calls and the variable assignments that take place in each case: the values of the variables inside the method definition block when the method with the given signature is called with the given arguments. (The square brackets indicate an array: a = [1,2,3], for example, means that an array containing three elements has been assigned to the variable a.)

Table 4.2 Sample method signatures with required, optional, and default-valued arguments

Argument type(s)	Method signature	Sample call(s)	Variable assignments
Required (Req)	def m(a,b,c)	m(1,2,3)	a = 1, b =2, c = 3
Optional (Opt)	def m(*a)	m(1,2,3)	a = [1,2,3]
Default-valued (Def)	def m(a=1)	m	a = 1
		m(2)	a = 2

Table 4.2   Sample method signatures with required, optional, and default-valued arguments *(continued)*

Argument type(s)	Method signature	Sample call(s)	Variable assignments
Req/Opt	`def m(a,*b)`	`m(1)`	`a = 1, b = []`
Req/Def	`def m(a,b=1)`	`m(2)`	`a = 2, b = 1`
		`m(2,3)`	`a = 2, b = 3`
Def/Opt	`def m(a=1,*b)`	`m`	`a = 1, b = []`
		`m(2)`	`a = 2, b = []`
Req/Def/Opt	`def m(a,b=2,*c)`	`m(1)`	`a = 1, b = 2, c = []`
		`m(1,3)`	`a = 1, b = 3, c = []`
		`m(1,3,5,7)`	`a = 1, b = 3, c = [5,7]`

As you can see from table 4.2, the arguments you send to methods are assigned to variables, and those variables can then be used throughout the duration of the execution of the method. You've seen variable assignment in a number of contexts, and the time is ripe to look at that process in its own right.

4.4   *Local variables and variable assignment*

You've seen many examples of Ruby variables in action—specifically, *local variables*—and we've been describing assignment of values to variables with some slightly loose (although convenient) terminology. It's time to consolidate and formalize our coverage of this topic.

Local variables are variables that hold their value only during the execution of a particular section of code. They're called *local* precisely because once program execution leaves the *scope* where the variable was created, the variable's name no longer has any meaning.

Local variables give you a kind of scratch-pad facility. You can use, say, the variable name x in more than one place; as long as those places have different scopes, the two x variables are treated as completely separate.

The classic case is a method definition. Watch what happens with x in this example:

```
def say_goodbye
  x = "Goodbye"
  puts x
end
```

```
def start_here
  x = "Hello"
  puts x
  say_goodbye
  puts "Let's check whether x remained the same:"
  puts x
end

start_here
```

The output from this program is as follows:

```
Hello
Goodbye
Let's check whether x remained the same:
Hello
```

When you call start_here (the last line of the program), the method start_here is executed. Inside that method, the string "Hello" is assigned to x—that is, to *this* x, the x in scope at the time.

start_here prints out its x ("Hello") and then calls the method say_goodbye. In say_goodbye, something similar happens: a string ("Goodbye") is assigned to x. But this is a different x—as we see when the call to say_goodbye is finished and control returns to start_here: We print out this x, and the value is still "Hello". Using x as a local variable name in the scope of one method didn't affect its value in the scope of the other.

Learning how local variables behave is a side effect of learning about how Ruby handles scope—a topic we'll look at in much greater depth in chapter 7. You've already learned the first lesson: Every method definition establishes a new local scope, starting with def and ending with end. Scope is a matter of which identifiers have what meaning at what point in the program, like the two x identifiers in our example.

Local variables can come into being in either of two ways:

- Through assignment: x = object
- As an entry in the method's argument list, initialized when the method is called

You've seen both of these in action already. But what *exactly* happens when the assignment or initialization takes place? What does the variable contain?

4.4.1 *Variable assignment in depth*

When you assign to a variable, you appear to be causing the variable to equal the object on the right-hand side of the assignment:

```
str = "Hello"
```

At this point, you can do `puts str` and other operations, and `str` will deliver the string "Hello" for printing and other processing.

Now look at this example:

```
str = "Hello"
abc = str
puts abc
```

This, too, prints "Hello". Apparently the variable `abc` also contains "Hello", thanks to having had `str` assigned to it.

The next example involves a method called `replace`, which does an in-place replacement of a string's content with new text:

```
str = "Hello"
abc = str
str.replace("Goodbye")
puts str
puts abc
```

Look closely at the output:

```
Goodbye
Goodbye
```

The first "Goodbye" is `str`; the second is `abc`. But we only replaced `str`. How did the string in `abc` get replaced?

The answer is that variables in Ruby (with some exceptions we'll show later) don't hold object values. `str` doesn't contain "Hello". Rather, `str` contains a *reference* to a *string object*. It's the string object that has the characteristic of containing the letters that make up "Hello".

When you perform an assignment with a variable name on the left and an object on the right, the variable receives *a reference* to the object. When you perform an assignment with a variable on the left *and* a variable on the right, the variable on the left receives *a reference to the same object that the right-hand variable refers to*.

When you do this

```
str.replace("Goodbye")
```

you're asking `str` to do the following:

```
Replace the contents of the string object to which you are
a reference with "Goodbye".
```

The variable `abc` contains *another* reference to *the same* string object. Even though the `replace` message went to `str`, it has caused a change to the object that `abc` is a reference to.

Consequently, when we print out `abc`, we see the result: The contents of the string to which `abc` is a reference have been changed.

Grasping references

If you've done programming in languages with pointers or references or anything in that vein, Ruby references won't be hard to understand. If you haven't, you'll need to contemplate them a little.

For every object in Ruby, there can and must be one or more references to that object. (If there are no references, the object is considered defunct, and its memory space is released and reused.)

If you act on the object (change it) through one of its references, *the object itself changes*. Because all the references still point *to the same object*, the changes you make through one reference are reflected if you examine the object through another reference later. (That's what happened with `str` and `abc` in the previous example.)

Variables contain references to objects. The message-sending notation (the dot operator), when a variable appears to the left of the dot, sends a message to the object to which the variable contains a reference. If *other* variables also contain references to *that* object, the effect of sending a message to one variable is the same as sending it to another. For example, if we used `abc.upcase!` instead of `str.upcase!`, the results would be the same: the single string, to which both references refer, would be changed.

Reassigning to variables

Every time you assign to a variable—every time you put a variable name to the left of an equal sign and something else on the right—you start from scratch: The variable is wiped clean, and a new assignment is made.

Here's a new, different version of our earlier example, illustrating this point:

```
str = "Hello"
abc = str
str = "Goodbye"
puts str
puts abc
```

This time the output is as follows:

```
Goodbye
Hello
```

When we do the second assignment to `str`, we give `str` a reference to a different string object. `str` and `abc` part company at that point. `abc` still refers to the old string (the one whose contents are "Hello"), but `str` now refers to a different string (a string whose contents are "Goodbye").

In the first version of the program, we changed a single string; but in the second version, we have two separate strings. Once we reuse the variable `str`, it has nothing further to do with the object it referred to previously.

4.4.2 *Local variables and the things that look like them*

Local variables have the quality of *barewords*; they must start with either a lowercase letter or the underscore character (_), and they must consist entirely of letters, numbers, and underscores. (You'll see later that other types of variables start with punctuation marks, to differentiate them from local variables.) However, local variables aren't the only things that look like barewords.

When Ruby sees a plain word sitting there, it interprets it as one of three things: a local variable, a method call, or a keyword.

Keywords are special reserved words that you can't use as variable names. `def` is a keyword; the only thing you can use it for is to start a method definition. `if` is also a keyword; lots of Ruby code involves conditional clauses that start with `if`, so it would be too confusing to also allow the use of `if` as a variable name.

Method calls can be barewords, such as `start_here` in the previous example. `puts` is a method call; so is `print`.

Here's how Ruby decides what it's seeing when it encounters a bareword:

1.   If there's an equal sign (=) to the right of the bareword, it's a local variable undergoing an assignment.

2.   If the bareword is a keyword, it's a keyword (Ruby has an internal list of these and recognizes them).

3.   Otherwise, the bareword is assumed to be a method call.

There's a fourth possibility: that Ruby won't recognize the bareword. Try running this script (using the -e switch, which as you'll recall lets you feed code directly to Ruby from the command line):

```
$ ruby -e "x"
```

You're not assigning to a variable, x isn't a keyword, and there's no method called x. Therefore, you get an error message:

```
-e:1: undefined local variable or method 'x' for
main:Object (NameError)
```

Don't worry about the bells and whistles in this message; the gist of it is that Ruby doesn't know what you mean by "x".

4.5 Summary

We've covered a lot of ground in this chapter. You've learned about creating a new object and defining methods for it. You've learned about the message-sending mechanism by which you send requests to objects for information or action. You also learned how to use some of the important built-in methods that every Ruby object comes with: `object_id`, `respond_to?`, and `send`. And we looked in some detail at the syntax for method argument lists, including the use of required, optional, and default-valued arguments.

Finally, we examined local variables and variable assignment. You saw that keywords and method calls can look like local variables; and Ruby has ways of figuring out what it's seeing. You also learned that variables receive references to objects, and more than one variable can refer to the same object.

The chapter started with some comments about domains, entities, models, and objects; and we'll end there, too. Writing a Ruby program consists largely of thinking about how you might map elements of a domain (even a modest one-entity domain like "a ticket to an event") onto a system of objects: objects that can know things and perform tasks. In this regard, object-oriented programming has a lot in common with database design. Both involve creating symbolic structures—tables and fields in one case, objects and methods and names (and more, as you'll see) in the other—that encapsulate domain characteristics and behavior.

And Rails, of course, stands between these two worlds, directing database traffic into object-oriented, Ruby-space form, and back again. We're dealing with a number of layers, but they converge nicely on the realm of modeling domains and representing entities.

Creating Ruby objects one by one, as we've done here, isn't much more than the tip of the iceberg. We'll open up the discussion exponentially next, by looking at how to create objects on a multiple, factory basis using Ruby classes.

5

Organizing objects with classes

Creating a new object with `Object.new`—and equipping that object with its own methods, one method at a time—is a great way to get a feel for the object-centeredness of Ruby programming. But this approach doesn't exactly scale; if you're running an online box office and your database has to process records for tickets by the hundreds, you've got to find another way to create and manipulate ticket-like objects in your Ruby programs.

Sure enough, Ruby gives you a full suite of programming techniques for creating objects on a batch or factory basis. You don't have to define a separate `price` method for every ticket. Instead, you can define a ticket *class*, engineered in such a way that every individual ticket object automatically has the `price` method.

Defining a class lets you group behaviors (methods) into convenient bundles, so that you can quickly create many objects that behave essentially the same way. You can also add methods to individual objects, if that's appropriate for what you're trying to do in your program. But you don't *have* to do that with every object, if you model your domain into classes.

Everything you handle in Ruby is an object; and every object is an *instance* of some class. This fact holds true even where it might at first seem a little odd. For example, when you manipulate an ActiveRecord object in a model file, that object is an instance of a class (`Composer`, perhaps)—while, at the same time, the class itself is also an object. You'll learn in this chapter how this closely interwoven aspect of the design of Ruby operates.

5.1 Classes and instances

In most cases, a class consists chiefly of a collection of method definitions. The class exists (also in most cases) for the purpose of being *instantiated*: that is, of having objects created that are *instances* of the class.

Have you guessed that you've already seen instantiation in action? It's our old signature tune:

```
obj = Object.new
```

`Object` is a built-in Ruby class. When you use the dot notation on a class, you send a message to the class. Classes can respond to messages, just like objects; in fact, as you'll see in more detail later, classes *are* objects. The `new` method is called a *constructor*, meaning a method whose purpose is to manufacture and return to you a new instance of a class, a newly minted object.

5.1.1 *A first class*

Let's break the class ice with a first class of our own creation. You define a class with the `class` keyword. It's like the `def` keyword you've been using to define methods, but the naming scheme is different. Classes are named with *constants*. A constant is a special type of identifier, recognizable by the fact that it begins with a capital letter. Constants are used to store information and values that don't change over the course of a program run.

> **WARNING** CONSTANTS AREN'T ALL THAT CONSTANT   Constants *can* change: They're not as constant as their name implies. But if you assign a new value to a constant, Ruby prints a warning. The best practice is to avoid assigning new values to constants that you've already assigned a value to. (See section 5.6.2 for more information on reassignment to constants.)

Let's define a `Ticket` class. Inside the class definition, we define a single, simple method.

```
class Ticket
  def event
    "Can't really be specified yet..."
  end
end
```

Now we can create a new ticket object and ask it (pointlessly, but just to see the process) to describe its event:

```
ticket = Ticket.new
puts ticket.event
```

The method call `ticket.event` results in the execution of our `event` method and, consequently, the printing out of the (rather uninformative) string specified inside that method.

Instance methods

The examples of method definitions in chapter 4 tended to involve a specific object, connected directly with a method name and definition:

```
def ticket.event
```

The `event` method in the previous example, however, is defined in a general way:

```
def event
```

That's because this `event` method will be shared by all tickets—that is, by all instances of the `Ticket` class. Methods of this kind, defined inside a class and intended for use by all instances of the class, are called *instance methods*. They don't belong only to one object. Instead, every instance of the class can call them.

(Methods that you define for one particular object—as in `def ticket.price`—are called *singleton methods*. You've already seen examples, and we'll look in more depth at how singleton methods work in chapter 7. Just keep in mind that methods written inside a class, for the benefit of all of that class's instances, are instance methods, whereas a method defined for a specific object (`def ticket.event`) is a singleton method of that object.)

Redefining methods

Nothing stops you from defining a method twice, or *overriding* it:

```
class C
  def m
    puts "First definition of method m"
  end

  def m
    puts "Second definition of method m"
  end
end
```

What happens when we call `m` on an instance of `C`? Let's find out:

```
C.new.m
```

The printed result is `Second definition of method m`. The second definition has prevailed: We see the output from that definition, not from the first. When you override a method, the new version takes precedence.

Reopening classes

In most cases, when you're defining a class, you create a single class definition block:

```
class C
  # class code here
end
```

It's possible, however, to *reopen* a class and make additions or changes. Here's an example:

```
class C
  def x
  end
end

class C
```

```
    def y
    end
  end
```

We open the class definition body, add one method, and close the definition body. Then, we reopen the definition body, add a second method, and close the definition body.

The previous example is equivalent to this:

```
class C
  def x
  end

  def y
  end
end
```

Here we open the class only once and add both methods. Of course, you're not going to break your class definitions into separate blocks just for fun. There has to be a reason—and it should be a good reason, because separating class definitions can make it harder for people reading or using your code to follow what's going on.

One reason to break up class definitions is to spread them across multiple files. If you `require` a file that contains a class definition (perhaps you load it from the disk at runtime from another file, and you also have a partial definition of the same class in the file from which the second file is required), the two definitions are merged. This isn't something you'd do arbitrarily: It must be a case where a design reason requires defining a class partially in one place and partially in another.

Here's a real-life example. Ruby has a `Time` class. It lets you manipulate times, format them for timestamp purposes, and so forth. You can use UNIX-style date format strings to get the format you want. For example, this command

```
puts Time.new.strftime("%m-%d-%y")
```

prints the string "01-07-06" (representing the date on the day I made the method call and saved its output).

In addition to the built-in `Time` class, Ruby *also* has a program file called `time.rb`, inside of which are various enhancements of, and additions to, the `Time` class.

`time.rb` achieves its goal of enhancing the `Time` class by reopening that class. If you look for the file `time.rb` either in the `lib` subdirectory of the Ruby source tree or in your Ruby installation, you'll see this on line 49 (at least, for the version of the file shipped with Ruby 1.8.4):

```
class Time
```

That's a reopening of the `Time` class, done for the purpose of adding new methods.

You can see the effect best by trying it, using `irb --simple-prompt`. irb lets you call a nonexistent method without causing the whole thing to terminate, so you can see the effects of the `require` command all in one session:

```
>> t = Time.new
=> Mon Sep 12 08:19:52 EDT 2005
>> t.xmlschema
NoMethodError: undefined method 'xmlschema'    <——— ❶
for Mon Sep 12 08:19:52 EDT 2005:Time
        from (irb):8
>> require 'time'    <——— ❷
=> true
>> t.xmlschema
=> "2005-09-12T08:19:52-04:00"
```

Here we send the unrecognized message `xmlschema` to our `Time` object ❶. Then we load the `time.rb` file ❷—and, sure enough, our `Time` object now has an `xmlschema` method. (That method, according to its documentation, "returns a string which represents the time as dateTime defined by XML Schema.")

You can spread code for a single class over multiple files or over multiple locations in the same file. Be aware, however, that it's considered better practice not to do so, when possible. In the case of the `Time` extensions, people often suggest the possibility of unification: giving `Time` objects all the extension methods in the first place, and not separating those methods into a separate library. It's possible that such unification will take place in a later release of Ruby.

Ruby is about objects; objects are instances of classes. That means it behooves us to dig deeper into what the life of an instance consists of. We'll look next at *instance variables*, a special language feature designed to allow every instance of every class in Ruby to set and maintain its own private stash of information.

5.1.2 *Instance variables and object state*

When we created individual objects and wrote methods for each action or value we needed, we hard-coded the value into the object through the methods. With this technique, if a ticket costs $117.50, then it has a method called `price` that returns precisely that amount:

```
ticket = Object.new
def ticket.price
  117.50
end
```

Now, however, we're moving away from one-at-a-time object creation with `Object.new`, and setting our sights instead on the practice of designing classes and creating many objects from them.

This means we're changing the rules of the game, when it comes to information like the price of a ticket. If you create a `Ticket` class, you can't give it a `price` method that returns $117.50, for the simple reason that not all tickets cost $117.50. Similarly, you can't give every ticket the event-name Benefit Concert, nor can every ticket think that it's for Row G, Seat 33.

Instead of hard-coding values into every object, we need a way to tell *different* objects that they have *different* values. We need to be able to create a new `Ticket` object and store *with that object* the information about event, price, and other properties. When we create another ticket object, we need to store different information with *that* object. And we want to be able to do this without having to hand-craft a method with the property hard-coded into it.

Information and data associated with a particular object is called the *state* of the object. We need to be able to do the following:

- Set, or reset, the state of an object (say to a ticket, "You cost $11.99")
- Read back the state (ask a ticket, "How much do you cost?")

Conveniently, Ruby objects come with their own value-storage mechanism. You can make arrangements for an object to remember values you give it. And you can make that arrangement up front in the design of your classes, so that every object—every instance—of a given class has the same ability.

Instance variables

The *instance variable* enables individual objects to remember state. Instance variables work much like other variables: You assign values to them, and you read those values back; you can add them together, print them out, and so on. However, instance variables have a few differences.

- Instance variable names always start with @ (the at sign). This enables you to recognize an instance variable at a glance.
- Instance variables are only visible to the object to which they belong.
- An instance variable initialized in one method definition, inside a particular class, is the same as the instance variable of the same name referred to in other method definitions of the same class.

Listing 5.1 shows a simple example of an instance variable, illustrating the way the assigned value of an instance variable stays alive from one method call to another.

Listing 5.1 Illustration of an instance variable's maintenance of its value between method calls

```
class C
  def inst_var_init(value)
    puts "Setting an instance variable...."
    @ivar = value    ⟵———❶
  end

  def inst_var_report
    puts "Inspecting the value of the instance variable...."
    puts @ivar
  end
end

c = C.new
c.inst_var_init("Just some string")    ⟵———❷
c.inst_var_report    ⟵———❸
```

Thanks to the assignment ❶ that happens as a result of the call to inst_var_init ❷, when you ask for a report ❸, you get back what you put in: the phrase "Just some string". Unlike a local variable, the instance variable @ivar retains the value assigned to it even after the method in which it was initialized has terminated. This property of instance variables—their survival across method calls—makes them suitable for maintaining state in an object.

Initializing an object with state

The scene is set to do something close to useful with our Ticket class. The missing step, which we'll now fill in, is the *object initialization* process.

When you create a class (like Ticket), you can, if you wish, include a special method called initialize. If you do so, that method will be executed *every time you create a new instance of the class.*

For example, if you write an initialize method that prints a message

```
class Ticket
  def initialize
    puts "Creating a new ticket!"
  end
end
```

then you'll see the message "Creating a new ticket!" every time you create a new ticket object by calling `Ticket.new`.

You can deploy this automatic initialization process to set an object's state at the time of the object's creation. Let's say we want to give each ticket object a *venue* and *date* when it's created. We can send the correct values as arguments to `Ticket.new`, and those same arguments will be sent to `initialize` automatically. Inside `initialize`, we'll thus have access to the venue and date information, and we'll need to save it. We do the saving by means of instance variables:

```
class Ticket
  def initialize(venue,date)
    @venue = venue
    @date = date
  end
```

Before closing the class definition with `end`, we should add something else: a way to read back the venue and date. All we need to do is create methods that return what's in the instance variables:

```
  def venue
    @venue
  end

  def date
    @date
  end
end
```

Each of these methods echoes back the value of the instance variable. In each case, that variable is the last (and only) expression in the method and therefore also the method's return value.

> **NOTE** NAMING CONVENTIONS VS. NAMING NECESSITIES The names of the instance variables, the methods, and the arguments to `initialize` don't have to match. You could use `@v` instead of `@venue`, for example, to store the value passed in the argument `venue`. However, it's usually good practice to match the names, to make it clear what goes with what.

Now we're ready to create a ticket (or several tickets) with *dynamically set* values for venue and date, rather than the hard-coded values of our earlier examples:

```
th = Ticket.new("Town Hall", "11/12/13")
cc = Ticket.new("Convention Center", "12/13/14")

puts "We've created two tickets."
puts "The first is for a #{th.venue} event on #{th.date}."
puts "The second is for an event on #{cc.date} at #{cc.venue}."
```

Run this code, along with the previous class definition of `Ticket`, and you'll see the following:

```
We've created two tickets.
The first is for a Town Hall event on 11/12/13.
The second is for an event on 12/13/14 at Convention Center.
```

The phrase "at Convention Center" is a bit stilted, but the process of saving and retrieving information for individual objects courtesy of instance variables operates perfectly. Each ticket has its own state (saved information), thanks to what our `initialize` method does; and each ticket lets us query it for the venue and date, thanks to the two methods with those names.

This opens up our prospects immensely. We can create, manipulate, compare, and examine any number of tickets at the same time, without having to write separate methods for each of them. All the tickets share the resources of the `Ticket` class. At the same time, each ticket has its own set of instance variables to store state information.

So far we've arranged things in such a way that we set the values of the instance variables at the point where the object is created and can then retrieve those values at any point during the life of the object. That arrangement is often adequate, but it's not symmetrical: What if you want to *set* values for the instance variables at some point other than object-creation time? What if you want to change an object's state after it's already been set once?

5.2 *Setter methods*

When you need to change an object's state once it's been set, or if you want to set an object's state at some point in your program other than the `initialize` method, the heart of the matter is assigning (or reassigning) values to instance variables. For example, if we want tickets to have the ability to discount themselves, we could write an instance method like this inside the `Ticket` class definition:

```
def discount(percent)
  @price = @price - (percent * 10) / 100
end
```

This method represents a limited scenario, though. It isn't a general-purpose method for setting or changing an object's price.

Writing such a method, however, is perfectly possible. Ruby provides some nice facilities for writing setter methods, as we'll now see.

5.2.1 *The equal sign (=) in method names*

Let's say we want a way to set the price of a ticket. As a starting point, price can be set along with everything else at object creation time:

```
class Ticket
  def initialize(venue,date,price)
    @venue = venue
    @date = date
    @price = price
  end
  # etc.
  def price
    @price
  end
  # etc.
end
```

```
th = Ticket.new("Town Hall", "11/12/13", 65.00)
```

But the initialization command is getting awfully long. There's nothing technically wrong with a long method, but it looks cluttered. We also have to remember what order to put the many arguments in, so we don't end up with a ticket whose price is "Town Hall". And what if want to change a ticket's price later? True, we could create a new ticket object with the same specifications, except for a different price; but it would be nicer to be able to tell the ticket we've already created, "Your price has changed; here's the new value."

Let's write a set_price method that allows us to set, or reset, the price of an existing ticket. We'll also rewrite the initialize method so that it doesn't expect a price figure:

```
class Ticket
  def initialize(venue, date)
    @venue = venue
    @date = date
  end

  def set_price(amount)
    @price = amount
  end

  def price
    @price
  end
end
```

Here's some price manipulation in action:

```
ticket = Ticket.new("Town Hall", "11/12/13")
ticket.set_price(65.00)
puts "The ticket costs $#{"%.2f" % ticket.price}."      Format price to two
ticket.set_price(72.50)                                  decimal places
puts "Whoops -- it just went up. It now costs $#{"%.2f" % ticket.price}."
```

The output is as follows:

```
The ticket costs $65.00.
Whoops -- it just went up. It now costs $72.50.
```

We've set and reset the price, and the change is reflected in the object's view of its own state.

This technique works: You can write all the set_*property* methods you need, and the instance variable-based retrieval methods to go with them. But there's a nicer way.

The nicer way to change object state dynamically

Ruby allows you to define methods that end with an equal sign (=). Let's replace set_price with a method called price=:

```
def price=(amount)
  @price = amount
end
```

price= does exactly what set_price did, and in spite of the slightly odd method name, you can call it just like any other method:

```
ticket.price=(65.00)
```

The equal sign gives you that familiar "assigning a value to something" feeling, so you know you're dealing with a setter method. It still looks odd, but Ruby takes care of that, too.

Syntactic sugar

Programmers use the term *syntactic sugar* to refer to special rules that let you write your code in a way that doesn't correspond to the normal rules but that is easier to remember how to do and looks better.

Ruby gives you some syntactic sugar for calling setter methods. Instead of this

```
ticket.price=(65.00)
```

you're allowed to do this:

```
ticket.price = 65.00
```

When the interpreter sees the message "price" followed by " =", it automatically ignores the space before equal sign and reads the single message "price="—a call to the method whose name is price=, which we've defined. As for the right-hand side: parentheses are optional on single arguments to methods, so you can just put 65.00 there and it will be picked up as the argument to the price= method.

The more you use this kind of setter style of method, the more you'll appreciate how much better the sugared version looks. This kind of attention to appearance is typical of Ruby. It also looms fairly large in Rails application code. Accordingly, we'll use some ActiveRecord idioms as a touchstone for a deeper look at setter methods.

5.2.2 *ActiveRecord properties and other =-method applications*

In section 5.3 we'll look at techniques for generating getter and setter methods automatically. As you'll see when we get there, automatic generation of these methods is convenient, but it also always gives you methods that work in the simplest possible way: value in, value out.

Before we get to method automation, a word is in order about how much power you can derive from getter and setter methods—especially setter—in cases where you need something beyond the simplest case of storing and retrieving a value.

The power of =

The ability to write your own =-terminated methods, and the fact that Ruby provides the syntactic sugar way of calling those methods, opens up some interesting possibilities.

One possibility is abuse. It's possible to write =-methods that look like they're going to do something involving assignment, but don't:

```
class Silly
  def price=(x)
    puts "The current time is #{Time.now}"
  end
end

s = Silly.new
s.price = 111.22
```

This example discards the argument it receives (111.22) and prints out the time:

```
Fri Jan 13 12:44:05 EST 2006
```

This example is a caricature of what you might do. But the point is important. Ruby checks your syntax but doesn't police your semantics. You're allowed to write methods with names that end with =, and you'll always get the assignment-syntax sugar.

The matter of having the method's name make any sense in relation to what the method does is entirely in your hands.

Equal-sign methods can serve as filters or gatekeepers. Let's say we want to set the price of a ticket only if the price makes sense as a dollar-and-cents amount. We can add some intelligence to the price= method to ensure the correctness of the data. Here, we multiply the number by 100, lop off any remaining decimal-place numbers with the to_i (convert to integer) operation, and compare the result with the original number multiplied by 100. This should expose any extra decimal digits beyond the hundredths column:

```
class Ticket
  def price=(amount)
    if (amount * 100).to_i == amount * 100
      @price = amount
    else
      puts "The price seems to be malformed"
    end
  end

  def price
    @price
  end

end
```

You can also use this kind of filtering technique to normalize data—that is, to make sure certain data always takes a certain form. For example, let's say you have a travel-agent Web site, where the user needs to type in the desired date of departure. You want to allow both *mm/dd/yy* and *mm/dd/yyyy*, and perhaps even *mm/dd/y* (because we're still in the single digits of the twenty-first century).

If you have, say, a Ruby CGI script that's processing the incoming data, you might normalize the year by writing a setter method like this:

```
class TravelAgentSession
  def year=(y)
    if y.to_i < 100      ⟵———┐ Handles one- or two-digit number
      @year = y.to_i + 2000     by adding the century to it
    else
      @year = y.to_i
    end
  end
  # etc.
end
```

Then, assuming you have a variable called `date` in which you've stored the date field from the form (using Ruby's CGI library), you can get at the components of the date like this:

```
month, day, year = date.split('/')
self.year = year
```

The idea is to split the date string into three strings using the slash character (/) as a divider, courtesy of the built-in `split` method, and then to store the year value in the `TravelAgentSession` object using that object's `year=` method.

Methods ending with = are, from Ruby's perspective, just methods. But the fact that they also give you the syntactic sugar assignment–like syntax makes them versatile and handy.

Setter methods in ActiveRecord

Method calls using the equal-sign syntax are common in Rails applications. You'll see (and write) a lot of statements that follow the basic `x.y = z` visual formula. Most of the ones you see will be in controller methods; some will be in model definitions.

When and if you write your own special-purpose setter methods, you'll do so in the model files. You'll see some examples in part 4, when we return to the music store application and extend it.

Meanwhile, in the context of learning Ruby and getting a sense of Rails's deployment of Ruby facilities, two items are worth noting about setter methods in ActiveRecord.

First, you don't have to write the majority of these methods yourself. ActiveRecord automatically creates setter methods for you that correspond to the field names of your database tables. If you have a *tickets* table, and it has a *venue* field, then when you create a ticket object, that object *already has* a `venue=` method (venue setter). You don't have to write it. (Nor would you want to; ActiveRecord setter methods do a great deal more than stash a value, integrity-checked or otherwise, in an instance variable.) Rails leverages the power of Ruby's setter-method syntax, including the associated syntactic sugar, to make life easy for you when it comes to database interaction in the course of application development.

Second, you often don't need to use these setter methods, because there are more automatic ways to populate your object with the values you want it to have. In particular, when you're writing a Rails action that processes a Web form, you can deposit a set of values into an object at once by providing the name of a field you've used in your form template.

For example, say you have the following fields in a form (using the ActionView form helper method text_field to create the correct HTML automatically):

```
<%= text_field "customer", "first_name" %>
<%= text_field "customer", "last_name" %>
```

In the controller action that processes the form, you can do this:

```
customer = Customer.new(params[:customer])
```

From the magic (that is, automatically initialized by Rails) params method, which gives you access to incoming CGI data, ActiveRecord gleans all the values pertaining to customer and transfers them in bulk to the new Customer object you've created.

You can use setter methods in Rails applications, and you often will; but you'll also find that Rails has anticipated your needs and doesn't make you trudge through

```
customer.first_name = params[:first_name]
customer.last_name = params[:last_name]
# etc.
```

when a shortcut can be arranged.

Setter methods, as well as their getter equivalents (v = ticket.venue, for example), are important concepts to understand in both Ruby and Rails and also a good illustration of the way Rails layers its own functionality, and even its own philosophy of design, on top of Ruby.

Ruby also layers its design philosophy on top of Ruby, so to speak—meaning, in this case, that Ruby provides shortcuts of its own for reaping the benefits of getter and setter methods.

5.3 *Attributes and the attr_* method family*

In Ruby terminology (and this would be understood by anyone familiar with object-oriented programming principles, even though it might operate differently in other languages), properties or characteristics of objects that you can set (write) and/or get (read) are called *attributes*. In the case of ticket objects, we would say that each ticket has a price attribute as well as a date attribute and a venue attribute.

Note the sneaking in of *read/write* as synonyms for *set/get* in the realm of attributes. Ruby usage favors *read/write*. For instance, our price= method would usually be described as an *attribute writer* method. date and venue are *attribute reader* methods. The read/write terminology can be a little misleading at first, because it sounds like there might be terminal or file I/O going on. But once you see how the set/get mechanism works, it's easy to understand how reading and writing can apply to internal object data as well as files and screens.

5.3.1 *Automating the creation of attribute handlers*

So common are attributes, and so frequently do we need a combination of reader and writer methods, that Ruby provides a set of techniques for creating those methods automatically. Consider, first, listing 5.2's full picture of what we have, by way of attribute reader and/or writer methods, in our `Ticket` class. (There's nothing new here; it's just being pulled together in one place.)

Listing 5.2 `Ticket` class, with the attribute reader/writer methods spelled out

```ruby
class Ticket
  def initialize(venue, date)
    @venue = venue
    @date = date
  end

  def price=(price)
    @price = price
  end

  def venue
    @venue
  end

  def date
    @date
  end

  def price
    @price
  end
end
```

You'll notice a certain amount of repetition creeping into the code. We have three methods that look like this:

```ruby
def something
  @something
end
```

There's repetition on top of repetition: Not only do we have three such methods, but each of those three methods repeats its name in the name of the instance variable it uses. And there are three of them. We're repeating a repetitive pattern.

Any time you see repetition on that scale, you should try to trim it—not by reducing what your program does, but by finding a way to express the same thing more concisely. In pursuit of this conciseness, Ruby is one step ahead of us. A built-in shortcut lets us create that style of method: a method that reads and returns the value of the instance variable with the same name as the method (give or take a @). We do it like this:

```
class Ticket
  attr_reader :venue, :date, :price
end
```

(The elements that start with colons (:venue, and so on) are *symbols*. Symbols are a kind of naming or labeling facility. They're a cousin of strings, although not quite the same thing. We'll look at symbols in more depth in chapter 10. For the moment, you can think of them as functionally equivalent to strings.)

The attr_reader (attribute reader) method *automatically writes for you* the kind of method we've just been looking at. And there's an attr_writer method, too:

```
class Ticket
  attr_writer :price
end
```

With that single line, we wrote (or, rather, Ruby wrote for us) our price= setter method. One line takes the place of three. In the case of the reader methods, one line took the place of nine. That means our whole program now looks like listing 5.3.

Listing 5.3   Ticket class, with getter and setter methods defined via attr_* calls

```
class Ticket
  attr_reader :venue, :date, :price
  attr_writer :price

  def initialize(venue, date)
    @venue = venue
    @date = date
  end
end
```

Not only is that code shorter; it's also more informative—*self-documenting*, even. You can see at a glance that ticket objects have venues, dates, and prices. The first two are readable attributes, and price can be read or written.

5.3.2 *Two (getter/setter) for one*

In the realm of object attributes, combination reader/writer attributes, like price, are common. Ruby provides a single method, attr_accessor, for creating both a reader and a writer method for an attribute. attr_accessor is the equivalent of `attr_reader` plus `attr_writer`. We can use this combined technique for `price`, because we want both operations:

```
class Ticket
  attr_reader :venue, :date
  attr_accessor :price
end
```

There's an alternate way to achieve `attr_accessor` functionality, namely with the plain `attr` method, used in the following way:

```
attr :price, true
```

Calling `attr` with `true` as the second argument triggers the creation of both reader and writer attributes, just like `attr_accessor`. However, `attr_accessor` is generally considered more readable, and it also has the advantage that you can give it more than one accessor name at a time (whereas `attr` only takes one, plus the optional `true` argument). Without the second argument, `attr` just provides a reader attribute.

5.3.3 *Summary of attr_* methods*

The `attr_*` family of methods is summarized in table 5.1.

Table 5.1   Summary of the `attr_*` family of getter/setter creation methods

Method name	Effect	Example	Equivalent code

attr_reader	Creates a reader method	attr_reader :venue	`def venue`
			`@venue`
			`end`

attr_writer	Creates a writer method	attr_writer :price	`def price=(price)`
			`@price = price`
			`end`

attr_accessor	Creates reader and writer methods	attr_accessor :price	`def price=(price)`
			`@price = price`
			`end`
			
			`def price`
			`@price`
			`end`

attr	Creates a reader and optionally a writer method (if the second argument is true)	1. attr :venue 2. attr :price, true	1. See attr_reader 2. See attr_accessor

At this point, you've had a good overview of instance methods—the methods defined inside class definitions and made available to all instances of the class. Classes have another kind of method, the *class method*, and we'll round out the picture by looking at class methods now.

5.4   Class methods and the Class class

When you call methods on objects, you use this message-sending syntax:

```
object.message
```

You may have noticed that the object creation calls we've done have conformed to the standard *object-dot-method* syntax:

```
Ticket.new
```

Analyzing this call in the light of the message-sending formula, we can quickly draw two conclusions:

- We're sending the message new.
- We're sending that message to *an object called* Ticket, *which we know to be a class.* (We know it's a class because of having written it previously.)

The first of these conclusions is unremarkable; messages get sent all the time. The second—the fact that the receiver of the message is a class—merits close attention. Because classes are object factories, thinking of them as objects in their own right takes a leap of imagination. Thinking of classes as receivers of messages also feels odd at first—although, as you'll see, it falls into place easily once you get over the "classes are objects" hurdle.

5.4.1   Classes are objects too!

Classes are special objects: They're the only kind of object that has the power to spawn new objects (instances). Nonetheless, they are objects. When you create a class, like Ticket, you can send messages to it, add methods to it, pass it around to other objects as a method argument, and generally do anything to it you would another object.

Here's an example. Let's say we've created our Ticket class. At this point, Ticket isn't only a class from which objects (ticket instances) can arise. Ticket (the class) is also an object in its own right. As we've done with other objects, let's add a method to it.

Our method will tell us which ticket, from a list of ticket objects, is the most expensive. There's some black-box code here. Don't worry about the details; the basic idea is that the `sort_by` operation sorts by price, with the most expensive ticket ending up last:

```
def Ticket.most_expensive(*tickets)
  tickets.sort_by {|t| t.price }.last
end
```

Now we can use this method to tell us which of several tickets is the most expensive (we'll avoid having two tickets with the same price, because our method doesn't deal gracefully with that situation):

```
th = Ticket.new("Town Hall","11/12/13")
cc = Ticket.new("Convention Center","12/13/14/")
fg = Ticket.new("Fairgrounds", "13/14/15/")

th.price = 12.55
cc.price = 10.00
fg.price = 18.00

highest = Ticket.most_expensive(th,cc,fg)

puts "The highest-priced ticket is #{highest.venue}."
```

We have used the *class method* most_expensive, a class method of the class `Ticket`, to select the most expensive ticket from a list.

5.4.2 *When, and why, to write a class method*

The idea of a class method is that you send a message to the object that is the class rather than to one of the class's instances. You send the message most_expensive to the class `Ticket`, not to a particular ticket.

Why would you want to do that? Doesn't it mess up the underlying order: the creation of ticket objects and the sending of messages to those objects?

Class methods serve a purpose. Some operations pertaining to a class can't be performed by individual instances of that class. new is an excellent example. We call `Ticket.new` because, until we've created an individual ticket, we can't send it *any* messages! Besides, the job of spawning a new object logically belongs to the class. It doesn't make sense for instances of `Ticket` to spawn each other. It does make sense, however, for the instance-creation process to be centralized as an activity of the class `Ticket`.

Another similar case is the built-in Ruby method `File.open`—a method which, as its name implies, opens a file. The open operation is a bit like new: It initiates file input and/or output and gives you a *filehandle* (a pointer to the stream of file data) with which you can read from and/or write to the file. It makes sense for this to be a class method of `File`: You're requesting the creation of an individual object (a filehandle, in this case) from the class. The class is acting as a dispatcher for the objects it creates.

Similarly, finding the most expensive ticket in a list of tickets can be viewed as an operation from above, something you do in connection with the realm of tickets in general, rather than something that is done *by* an individual ticket object. We have a task—finding the most expensive ticket—that depends on knowledge of ticket objects (you have to know that they have a `price` method), yet it doesn't logically belong at the individual ticket level. Writing `most_expensive` as a class method of `Ticket` lets us keep the method in the family, so to speak, while assigning it to the abstract, supervisory level represented by the class.

Converting the converter

It's not unheard of to create a class *only* for the purpose of giving it some class methods. We can do so in the case of our earlier temperature conversion exercises. Let's convert the converter to a converter class:

```
class Temperature
  def Temperature.c2f(c)
    c * 9 / 5 + 32
  end

  def Temperature.f2c(f)
    (f - 32) * 5 / 9
  end
end
```

And let's try it out:

```
puts Temperature.c2f(100)
```

Sure enough, it works.

The idea is that we have *temperature-related utility methods*—methods pertaining to temperature that don't pertain to a *specific* temperature. The `Temperature` class is a good choice of object to own those methods. We could get fancier and have `Temperature` instances that knew whether they were C or F, and could convert themselves; but practically speaking, having a `Temperature` class with class methods to perform the conversions is adequate and is an acceptable design.

5.4.3 *Class methods vs. instance methods, clarified*

It's vital to understand that by defining `Ticket.most_expensive`, we have defined a method that we can access through the class object `Ticket` *but not through its instances.* Individual ticket objects (instances of the class `Ticket`) *do not have this method.* You can test this easily. Try adding this to the code from section 5.4.1, where the variable `fg` referred to a `Ticket` object (for an event at the fairgrounds):

```
puts "Testing the response of a ticket instance...."
wrong = fg.most_expensive
```

You'll get an error message, because `fg` has no method called `most_expensive`. The *class* of `fg`—namely, `Ticket`—has such a method. But `fg`, which is an instance of `Ticket`, doesn't.

Remember:

- Instances created by classes are objects.

- Classes are objects too.

- A class object (like `Ticket`) has its own methods, its own state, its own identity. It doesn't share these things with instances of itself. Sending a message to `Ticket` *is not the same thing* as sending a message to `fg` or `cc` or any other instance of `Ticket`.

If you ever get tangled up over what's a class method and what's an instance method, you can usually sort out the confusion by going back to these three principles.

> **TIP** SEEING CLASS METHODS AS SINGLETON METHODS ON CLASS OBJECTS
> You've seen that you can add a *singleton* method to any object (that is, a method defined in connection with, and for the exclusive use of, that object). Examples that follow the `def ticket.price` pattern illustrate the creation of singleton methods. A class method is basically just a method added to an individual object, where the object getting the method happens to be a class object. There's a special term for this case because it's common; many classes, including many in the core Ruby language, have methods attached to them. Also, class methods (or something similar) are common in object-oriented languages—Ruby comes by the term naturally, so to speak, even though class methods aren't a separate construct in the language in Ruby's case, just a particular case of a general construct.

A note on notation

In writing about and referring to Ruby methods (outside of code, that is), it's customary to refer to instance methods by naming the class (or module, as the case may be, and as you'll see in chapter 6) in which they are defined, followed by a hash mark (#) and the name of the method; and to refer to class methods with a similar construct but using a period instead of the hash mark. Sometimes you'll see a double colon (::) instead of a period in the class method case.

Here are some examples of this notation:

Notation	Method referred to
Ticket#price	The instance method price in the class Ticket
Ticket.most_expensive	The class method most_expensive, in the class Ticket
Ticket::most_expensive	Another way to refer to the class method most_expensive

From now on, when you see this notation (in this book or elsewhere), you'll know what it means. (The second example (class method reference using a dot) looks the same as a call to the method, but you'll know from the context whether it's a method call or a reference to the method in a discussion.)

Objects come from classes. If classes are objects, that implies that they, too, come from a class. A class can be created with a call to the class method new of its class.

And what *is* the class of a class? It's a class called Class. Yes, there's a bit of "Who's on first?" here, but the concept is by no means impenetrable. We'll round out this discussion with a look at the class Class and its new method.

5.4.4 *The Class class and Class.new*

Classes are objects; specifically, they are instances of the class Class. As you've already seen, you can create a class object with the special class keyword formula:

```
class Ticket
  # code here
end
```

That formula is a special provision by Ruby—a way to make class definition blocks look nice and give you easy access to them.

The other way to create a class is this, which leaves you with a new Class object in the variable my_class:

```
my_class = Class.new
```

Class.new corresponds precisely to other constructor calls (calls to methods that create objects), such as Object.new and Ticket.new. When you instantiate the class Class—when you create an instance of it—you've created a class. That class, in turn, can create instances of its own:

```
instance_of_my_class = my_class.new
```

In section 5.1.1, you saw that class objects are usually stored in constants (like `Ticket` or `Object`). In the scenario in the previous example, however, we've stored a class in a regular variable (`my_class`). When we call the new method, we send the message `new` to the class through that variable

And yes, there is a paradox here. The class `Class` *is an instance of itself;* that is, it's a `Class` object. And there's more. Remember the class `Object`? Well, `Object` is a class ... but classes are objects. So `Object` is an object. And `Class` is a class. And `Object` is a class, and `Class` is an object.

Which came first? How can the class `Class` be created unless the class `Object` already exists? But how can there *be* a class `Object` (or any other class) until there's a class `Class` of which there can be instances?

The best way to deal with this paradox, at least for now, is to ignore it. Ruby has to do some of this chicken-or-egg stuff in order to get the class and object system up and running—at which point the circularity and paradoxes don't matter. In the course of programming, you just need to know that classes are objects, and the class of which class-objects are instances is the class called `Class`.

The proliferation of names of constants in the last few paragraphs is a graphic reminder of the fact that we haven't yet looked at constants in more than a place-holder way. We'll discuss them a little more deeply now.

5.5 Constants up close

Most classes consist principally of instance methods and/or class methods. Constants, however, are an important and common third ingredient in many classes. You've already seen constants used as the names of classes. Constants can also be used to set and preserve important data values *in* classes.

5.5.1 Basic usage of constants

The name of every constant begins with a capital letter. You assign to constants much as you would to variables. Let's say we decide to establish a list of predefined venues for the `Ticket` class—a list that every ticket object can refer to and select from. We can assign the list to a constant. Constant definitions usually go at or near the top of a class definition:

```
class Ticket
  VENUES = ["Convention Center", "Fairgrounds", "Town Hall"]
```

We can then use this list in instance methods or in class methods (constants are visible anywhere in the class definition). We can also refer to the constant from outside the class definition. To do this, we have to use a special *path* notation: a double colon (::). Here's an example where, for the sake of illustration, the class consists only of a constant assignment:

```
class Ticket
  VENUES = ["Convention Center", "Fairgrounds", "Town Hall"]
end

puts "We've closed the class definition."
puts "So we have to use the path notation to reach the constant."
puts "The venues are:"
puts Ticket::VENUES
```

The double-colon notation pinpoints the constant VENUES inside the class known by the constant Ticket, and the list of venues is printed out.

Ruby's built-in constants

Ruby comes with some predefined constants that you can access this way, and that you may find useful. Try typing this into irb:

```
Math::PI
```

Math is a *module,* rather than a class (you'll learn about modules in the next chapter), but the principle is the same: You're using the :: connector to do a lookup on the constant PI defined by Math.

One peculiarity of Ruby constants is that they aren't constant. You can change them, in two senses of the word *change*—and therein lies an instructive lesson.

5.5.2 *Reassigning vs. modifying constants*

It's possible to perform an assignment on a constant to which you've already assigned something—that is, to reassign to the constant. However, you'll get a warning if you do this (even if you're not running with the -w command-line switch). Try this in irb:

```
A = 1
A = 2
```

You'll receive the following message:

```
warning: already initialized constant A
```

The fact that constant names are reusable but the practice of reusing them is a warnable offense represents a compromise. On the one hand, it's useful for the language to have a separate category for constants, as a way of storing data that remains visible over a longer stretch of the program than a regular variable.

(You'll learn more about the visibility of variables and constants in chapter 7, when we talk about scope.) On the other hand, Ruby is a dynamic language, in the sense that anything can change during runtime. Engineering constants to be an exception to this would theoretically be possible, but doing so would introduce an anomaly into the language.

In addition, because you can reload program files you've already loaded, and program files can include constant assignments, forbidding reassignment of constants would mean that many file-reloading operations would fail with a fatal error.

So, you *can* reassign to a constant, but it's not considered good practice. If you want a reusable identifier, you should use a variable.

You can also make changes to the object *assigned to* the constant. For example, suppose you've assigned an empty array to a constant:

```
A = []
```

You can add elements to that array (here, using the << method, which adds a single element to the end of an array)

```
A << "New York"
A << "New Jersey"
```

and you won't receive a warning.

You can find examples of this kind of operation in the Rails source code, where constants figure prominently and the objects they represent undergo fairly frequent changes. For example, in the file `routing.rb` (in the `lib/action_controller` subdirectory of the ActionPack source tree), is

```
Helpers = []
```

and then, a little later, this:

```
Helpers << url_helper_name(name).to_sym
Helpers << hash_access_name(name).to_sym
```

You're seeing the creation of an array that's designed to store names of helper methods, followed by the insertion of a couple of such names into the array. No warning occurs, because the constant name, `Helpers`, isn't being reused. Rather, the object assigned to that name (an array) is having items added to it.

The difference between *reassigning* a constant name and *modifying* the object referenced by the constant is important, and it gives you a useful lesson in two kinds of change in Ruby: changing the mapping of identifiers to objects (assignment), and changing the state or contents of an object. With regular variable names, you aren't warned when you do a reassignment—but reassignment is still different from making changes to an object, for any category of identifier.

We'll return now to classes and look at more techniques involved in their creation and use. You've already seen some of the advantages of creating objects with a class—certainly in comparison with creating one object at a time and having to start again when we want (say) a ticket with a different price. But even classes, individually and in isolation, can only do so much. The next level of functionality, *inheritance*, adds another axis along which your programming capability can expand.

5.6 *Inheritance*

Without getting too philosophical, it's reasonable to say that in many cases, two or more material objects or ideas relate to each other according to the principle of *the general* and *the specific*:

- *Musical instrument* is general; *piano* is specific.
- *Publication* is general; *magazine* is specific.
- *Vehicle* is general; *bicycle* is specific.

And so forth.

Object-oriented programming involves mapping real-world entities and their relationships onto computer data structures. And just as the general/specific ratio looms large in the real world, it surfaces in object-oriented class design.

The relation between a general case and a specific case can be expressed through the technique known as *inheritance*. Inheritance is a relation between two classes. To start with the notation, it looks like this:

```
class Publication
  attr_accessor :publisher
end

class Magazine < Publication
  attr_accessor :editor
end
```

In this example, `Magazine` is a *subclass* of `Publication`. Conversely, `Publication` is the *superclass* of `Magazine`. When it comes to instance methods, each class can have its own, and the classes lower on the inheritance chain also get the methods defined above. The model cascades:

- At the top, in `Publication`, you put all the methods and accessors (which, as you'll recall, are shortcuts for methods) that you want *every* publication to have.

- In each subclass, you define the methods you want *that particular type of publication* to have. Instances of the subclass—in our example, an instance of `Magazine`—have access to *all* the methods you've defined: those in the superclass as well as those in the subclass.

We can continue the cascade downward:

```
class Ezine < Magazine
end
```

Instances of `Ezine` will have both publisher and editor accessors, as defined in the superclass and super-superclass of `Ezine`.

Collectively, all the classes in the upward chain (a class's superclass, super-superclass, and so on) are known as the class's *ancestors*. (Ancestry also includes *modules*, a close relative of classes that we'll cover in the next chapter.)

Rails applications provide as good an illustration as any (and better than many) of inheritance in practice. We'll look in that direction next to put some flesh on the inheritance bones.

5.6.1 *Inheritance and Rails engineering*

Inheritance is one of the key organizational techniques for Rails program design and the design of the Rails framework. You can see key cases of the use of inheritance as a structuring principle if you look at any Rails controller file, such as `app/controllers/composer_controller.rb` from the music store application:

```
class ComposerController < ApplicationController
end
```

This code opens a definition block for a class called `ComposerController`, which is a subclass of the class `ApplicationController`. That latter class, in turn, is defined in a file (automatically created by Rails; it's the only file in the controllers directory other than the ones you create) called `application_controller.rb`, which at the time of its creation looks like this:

```
class ApplicationController < ActionController::Base
```

This call creates a new class, `ApplicationController`, which inherits from the class `ActionController::Base`. (Remember that the `::` connector performs lookups of constants. The constant `Base` refers to a class defined inside `ActionController`, which is a module.) The class `ActionController::Base` is predefined in the source code for the Rails framework, in the ActionController library inside the Action-Pack multi-library package.

Seeing this inheritance chain, and knowing what you know about classes as the factories from which objects are created, you can deduce that a *controller* in Rails is an *object*. Somewhere along the line, something like this happens:

```
controller = ComposerController.new
```

At this point, `controller` contains an instance of `ComposerController`. And because `ComposerController` descends, ultimately, from `ActionController::Base`, it can be further assumed that the instance of it is endowed with whatever instance methods are defined in `ActionController::Base`.

In fact, no specific line of code in the Rails source contains a call to `Composer-Controller.new`. The creation of a controller object is a little more complicated, mainly because, to make life easier for the developers (and the users), Rails takes it upon itself to figure out that a URL with *composer* in the controller position (like http://www.r4rmusic.com/composer/show/1) requires that a file called `composer_controller.rb` be tracked down and an object of the class `Composer-Controller` be created. There's some magic involved.

But the principle that a Rails controller is an object holds. To get it to accomplish things that a controller is supposed to accomplish, you send it messages. Some of these messages correspond to instance methods of the `ActionController::Base` class. Some correspond to instance methods you write: your application's *actions*.

When you define an action, you're adding an instance method to your controller class, which is a descendant class of `ActionController::Base`. Model classes, too, inherit from a predefined Rails core class. At the top of each model file (for example, `app/models/composer.rb`) is the following:

```
class Composer < ActiveRecord::Base
```

There's no automatically placed intermediate class, as there was between the base level of `ActionController` and your controller class: Models inherit directly from the class `ActiveRecord::Base`. (In many applications, however, model classes inherit from other model classes—Teacher from Employee, perhaps—but you have to program that kind of model cascading yourself.) Whatever the details, though, the engineering of both models and controllers provides a good example of the kind of central role inheritance can play.

Objects get their behaviors from their classes, and from their individual or singleton methods. Classes endow their instances with their own instance methods, as well as those of their superclass and more remote ancestors. All in all, Ruby objects lead interesting and dynamic lives. We'll conclude this chapter by pulling some of the threads together with some observations about how objects, classes, and methods interact.

5.6.2 *Nature vs. nurture in Ruby objects*

The world is full of pairs of entities exhibiting the general/specific relationship. We're used to seeing the animal kingdom this way, as well as everything from musical instruments to university departments to libraries' shelving systems to pantheons of gods.

To the extent that a programming language helps you model the real world (or, conversely, that the real world supplies you with ways to organize your programs), you could do worse than to rely heavily on the general-to-specific relationship. As we've seen, inheritance—the superclass-to-subclass relationship—mirrors the general/specific ratio closely. If you hang out in object-oriented circles, you'll pick up some shorthand for this relationship: the phrase *is a*. If, say, `Ezine` inherits from `Magazine`, we say that "an ezine *is a* magazine". Similarly, a `Magazine` object *is a* `Publication`, if `Magazine` inherits from `Publication`.

Ruby lets you model this way. You can get a lot of mileage out of thinking through your domain as a cascaded, inheritance-based chart of objects.

On the other hand, Ruby objects (unlike objects in some other object-oriented languages) can be individually modified. You can always add methods on a per-object basis, as we've seen from our earliest examples.

In languages where you can't do this, an object's class (and the superclass of that class, and so forth) tells you everything you need to know about the object. If the object is an instance of `Magazine`, and you're familiar with the methods provided by the class `Magazine` for the use of its instances, you know exactly how the object behaves.

In Ruby, however, the behavior or capabilities of an object can deviate from those supplied by its class. We can make a magazine sprout wings:

```
mag = Magazine.new
def mag.wings
  puts "Look! I can fly!"
end
```

This demonstrates that the capabilities the object was born with aren't necessarily the whole story.

Thus the inheritance tree—the upward cascade of class to superclass to super-class—isn't the only determinant of an object's behavior. If you want to know what a brand-new magazine object does, look at the methods in the `Magazine` class and its ancestors. If you want to know what a magazine object can do *later*, you have to know what's happened to the object *since* its creation. (And `respond_to?`—the method that lets you determine in advance whether an object knows how to handle a particular method—can come in handy.)

Ruby objects are tremendously flexible and dynamic. That flexibility translates into programmer power: You can make magazines fly, make cows tell you who published them, and all the rest of it. As these silly examples make clear, the power entails responsibility: When you make changes to an individual object—when you add methods to that object, and that object alone—you have to have a good reason.

Most Ruby programmers are conservative in this area. You'll see less adding of methods to individual objects than you might expect. Methods are most often added to `Class` objects; those methods are class methods, which are, as we've seen, a good design fit in many cases.

Adding methods to other objects (magazines, tickets, composers, and so on) is also possible. But you have to do it carefully and selectively, and with the design of the program in mind.

The not-so-missing link: class Object

In numerous examples in this chapter, we've done the following:

```
obj = Object.new
```

You're now in a position to understand more deeply what's going on.

The class `Object` is at the top of the inheritance chart. Every class is either a subclass of `Object` or a sub-subclass of `Object` or, at some distance, a direct descendant of `Object`:

```
class C
end

class D < C
end

puts D.superclass
puts D.superclass.superclass
```

The output is

```
C
Object
```

because C is D's superclass (that's our doing) and Object is C's superclass (that's Ruby's doing).

If you go up the chain far enough from any class, you hit Object. Any method available to a bare instance of Object is available to every object. This follows the principle that an object has access to the instance methods of its class and to those of its class's ancestors.

You already know that every object is born with certain capabilities, including send, object_id, and respond_to?. You now know that every object is born with the capabilities defined for instances of Object. You might conclude that send and friends are instance methods of Object.

They're not. Yes, Object is the ultimate great-great-...-grandparent class of all classes. But it turns out that classes aren't the whole story. We'll explore this in depth in the next chapter.

5.7 *Summary*

In this chapter, you've learned the basics of Ruby classes. You've seen how writing a class, and then creating instances of that class, allows you to share behaviors among numerous objects. Through the use of setter methods, either written out or automatically created with the attr_* family of methods, we've demonstrated how to create object attributes, which store object state in instance variables.

From there, we moved to the matter of classes as objects, as well as object factories. Class methods (methods added individually to class objects) can provide general utility functionality connected with the class.

We then looked at Ruby constants, which are a special kind of data container usually residing inside class definitions. Finally, we examined inheritance: a hierarchical, cascading relationship between a superclass and one or more subclasses.

This gives you a firm foundation for understanding how objects come into being and relate to each other in Ruby. Next, we'll build on that foundation by looking at another important building-block: modules.

Modules and
program organization

6

This chapter will introduce you to a Ruby construct that's closely related to classes: namely, *modules*. Like classes, modules are bundles of methods and constants. Unlike classes, modules don't have instances; instead, you specify that you want the functionality of a particular module to be added to the functionality of a class, or of a specific object.

The greatest strength of modules is that they help you with program design and flexibility. You'll see evidence of this, both in examples of modules you can write yourself and in the workings of modules that come built into Ruby. As their name suggests, modules encourage *modular design*: program design that breaks large components into smaller ones and lets you mix and match object behaviors.

It's no accident that modules are similar in many respects to classes: The class `Class` is a subclass of `Module`. Judging by the family tree of classes, classes are a specialized form of module. (We discussed classes first because Ruby is object-centric and objects are instances of classes.) In the realm of Rails, modules hold considerable sway, particularly in the design and organization of the framework. You need to understand modules and modularization in order to understand even the two or three lines of boilerplate code that Rails inserts into all model and controller templates. (We'll take a close look at this in section 6.3.2.) Because Rails does a lot of code organizing and templating for you, you may not need to create new modules from scratch in your application; but in cases where you add large segments of code that don't fit into any predefined Rails slots, and also in cases where you want to abstract code for reuse, modularization can come in handy.

Looking at modules takes us further along several paths we partially walked in the previous chapter. We saw that `Object` is the highest class; here, we'll meet the highest module: `Kernel`. We've touched on the fact that objects seek their methods in both class and superclass; here, we'll look in considerable detail at how this method-lookup process works when both classes and modules are involved.

6.1 *Basics of module creation and use*

Writing a module is similar to writing a class, except you start your definition with the `module` keyword instead of the `class` keyword:

```
module MyFirstModule
  def say_hello
    puts "Hello"
  end
end
```

When you write a class, you then create instances of the class. Those instances can execute the class's instance methods. Modules, however, don't have instances. Instead, modules get *mixed in* to classes. (Modules are sometimes referred to as *mix-ins*.) When this happens, the instance of the class has the ability to call instance methods defined in the module.

For example, using the little module from the previous example, you can go on to do this:

```
class ModuleTester
  include MyFirstModule
end

mt = ModuleTester.new
mt.say_hello
```

Your `ModuleTester` object will call the appropriate method (`say_hello`). Notice that `say_hello` isn't defined in the class of which the object is an instance. Instead, it's defined in a module that the class mixes in.

The mix-in operation is achieved with the `include` statement. `include` is actually a method. You'll see in detail later how the mixing of a module into a class, via `include`, operates.

You may notice that mixing in a module bears a strong resemblance to inheriting from a superclass. In a case where, say, class B inherits from class A, instances of class B can call instance methods of class A. In cases where, say, class C mixes in module M, instances of C can call instance methods of module M. In both cases, the instances of the class at the bottom of the list reap the benefits: They get to call not only their own class's instances methods, but also those of (in one case) a superclass or (in the other case) a mixed-in module.

The main difference between inheriting from a class and mixing in a module is that you can mix in more than one module. No class can inherit from more than one class. In cases where you want numerous extra behaviors for a class's instances—and you don't want to stash them all into the class's superclass—you can use modules to organize your code in a more granular way. Each module can add something different to the methods available through the class.

Modules open up lots of possibilities, particularly for sharing code among more than one class (because any number of classes can mix in the same module). We'll look next at some further examples, and you'll get a sense of the possibilities.

6.1.1 *A module encapsulating "stack-like-ness"*

Modules give you a way of collecting and encapsulating behaviors. A typical module contains methods connected to a particular subset of what will be, eventually, the full capabilities of an object.

By way of fleshing out this statement, we'll write a module that encapsulates the characteristic of *being like a stack*, or *stack-like-ness* (henceforth written without the hyphens, now that the word has been coined and introduced into the discussion). We'll then use that module to impart stacklike behaviors to objects, via the process of mixing the stacklike module into one or more classes.

As you may know from previous studies, a *stack* is a data structure that operates on the LIFO (last in, first out) principle. The classic example is a (physical) stack of plates. The first plate to be used is the last one placed on the stack. Stacks are usually discussed as a pair with *queues*, which exhibit FIFO (first in, first out) behavior. Think of a cafeteria: The plates are in a stack; the customers are in a queue.

Numerous items behave in a stacklike, LIFO manner. The last sheet of printer paper you put in the tray is the first one printed on. Double-parked cars have to leave in an order that's the opposite of the order of their arrival. The quality of being *stacklike* can manifest itself in a wide variety of collections and aggregations of entities.

That's where modules come in. When you're designing a program and you identify a behavior or set of behaviors that may be exhibited by more than one kind of entity or object, you've found a good candidate for a module. Stacklikeness fits the bill: More than one entity, and therefore imaginably more than one class, exhibits stacklike behavior. By creating a module that defines methods that *all* stacklike objects have in common, you give yourself a way to summon stacklikeness into any and all classes that need it.

Listing 6.1 shows a simple implementation of stacklikeness, in Ruby module form. (The code uses a few unfamiliar techniques; they're explained after the listing.) This example, although simple, involves a couple of different program files, which you can save to your *Ruby for Rails* scratchpad directory. Save listing 6.1 in a file called `stacklike.rb`.

Listing 6.1 The `Stacklike` module, encapsulating stacklike structure and behavior

```
module Stacklike
  attr_reader :stack

  def initialize
    @stack = Array.new    <——①
```

```
    end

    def add_to_stack(obj)    ◁──── ❷
      @stack.push(obj)
    end

    def take_from_stack    ◁──── ❸
      @stack.pop
    end
  end
```

The `Stacklike` module in listing 6.1 uses an *array* (an ordered collection of objects) to represent the stack. Upon initialization, a `Stacklike` object's instance variable `@stack` is initialized to a new, empty array ❶. When an object is added to the stack ❷, the operation is handled by pushing the object onto the array—that is, adding it to the end. Removing an object from the stack ❸ involves popping an element from the array—that is, removing it from the end. (`push` and `pop` are instance methods of the `Array` class. You'll see them again when we look at container objects, including arrays, in chapter 11.)

The module `Stacklike` thus implements stacklikeness by selectively deploying behaviors that already exist for `Array` objects: Add an element to the end of the array; take an element off the end. Arrays are more versatile than stacks; a stack can't do everything an array can. For example, you can remove elements from an array in any order, whereas by definition the only element you can remove from a stack is the one that was added most recently. But an array can do everything a stack can. As long as we don't ask it to do anything *un*stacklike, using an array as a kind of agent or proxy for the specifically stacklike add/remove actions makes sense.

We now have a module that implements stacklike behavior: maintaining a list of items, such that new ones can be added to the end and the most recently added one can be removed. The next question is, what can we do with this module?

6.1.2 *Mixing a module into a class*

As you've seen, modules don't have instances; so we *cannot* do this:

```
    s = Stacklike.new    ◁──────  Wrong!
```

In order to create instances (objects) we need a class; and in order to make those objects stacklike, we need to mix our module into that class. But what class? The most obviously stacklike thing is probably a `Stack`. Save the code in listing 6.2 to `stack.rb`, in the same directory as `stacklike.rb`.

Listing 6.2   Mixing the `Stacklike` **module into the** `Stack` **class**

```
require "stacklike"
class Stack
  include Stacklike   ◁——————❶
end
```

The business end of the `Stack` class in listing 6.2 is the `include` statement ❶ with which we have mixed in the `Stacklike` module. It ensures that instances of `Stack` will exhibit the behaviors defined in `Stacklike`.

> **NOTE**   SYNTAX OF require/load VS. SYNTAX OF include   You may have noticed that when you use `require` or `load`, you put the name of the item you're requiring or loading in quotation marks, but with `include`, you don't. `require` and `load` take strings as their arguments, whereas `include` takes the name of a module, in the form of a constant. The requirements to `require` and `load` are usually literal strings (in quotation marks), but a string in a variable will also work.

Notice that our class's name is a noun, whereas the module's name is an adjective. Neither of these practices is mandatory, but they're both common. What we end up with, expressed in everyday language, is a kind of predicate on the class:

```
Stack objects are stacklike.
```

That's English for

```
class Stack
  include Stacklike
end
```

To see the whole thing in action, let's create a `Stack` object and put it through its paces. The code in listing 6.3 creates a `Stack` object and performs some operations on it; you can enter this code at the end of your `stack.rb` file.

Listing 6.3   Creating and using an instance of class `Stack`

```
s = Stack.new   ◁——————❶

s.add_to_stack("item one")        ❷
s.add_to_stack("item two")
s.add_to_stack("item three")

puts "Objects currently on the stack:"
puts s.stack
```

```
taken = s.take_from_stack      ◁────❸
puts "Removed this object:"
puts taken

puts "Now on stack:"
puts s.stack
```

Listing 6.3 starts with the innocent-looking (but powerful) instantiation ❶ of a new Stack object, which we've assigned to the variable s. That Stack object is born with the knowledge of what to do when we ask it to perform stack-related actions, thanks to the fact that its class mixed in the Stacklike module. The rest of the code involves asking it to jump through some stacklike hoops: adding items (strings) to itself ❷, and popping the last one off itself ❸. Along the way, we ask the object to report on its state.

Now let's run the program. Here's an invocation of stack.rb, together with the output from the run:

```
$ ruby stack.rb
Objects currently on the stack:
item one
item two
item three
Removed this object:
item three
Now on stack:
item one
item two
```

Sure enough, our little Stack object knows what to do. It is, as advertised, stacklike.

The Stack class is fine as far as it goes. But it may leave you wondering: Why did we bother writing a module?

6.1.3 *Leveraging the module further*

It would be possible to pack all the functionality of the Stacklike module directly in the Stack class without writing a module. Listing 6.4 shows you what the class would look like.

Listing 6.4 A nonmodular rewrite of the Stack class

```
class Stack
  attr_reader :stack

  def initialize
    @stack = Array.new
```

```
  end

  def add_to_stack(obj)
    @stack.push(obj)
  end

  def take_from_stack
    @stack.pop
  end
end
```

As you'll see if you add the code in listing 6.3 to listing 6.4 and run it all through Ruby, it produces the same results as the implementation that uses a module.

Before you end up concluding that modules are pointless, remember what the modularization buys you: It lets you apply a general concept like *stacklikeness* to several cases, not just one.

What else is stacklike?

A few examples came up earlier: plates, printer paper, and so forth. Let's use a new one, though, borrowed from the world of urban legend.

Lots of people believe that if you're the first passenger to check in for a flight, your luggage will be the last off the plane. Real-world experience suggests that it doesn't work this way. Still, for stack practice, let's see what a Ruby model of an urban-legendly correct cargo hold would look like.

To model it reasonably closely, we'll include a barebones `Suitcase` class—a placeholder that doesn't fully model suitcase behavior (there are no `pack` or `snap_shut` methods) but that lets us create suitcase objects to fling into the cargo hold. Also for the sake of real-world resemblance, we'll give our cargo hold two methods: `load_and_report` and `unload`. `load_and_report` prints a message reporting that it's adding a suitcase to the cargo hold, and it gives us the suitcase object's id number (which will help us trace what happens to each suitcase). The `unload` method calls `take_from_stack`. (We could call `take_from_stack` directly, but *unload* sounds more like a term you might use to describe removing a suitcase from a cargo hold.)

Put the code in listing 6.5 into `cargohold.rb`, and try it.

Listing 6.5   Using the `Stacklike` module a second time, for a different class

```
require "stacklike"

class Suitcase
end
```

```
class CargoHold
  include Stacklike     ◁────❶
  def load_and_report(obj)
    print "Loading object "
    puts obj.object_id
    add_to_stack(obj)   ◁────❷
  end
  def unload
    take_from_stack     ◁────❸
  end
end

ch = CargoHold.new      ◁────❹
sc1 = Suitcase.new
sc2 = Suitcase.new
sc3 = Suitcase.new

ch.load_and_report(sc1)
ch.load_and_report(sc2)
ch.load_and_report(sc3)

first_unloaded = ch.unload

print "The first suitcase off the plane is...."
puts first_unloaded.object_id
```

At its heart, the program in listing 6.5 isn't all that different from those in listings 6.2 and 6.3 (which you saved incrementally to stack.rb). It follows much the same procedure: mixing Stacklike into a class ❶, creating an instance of that class ❹, and adding items to ❷, and removing them from ❸, that instance (the stacklike thing—the cargo hold, in this case). It also does some reporting of the current state of the stack ❶, as the other program did.

The output from the cargo hold program looks like this (remember that suitcases are referred to by their object id numbers, which may be different on your system):

```
Loading object 942912
Loading object 942892
Loading object 942882
The first suitcase off the plane is....942882
```

The cargo hold example shows how you can use an existing module for a new class. Sometimes it pays to wrap the methods in new methods with better names for the new domain (like unload instead of take_from_stack), although if you find yourself changing too much, it may be a sign that the module isn't a good fit.

In the next section, we're going to put together several of the pieces we've looked at more or less separately: method calls (message sending), objects and their status as instances of classes, and the mixing of modules into classes. All of these concepts come together in the process by which an object, upon being sent a message, looks for and finds (or fails to find) a method to execute whose name matches the message.

6.2 Modules, classes, and method lookup

You already know that when an object receives a message, the result may be the execution of a method with the same name as the message in the object's class, or a method in that class's superclass—and onward, up to the Object class—or a method in a module that has been mixed into any of those classes. But how *exactly* does this come about? And what happens in ambiguous cases—for example, if a class and a mixed-in module both define a method with a given name? Which one does the object choose to execute?

It pays to answer these questions precisely. Imprecise accounts of what happens are easy to come by. Sometimes they're even adequate: If you say, "This object has a push method," you may well succeed in communicating what you're trying to communicate, even though objects don't "have" methods but, rather, find them by searching classes and modules.

But an imprecise account won't scale. It won't help you understand what's going on in more complex cases, and it won't support you when you're designing your own code. Your best course of action is to learn what *really* happens when you send messages to objects.

Fortunately, the way it works turns out to be straightforward.

6.2.1 Illustrating the basics of method lookup

In the interest of working toward a clear understanding of how objects find methods, let's back-pedal on the real-world references and, instead, write some classes and modules with simple names like C and M. Doing so will help you concentrate on the logic and mechanics of method lookup without having to think simultaneously about modeling a real-world domain. We'll also write some methods that don't do anything except print a message announcing that they've been called. This will help track the order of method lookup.

Look at the program in listing 6.6.

Listing 6.6   Demonstration of module inclusion and inheritance

```
module M
  def report
    puts "'report' method in module M"
  end
end

class C
  include M
end

class D < C
end

obj = D.new
obj.report
```

The instance method report is defined in module M. Module M is mixed into class C. Class D is a subclass of C. obj is an instance of D. Through this cascade, the object (obj) gets access to the report method.

Still, *gets access*, like *has*, is a vague way to put it. Let's try to get more of a fix on the process by considering an object's-eye view of it.

An object's-eye view of method lookup

You're the object, and someone sends you a message. You have to figure out how to respond to it—or whether you *can* respond to it. Here's a bit of object stream-of-consciousness:

> *I am a Ruby object, and I've been sent the message "report". I have to try to find a method called report in my method lookup path. report, if it exists, resides in a class or module.*
>
> *I am an instance of a class called D. Does D define an instance method report?*

No.

> *Does D mix in any modules?*

No.

> *Does D's superclass (C) define a report instance method?*

No.

> *Does C mix in any modules?*

Yes: M.

> *Does M define a report method?*

Yes! I'll execute that method.

The search ends when the method being searched for is found, or with an error condition if it isn't found.

NOTE   `method_missing`   When you send an object a message it doesn't understand, the situation triggers execution of a built-in method called `method_missing`. The default version of this method treats the problem as a fatal error. However, you can override `method_missing` as an instance method in your class. Your version will be then be executed when instances of that class receive unknown messages.

  `method_missing` is the key to much of the behavior of objects in Rails applications: They receive messages they don't understand, and then their `method_missing` facilities look among the database fields for matching names and create the corresponding methods on the spot.

This example gives you much of what you need to know about how objects look for methods to call when they're asked to call methods. It doesn't give you all the information you need; a couple of concepts will materialize down the road. But it gives you what you need to understand the rest later on.

  Let's move from object stream-of-consciousness to specifics about the method search scenario, and in particular the question of how far it can go.

How far does the method search go?

Ultimately, every object in Ruby is an instance of some class descended from the big class in the sky: `Object`. That means however many classes and modules it may cross along the way, the search for a method can always go as far up as `Object`. It can even go one step further: the class `Object` mixes in a module more primal than itself: `Kernel`. If you get to `Kernel` and you still haven't found the method you're asking the object to execute, that means you're not going to find it.

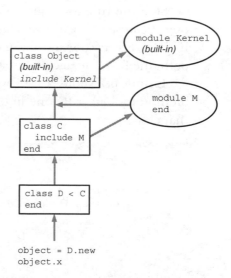

  Figure 6.1 illustrates the method search path from our earlier example (the class `D` object), up to and including `Kernel`. (In the example, the search for the method succeeds at module `M`; the

Figure 6.1   Diagram of the method lookup process for an instance of `D`

diagram shows how far the object would look if it didn't find the method there.) When the message "x" is sent to the object, the method search begins, hitting the various classes and mix-ins (modules) as shown by the arrows.

`Kernel` is where the methods common to all Ruby objects are defined, including the ones we looked at earlier (`respond_to?`, `object_id`, and `send`). Now you know why every object has these methods: They're defined in `Kernel`, `Object` mixes in `Kernel`, and `Object` is an ancestor of every class in Ruby.

6.2.2 *Defining the same method more than once*

You learned in chapter 5 that if you define a method twice inside the same class, the second definition takes precedence over the first. The same is true of modules. The rule comes down to this: There can be only one method of a given name per class or module at any given time.

That's how classes and modules keep house. When we flip to an object's-eye view, however, the question of having access to two or more methods with the same name becomes more involved.

An object's methods can come from any number of classes and modules. True, any *one* class or module can have only one `report` method (to use that name as an example). But an object can have *multiple* `report` methods in its method search path, because the method search path passes through multiple classes or modules.

Still, the rule for objects is analogous to the rule for classes and modules: An object can see only one version of a method with a given name at any given time. If there are two or more same-named methods in the object's method lookup path, the first one encountered is the winner and will be executed.

Listing 6.7 shows a case where two versions of a method lie on an object's method lookup path: one in the object's class, and one in a module mixed in by that class.

Listing 6.7   Two same-named methods on a single search path

```
module M
  def report
    puts "'report' method in module M"
  end
end

class C
  include M
  def report
    puts "'report' method in class C"
```

```
      end
  end

  c = C.new
  c.report
```

When you run listing 6.7, you get the following output:

```
'report' method in class C.
```

Two `report` methods lie on the method lookup path of the object `c`. But the lookup hits the class `C` (c's class) before it hits the module `M` (a mix-in of class `C`). Therefore, the report method it executes is the one defined in `C`.

An object may have two methods with the same name on its method lookup path in another circumstance: When a class mixes in two or more modules, more than one of which implement the method being searched for, the modules are searched in *reverse order of inclusion*—that is, the most recently mixed-in module is searched first.

For example, consider a case where two modules, `M` and `N`, both define a `report` method and are both mixed into a class, as in listing 6.8.

Listing 6.8   Mixing in two modules with a same-named method defined

```
module M
  def report
    puts "'report' method in module M"
  end
end

module N
  def report
    puts "'report' method in module N"
  end
end

class C
  include M
  include N
end
```

What does an instance of this class do when you send it the "`report`" message and it walks the lookup path, looking for a matching method? Let's ask it:

```
c = C.new
c.report
```

The answer is, "`'report'` method in module N`'`". The first `report` method encountered in C's method lookup path is the one in the *most recently mixed-in* module. In this case, that means N—so N's `report` method wins over M's method of the same name.

The double-barreled rule, then, is this:

- If you're a class or module, you can only have one method of a given name at a given time.

- If you're an object, you can look for a method in multiple classes and/or modules, but your search stops when you find the first matching method.

Except…

6.2.3 *Going up the method search path with super*

There is a special way, inside the body of a method definition, to reach upward and execute the next method with the same name, higher up in the lookup path. You do this with the `super` keyword.

Listing 6.9 shows a basic example (after which we'll get to the "why would you do that?" aspect).

Listing 6.9 Using the `super` keyword to reach up one level in the lookup path

```
module M
  def report        <----1
    puts "'report' method in module M"
  end
end


class C
  include M
  def report        <----2
    puts "'report' method in class C"
    puts "About to trigger the next higher-up report method..."
    super      <----3
    puts "Back from the 'super' call."
  end
end

c = C.new
c.report      <----4
```

The output from running listing 6.9 is as follows:

```
'report' method in class C
About to trigger the next higher-up report method...
```

```
'report' method in module M
Back from the 'super' call.
```

The instance of C (namely, c) receives the "report" message ❹. The method-lookup process starts with c's class (C)—and, sure enough, there is a report method ❷. That method is executed.

Inside the method, however, is a call to super ❸. That means even though you found a method corresponding to the message ("report"), you must keep looking and find *the next match*. The next match for "report", in this case, is the report method defined in module M ❶.

Note that M#report *would have been* the first match in a search for a report method, if C#report didn't exist. The super keyword gives you a way to call what would have been the applicable version of a method, in cases where that method has been overridden later in the lookup path. Why would you want to do this?

Sometimes, particularly when you're writing a subclass, a method in an existing class does *almost* what you want, but not quite. With super, you can have the best of both, by hooking into or wrapping the original method, as listing 6.10 illustrates.

Listing 6.10   Using super to wrap a method in a subclass

```
class Bicycle
  attr_reader :gears, :wheels, :seats

  def initialize(gears = 1)    ⬅━━━❶
    @wheels = 2
    @seats = 1
    @gears = gears
  end
end

class Tandem < Bicycle
  def initialize(gears)
    super
    @seats = 2    ⬅━━━❷
  end
end
```

super gives us a nice clean way to make a tandem *almost* like a bicycle. We change only what needs to be changed (the number of seats ❷), and we use super to trigger the earlier initialize method ❶, which sets bicycle-like default values for the other properties of the tandem.

When we call super, we don't explicitly forward the gears argument that is passed to initialize. Yet when the original initialize method in Bicycle is called, any arguments provided to the Tandem version are visible. This is a special behavior of super. The way super handles arguments is as follows:

- Called as a bareword, super automatically forwards the arguments that were passed to the method from which it's called.

- Called with an empty argument list—super()—it sends *no* arguments to the higher-up method, even if arguments were passed to the current method.

- Called with specific arguments—super(a,b,c)—it sends exactly those arguments.

This unusual treatment of arguments exists because the most common case is the first one, where you want to bump up to the super method with the same arguments as those received by the method from which super is being called. That case is given the simplest syntax; you just type super.

You now have a good grasp of both classes and modules, and how individual objects, on receiving messages, look for a matching method by traversing their class/module family tree. Next, we'll look at what you can do with this system—specifically, the kinds of decisions you can and should make as to the design and naming of your classes and modules, in the interest of writing clear and comprehensible programs.

6.3 *Class/module design and naming*

The fact that Ruby has classes and modules—along with the fact that from an object's perspective, all that matters is whether a given method exists, not what class or module the method's definition is in—means that you have a lot of choice when it comes to your programs' design and structure. This richness of design choice raises some considerations you should be aware of.

We've already looked at one case (the Stack class) where it would have been possible to put all the necessary method definitions into one class but was advantageous to yank some of them out, put them in a module (Stacklike), and then mix the module into the class. There's no rule for deciding when to do which. It depends on your present and (to the extent you can judge them) future needs. It's sometimes tempting to break everything out into separate modules, because modules you write for one program may be useful in another ("I just know I'm going to need that ThreePronged module again some day!" says the packrat voice in your head). But there's such a thing as over-modularization. It depends on the situation. And you have more than one program architecture design tool at your disposal.

6.3.1 *Mix-ins and/or inheritance*

Module mix-ins are closely related to class inheritance. In both cases, one entity (class or module) is establishing a close connection—becoming neighbors on a method lookup path—with another. In some cases, you may find that you can design part of your program *either* with modules *or* with inheritance.

Our CargoHold class is an example. We implemented it by having it mix in the Stacklike module. But had we gone the route of writing a Stack class instead of a Stacklike module, we still could have had a CargoHold. It would have been a subclass of Stack, as illustrated in listing 6.11.

Listing 6.11 CargoHold, inheriting from Stack instead of mixing in Stacklike

```ruby
class Stack
  attr_reader :stack

  def initialize
    @stack = []
  end

  def add_to_stack(obj)
    @stack.push(obj)
  end

  def take_from_stack
    @stack.pop
  end
end

class Suitcase
end

class CargoHold < Stack
  def load_and_report(obj)
    print "Loading object "
    puts obj.object_id
    add_to_stack(obj)
  end
  def unload
    take_from_stack
  end
end
```

From the point of view of an individual CargoHold object, the process works in listing 6.11 exactly as it worked in the earlier implementation, where CargoHold mixed in the Stacklike module. The object is concerned with finding and executing methods that correspond to the messages it receives. It either finds such methods on its method lookup path, or it doesn't. It doesn't care whether the methods were defined in a module or a class. It's like searching a house for a screwdriver: You don't care which room you find it in, and which room you find it in makes no difference to what happens when you subsequently employ the screwdriver for a task.

There's nothing wrong with this inheritance-based approach to implementing `CargoHold`, except that it eats up the one inheritance opportunity `CargoHold` has. If another class might be more suitable than `Stack` to serve as `CargoHold`'s superclass (like, hypothetically, `StorageSpace` or `AirplaneSection`), we might end up needing the flexibility we'd gain by turning at least one of those classes into a module.

There's no single rule or formula that always results in the right design. But it's useful to keep a couple of considerations in mind when you're making class-versus-module decisions:

- *Modules don't have instances.* It follows that entities or things are generally best modeled in classes, and characteristics or properties of entities or things are best encapsulated in modules. Correspondingly, as noted in section 6.1.1, class names tend to be nouns, while module names are often adjectives (like `Stack` versus `Stacklike`).

- *A class can have only one superclass, but it can mix in as many modules as it wants.* If you're using inheritance, give priority to creating a sensible superclass/subclass relationship. Don't use up a class's one and only superclass relationship to endow the class with what might turn out to be just one of several sets of characteristics.

Summing up these rules in one example, here is what you should *not* do:

```
module Vehicle
...
class SelfPropelling
...
class Truck < SelfPropelling
  include Vehicle
...
```

Rather, you should do this:

```
module SelfPropelling
...
class Vehicle
  include SelfPropelling
...
class Truck < Vehicle
...
```

The second version models the entities and properties much more neatly. `Truck` descends from `Vehicle` (which makes sense), whereas `SelfPropelling` is a characteristic of vehicles (at least, all those we care about in this model of the world)—a characteristic that is passed on to trucks by virtue of `Truck` being a descendant, or specialized form, of `Vehicle`.

Nesting modules and classes

You can nest modules and classes inside each other—for example, start a class definition inside a module definition, like this:

```
module Tools
  class Hammer
```

To create an instance of the `Hammer` class defined inside the `Tools` module, you use the double-colon constant lookup token (`::`) to point the way to the name of the class :

```
h = Tools::Hammer.new
```

Nested module/class chains like `Tools::Hammer` are sometimes used to create separate *namespaces* for classes, modules, and methods. This technique can help if two classes have a similar name but aren't the same class. For example, if you have got a `Tool::Hammer` class, you can also have a `Piano::Hammer` class, and the two `Hammer` classes won't conflict with each other because each is nested in its own namespace (`Tool` in one case, `Piano` in the other).

(An alternative way to achieve this separation would be to have a `ToolsHammer` class and a `PianoHammer` class, without bothering to nest them in modules. However, stringing names together like that can quickly lead to visual clutter, especially when elements are nested deeper than two levels.)

We'll look further at nested classes, modules, and other constants in the next chapter, when we talk in more detail about the subject of *scope*. Meanwhile, note that this ability to nest modules and classes inside each other (to any depth, in any order) gives you yet another axis along which you can plan your program's design and structure.

6.3.2 *Modular organization in Rails source and boilerplate code*

Even if it weren't the main impetus for learning Ruby in this book, Rails would be a great source of examples of modularization at work. We'll look here at how modules manifest themselves in two Rails contexts: the source code of the framework, and the boilerplate code generated when you initialize an application with the `rails` command. Both of these are sneak peeks; we'll look more closely at the process of examining the source code in chapter 17, and the discussion of model and controller files will extend in chapters 14–16 well beyond the point of noting what's a class and what's a module. This is a limited-agenda subsection, but it's a useful illustration of the front-and-center status of modules in Rails.

Modularization in the Rails source

The Rails source code makes heavy use of modules, in particular the technique of *reopening* the definition bodies of both classes and modules. For a glimpse, go to your `action_controller` directory, which resides deep in the `gems` directory of your Ruby installation. Its path will look something like this, depending on your setup and version numbers:

```
gems/1.8/gems/actionpack1.7.0/lib/action_controller
```

Once you're there, try this:

```
$ grep "module ActionController" *
```

Watch `grep` show you all the files that contain this line. (You'll probably see the tag `#:nodoc:` on most of them; this is a directive to the Ruby Documentation (RDoc), and you can ignore it.) If you don't have `grep` on your system, you can use the following command-line Ruby script instead. (The backslash at the end of the first line of the script tells Ruby that the following line is a continuation of the current one. You could also remove the backslash and type the whole command on one line.)

```
$ ruby -ne 'puts ARGF.filename + ":" + $_ \
   if $_ && /module ActionController/' *.rb
```

For every line displayed by `grep` (or the Ruby substitute), the `ActionController` module is being reopened, and new functionality—nested classes and/or modules, with their methods—is being added.

To see some nesting in the wild, a good file to look at is `routing.rb` (in the same `/usr/local/..../action_controller` directory where you did the grepping). The first few lines (with some comments trimmed) are as follows:

```
module ActionController
  module Routing
    class Route
```

If you had occasion to create an instance of that `Route` class, what would you do? You'd do this:

```
ActionController::Routing::Route.new
```

That would take you down the chain of nested definitions to the right one: You're asking for a new instance of the class `Route`, which is defined in the module `Routing` of the module `ActionController`.

> **NOTE** CLASS OR MODULE? When you see a construct like
>
> `ActionController::Routing::Route`
>
> you can't tell from that construct what's a class and what's a module. If there's a call to `new`, you can be pretty sure the last element in the chain is a class, but otherwise the last element could be any constant—class, module, or other—and the elements on the left could be either classes or modules. In many cases, the fact that you can't tell classes from modules in this kind of context doesn't matter; what matters is the nesting or chaining of names in a way that makes sense. That's just as well, because you can't tell what's what without looking at the source code or the documentation. This is a consequence of the fact that *classes are modules*—the class `Class` is a subclass of the class `Module`—and in many respects (with the most notable exception being the fact that classes can be instantiated), their behavior is similar.

Some of the deep nesting of classes and modules in the Rails libraries bubbles to the surface of your application in the code that Rails inserts into your application files when they're first created. Now you can understand the syntax and semantics behind it, which we'll examine next.

Modularization in Rails boilerplate code

As you'll recall from chapter 5, as well as from the sample application developed in chapter 2, each file in the `app/models` subdirectory of your application looks something like this when it's first created with the `generate` script:

```
class Composer < ActiveRecord::Base
end
```

You're now in a position to decipher this code completely:

- `Composer` is a class.
- The superclass of `Composer` is `ActiveRecord::Base`—which must, therefore, be a class.
- There's a class called `Base`, nested inside a class or module called `ActiveRecord`. You can't tell whether the latter is a class or module just by looking at the wording in the file. (It's a module, as it happens.)

Understanding what the boilerplate code means will help you be aware of what you're doing when you add code to the model file.

When you create your application, there's nothing in the models directory; you create all the models with the `generate` script. However, you get a free controller file: the generic file `app/controllers/application.rb`, which serves as an umbrella controller file for all the other controllers. Upon the automatic creation of this file, you see something similar to what you saw in the newly minted model files:

```
class ApplicationController < ActionController::Base
end
```

This code creates a class (or perhaps reopens a class; you can't tell by looking, although in this case the action is creation) called `ApplicationController`, which is a subclass of a class called `Base` that is nested inside a class or module (module, as it happens) called `ActionController`. The new class created here ends up serving as the superclass for the other controller classes you create later with the `generate` script—as you can see if you look in one of the application-specific controller files:

```
class ComposerController < ApplicationController
```

We'll come back and flesh out the ramifications of this discussion, particularly in part 4 when we revisit the music store application and bear down on further details of coding inside the model and controller files. Meanwhile, you now have a good sense of the centrality of modules as well as classes (which, again, are a specialized form of module) to Ruby programming in general and the Rails framework specifically.

6.4 Summary

This chapter has been both a companion to and a continuation of the previous chapter on classes. We've looked in detail at modules, which are similar to classes in that they bundle methods and constants together, but which can't be instantiated. You've seen examples of how you might use modules to express the design of a program. We've taken an object's-eye view of the process of finding and executing a method in response to a message. We've also looked at some techniques you can use—including nesting classes and modules inside each other, which can have the benefit of keeping namespaces separate and clear. Finally, we discussed aspects of modular organization in the Rails framework source and in some of the boilerplate code created by Rails when you initialize your application.

Now that we're nesting elements inside each other, the next topic we should and will examine in detail is *scope*: what happens to data and variables when your program moves from one code context to another.

The default object (self) and scope

In describing and discussing computer programs, we often use spatial and, sometimes, human metaphors. We talk about *being in* a class definition, or *returning from* a method call. Sometimes there's a sense of addressing objects in the second person, as in obj.respond_to?("x") (that is, "Hey obj, do you respond to 'x'?"). As your program runs, the context and orientation change again and again.

This chapter is about knowing what's going on in a Ruby program, based on understanding what different elements mean, and why, in certain contexts.

A few components mean the same thing everywhere. Integers, for example, mean what they mean wherever you see them. The same is true for keywords: You can't use keywords like def and class as variable names, so when you see them, you can easily glean what they're doing.

But most elements depend on context for their meaning. Most words and tokens can mean different things at different times. If you understand what can change from one context to another, and also what triggers a change in context (for example, starting a method definition), you can always get your bearings in a Ruby program. And it's not just a matter of passive Ruby literacy: You also need to know about contexts and how they affect the meaning of what you're doing when you're writing Ruby.

This chapter focuses primarily on two topics: *scope* and *self*. As we discussed briefly a little earlier, the rules of scope govern the visibility of variables (and other elements, but largely variables). It's important to know what scope you're in, so that you can tell what the variables refer to and not confuse them with variables from different scopes that have the same name.

Unlike scope, *self* isn't so much a concept as an object. However, self changes in the course of program. At every moment, only one object is playing the role of self. But it's not necessarily the same object from one moment to the next. Self is like the first person or *I* of the program. As in a book with multiple first-person narrators, the I role can get passed around. There's always one I, but who it is—what object it is—will vary.

Both of these components of Ruby pertain directly and centrally to the matter of staying correctly oriented in a program. In order to know what you're looking at, you need to know what scope you're in. And in order to understand what the things you're looking at do, you need to know which object is self.

The third subtopic of this chapter is *method access*. Ruby provides mechanisms for making distinctions among access levels of methods. Basically, this means rules limiting the calling of methods depending on what self is. Method access is therefore a meta-topic, grounded in the study of self and scope. We'll look at Ruby's method-access rules both as a general matter and in their role as a mechanism for creating layers of access to Rails controller actions.

Finally, we'll discuss a topic that pulls together several of these threads: top-level methods, which are written outside of any class or module definition.

7.1 Understanding self, the current/default object

One of the cornerstones of Ruby programming—the backbone, in some respects—is the *default object* or *current object*, accessible to you in your program through the keyword self. At every point when your program is running, there is one and only one self. Being self has certain privileges, as you'll see. In this section, we'll look at how Ruby determines which object is self at a given point and what privileges are granted to the object that is self.

7.1.1 Who gets to be self, and where

There is always one (and only one) current object or self. You can tell which object it is by following a small set of rules. These rules are summarized in table 7.1; the table's contents will be explained and illustrated as we go along.

To know which object is self, you need to know what context you're in. In practice, there aren't all that many contexts to worry about. There's the top level (before you've entered any other context, such as a class definition). There are class definition blocks, module definition blocks, and method definition blocks. Aside from a few subtleties in the way these contexts interact, that's about it. As shown in table 7.1, self is determined by which of these contexts you're in (class and module definitions are similar and closely related).

Figure 7.1 gives you a diagrammatic summary of the information from table 7.1. Both show you that some object is always self, and that *which* object is self depends on where you are in the program.

The most basic and, in some respects, unique program context is the top level, the context of the program before any class or module definition has been opened, or after they've all been closed. We'll look next at the top level's ideas about self.

Table 7.1   How the current object (self) is determined

Context	Example	Which object is self?
Top level of program	*Any code outside of other blocks*	`main` (*built-in top-level default object*)
Class definition	`class C`	The class object `C`
Module definition	`module M`	The module object `M`
Method definitions	1. Top level `def method_name`	`main` (*built-in top-level default object*)

	2. Instance method definition
	   `class C`
	     `def method_name`
		An instance of `C`, responding to `method_name`

	3. Instance method definition in module
	   `module M`
	     `def method_name`
		I. Individual object extended by `M`
		II. Instance of class that mixes in `M`

	4. Singleton method (including class methods) `def obj.method_name`	`obj`

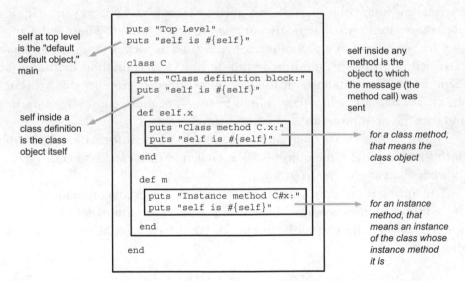

Figure 7.1   Diagrammatic view of the determination of self in different contexts

The top-level self object

The term *top level* refers to program code written outside of any class or module definition block. If you open a brand-new text file and type

```
x = 1
```

you have created a *top-level local variable* x. If you type

```
def m
end
```

you have created a *top-level method*—a method that isn't defined as an instance method of a particular class or module nor associated uniquely with an individual object (it isn't a singleton method).

A number of our examples, particularly in the early chapters, involved top-level code. Once we started writing class and module definitions, more of our code began to appear inside those definitions. The way self shifts in class, module, and method definitions is uniform: The keyword (`class`, `module`, or `def`) marks a switch to a new self. But what is self when you haven't yet entered any definition block?

The answer is that Ruby provides you with a start-up self at the top level. If you ask it to identify itself

```
ruby -e 'puts self'
```

it will tell you that it's called `main`.

`main` is a special term the default self object uses to refer to itself. You can't refer to it as `main`. If you want to grab `main` for any reason, you need to assign it to a variable at the top level:

```
m = main
```

(It's not likely that you'd need to do this, but this is how it's done.)

Self inside class and module definitions

In a class or module definition, self is *the class or module object*. This innocent-sounding rule is important. If you master it, you'll save yourself from several of the most common mistakes that people make when they're learning Ruby.

You can see what self is at various levels of class and/or module definition by using `puts` explicitly, as shown in listing 7.1.

Listing 7.1 Examining self via calls to puts in class and module definitions

```
class C
  puts "Just started class C:"
  puts self    ◁——— Output: C
  module M
    puts "Nested module C::M:"
    puts self    ◁——— Output: C::M
  end
  puts "Back in the outer level of C:"
  puts self    ◁——— Output: C
end
```

As soon as you cross a class or module keyword boundary, the class or module whose definition block you've entered—the Class or Module object—becomes self. Listing 7.1 shows two cases: entering C, and then entering C::M. When you leave C::M but are still in C, self is once again C.

Of course, class and module definition blocks do more than just begin and end. They also contain method definitions; and method definitions, for both instance methods and class methods, have rules determining self.

The determination of self in instance method definitions

The notion of self inside an instance method definition is subtle, for the following reason: When the interpreter encounters a def/end block, it defines the method immediately; but the code *inside* the method definition isn't executed until later, when an object capable of triggering its execution receives the appropriate message.

When you're looking at a method definition on paper or on the screen, you can only know in principle that, when the method is called, self will be the object that called it (the receiver of the message). At the time the method *definition* is executed, the most you can say is that self inside this method will be some future object that has access to this method.

You can rig a method to show you its self as it runs:

```
class C
  def x
    puts "Class C, method x:"
    puts self
  end
end

c = C.new
c.x
```

which outputs:

```
Class C, method x:
#<C:0xbf4c294c>
```

The weird-looking item in the output (#<C:0xbf4c294c>) is Ruby's way of saying "an instance of C." (The hexadecimal number after the colon is a memory location reference. When you run the code on your system, you'll probably get a different number.) As you can see, the object we created (obj) takes on the role of self during execution of the method x.

Self in singleton-method and class-method definitions

Instance methods are made to be shared. But *singleton methods*—those attached to a particular object, like the method talk in def obj.talk—can be called by only one object.

As you might expect, when a singleton method is executed, self is the object that owns the method, as an object will readily tell you:

```
obj = Object.new
def obj.show_me
  print "I'm an object; "
  puts "here's self inside a singleton method of mine:"
  p self
end

obj.show_me
print "And inspecting obj from outside, "
puts "to be sure it's the same object:"
p obj
```

The output of this example is as follows:

```
I'm an object; here's self inside a singleton method of mine:
#<Object:0x40193d40>
And inspecting obj from outside, to be sure it's the same object:
#<Object:0x40193d40>
```

(As always, the exact hexadecimal number in the object's inspection string will probably be different on your run of the code.)

It makes sense that if a method is written to be called by only one object, that object gets to be self. Moreover, this is a good time to remember *class methods*—defined as singleton methods for class objects. The following example reports on self from inside a class method of C:

```
class C
  def C.x
    puts "Class method of class C"
```

```
      p self
    end
  end

C.x
```

Here's what it reports:

```
Class method of class C
C
```

Sure enough, self inside a singleton method (a class method, in this case) is the object whose singleton method it is.

By way of a little programming tip, here's a variation on the last example:

```
class C
  def self.x    ◁────── ❶
    puts "Class method of class C"
    p self
  end
end
```

Note the use of self.x ❶ rather than C.x. This way of writing a class method takes advantage of the fact that in the class definition, self is C. So, def self.x is the same as def C.x. The self.x version offers a slight advantage: If you ever decide to rename the class, self.x will adjust automatically to the new name. If you hard-code C.x, you'll have to change C to your class's new name.

Being self at a given point in the program comes with some privileges. The chief privilege enjoyed by self is that of serving as the *default receiver of messages*, as you'll see next.

7.1.2 *Self as default receiver of messages*

Calling methods (that is, sending messages to objects) usually involves the dot notation:

```
obj.talk
ticket.venue
"abc".capitalize
```

That's the normal, full form of the method-calling syntax in Ruby. However, a special rule governs method calls: If the receiver of the message is self, *you can omit the receiver and the dot*. Ruby will use self as the default receiver, meaning the message you send will be sent to self, as the following equivalencies show:

```
talk        ◁─────── Same as self.talk
venue       ◁─────── Same as self.venue
capitalize  ◁─────── Same as self.capitalize
```

NOTE GIVING METHODS AND VARIABLES THE SAME NAMES You can (but really shouldn't) give a method and a variable the same name. If both exist, and you use the bare identifier (like talk), the variable takes precedence. To force Ruby to see the identifier as a method name, you'd have to use self.talk or call the method with an empty argument list: talk(). Because variables don't take arguments, the parentheses establish that you mean the method rather than the variable. Again, it's best to avoid these name clashes if you can.

Let's see this concept in action by inducing a situation where we know what self is and then testing the dot-less form of method calling. In the top level of a class definition block, self is the class object. And we know how to add methods directly to class objects. So, we have the ingredients to do a default receiver demo:

```
class C
  def C.no_dot
    puts "As long as self is C, you can call this method with no dot"
  end

  no_dot    ←————❶
end

C.no_dot    ←————❷
```

The first call to no_dot ❶ doesn't have an explicit receiver; it's a bareword. When Ruby sees this (and determines that it's a method call, rather than a variable or keyword), it figures that you mean it as shorthand for

```
self.no_dot
```

In the case of our example, self.no_dot is the same as C.no_dot, because we're inside C's definition block and, therefore, self is C. The result is that the method C.no_dot is called, and we see the output.

The second time we call the method ❷, we're back outside the class definition block. C is no longer self. Therefore, to call no_dot, we need to specify the receiver: C.

The most common use of the dotless method call occurs when you're calling one instance method from another. Here's an example:

```
class C
  def x
    puts "This is method 'x'"
  end

  def y
    puts "This is method 'y', about to call x without a dot."
```

```
      x
    end
  end

  c = C.new
  c.y
```

The output is as follows:

```
  This is method 'y', about to call x without a dot.
  This is method 'x'.
```

Upon calling c.y, the method y is executed, with self set to c (which is an instance of C). *Inside* y, the bareword reference to x is interpreted as a message to be sent to self. That, in turn, means the method x is executed.

> **WARNING** DON'T LEAVE OUT THE DOT WHEN IT'S NEEDED In one situation, you *must* use the full object-dot-message notation, even if you're sending the message to the current self: when the method is a setter method—a method whose name ends with an equal sign. You have to do self.venue = "Town Hall" rather than venue = "Town Hall", if you want to call the method venue=. The reason is that Ruby always interprets the sequence: *bareword = value* as an assignment to a local variable. To call the method venue= on the current object, you need to include the explicit self. Otherwise, you'll end up with a variable called venue and no call to the setter method.

7.1.3 Instance variables and self

One of the most useful and important rules to learn in Ruby is this: Every instance variable you'll ever see in a Ruby program belongs to whatever object is the current object (self) *at that point in the program.*

Here's a classic case where this knowledge comes in handy. See if you can figure out what this code will print, before you run it:

```
  class C
    def show_var
      @v = "I am an instance variable initialized to a string."   ⟵ ❶
      puts @v
    end
    @v = "Instance variables can appear anywhere...."   ⟵ ❷
  end

  C.new.show_var
```

The code prints the following:

```
  I am an instance variable initialized to a string.
```

The trap is that you may think it will print "Instance variables can appear any-where...." The code prints what it does because the @v in the method definition ❶ and the @v outside it ❷ are *completely unrelated* to each other. They are both instance variables, and both are named @v, but they aren't the same variable. They belong to different objects.

Whose are they?

The first @v lies inside the definition block of an instance method of C. That fact has implications, not for a single object, but for instances of C in general: Each instance of C that calls this method will have its own instance variable @v.

The second @v belongs to *the class object* C. This is one of the many occasions where it pays to remember that classes are objects. Any object may have its own instance variables—its private stash of information and object state. Class objects enjoy this privilege as much as any other object.

The logic required to figure out what object owns a given instance variable is simple and consistent: Every instance variable belongs to whatever object is play-ing the role of self (the current object) at the moment the code containing the instance variable is executed.

Let's do a quick rewrite of the example, this time making it a little more chatty about what's going on. Listing 7.2 shows the rewrite.

Listing 7.2 Chatty examination of the relationship between instance variables and self

```
class C
  puts "Just inside class definition block. Here's self:"
  puts self

  @v = "I am an instance variable initialized to a string"
  puts "And here's the instance variable @v, belonging to self:"
  puts @v

  def show_var
    puts "Inside an instance method definition block. Here's self:"
    puts self
    puts "And here's the instance variable @v, belonging to self:"
    puts @v
  end
end

c = C.new
c.show_var
```

The output from this version is as follows:

```
Just inside class definition block. Here's self:
C
And here's the instance variable @v, belonging to self:
I am an instance variable initialized to a string
Inside an instance method definition block. Here's self:
#<C:0x401c2ac0>
And here's the instance variable @v, belonging to self:
nil
```

Sure enough, each of these two different objects (the class object C and the instance of C, c) has its own instance variable @v.

Understanding self—both the basic fact that such a role is being played by some object at every point in a program, and knowing how to tell *which* object is self—is one of the most vital aspects of understanding Ruby. Another equally vital aspect is the understanding of *scope*, to which we will turn now.

7.2 Determining scope

Scope refers to the reach or visibility of variables. Different types of variables have different scoping rules. We'll be talking chiefly about two types: *global* and *local* variables.

Like the role of self, scope changes over the course of a program. Also as with self, you can deduce what's in what scope by reading the program as well as running it. But scope and self aren't the same thing. You can start a new local scope without self changing. Sometimes scope and self change together. They have in common the fact that they are both necessary to make sense of what you're seeing. Like knowing who self is, knowing what scope you're in tells you the significance of the code.

We'll talk first about global scope and then about local scope. Constants also have scoping rules, which we'll look at as well.

7.2.1 Global scope and global variables

We're starting with the scope that's used least often, but which you need to be aware of: *global scope*, meaning scope that covers the entire program. Global scope is enjoyed by *global variables*, which we haven't looked at yet. Global variables are distinguished by starting with a dollar-sign ($) character. They are available everywhere in your program. They walk through walls: Even if you start a new class or method definition, even if the identity of self changes, the global variables you've initialized will still be available to you.

In other words, global variables never go out of scope. In this example, a method defined inside a class definition body (two scopes removed from the outer or top-level scope of the program) has access to a global variable initialized at the top:

```
$gvar = "I'm a global!"
class C
  def examine_global
    puts $gvar
  end
end

c = C.new
c.new.examine_global
```

You'll be told by $gvar, in no uncertain terms, "I'm a global!" If you change all the occurrences of $gvar to a nonglobal, such as var, you'll see that the first var goes out of scope inside the method definition block.

Built-in global variables

The Ruby interpreter starts up with a fairly large number of global variables already initialized. These variables store information that's of potential use anywhere and everywhere in your program. For example, the global variable $0 contains the name of the file Ruby is executing. The global $: (dollar sign followed by a colon) contains the directories that make up the path Ruby searches when you load an external file. $$ contains the process id of the Ruby process. And there are more.

> **TIP**   LOOK AT English.rb FOR GLOBAL VARIABLE DESCRIPTIONS   A good place to see descriptions of all the built-in global variables you're likely to need—and then some—is the file English.rb in your Ruby installation. This file provides less cryptic names for the notoriously cryptic global variable set. (Don't blame Ruby for the names—most of them come from shell languages and/or Perl and awk.) If you want to use the slightly more friendly names in your programs, you can do require "English", after which you can refer to $IGNORECASE instead of $=, $PID instead of $$, and so forth.

The pros and cons of global variables

Global variables are tempting for beginning programmers and people learning a new language (not just Ruby, either). They appear to solve lots of design problems: You don't have to worry about scope, and multiple classes can share information by stashing it in globals rather than designing objects that have to be queried with method calls. Without doubt, global variables have a certain allure.

However, they're used very little by experienced programmers. The reasons for avoiding them are similar to the reasons they are tempting. Using global variables tends to end up being a substitute for solid, flexible program design, rather than contributing to it. One of the main points of object-oriented programming is that data and actions are encapsulated in objects. You're *supposed* to have to query objects for information and to request that they perform actions.

And objects are supposed to have a certain privacy. When you ask an object to do something, you're not supposed to care what the object does internally to get the job done. Even if *you* wrote the code for the object, when you send the object a message, you treat the object as a black box that works behind the scenes and provides a response.

Global variables distort the landscape by providing a layer of information shared by every object in every context. The result is that objects stop talking to each other and share information by setting global variables.

Here's a small example. Let's go back to our music store. We pick up the action in mid-program; let's say we have a `Work` object, and we want information from it. We'll assume the `Work` class already exists. Here, we're adding a method called `show_info` to it. Then we create a `Work` object, add some information to it, and ask it to show its information:

```
class Work      ◄────❶
  def show_info
    puts "Title and composer: #{title}, #{composer}"
  end
end

work = Work.new    ◄────❷
work.composer = "Giuseppe Verdi"    ◄──── Shortcut composer
work.title = "La Traviata"                object by using name
work.show_info
```

The `Work` class ❶ provides its instance (`work`) ❷ with the ability to store and retrieve information about itself (its state). From outside the class, we organize our code so that our queries and requests are all directed toward the `work` object.

Here's another version, using global variables:

```
class Work
  def show_info
    puts "Title and composer: #{$title}, #{$composer}"
  end
end

work = Work.new
$composer = "Giuseppe Verdi"
$title = "La Traviata"
work.show_info
```

This version still has a `Work` class and an instance of `Work`. But the information is handed around over the heads of the objects, so to speak, in a separate network of global variables. It's concise and easy, but it's also drastically limited. What would happen if you had lots of works? Or wanted to save a work, with all its internal information, to a database? Your code would quickly become tangled.

Globally scoped data is fundamentally in conflict with the object-oriented philosophy of endowing objects with abilities and then getting things done by sending requests to those objects. Some Ruby programmers work for years and never use a single global variable (except perhaps a few of the built-in ones). That may or may not end up being your experience, but it's not a bad target to aim for.

7.2.2 *Local scope*

Now that we've finished with the "try not to do this" part, let's move on to a detailed consideration of *local scope*. Local scope is part of the bread-and-butter of Ruby programming. At any given moment, *your program is in a particular local scope.* The main thing that changes from one local scope to another is your supply of local variables. When you leave a local scope—by returning from a method call, or by doing something that triggers a new local scope—you get a new supply. Even if you've assigned to a local variable x in one scope, you can assign to a new x in a new scope, and the two xs won't interfere with each other.

You can tell by looking at a Ruby program where the local scopes begin and end, based on a few rules:

- The top level (outside of all definition blocks) has its own local scope.
- Every class or module definition block (class, module) has its own local scope, *even nested class/module definition blocks.*
- Every method definition (def) has its own local scope.

Exceptions and additions to these rules exist, but they are fairly few and won't concern us right now.

Figure 7.2 shows the creation of a number of local scopes.Note that every time you cross into a class, module, or method definition block—every time you step over a def, class, or module keyword—you start a new local scope. Here's an example:

```
class C
  a = 1    ◁———❶
  def local_a
    a = 2    ◁———❷
    puts a
  end
  puts a    ◁———❸
end

c = C.new
c.local_a    ◁———❹
```

This code shows the following output:

```
1
2
```

The variable a that gets initialized in the local scope of the class definition ❶ is in a different scope than the variable a inside the method definition ❷. When you get to the puts a statement *after* the method definition ❸, you're back in the class definition local scope; the a that gets printed is the a you initialized back at the top, not the a that's in scope in the method definition. Meanwhile, that a isn't printed until later, when you've created a C instance and sent the message local_a to it ❹.

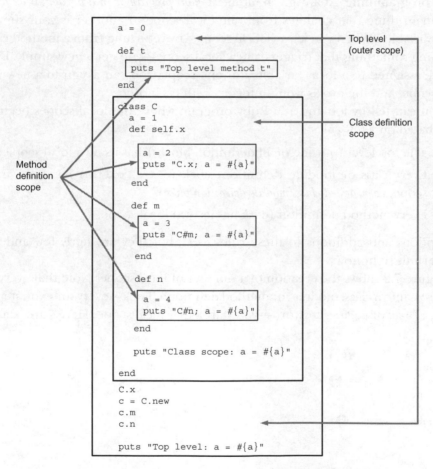

Figure 7.2   Schematic view of local scopes at the top level, the class-definition level, and the method-definition level

Keep in mind that a new local scope begins *every* time you introduce a definition block with the def, class, or module keyword. This is true no matter how they're nested. Listing 7.3 shows some deep nesting of classes and modules, with a number of variables called a being initialized and printed out along the way.

Listing 7.3   Reuse of a variable name in nested local scopes

```
class C
  a = 5
  module M
    a = 4
    module N
      a = 3
      class D
        a = 2
        def show_a
          a = 1
          puts a
        end
        puts a      <───── Output: 2
      end
      puts a      <───── Output: 3
    end
    puts a      <───── Output: 4
  end
  puts a      <───── Output: 5
end

d = C::M::N::D.new
d.show_a      <───── Output: 1
```

Every definition block, whether for a class, a module, or a method, starts a new local scope—a new local variable scratchpad—and gets its own variable a.

Local scope changes often, as you can see. So does the identity of self. Sometimes, but only sometimes, they vary together. The relationship between scope and self will be the focus of attention next.

Local scope and self

When you start a definition block (method, class, module), you start a new local scope, and you also create a block of code with a particular self. However, local scope and self don't operate entirely in parallel, not only because they're not the same thing but also because they're not the same *kind* of thing.

Consider this code snippet:

```
class C
  def x
    print "Here's the inspect-string for 'self':"
    p self
    a = "And I'm a different variable called 'a' each time!"
    puts a
  end
end

c = C.new
c.x
c.x
```

Yes, we've called x twice. Both times, inside the definition block, self is our object c. But *each time* the method is called, a new local scope is created. We call it once; we get a new local scope, in which we initialize a variable called a. That execution of the method ends, at which point that variable is no longer in scope and ceases to exist. Then we call the method again—and the same thing happens: a *new* local scope, with new, fresh variables. Once again we initialize a, but this a is unrelated to the a created when we called the method the first time. Self is the same object both times, as the snippet informs us:

```
Here's the inspect-string for 'self':#<C:0x40193c3c>
And I'm a different variable called 'a' each time!
Here's the inspect-string for 'self':#<C:0x40193c3c>
And I'm a different variable called 'a' each time!
```

It's also possible to change self without entering a new local scope, although that's a more advanced technique, and we won't look at it until somewhat later. The bottom line is that both scope and self tend to go through changes when program execution hits a definition block, and they always do so in logical and consistent ways—but not always in sync with each other.

Like variables, constants are governed by rules of scope. We'll look next at how those rules work.

7.2.3 *Scope and resolution of constants*

As you've seen, constants can be defined inside class and method definition blocks. If you know the chain of nested definitions, you can access a constant from anywhere:

```
module M
  class C
    class D
      module N
        X = 1
```

```
        end
      end
    end
end

puts M::C::D::N::X
```

This code digs all the way down the nest of modules and classes and prints the value you've asked for: 1.

Constants have a quasi-global nature: If you know the path to a constant through the classes and/or modules in which it's nested, you can find it from anywhere. However, on their own, constants are definitely not globals. The constant X in one scope isn't the constant X in another:

```
module M
  class C
    X = 2
    class D
      module N
        X = 1
      end
    end
  end
end

puts M::C::D::N::X
puts M::C::X
```

As per the nesting, the first `puts` gives you 1; the second gives you 2. A particular constant identifier (like X) doesn't have an absolute meaning the way a global variable (like $x) does.

Constant lookup—the process of resolving a constant identifier, finding the right match for it—bears a close resemblance to searching a filesystem for a file in a particular directory. For one thing, constants are identified *relative* to the point of execution. Another variant of our example illustrates this:

```
module M
  class C
    class D
      module N
        X = 1
      end
    end
    puts D::N::X
  end
end
```

Here, the identifier `D::N::X` is interpreted relative to where it occurs: inside the definition block of the class `M::C`. From `M::C`'s perspective, `D` is just one level away. There's no need to do `M::C::D::N::X`, when just `D::N::X` points the way down the path to the right constant. Sure enough, we get what we want: a printout of the number 1.

Forcing an absolute constant path

Sometimes you don't want a relative path. Sometimes you really want to start the constant lookup process at the top level—just as you sometimes need to use an absolute path for a file.

This may happen if you create a class or module with a name that's similar to the name of a Ruby built-in class or module. For example, Ruby comes with a `String` class. But if you create a `Violin` class, you may also have `String`s:

```
class Violin
  class String
    attr_accessor :pitch
    def initialize(pitch)
      @pitch = pitch
    end
  end

  def initialize
    @e = String.new("E")    ⟵ ❶
    @a = String.new("A")
    # etc.
```

The constant `String` in this context ❶ resolves to `Violin::String`, as defined. Now let's say that elsewhere in the overall `Violin` class definition, you need to refer to Ruby's built-in `String` class. If you have a plain reference to `String`, it will resolve to `Violin::String`. To make sure you're referring to the built-in, original `String` class, you need to put the constant path separator `::` (double colon) at the beginning of the class name:

```
def history
  ::String.new(maker + ", " + date)
end
```

This way, you'll get a Ruby `String` object instead of a `Violin::String` object. Like the slash at the beginning of a pathname, the `::` in front of a constant means *start the search for this at the top level*.

We have one more major subtopic to cover in the realm of who gets to do what where, and how, in Ruby programs. That subtopic is Ruby's system of *method access rules*.

7.3 *Deploying method access rules*

As you've seen, the main business of a Ruby program is to send messages to objects. And the main business of an object is to respond to messages. Sometimes an object wants to be able to send *itself* messages that it doesn't necessarily want anyone else to send it. For this scenario, Ruby provides the ability to make a method *private*.

There are two access levels other than private: *protected* and *public*. Public is the default access level; if you don't specify that a method is protected or private, then it's public. Public instance methods are the common currency of Ruby programming. Most of the messages you send to objects are calling public methods.

We'll focus here on methods that aren't public. Protected methods are a slight variant of private methods, so we'll look most closely at private methods.

7.3.1 *Private methods*

Think of an object as someone you ask to perform a task for you. Let's say you ask someone to bake you a cake. In the course of baking you a cake, the baker will presumably perform a lot of small tasks: measure sugar, crack an egg, stir batter, and so forth.

The baker can do, and does do, all these things. But not all of them have equal status when it comes to what the baker is willing to do *for other people, like you*. It would be weird if you called a baker and said, "Please stir some batter" or "Please crack an egg." What you say is, "Please bake me a cake," and you let the baker deal with the details. Object orientation is all about modeling behaviors, so let's model that behavior (loosely). We'll use minimal, placeholder classes for some of the objects in our domain, but we'll develop the Baker class a little further.

Save the code in listing 7.4 to a file called baker.rb.

Listing 7.4 Baker and other baking-domain classes

```
class Cake
  def initialize(batter)
    @batter = batter
    @baked = true
  end
end

class Egg
end

class Flour
end
```

```
class Baker
  def bake_cake
    @batter = []          ◁━━━━━━  Implement @batter as array
    pour_flour                     of objects (ingredients)
    add_egg
    stir_batter
    return Cake.new(@batter)  ◁━━━━  Return new Cake object
  end

  def pour_flour
    @batter.push(Flour.new)  ◁━━┓  Add element
  end                           ┗━ (ingredient) to @batter

  def add_egg
    @batter.push(Egg.new)
  end

  def stir_batter
  end

  private :pour_flour, :add_egg, :stir_batter  ◁━━━━ ❶

end
```

There's something new in this code: the `private` method ❶. As arguments to this method, you supply a list of methods you want to make private. (If you don't supply any arguments, the call to `private` will act like an "on-switch": all the instance methods you define below it, until you reverse the effect by calling `public` or `protected`, will be private.)

Private means that *the method can't be called with an explicit receiver.* You can't say

```
b = Baker.new
b.add_egg
```

As you'll see, calling `add_egg` this way results in a fatal error. `add_egg` is a private method, but you've specified the receiving object (`b`) explicitly. That's not allowed.

OK; let's go along with the rules. We won't specify a receiver. We'll just say

```
add_egg
```

But wait. Can we call `add_egg` in isolation? Where will the message go? How can a method be called if there's no object handling the message?

A little detective work will answer this question.

If you don't use an explicit receiver for a method call, Ruby assumes that you want to send the message to *the current object, self.* Thinking logically, we can conclude that add_egg has an object to go to only if self is an object that responds to "add_egg". In other words, you can only call the add_egg instance method of Baker when self is an instance of Baker.

And when is self an instance of Baker?

When any instance method of Baker is being executed. Therefore, inside the definition of bake_cake, you can call add_egg, and Ruby will know what to do. Whenever Ruby hits that call to add_egg inside that method definition, it will send the message "add_egg" to self, and self will be a Baker object.

It comes down to this: By tagging add_egg as private, you're saying the Baker object gets to send this message to itself (the baker can tell himself to add an egg to the batter), but no one else can send the message to the baker (you, as an outsider, can't tell the baker to add an egg to the batter). Ruby enforces this privacy through the mechanism of forbidding an explicit receiver. And the only circumstances under which you can omit the receiver arc precisely the circumstances in which it's OK to call a private method. It's all elegantly engineered.

WARNING PRIVATE AND SINGLETON ARE DIFFERENT It's important to note the difference between a *private method* and a *singleton method*. A singleton method is "private" in the loose, informal sense that it belongs to only one object, but it isn't private in the technical sense. (You can make a singleton method private, but by default it isn't.) A private, non-singleton instance method, on the other hand, may be shared by any number of objects but can only be called under the right circumstances. What determines whether you can call a private method isn't the object you're sending the message to, but which object is self at the time you send the message.

7.3.2 *Private methods as ActionController access protection*

Rails applications provide a great example of a place you may want to use private methods. A Rails *controller* object has a lot in common with a baker. Just as a baker has to know how to break eggs but doesn't field direct requests for breaking eggs, so a controller (in some cases) has to know how to do things for which it doesn't field direct requests.

Here's an example from a Rails-based site: http://www.rcrchive.net, the official site for Ruby Change Requests (RCRs). When you sign up for a new user account on RCRchive (which you're welcome to do, by the way, if you're interested in following the progress of discussions about possible changes to Ruby, or suggesting changes), you first connect to http://www.rcrchive.net/user/register, which you can reach directly or from a link on the homepage. Doing so triggers the `register` action in the user controller file (`user_controller.rb`). To register, you enter the username and password you want to use, and submit the form.

Assuming you haven't chosen a username that's already in use, the next thing you see is an acknowledgment screen, letting you know that you'll get confirmation email with instructions on how to activate your registration. This screen appears courtesy of the fact that the Submit button for registering triggers an `acknowledge` action, also in the user controller file.

The `acknowledge` action is associated with the `acknowledge` view (the template stored in `acknowledge.rhtml`), and that view contains the message about receiving email. In addition to rendering the view, `acknowledge` also triggers the sending of the email. This is done by calling another method, `invite`, which is also in the user controller file.

In abbreviated form (just the most relevant lines), the user controller file looks like this:

```
class UserController < ApplicationController
  def register
  end

  def acknowledge     ◁━━━━❶
    # here, create a new "applicant" object called "app"; then:
    invite(app)       ◁━━━━❷
  end

  # etc.
```

Note the call to the `invite` method ❷. This method sends the email to the applicant. It then returns (assuming it worked), and `acknowledge` ❶ proceeds to render its own ERb template. `invite` is a utility method, like `add_egg`. It's only of use to the `UserController` object that's handling the tasks. It would be pointless to allow the `invite` method to be triggered by itself. Just as you wouldn't ask a baker to crack an egg, you shouldn't ask the RCRchive Rails application to invite someone (send them email). That's the application's business.

The problem is, if you use the URL http://www.rcrchive.net/user/invite, the application's default behavior is to look inside the user controller and try to call a method called `invite` (just as it does with the methods you want it to call, like `acknowledge`). Called directly like that, the method will fail: It expects an argument, and calling it without one, via a URL, will cause a fatal error.

But there's another issue: security. What if someone figures out a way to get `invite` to execute? What if the method is rewritten in such a way that it doesn't crash when it's called from the outside world? By letting people connect to the `user/invite` action, you're doing the equivalent of letting them instruct a baker to break eggs. It isn't something they should be doing.

As with the baker and the eggs, the way around this situation is to make `invite` a private method. We'll continue where the previous code snippet left off. This second snippet also illustrates the "on-switch" use of `private` with no arguments.

```
private
def invite(app)
  # handle sending of email here
end
```

Being private, `invite` can only be called internally by the `UserController` instance. During execution of `acknowledge`, the call to `invite` works. But trying to trigger it from outside won't.

Ruby's private method mechanism makes it easy to layer your methods into those that the outside world should have access to and those that it shouldn't. Rails gives you ways to authenticate users and protect your application from rogue requests. But you can gatekeep at an early point with Ruby's rules for method access.

The most common access level is the public level. The second most common is probably private. There's one more access level, though, which serves a narrow but sometimes important purpose: protected.

7.3.3 Protected methods

A *protected method* is like a slightly kinder, gentler private method. The rule for protected methods is as follows: You can call an object's protected methods as long as the default object (self) is an instance of the same class as the object whose method you're calling.

This approach sounds convoluted. But it's generally used for a particular reason: You want one instance of a certain class to do something with another instance of its class. Listing 7.5 shows you such a case.

Listing 7.5 Example of a protected method and its use

```
class C

  def initialize(n)
    @n = n
  end

  def n
    @n
  end
```

```
  def compare(c)
    if c.n > n
      puts "The other object's n is bigger."
    else
      puts "The other object's n is the same or smaller."
    end
  end

  protected :n
end

c1 = C.new(100)
c2 = C.new(101)

c1.compare(c2)
```

The goal in listing 7.5 is to compare one C instance with another C instance. The comparison, however, depends on the result of a call to the method n. The object doing the comparing (c1, in the example) has to ask the other object (c2) to execute its n method. So, n can't be private.

That's where the protected level comes in. With n protected rather than private, c1 can ask c2 to execute n, because c1 and c2 are both instances of the same class. But if you try to call the n method of a C object when self is anything other than a C object, the method will fail.

A protected method is thus like a private method, but with an exemption for cases where the class of self (c1) and the class of the object having the method called on it (c2) are the same.

Inheritance and private methods

Subclasses inherit the method-access rules of their superclasses. Given a class C with a set of access rules, and a class D that's a subclass of C, instances of D will exhibit the same access behavior as instances of C. You can, however, set up new rules inside the class definition of D, in which case the new rules will take precedence for instances of D over the rules inherited from C.

The next and last topic we'll cover in this chapter is top-level methods. As you'll see, top-level methods enjoy a special case status. But even this status meshes logically with the aspects of Ruby's design we've encountered in this chapter.

7.4 *Writing and using top-level methods*

The most natural thing to do with Ruby is to design classes and modules, and instantiate your classes. But sometimes you just want to write a quick script—a few commands stuffed in a file and executed.

The files in the `script` directory of any Rails application give you some examples of scripts that consist solely of top-level programming instructions with no class or module definitions. These scripts perform tasks like starting up a Web server; creating a new controller, model, or view; or initiating an irb console session so you can test your program interactively. These more complex tasks rely on code with lots of class and modules definitions. The script files themselves configure a few settings and then fire up the larger software components.

A quick review of `main`: When you write code at the top level, Ruby provides you automatically with a default self—a default default object, so to speak. This object is a direct instance of `Object`. When you ask it to describe itself

```
puts self
```

it says:

```
main
```

The object `main` is like the backstop of a Ruby program: It's the farthest back you can fall. `main` is the current object as soon as your program starts up.

7.4.1 *Defining a top-level method*

Suppose you define a method at the top level:

```
def talk
  puts "Hello"
end
```

Who, or what, does the method belong to? It's not inside a class or module definition block, so it doesn't appear to be an instance method of a class or module. It's not attached to any particular object (as in `def obj.talk`), so it's not a singleton method. What is it?

By special decree (this is just the way it works!), top-level methods are *private instance methods of the* `Kernel` *module.*

That decree tells you a lot.

Because top-level methods are private, you can't call them with an explicit receiver; you can only call them by using the implied receiver, self. That means self must be an object on whose method search path the given top-level method lies.

But *every* object's search path includes the `Kernel` module, because the class `Object` mixes in `Kernel`, and every object's class has `Object` as an ancestor. That means you can *always* call any top-level method, wherever you are in your program. It also means you can *never* use an explicit receiver on a top-level method.

To illustrate this, let's extend the `talk` example. Here it is again, with some code that exercises it:

```
def talk
  puts "Hello"
end

puts "Trying 'talk' with no receiver..."
talk
puts "Trying 'talk' with an explicit receiver..."
obj = Object.new
obj.talk
```

The first call to `talk` succeeds; the second fails, because you're trying to call a private method with an explicit receiver.

The rules concerning definition and use of top-level methods brings us all the way back to some of the bareword methods we've been using since as early as chapter 1. You're now in a position to understand exactly how those methods work.

7.4.2 *Predefined (built-in) top-level methods*

From our earliest examples onward, we've been making bareword-style calls to `puts` and `print`, like this one:

```
puts "Hello"
```

`puts` *and* `print` *are built-in private instance methods of* `Kernel`. That's why you can—indeed, must—call them without a receiver. This constraint is a bit out of character for Ruby (where *object.method* is the usual idiom). On the other hand, it creates a category of general utility methods, like `puts` and `print`, that increase the power of Ruby as a scripting language. You can get a lot done with Ruby scripts that don't have any class, module, or method definitions, because you can do so much (print, read and write files, run system commands, exit your program, and so on) with Ruby's top-level methods.

If you want to see all of them, try this:

```
$ ruby -e 'print Kernel.private_instance_methods.sort'
```

You can add to the mix by writing your own top-level methods.

7.5 *Summary*

This chapter covered several important topics pertaining to the art of understanding *exactly* what's going on at a given point in a Ruby program. We talked about the rotating role of self (the current or default object) which serves as the receiver for method calls if no other receiver is explicitly named and which is the owner of all instance variables. We also looked closely at variable scope in Ruby—the matter of the visibility of variables, and the rules governing the separation of variables of the same name from each other—and at the rules for looking up constants from any scope.

We then examined Ruby's method access rules (public, private, protected), and saw that these rules are defined in terms of self, the class of self, and the identity and/or class of the receiver. Both self and method access also played key roles in the chapter's final topic: the workings of top-level methods.

The techniques in this chapter are of great importance to Ruby. Concepts like the difference between instance variables in a class definition and instance variables in an instance method definition are crucial and can easily be a source of misunderstanding. It's easy to look at a Ruby program and get a general sense of what's going on. But to understand a program in depth—and to write well-organized, robust programs—you need to know how to detect where the various local scopes begin and end, and how to evaluate the impact of Ruby's assignment of the role of self to a given object.

This chapter has shown you how to get your bearings in a Ruby program. It's also shown you some techniques you can use more accurately and effectively in your code by virtue of having your bearings. But there's more to explore, relating to what you can *do* in the landscape of a program, beyond understanding it. The next chapter, on the subject of *control flow*, will address some of these techniques.

Control flow techniques

In this chapter

- Conditional execution
- Loops and looping techniques
- Iterators
- Exceptions and error handling

206

As you've already seen in the case of method calls—where *control* of the program jumps from a line where the call is made, to the line or lines inside a method definition somewhere else—programs don't run in a straight line. Instead, execution order is determined by a variety of rules and programming techniques collectively referred to as *control flow* techniques.

Control flow techniques include the following:

- *Conditional execution*—Execution depends on the truth of an expression.
- *Looping*—A single segment of code is executed repeatedly.
- *Iteration*—A call to a method is supplemented with a block of code, which the method can call one or more times during its own execution.
- *Exceptions*—Error conditions are handled by special control-flow rules.

We'll look at each of these in turn. They are all indispensable to both the understanding and the practice of Ruby. The first, conditional execution (`if` and friends) is a fundamental (and easily understood) programming tool in almost any programming language. Looping is a more specialized but closely related technique, and Ruby provides you with several ways to do it.

When we get to iteration, we'll be in true Ruby hallmark territory. The technique isn't unique to Ruby, but it's a relatively rare programming language feature that figures prominently in Ruby. Finally, we'll look at Ruby's extensive mechanism for handling error conditions through exceptions. Exceptions stop the flow of a program, either completely or until the error condition has been dealt with. Exceptions are objects, and you can create your own exception classes, inheriting from the ones built in to Ruby, for specialized handling of error conditions in your programs. We'll discuss how the Rails framework uses this technique: A large number of exception classes are created to match, by name, the problems that can arise in the course of running a Rails application.

8.1 Conditional code execution

Allow a user access to a site if the password is correct. Print an error message unless the requested item exists. Concede defeat if the king is checkmated. The list of uses for controlling the flow of a program conditionally—executing specific lines or segments of code only if certain conditions are met—is endless. Without getting too philosophical, we might even say that decision-making based on unpredictable but discernible conditions is as common in programming as it is in life.

Ruby gives you a number of ways to control program flow on a conditional basis.

8.1.1 *The if keyword and friends*

The bread-and-butter tool of conditional execution, not surprisingly, is the `if` keyword. `if` clauses can take several forms. The simplest is the following:

```
if condition
  # code here, executed if condition evaluates to true
end
```

The code inside the conditional can be of any length, and can include nested conditional blocks.

You can also put an entire `if` clause on a single line. To do that, you need to insert a `then` keyword after the condition:

```
if x > 10 then puts x end
```

You can also use semicolons to mimic the line breaks, and to set off the `end` keyword:

```
if x > 10; puts x; end
```

As a special dispensation from Ruby, you can use a colon instead of `then`:

```
if x > 10: puts x; end
```

Conditional execution often involves more than one branch; you may want to do one thing if the condition succeeds and another if it doesn't. For example, *if the password is correct, let the user in; otherwise, print an error message.* Ruby makes full provisions for multiple conditional branches.

else and elsif

You can provide an `else` branch in your `if` statement:

```
if condition
  # code executed if condition is true
else
  # code executed if condition is false
end
```

There's also an `elsif` keyword (spelled like that, with no second e). `elsif` lets you cascade your conditional logic to more levels than you can with just `if` and `else`:

```
if condition1
  # code executed if condition1 is true
elsif condition2
  # code executed if condition1 is false
  # and condition2 is true
elsif condition3
  # code executed if neither condition1
  # nor condition2 is true, but condition3 is
end
```

You can have any number of `elsif` clauses in a given `if` statement. The code segment corresponding to the first successful `if` or `elsif` is executed, and the rest of the statement is ignored:

```
print "Enter an integer: "
n = gets.to_i
if n > 0
  puts "Your number is positive."
elsif n < 0
  puts "Your number is negative."
else
  puts "Your number is zero."
end
```

Note that you can use a final `else` even if you already have one or more `elsifs`. The `else` clause is executed if none of the previous tests for truth has succeeded. If none of the conditions is true and there is no `else` clause, the whole `if` statement terminates with no action.

unless

Sometimes you want an `if` condition to be negative: *if something isn't true, then execute a given segment of code.* You can do this in several ways. One of them is to use the `not` keyword:

```
if not (x == 1)
```

The parentheses help keep the code clear when keywords proliferate.

You can also use the negating `!` (exclamation point, or *bang*) operator:

```
if !(x == 1)
```

A third way to express a negative condition uses `unless`:

```
unless x == 1
```

This syntax gives you a more natural-sounding way to express `if not` or `if !`.

Some else tips

It pays to keep careful track of your `else` and `elsif` statements. In particular, note that `else if`—a legitimate expression, which starts a new `if` statement inside an `else` clause—isn't the same as `elsif`, which is a branch of the `if` statement that's already open.

You also have to keep track of your `elses`. The fact that Ruby requires an `end` keyword at the end of every `if` clause can help you see what's going on, in cases that might otherwise be ambiguous. This applies, for example, to the oft-cited if/else ambiguity that arises when you have nested ifs. In some languages, you can't tell without a special rule what belongs with what. In C, for example, an if statement might look like this:

```
if (x)
    if (y) { execute this code }
    else   { execute this code };   ◁──────  x is true, but y isn't
```

But wait: Does the code behave the way the indentation indicates (the else belongs to the second if)? Or does it work like this:

```
if (x)
    if (y){ execute this code }
else { execute this code };   ◁──────  x isn't true
```

All that's changed is the indentation of the third line—and that won't matter to the C compiler, but it indicates the ambiguity visually. Which if does the else belong to? And how do you tell?

You tell by knowing the rule in C: A dangling else goes with the last unmatched if (the first of the two behaviors in this example). In Ruby, you have end to help you out:

```
if x > 50
  if x > 100
    puts "Big number"
  else
    puts "Medium number"
  end
end
```

The single else in this statement has to belong to the second if, because that if hasn't yet hit its end. The first if and the last end always belong together, the second if and the second-to-last end always belong together, and so forth. The if/end pairs encircle what belongs to them, including else. Of course, this means you have to place your end keywords correctly.

Also watch out for else with unless. You can use this combination, but it looks and sounds a little weird:

```
unless x > 100
  puts "Small number!"
else
  puts "Big number!"
end
```

unless/else doesn't harmonize with regular English-language usage the way if/else does, and it's easy to trip over the logic of unless/else (especially if it's nested). In general, if/else reads better than unless/else—and by flipping the logic of the condition, you can always replace the latter with the former:

```
if x <= 100
  puts "Small number!"
else
  puts "Big number!"
end
```

If you come across a case where negating the logic seems more awkward than pairing unless with else, then keep unless. Otherwise, if you have an else clause, if is generally a better choice than unless.

8.1.2 Conditional modifiers

You can put conditionals in a *modifier* position, directly after a statement, in which case they operate on the statement. For example:

```
puts "Big number!" if x > 100
```

This is the same as

```
if x > 100
  puts "Big number!"
end
```

You can also do this with unless:

```
puts "Big number!" unless x <= 100
```

Conditional modifiers have a conversational tone. There's no end to worry about. You can't do as much with them (no else or elsif branching), but when you need a simple conditional, they're often a good fit.

8.1.3 Case statements

Ruby has another way to make code branch on the truth or falsehood of conditions: the case statement. A case statement starts with an expression—usually a single object or variable, but any expression can be used—and walks it through a list of possible matches. Each possible match is contained in a when expression consisting of one or more possible matches and a segment of code. When a given when expression matches, it's considered to have won, and its code segment is executed.

case statements are easier to grasp by example than description. Listing 8.1 shows a case statement that tests a line of keyboard input and branches based on its value.

Listing 8.1 Interpreting user input with a `case` statement

```
print "Exit the program? (yes or no): "
answer = gets.chomp
case answer         ←——————1
when "yes"          ←———————2
  puts "Good-bye!"
  exit
when "no"
  puts "OK, we'll continue"
else  ←————3
  puts "That's an unknown answer -- assuming you meant 'no'"
end  ←————4
```

The `case` statement begins with the `case` keyword **1**, continues through all the
`when` blocks **2** and an `else` clause **3**, and ends with the `end` keyword **4**. At most,
one match will succeed; only one `when` expression will be executed.

You can put more than one possible match in a single `when`, as this snippet shows:

```
case answer
when "y", "yes"
  puts "Good-bye!"
  exit
# etc.
```

This code will say "Good-bye!" and exit if `answer` is either "y" or "yes".

How when works

The basic idea of the `case`/`when` structure is that you take an object and cascade
through a series of tests for a match, taking action based on the test that succeeds.
But what does *match* mean in this context? What does it mean, in our example, to
say that `answer` matches the word "yes", or the word "no", or neither?

Ruby has a concrete definition of match when it comes to `when` statements.
Every Ruby object has a *case equality* method called `===` (three equal signs, sometimes called the "threequal operator"). The outcome of calling the method determines whether a `when` clause has matched.

You can see this clearly if you look first at a `case` statement and then at a translation of this statement into threequal terms. Look again at the `case` statement in
our previous example. Here's the same thing (in effect, the same program code)
rewritten to show how the threequal method works, and also to illustrate some
nice syntactic sugar you get when you use the `===` method:

```
if "yes" === answer  ←       Syntactic sugar for the method call:
  puts "Good-bye!"             if "yes".===(answer)
```

```
   exit
elsif "no" === answer
  puts "OK, we'll continue"
else
  puts "That's an unknown answer—assuming you meant 'no'"
end
```

when is really a wrapper—syntactic sugar on top of sugar, if you like—for a call to the method ===. But why does

```
"yes" === answer
```

return true when answer contains "yes"?

It happens because of how the threequal method is defined for strings. When you ask a string to threequal against another string (string1 === string2), you're asking it to compare its own contents character by character against the other string and report back true for a perfect match or false otherwise.

The most important point in this explanation is the phrase *for strings*. Every class (and, in theory, every individual object, although it's usually handled at the class level) can define its own === method. Objects of that class will then perform the threequal test (the case equality test) based on how === is defined. For strings, === works the same as == (the basic string-equals-some-other-string test method). But other classes can define the threequal test any way they want.

case/when logic is object === other_object logic in disguise; and object === other_object is object.===(other_object) in disguise. By defining the threequal method however you wish for your own classes, you can exercise complete control over the way your objects behave inside a case statement.

Programming objects' case statement behavior

Let's say we decide that a Ticket object should match a *when* clause in a case statement based on its venue. We can bring this about by writing the appropriate threequal method. Listing 8.2 shows such a method, bundled with enough ticket functionality to make a complete working example.

> **Listing 8.2   Implementing case statement behavior for the Ticket class**

```
class Ticket
  attr_accessor :venue, :date
  def initialize(venue, date)
    self.venue = venue
    self.date = date
  end

  def ===(other_ticket)    ◁——❶
```

```
      self.venue == other_ticket.venue
    end
  end

ticket1 = Ticket.new("Town Hall", "07/08/06")
ticket2 = Ticket.new("Conference Center", "07/08/06")
ticket3 = Ticket.new("Town Hall", "08/09/06")

puts "ticket1 is for an event at: #{ticket1.venue}."

case ticket1
  when ticket2    <------②
    puts "Same location as ticket2!"
  when ticket3    <------③
    puts "Same location as ticket3!"
  else
    puts "No match"
end
```

The output from listing 8.2 is as follows:

```
ticket1 is for an event at: Town Hall.
Same location as ticket3!
```

The match was found through the implicit use of the === instance method of the Ticket class ①. Inside the case statement, the first when expression ② triggers a hidden call to ===, equivalent to doing this:

```
if ticket2 === ticket1
```

Because the === method returns true or false based on a comparison of venues, and ticket2's venue isn't the same as ticket1's, the comparison between the two tickets returns false. The body of the corresponding when clause is therefore not executed.

The next test is then performed: another threequal or case-equality comparison between ticket1 and ticket3 ③. This test returns true; that when expressions succeeds, and the code in its body is executed.

This kind of interflow between method definitions (===) and code that doesn't look like it's calling methods (case/when) is typical of Ruby. The case/when structure provides an elegant way to perform cascaded conditional tests; and the fact that it's a bunch of === calls means you can make it do what you need by defining the === method in your classes.

Conditionals like if and case/when let you control program flow by doing one thing instead of another. Sometimes, however, you need to perform a single task again and again. This kind of repetition can be accomplished with loops, which we'll look at next.

8.2 *Repeating actions with loops*

Ruby's facilities for looping repeatedly through code also allow you to incorporate conditional logic: You can loop *while* a given condition is true (such as a variable being equal to a given value), and you can loop *until* a given condition is true. You can also break out of a loop *unconditionally*, terminating the loop at a certain point and resume execution of the program after the loop.

We'll look at several ways to loop—starting, appropriately, with a method called `loop`.

8.2.1 *Unconditional looping with the loop method*

The `loop` method doesn't take any normal arguments: You just call it. However, it does take a special type of argument called a *code block*. This code block contains the code you want to loop through. Code blocks can be written in one of two ways: either in curly braces (`{}`) or with the keywords `do` and `end`. The following two snippets are equivalent:

```
loop { puts "Looping forever!" }
loop do puts "Looping forever!" end
```

A loose convention holds that one-line code blocks use the curly braces, and multi-line blocks use `do`/`end`. (If we were observing that convention, we'd use the first of the versions shown here in preference to the second.) But Ruby doesn't enforce this convention.

> **NOTE** THE DIFFERENCE BETWEEN do/end AND {} The two ways of delimiting a code block (`do`/`end` and `{}`) aren't interchangeable: They differ in the matter of *precedence*. When you have a complex statement that involves multiple method calls chained together, and code blocks are involved, the choice of delimiter has a bearing on what is executed in what order and which method call goes with which block. In the vast majority of cases, you don't have to worry about this. But it's useful to know that the two approaches aren't quite identical, as you start to use code blocks more (see section 8.3).

Code blocks will loom large as we proceed through the book—indeed, by the end of this chapter. You'll learn much more about what they are, when you use them, and what they enable you to do. For now, though, we'll just plug them in and watch them go.

Controlling the loop

Generally, you don't want a loop to loop forever; you want it to stop at some point. One way to stop the loop is with the `break` keyword, as in this admittedly verbose approach to setting n to 10:

```
n = 1
loop do
  n = n + 1
  break if n > 9
end
```

Another technique skips to the next iteration of the loop without finishing the current iteration. To do this, you use the keyword `next`:

```
n = 1
loop do
  n = n + 1
  next unless n == 10
  break
end
```

Here, control falls through to the `break` statement only if n == 10 is true. If n == 10 is *not* true (`unless n == 10`), the `next` is executed, and control jumps back to the beginning of the loop before it reaches `break`.

You can also loop conditionally: *while* a given condition is true, or *until* a condition becomes true.

8.2.2 Conditional looping with the while and until keywords

Conditional looping is achieved via the keywords `while` and `until`, which, like `if` and `unless`, branch on the truth or falsehood of a condition but can go through the process more than once.

while

The `while` keyword allows you to run a loop while a given condition is true. `while` has to be paired with `end`. The code between the `while` clause and `end` is the body of the loop. Here's an example:

```
n = 1
while n < 11
  puts n
  n = n + 1
end
puts "Done!"
```

This code prints the following:

```
1
2
3
4
5
6
7
8
9
10
Done!
```

As long as the condition n < 11 is true, the loop executes. Inside the loop, n is incremented by one. The eleventh time the condition is tested, it's false (n is no longer less than 11), and the execution of the loop terminates.

You can also place `while` at the end of a loop. In this case, you need to use the keyword pair `begin`/`end` to mark where the loop is (otherwise, Ruby won't know how many of the lines previous to the `while` you want to include in the loop):

```
n = 1
begin
  puts n
  n = n + 1
end while n < 11
puts "Done!"
```

The output from this example is the same as the output from the previous example.

There is a difference between putting `while` at the beginning and putting it at the end. If you put `while` at the beginning, and if the `while` condition is false, the code isn't executed:

```
n = 10
while n < 10
  puts n
end
```

Because n is already greater than 10 when the test n < 10 is performed the first time, the body of the statement isn't executed. However, if you put the `while` test at the end:

```
n = 10
begin
  puts n
end while n < 10
```

the number 10 is printed. Obviously n isn't less than 10 at any point. But because the `while` test is positioned at the end of the statement, the body is executed once before the test is performed.

until

Like `if` and `unless`, the conditional loop keywords come as a pair: `while` and `until`. `until` is used the same way as `while`, but with reverse logic. Here's another labor-intensive way to print out the integers from one to 10, this time illustrating the use of `until`:

```
n = 1
until n > 10
  puts n
  n = n + 1
end
```

The body of the loop (the printing and incrementing of n, in this example) is executed repeatedly *until* the condition is true.

while and until as modifiers

You can use `while` and `until` as modifiers at the end of a statement, like `if` and `unless`:

```
n = 1
n = n + 1 until n == 10
puts "We've reached 10!"
```

In place of the `until` statement, you could also use `while n < 10`.

8.2.3 *Looping based on a list of values*

We've looked at unconditional looping (`loop`) and conditional looping (`while`, `until`). Another way to loop is to go through a list of values, running the loop once for each value. For example, let's say you want to print a chart of Fahrenheit equivalents of Celsius values. You can do this by putting the Celsius values in an array and then looping through the array using the `for/in` keyword pair. The loop runs once *for* each value *in* the array; each time through, that value is assigned to a variable you specify:

```
celsius = [0, 10, 20, 30, 40, 50, 60, 70, 80, 90, 100]
puts "Celsius\tFahrenheit"          ◁          Header for chart
for c in celsius                               (\t prints a tab)
  puts "c\t#{Temperature.c2f(c)}"
end
```

The body of the loop (the `puts` statement) runs 11 times. The first time through, the value of c is 0. The second time, c is 10; the third time, it's 20; and so forth.

`for` is a powerful tool. Oddly enough, though, on closer inspection it turns out that `for` is just an alternate way of doing something even more powerful….

8.3 *Code blocks, iterators, and the yield keyword*

The control-flow techniques we've looked at so far involve controlling how many times, or under what conditions, a segment of code gets executed. In this section, we'll examine a different kind of flow control facility. The techniques we'll discuss here don't just perform an execute-or-skip operation on a segment of code; they bounce control of the program from one scope to another, and back again.

It may sound like we've gone back to talking about method calls. After all, when you call a method on an object, control is passed to the body of the method (a different scope), and when the method has finished executing, control returns to the point right after the point where the method call took place.

We *are* back in method-call territory, but we're exploring new aspects of it, not just revisiting the old. We're talking about a new construct called a *code block* and a keyword by the name of `yield`.

8.3.1 *The basics of yielding to a block*

We've seen method calls, both with and without arguments. What we haven't seen (or, more accurately, have only seen in passing, in some of the loop examples in section 8.2.2) is another optional component of a Ruby method call: the code block.

When you call a method—any method, any time, with or without arguments—you have the option of supplying a code block. The code block can consist of any number of lines of Ruby code. This code is wrapped either in curly braces, like this

```
object.method_name {
   # code inside block
}
```

or in a do/end keyword pair, like this:

```
object.method_name do
   # code inside block
end
```

But *why* would you add a block of code to a method call? You'd do it so that your method can yield.

The yield keyword in action

If you provide a code block when you call a method, then *inside the method*, you can yield control to that code block—suspend execution of the method; execute the code in the block; and return control to the method body, right after the call to `yield`.

It's like a backward method call. Calling a method causes control to jump from the line containing the call to the method body. The `yield` keyword causes control to jump from the method body back to the code block sitting next to the method call.

Listing 8.3 shows an example: a method called `demo_of_yield`, which performs a yield operation. We'll call it with a code block.

Listing 8.3   Demonstration of calling a method and yielding control back to the code block

```
def demo_of_yield
  puts "Executing the method body..."        <——❶
  puts "About to yield control to the block..."
  yield  <——❷
  puts "Back from the block—finished!"        <——❸
end

demo_of_yield { puts "> Control has been passed to the block!" }  <——❹
```

The output from this code is as follows:

```
Executing the method body...
About to yield control to the block...
> Control has been passed to the block!
Back from the block—finished!
```

When we call the method `demo_of_yield`, program control jumps to the body of the method, and the first two `puts` statements ❶ are executed. The method yields ❷ to the code block ❹; the code block is, syntactically, part of the *method call*, not part of the method, and therefore it's physically (or lexically) detached from the method.

The code inside the block (a single `puts` statement) is executed, after which the block is finished. Control returns to the body of the method at the point immediately after the `yield` ❸.

A method call in Ruby may involve passing around arguments, and it can also involve the transfer of control back and forth between the method body and the context of the method call. Any amount of back-and-forth is possible; a method can yield more than once, and, as you'll see, most methods that yield at all yield repeatedly.

Now, let's look more closely at the behavior of our new construct, the code block.

Passing arguments to a code block

Code blocks have a lot in common with methods. Both consist of lines of code; both get executed, one by being called directly, one by being yielded to. (There's a way to call code blocks directly, but we won't get into that until chapter 13.)

Like a method, a code block can take arguments. You send arguments to a code block by supplying them to `yield`. To yield three arguments to a block, you do this inside your method:

```
yield(x,y,z)
```

There is, however, a twist in the way the block specifies the arguments it wants. Methods do this with parenthetical lists of variable names for the arguments:

```
def meth(a,b,c)
```

Code blocks have a different syntax; instead of parentheses, they use a pair of pipes (| |):

```
some_method {|a,b,c|
  # code here
  }
```

In addition, there are differences between the way methods handle method arguments and the way blocks handle block arguments. We'll discuss that later. For the moment, you need to become accustomed to seeing code like this:

```
def yield_an_arg
  puts "Yielding 10!"
  yield(10)
end
```

```
yield_an_arg {|x| puts "> Code block received this argument: #{x}" }
```

The value 10 is yielded to the code block, where it's assigned to the variable x (as seen in the argument list, between the pipes).

Returning a value from a code block

Code blocks would be of limited use if they didn't have the ability to return values as well as accept arguments.

A code block's return value (like that of a method) is the value of the last expression evaluated in the code block. This return value is made available inside the method; it comes through as the return value of `yield`:

```
def more_yielding
  puts "The code block shall multiply a number by 10."
  result = yield(3)
  puts "The result of this operation is #{result}."
end
```

```
more_yielding {|x| x * 10 }
```

Here, the block receives an argument, assigns it to the variable x, and returns the value x * 10. In this example, the method is hard-coded to yield 3. You could write it so that it yielded a number input from the keyboard, a random number, or each number in a list. Whatever the method yields, the block multiplies by 10.

8.3.2 *Performing multiple iterations*

The process of yielding from a method to a block is called *iteration*, and any method that yields to a block is called an *iterator*. Iteration implies something repeated: You iterate through a list or over a collection of objects. And, as you'll see, most methods that use `yield` do yield multiple times. The method fires values at the code block like an automatic baseball-pitching machine. The code block does something with each value and returns the result.

We can see this pattern in action by rewriting our temperature chart to use `yield`. The new version is shown in listing 8.4.

Listing 8.4   Temperature conversion method using a code block to perform the conversion

```
def temp_chart(temps)        ❶
  for temp in temps           ❷
    converted = yield(temp)    ❸
    puts "#{temp}\t#{converted}"     ❹
  end
end


celsiuses = [0,10,20,30,40,50,60,70,80,90,100]     ❺
temp_chart(celsiuses) {|cel| cel * 9 / 5 + 32 }     ❻
```

Here's what's happening in this example:

- The method `temp_chart` ❶ takes an argument: a list (array) of Celsius temperatures.

- The temperatures we're going to convert are stashed in an array ❺ assigned to the variable `celsiuses`, and `temp_chart` is called ❻ with `celsiuses` as an argument—and with a code block provided.

- Inside the method, a `for` loop ❷ goes through the array of temperatures. Each time through the loop, the next value in the array is assigned to the variable `temp`. `temp` is then yielded ❸ to the code block. The return value from the block is assigned to the variable `converted`.

- Inside the code block ❻, the yielded argument is assigned to the variable `cel`. The first time through, `cel` is 0. The next time it's 10, and so forth.

- The code inside the block converts `cel` to Fahrenheit and returns the result.
- Back in `temp_chart`, the conversion results are printed ❹. We get one result printed out for each value in the array of Celsius temperatures.

In effect, we've split the work of temperature conversion between a method and a code block, and we get the work done by going back and forth between them.

This may not seem like much of a gain; after all, we could do the same thing using a method. But the division of labor between method and code block pays dividends when you start matching different blocks with a single method.

8.3.3 *Using different code blocks*

Ruby's code block mechanism means you can share the authorship of a method, even if you didn't write the method. The method farms out some of its own work to the code block you provide.

An important implication of this behavior is that you can use code blocks to put the finishing touches on methods that don't have completely defined behavior. That's what the yielding or iterating mechanism offers: a way to postpone final implementation of a method until you call the method and supply the missing bit of code.

Look at the temperature example. The method `temp_chart` *doesn't do any temperature conversion*. All it does is yield values to a code block and print out the results it gets back. The method operates in a partnership with the code block. It's in the code block that the conversion takes place.

We could use the same method to convert temperatures the other way:

```
fahrens = [32,62,92,122,152,182,212]
temp_chart(fahrens) {|fahr| (fahr - 32) * 5 / 9 }
```

`temp_chart` fires the values at the block and prints out a chart of what comes back. It doesn't care what the block does. C to F, F to C—it's all the same, as far as the method is concerned.

8.3.4 *More about for*

When you first learned about doing

```
for x in array of values
  code
end
```

you were told that, oddly enough, `for` is an alternate way of doing something even more powerful. That led us straight into iterators: `yield`. And yes, that means `for` is really an iterator in disguise.

`for` is an alternate way of calling a special iterator called `each`. A number of Ruby objects respond to the `each` message. `for` does it for them.

The following two snippets are equivalent:

```
for x in [1,2,3,4,5]
  puts x * 10
end
```

and

```
[1,2,3,4,5].each {|x| puts x * 10 }    ◁────❶
```

What you're not seeing is the method body of `each`—in this case, `Array#each` (because `[1,2,3,4,5]` is an array). `Array#each` is written in C; it's part of the core C implementation of Ruby (and it could be written in Ruby easily). It goes through the array, one item at a time, and *yields* the current item. In this example, the code block ❶ accepts each item as it's yielded and returns that item multiplied by 10.

Every `for` statement is a wrapper around a call to `each`. Some people prefer the look and feel of the `for` version. In particular, it seems to crop up a lot in ERb files. You may see code like this in an ActionView template file:

```
<% for s in @students %>
  <%= link_to s.name,
     :controller => "student",
     :action    => "grade",
     :id        => s.id %>
<% end %>
```

rather than this:

```
<% @students.each do |s| %>
 <%= link_to s.name,
   # etc.
<% end %>
```

although you'll definitely see both. The `for` idiom is more familiar to programmers accustomed to languages other than Ruby; `each`, on the other hand, blends a little better with other Ruby idioms. You can take your pick.

So far, we've been surveying a cooperative landscape. Everything works so nicely … but that's not always the way it goes. Unexpected results happen when programs run—and not just at the level of an `if` test returning false. When things go seriously wrong, programs need to react; and reacting to error conditions often involves special kinds of control flow intervention. We'll look next at Ruby facilities for reacting to, and handling, error conditions.

8.4 *Error handling and exceptions*

Way back in chapter 1, we looked at how to test code for syntax errors:

```
$ ruby -cw filename.rb
```

Passing the -cw test means Ruby can run your program. But it doesn't mean nothing will go wrong while your program is running. You can write a syntactically correct program—a program that the interpreter will accept and execute—that does all sorts of unacceptable things. Ruby handles unacceptable behavior at runtime by *raising an exception.*

8.4.1 *Raising and rescuing exceptions*

An *exception* is a special kind of object, an instance of the class Exception or a descendant of that class. *Raising* an exception means stopping normal execution of the program and either dealing with the problem that's been encountered or exiting the program completely.

Which of these happens—dealing with it or aborting the program—depends on whether you have provided a rescue clause. If you haven't provided such a clause, the program terminates; if you have, control flows to the rescue clause.

To see exceptions in action, try dividing by zero:

```
$ ruby -e '1/0'
```

Ruby raises an exception:

```
-e:1:in `/': divided by 0 (ZeroDivisionError)
        from -e:1
```

ZeroDivisionError is the name of this particular exception. More technically, it's the name of a class—a descendant class of the class Exception. Ruby has a whole family tree of exceptions, all of them going back eventually to Exception.

Some common exceptions

Table 8.1 shows some common exceptions (each of which is a class, descended from Exception) along with common reasons they are raised and an example of code that will raise each one.

You can try these examples in irb; you'll get an error message, but the session shouldn't terminate. The technique irb uses to make potentially fatal errors nonfatal is available to you, too.

Table 8.1 Common exceptions

Exception name	Common reason(s)	How to raise it
RuntimeError	This is the default exception raised by the `raise` method.	`raise`
NoMethodError	An object is sent a message it can't resolve to a method name.	`a = Object.new` `a.some_unknown_method_name`
NameError	The interpreter hits an identifier it can't resolve as a variable or method name.	`a = some_random_identifier`
IOError	This is caused by reading a closed stream, writing to a read-only stream, and similar operations.	`STDIN.puts("Don't write to STDIN!")`
Errno::error	This family of errors relates to file IO.	`File.open(-12)`
TypeError	A method receives an argument it can't handle.	`a = 3 + "can't add a string to a number!"`
ArgumentError	This is caused by using the wrong number of arguments.	`def m(x); end; m(1,2,3,4,5)`

rescue to the rescue!

Having an exception raised doesn't have to mean your program terminates. You can handle exceptions—deal with the problem and keep the program running—by means of the rescue keyword.

You rescue yourself from an exception by using a rescue *block*. There are two ways to create such a block:

- Wrap the code you want to protect in a begin/end pair.
- To protect an entire method definition, you only need a rescue clause, placed last inside the method definition body.

Here's an example of a rescue block with begin/end:

```
print "Enter a number: "
n = gets.to_i

begin
  result = 100 / n
rescue
  puts "Your number didn't work. Was it zero???"
  exit
end

puts "100/#{n} is #{result}."
```

If you run this program and enter 0 as your number, the division operation (100/n) raises a ZeroDivisionError. Because you've done this inside a rescue block, control is passed to the rescue part of the block. An error message is printed out, and the program exits.

If you enter something other than 0 and the division succeeds, program control skips over the rescue statement and block, and execution resumes thereafter (with the call to puts).

You can refine this technique by pinpointing the exception you want to trap. Instead of a generic rescue instruction, you tell rescue what to rescue:

```
rescue ZeroDivisionError
```

This traps a single type of exception, but not others. The advantage is that you're no longer running the risk of inadvertently covering up some other problem by rescuing it. An open-ended rescue may cast too wide a net.

In addition to trapping exceptions, you can also raise them in your own code. We'll look next at some techniques for doing this.

8.4.2 *Raising exceptions explicitly*

When it comes to Ruby's traditional flexibility and compact coding power, exceptions are, so to speak, no exception. You can raise exceptions in your own code, and you can create new exceptions to raise.

To raise an exception, you use raise plus the name of the exception you wish to raise. You can also give raise a second argument, which is used as the message string when the exception is raised:

```
def fussy_method(x)
  raise ArgumentError, "I need a number under 10" unless x < 10
end

fussy_method(20)
```

If run from a file called fussy.rb, this code prints out the following:

```
fussy.rb:2:in `fussy_method':
  I need a number under 10 (ArgumentError) from fussy.rb:5
```

You can also use rescue in such a case:

```
begin
  fussy_method(20)
rescue ArgumentError
  puts "That was not an acceptable number!"
end
```

By only rescuing `ArgumentError`, you ensure that if anything else goes wrong and some other exception is raised, you won't trap it. That way, you don't inadvertently mask problems by rescuing excessively.

Re-raising an exception is a useful technique. The idea is that your code has a `rescue` block, and thus handles the exception—but you also pass the exception along for further handling from wherever your code was called:

```
def reraiser(filename)
  file_handle = File.new(filename)
rescue Errno::ENOENT => e   ◁———————❶
  puts "Something's wrong with your filename...."   ◁————❷
  raise e
end
```

This is an example of how to rescue exceptions through the whole body of a method definition. You don't have to include explicit `begin`/`end` delimiters, as long as the `rescue` clause is the last thing in the method; the method's own `end` serves as the `end`, and the `begin` is implied. (If you want a rescue scenario for only part of a method definition, you need to reintroduce the `begin`/`end` delimiters.)

The major new technique introduced in this example (and the main point here) is the fancy `rescue` line ❶. The `=> e` construct puts the `Exception` object into the variable `e`. Once you've stored the exception in a variable, you can do whatever else you want inside your `rescue` clause (in this case, printing out a vague, ominous error message ❷) and then re-raise the exception by raising `e`. This re-raise bubbles up to wherever your method was called from. For example, this call to our method

```
reraiser("some_non_existent_filename")
```

outputs the following:

```
Something's wrong with your filename....   ◁———❶
reraiser.rb:2:in `initialize': No such file
  or directory - some_non_existent_filename
    (Errno::ENOENT)   ◁———❷
```

First, the `rescue` clause intercepts the exception and prints out its message ❶. Then, the exception is re-raised, and this time ❷ it isn't rescued.

When it comes to the types of exceptions you can raise and rescue, you aren't limited to Ruby's built-in exception classes. You can also create your own.

8.4.3 *Creating your own exception classes*

You create a new exception class by inheriting from `Exception` or from a descendant class of `Exception`:

```
class MyNewException < Exception
end
```

```
raise MyNewException, "some new kind of error has occurred!"
```

This technique offers two primary benefits. First, by letting you give new names to exception classes, it performs a self-documenting function: When a MyNew-Exception gets raised, it will be distinct from, say, a ZeroDivisionError or a plain vanilla RuntimeError.

Second, this approach lets you pinpoint your rescue operations. Once you've created MyNewException, you can rescue it by name:

```
class MyNewException < Exception
end

begin
  puts "About to raise exception..."
  raise MyNewException
rescue MyNewException => e
  puts "Just raised an exception: #{e}"
end
```

The output from this snippet is as follows:

```
About to raise exception...
Just raised an exception: MyNewException
```

Only MyNewException errors will be trapped by that rescue clause. If another exception is raised first for any reason, it will result in program termination without rescue.

Exceptions and their names in the Rails framework

Creating new exception classes with descriptive names can help document errors when they happen. In the Rails framework, the major components define a number of exception classes, each of which has a name that tells you what went wrong even before you see an associated message. For example, the ActiveController library defines exception classes called UnknownAction, UnknownController, and MissingTemplate, among others. (All of these descend from the intermediate class ActionControllerError, which is a subclass of the built-in StandardError class.) The names of the exceptions thus serve as documentation of what went wrong.

For example, in the method perform_action, which is the main control tower for directing the execution of the method corresponding to the action requested through the URL, you'll see this as one of several options:

```
raise UnknownAction,
  "No action responded to #{action_name}", caller
```

This option is executed if the controller can't find an action corresponding to the request or a same-named template it can render.

How much or how little of this you do in your own code will depend on your needs. A Rails application may not need to define any more exception classes than Ruby and Rails already provide. If you're writing other Ruby programs, you may want to create a new exception class. On the other hand, the exception classes Ruby provides are useable in a lot of situations, as the earlier examples with `ArgumentError` and `Errno::ENOENT` suggested.

If you think of new exception classes principally as a way of letting users and other programmers see your intentions and the nature of a problem more clearly, you'll be able to make reasonable decisions about how often to create them.

8.5   *Summary*

This chapter has covered several wide-ranging topics, all bundled together because they have in common the fact that they involve control flow. Conditionals (`if`/`unless` and `case`/`when`) move control around based on the truth or falsehood of expressions. Loops (`loop`, `for`, and `while`/`until`) repeat a segment of code either unconditionally, conditionally, or once for each item in a list.

Iterators—methods that yield to a code block you provide alongside the call to the method—are among Ruby's most distinctive features. You've learned how to write and call an iterator, techniques you'll encounter frequently later in this book (and beyond).

Finally, we looked at exceptions, Ruby's mechanism for handling unrecoverable error conditions. *Unrecoverable* is relative: You can rescue an error condition and continue execution, but you have to stage a deliberate intervention via a `rescue` block and thus divert and gain control of the program where otherwise it would terminate. You can also create your own exception classes through inheritance from the built-in Ruby exception classes. The Rails framework makes extensive use of this technique, creating a spectrum of exceptions with specific, informative names.

Equipped with knowledge of these techniques, we'll turn next to the exploration of a series of built-in Ruby classes and modules.

Part 3

Built-in classes and modules

In part 3, we'll look in detail at a number of the built-in classes and modules that are part of the Ruby language. Some of them—strings and integers, for example—you've seen before, at least briefly or in a usage context. Here, we'll go into depth about each of the classes and modules we look at, and you'll learn how to use several instance and/or class methods from each one.

The material presented here represents a selection of classes and modules, and a selection of the methods *of* those classes and modules. The selection is weighted toward those that are more, rather than less, likely to be of use to Rails developers. However, what's *really* of use to Rails developers is a grasp of the Ruby language as a system and a reasonably general Ruby literacy. A dual principle has guided the content of these chapters: not casting such a wide net that the Rails orientation gets diluted out of existence, but also not scrubbing Ruby clean of its integral, organic, systemic qualities.

Chapter 9 covers some preliminaries that will help you get your bearings in the subsequent chapters. It pulls together aspects that a lot of objects have in common, so those points don't have to be covered repeatedly or confined to one chapter when they really apply to all. From chapter 10 on, we'll discuss specific classes and modules. Chapter 10 deals with scalar objects: one-dimensional objects like strings and numbers. Chapter 11 covers Ruby's built-in collection classes: `Array` and `Hash`. In the course of these two chapters, you'll also learn about the `Comparable` and `Enumerable` modules, which are the source of searching, filtering, and sorting capabilities for many Ruby classes (and which you can mix into your own classes).

Chapter 12 discusses regular expressions and, with that material in place, circles back to discuss string- and array-related methods that use regular expressions as arguments. Finally, Chapter 13 introduces you to *dynamic Ruby*—an umbrella term for a number of subtopics having to do with Ruby's ability to change the programming environment almost arbitrarily during runtime.

As was the case with part 2, Rails-related examples will be used, where doing so makes sense, to illustrate and sometimes to illuminate Ruby points. (You'll see quite a few examples that use the `irb --simple-prompt` style of presentation, as described in the "Code conventions" section at the beginning of the book.) By the time we've finished this part, you'll be well equipped to move on to part 4 and the Ruby-informed redesign of the music store application.

Built-in essentials

9

The later chapters in this part of the book will cover specific built-in classes: what they are, what you can do with them, what methods their instances have. *This* chapter will discuss a selection of topics that cut across a number of built-in classes.

The goal is to collect in one place important material that applies to more than one of the chapters to come. That way, as you explore the built-in classes further, you'll have a grounding in the common material, and you'll be familiar with some recurrently important techniques.

The topics we'll cover here all have Ruby-wide relevance in common; learning about them up front can save you a lot of fragmentary effort later. However, they're a miscellaneous bunch of subjects—and therefore worth seeing listed in one place, before you begin reading the chapter:

- *Literal constructors*—Ways to create certain objects with syntax, rather than with a call to new
- *Recurrent syntactic sugar*—Things Ruby lets you do to make your code look nicer
- *Methods that change their receivers*—Cases where calling a method puts the receiver in a different state, and why it matters
- *Methods that convert among classes*—Methods that convert an object to a class
- *Iterators reiterated*—Further exploration of iterators and their uses
- *Boolean states, Boolean objects, and* nil—A close look at true and false and related concepts in Ruby
- *Comparing two objects*—Ruby-wide techniques, both default and customizable, for object-to-object comparison
- *Listing an object's methods*—An important set of techniques for runtime reflection on the capabilities of an object

You'll find all of these topics useful as you work through this book, and as you read and/or write Ruby code (including, but not limited to, Rails source and/or application code) in the future.

You may want to fire up an irb session for this chapter; it makes frequent use of the irb session format for the code examples, and you can often try the examples with small variations to get a feel for how Ruby behaves.

9.1 Ruby's literal constructors

Ruby has a lot of built-in classes. Most of them can be instantiated using new:

```
str = String.new
arr = Array.new
```

Some can't; for example, you can't create a new instance of the class `Integer`. But for the most part, you can create new instances of the built-in classes.

In addition, a lucky, select few built-in classes enjoy the privilege of having *literal constructors*. That means you can use special notation, instead of a call to `new`, to create a new object of that class.

The classes with literal constructors are shown in table 9.1. When you use one of these literal constructors, you bring a new object into existence.

Table 9.1 **Summary of literal constructors for those built-in Ruby classes that have them**

Class	Literal constructor	Example(s)
String	Quotation marks	`"new string"` or `'new string'`
Symbol	Leading colon	`:symbol` or `:"symbol with spaces"`
Array	Square brackets	`[1,2,3,4,5]`
Hash	Curly braces	`{"New York" => "NY", "Oregon" => "OR"}`
Range	Two or three dots	`0...10` or `0..9`
Regexp	Forward slashes	`/([a-z]+)/`

We'll look in considerable detail at most of these classes and the corresponding literal constructors. (The only class on the list to which we won't devote a whole section or more is `Range`; but you'll see an explanation of ranges along the way when we encounter them.) Meanwhile, try to begin getting used to these notations, so you can recognize these data types on sight. They're very common; you'll probably see `""` and `[]` more often than you'll see `String.new` and `Array.new`.

NOTE   LITERAL CONSTRUCTOR CHARACTERS WITH MORE THAN ONE MEANING Some of the notation used for literal constructors has more than one meaning in Ruby. Many objects have a method called `[]` that looks like a literal array constructor but isn't. Code blocks, as you've seen, can be delimited with curly braces—but they're still code blocks, not hash literals. This kind of *overloading* of notation is a consequence of the finite number of symbols on the keyboard. You can always tell what the notation means by its context, and there are few enough contexts that with a little practice, it will be easy to differentiate.

We'll turn next to some cases of syntactic sugar that you'll see, and possibly use, recurrently.

9.2 *Recurrent syntactic sugar*

As you know, Ruby sometimes let you use sugary notation in place of the usual
`object.method(args)` method-calling syntax. This lets you do nice-looking things,
such as using a plus sign between two numbers, like an operator:

```
x = 1 + 2
```

Here's the odd-looking method-style equivalent:

```
x = 1.+(2)
```

As you delve more deeply into Ruby and its built-in methods, be aware that certain
methods *always* get this treatment. Methods in this special group—whether
they're methods of built-in classes, or methods you write in your own classes—can
always be called with the syntactic sugar notation rather than the method-call
notation. For example, you can define the plus-sign method on an object you've
created. Here's a somewhat bizarre but perfectly valid example:

```
obj = Object.new
def obj.+(other_obj)
  "Trying to add something to me, eh?"
end

puts obj + 100   # output: Trying to add something to me, eh?
```

The plus sign in the `puts` statement is a call to the + method of `obj`, with the integer 100 as the single argument. If the method chooses to ignore the argument,
and not to perform addition of any kind, it can.

A number of Ruby's automatically sugared methods are collected in table 9.2.

Table 9.2   Methods with operator-style syntactic sugar calling notation

Category	Name	Definition example	Calling example	Sugared notation
Arithmetic method/ operators	+	def +(x)	obj.+(x)	obj + x
	-	def -(x)	obj.-(x)	obj - x
	*	def *(x)	obj.*(x)	obj * x
	/	def /(x)	obj./(x)	obj / x
	%	def %(x)	obj.%(x)	obj % x
Get/set/append data	[]	def [](x)	obj.[](x)	obj[x]
	[]=	def []=(x,y)	obj.[]=(x,y)	obj[x] = y
	<<	def <<(x)	obj.<<(x)	obj << x

Table 9.2   Methods with operator-style syntactic sugar calling notation *(continued)*

Category	Name	Definition example	Calling example	Sugared notation
Comparison method/ operators	==	def ==(x)	obj.==(x)	obj == x
	>	def >(x)	obj.>(x)	obj > x
	<	def <(x)	obj.<(x)	obj < x
	>=	def >=(x)	obj.>=(x)	obj >= x
	<=	def <=(x)	obj.<=(x)	obj <= x
Case equality operator	===	def ===(x)	obj.===(x)	obj === x

Remembering which methods get the sugar treatment is not difficult. They fall into several distinct categories, as table 9.2 shows. These categories are for convenience of grouping only; you can define []= to output *Hamlet*, if you feel like it. The category names indicate how these method names are used in Ruby's built-in classes, and how they're most often used, by convention, when programmers implement them in new classes.

The extensive use of this kind of syntactic sugar—where something *looks* like an operator but *is* a method call—tells you a lot about the philosophy behind Ruby as a programming language. The fact that you can define and even *re*define elements like the plus sign, the minus sign, and square brackets means that Ruby has a great deal of flexibility. No matter what domain you're modeling, you can decide that you want to be able to add two of your objects together; all you have to do is define the + method, after which you'll be able to use + as an operator.

There are limits to what you can redefine in Ruby. You can't redefine any of the literal object constructors: {} is always a hash literal (or a code block, in that context), "" will always be a string, and so forth.

9.2.1 *Special treatment of +=*

Another bit of syntactic sugar you'll see a lot is the += construct:

```
x = 1
x += 1
```

Ruby always interprets this to mean

```
x = x + 1
```

This approach works for all the arithmetic method/operators, as shown in table 9.3.

Table 9.3 Sugar notation for arithmetic method/operators

Sugar notation	How Ruby sees it
x += 1	x = x + 1
x -= 1	x = x - 1
x *= 2	x = x * 2
x /= 2	x = x / 2
x %= 2	x = x % 2

The sugar provides a way to make code more concise. You can use either form. The non-sugared version looks reasonably good in these cases (unlike some other instances of sugar, where you'd end up with code like x./(y) if you didn't have the option of writing x/y).

We'll look next at an important criterion by which methods in Ruby can be distinguished from each other: whether they bring about permanent changes to the content or state of the objects on which they are called.

9.3 *Methods that change their receivers (or don't)*

The basic scenario of calling a method is always the same:

1. A message is sent to a receiver (an object).
2. The object executes the first method on its method lookup path whose name matches the message (or handles the error condition if there's no such method).
3. The method returns a value.

That's what *always* happens. In addition, some things *sometimes* happen. The first two will be familiar; the third is what we'll focus on here:

- A method call may (or may not) include arguments.
- A method may (or may not) yield one or more times to a code block associated with the method call.
- A method may (or may not) *modify its receiver.*

What does it mean for a method to modify its receiver?

9.3.1 *Receiver-changing basics*

To gain perspective on methods that change their receivers, let's start with an example of one that doesn't. Let's say you have a string:

```
str = "hello"
```

You wish to print it out with the first letter capitalized. Ruby has a handy `capitalize` method for strings:

```
puts str.capitalize
```

The result is "`Hello`". Here, the call to `capitalize` gives you, as its return value, a new string. It's this new string that you print out with `puts`. The *original* string, which served as the receiver of the "`capitalize`" message, still starts with a small *h*. You can test this by printing it out:

```
puts str    # output: hello
```

`str` is still "hello," not "Hello".

Now, let's use another string method—this time, one that modifies its receiver. We'll check for changes to the original string after making this method call, too:

```
str = "hello"
str.replace("goodbye")
puts str
```

This time, you see "goodbye". You haven't manufactured a new string; rather, you've modified the old string. The `replace` method changes the content of its receiver. (We'll talk about `String#replace` in more detail in chapter 10.)

You should always be aware of whether the method you're calling changes its receiver. Neither option is always right or wrong. Which is best depends on what you're doing, but it's important to know. One consideration, weighing in on the side of modifying objects instead of creating new ones, is efficiency: Creating new objects (like a second string that's identical to the first except for one letter) is expensive, in terms of memory and processing. This doesn't matter much if you're dealing with a small number of objects. But when you get into, say, handling data from large files, and using loops and iterators to do so, creating new objects can be a drain on resources.

On the other hand, you need to be cautious about modifying objects in place because other parts of the program may depend on those objects not to change. For example, let's say you have a database of names. You read the names out of the database into an array. At some point, you need to process the names for printed output—all in capital letters. You may do something like this:

```
names.each do |name|    ◁────────    Iterate through array of names one at a time
  capped = name.upcase
  # ...code that does something with capped...
end
```

In this example, `capped` is a new object: an uppercase duplicate of `name`. When you go through the same array later, in a situation where you do *not* want the names in uppercase, such as saving them back to the database, the names will be the way they were originally.

By creating a new string (`capped`) to represent the uppercase version of each name, you avoid the side effect of changing the names permanently. The operation you perform on the names achieves its goals without changing the basic state of the data. Sometimes you'll want to change an object permanently, and sometimes you'll want *not* to; there's nothing wrong with that, as long as you know which you're doing, and why.

9.3.2 *bang (!) methods*

Ruby lets you define a method whose name ends with an exclamation point. The built-in classes have many such methods.

The exclamation point, or *bang*, has no significance to Ruby internally; bang methods are called and executed just like any other method. However, by convention, the bang labels a method as *dangerous*—specifically, as the dangerous equivalent of a method with the same name but without the bang.

Dangerous can mean whatever the person writing the method wants it to mean. In the case of the built-in classes, it usually (although not always) means *this method, unlike its non-bang equivalent, permanently modifies its receiver.*

You'll find a number of pairs of methods, one with the bang and one without. Those without the bang perform an action and return a freshly minted object, reflecting the results of the action (capitalizing a string, sorting an array, and so on). The bang versions of the same methods perform the action, but they do so *in place.* Instead of creating a new object, they transform the original object.

Examples of such pairs of methods include `sort`/`sort!` for arrays, `upcase`/`upcase!` for strings, `chomp`/`chomp!` for strings, and `reverse`/`reverse!` for strings and arrays. In each case, if you call the non-bang version of the method on the object, you get a new object. If you call the bang version, you operate in-place on the same object to which you sent the message.

In the rest of the book, you'll see mention made several times of methods that have bang equivalents. Unless otherwise specified, that means the bang version of the method replaces the original content of the object with the results of the method call. Again, no rule says that this is the case, but it's a common scenario.

Changing the receiver (or not) is by no means just the domain of built-in Ruby methods. Everyone who writes Ruby programs deals one way or another with object state—and that means dealing with the evolution of an object's state, including changes to that state brought about by method calls during program execution.

What *state* means—and, therefore, what it means for a method call to change its receiver—varies from one case, one class, to another. For a string object, state includes the characters in the string; for a ticket object, it's the venue, price, performer, and so forth. The case of ActiveRecord objects provides an interesting illustration of some of the ramifications of receiver-changing under complex—and, for our purposes, particular relevant—circumstances.

9.3.3 *Specialized and extended receiver-changing in ActiveRecord objects*

Depending how much, and what, you've done with Rails, and ActiveRecord in particular, you know that some methods you can call on an ActiveRecord object affect the object as it currently exists in program memory, and some methods affect the database record with which the object is connected. We'll examine a set of permutations of these methods in chapter 14, in a different context. But they're worth a look here, in connection with the topic of changing the receiver.

Listing 9.1 shows an example that makes two changes to an object's properties, with different effects.

Listing 9.1   Two ways to set an object property and save a database record

```
composer = Composer.new
composer.first_name = "Johann"
composer.save
composer.update_attribute("last_name","Bach")
```

The first change in listing 9.1, which sets the new composer's first name to "Johann", requires a manual save operation to save the new value to the database. The second change, however, performs an update_attribute operation, which changes the property in the in-memory object and *also* writes the record out to the database, all in one operation.

You can view what's going on in this example as an extended version of changing/not changing the receiver. All these operations change the receiver, because the Composer object ends up in a different state each time. But the `update_attribute` operation also changes the database record connected with the object: It performs a lateral or meta-change of the receiver, changing its representation not just in memory, but permanently.

This is a more complex, multilayered change/no change process than you'll usually encounter when you're dealing with the issue as it relates to built-in Ruby classes, but it's instructive. You can think of the basic receiver-changing question as a starting point for understanding the more elaborate behaviors exhibited by ActiveRecord objects. Being able to connect such a fundamental concept to the behaviors of a specialized system like ActiveRecord can help you organize your thoughts as you explore the more specialized system.

We'll rejoin the mainstream agenda here—the exploration of important Ruby-wide behaviors—by turning, next, to a family of methods that perform conversions of one class of object to another.

9.4 *Built-in and custom to_* (conversion) methods*

Ruby offers a number of built-in methods whose names start with `to_` and end with something that indicates a class *to* which the method converts an object: `to_s` (to string), `to_a` (to array), `to_i` (to integer), and `to_f` (to float). Not all objects respond to all of these methods. But many objects respond to a lot of them, and the principle is consistent enough to warrant looking at them collectively.

The most commonly used `to_` method is probably `to_s`. Every Ruby object responds to `to_s`; every Ruby object has a way of displaying itself as a string. What `to_s` does, as the following irb-session excerpts show, ranges from nothing, other than return its own receiver, when the object is already a string

```
>> "I am already a string!".to_s
=> "I am already a string!"
```

to a flattened, probably useless string representation of miscellaneous data

```
>> ["one", "two", "three", 4, 5, 6].to_s
=> "onetwothree456"
```

to an informative, if cryptic, descriptive string about an object:

```
>> Object.new.to_s
=> "#<Object:0x401f81a4>"
```

(The numbers in the string representing the new object may be different on your computer; they pertain to memory addresses.)

Another common and useful `to_` method is `to_i` (to integer). (It's so useful that we've already used it in earlier examples.) Unlike some programming languages, such as Perl, Ruby doesn't automatically convert from strings to integers. You can't do this

```
x = "We're number "
y = 1
puts x + y
```

because Ruby doesn't know how to add a string and an integer together. Similarly, you'll get a surprise if you do this:

```
print "Enter a number: "
n = gets.chomp
puts n * 100
```

You'll see the *string* version of the number printed out 100 times. (That, by the way, also tells you that Ruby lets you multiply a string—but it's always treated as a string, even if it consists of digits.) If you want the number, you have to turn it into a number explicitly:

```
n = gets.to_i
```

As you'll see if you experiment with converting strings to integers (which you can do easily in irb with expressions like `"hello".to_i`), strings that have no reasonable integer equivalent (including "hello") are always converted to 0 with `to_i`.

We'll look next at the creation of homemade `to_*` methods.

9.4.1 *Writing your own to_* methods*

In addition to using Ruby's built-in `to_*` conversion methods, you can write your own. Ruby will pick up on the ones you write: If you define your own `to_s` method for an object or class, then that `to_s` method will be called, for example, when an object that uses it is provided as an argument to `puts`.

Let's go back to our workhorse example class, C. Maybe we want the string representation of C objects to be a little nicer than a hexadecimal number inside angle brackets. Arranging for this result is as easy as writing a `to_s` method. We'll elaborate on the class, to give `to_s` something to do, as shown in listing 9.2.

Listing 9.2 Defining the `to_s` method for a class of your own

```
class C
  def initialize(name)
    @name = name
  end
  def to_s
    "A C object named #{@name}"
  end
```

244

```
end

c = C.new("Emma")
puts c
```

We've piggybacked here on the automatic calling of to_s by puts; puts is used on what we predefined in the to_s method, leading to the following output:

```
A C object named Emma
```

You can write arbitrarily many to_* methods that don't correspond to Ruby's, if you need them; for instance, if you were writing an application where it was meaningful to do so, you could have a to_c method that caused objects to represent themselves as instances of your class C. Most custom-written to_* methods, however, correspond to the ones that Ruby knows about and uses.

Next, we'll pick up on a topic we looked at first in chapter 8: iterators. There's always more to say about iterators; here, we'll look at them in light of what you've learned about method calls and return values.

9.5 *Iterators reiterated*

As we proceed with the core classes and modules, you'll see a ton of iterators. Consider this a reminder and a pep talk.

There's no doubt that iterators add twists and turns to the basic method call scenario. But it's additive: New things happen, but the old things *still* happen.

Every Ruby method call produces a return value. *That includes iterators.* This fact isn't always obvious. In many cases, everything you care about happens in the code block when the method yields to it. The eventual return value of the call to the iterator may be anticlimactic.

The best example of an anticlimactic return value is the array method each, a basic iterator method that walks through the array one item at a time and yields the item it's on to the code block. You can do a lot inside an each code block. But the return value of each is unexciting; each returns its own receiver, the original array:

```
array = [1,2,3,4,5]
other = array.each {|n| puts "Current element is #{n}" }
```

Here, other is just another reference to (another variable attached to) array. There's rarely any point in capturing the return value of each. The action is in the code block; the return value is a formality.

Yet in other iterator cases, the return value is crucial. The `map` method of `Array` is a perfect example. In some respects, `map` is a lot like `each`: It walks through the array, yielding one item at a time starting with the first and ending with the last. The difference is that the return value of `map` is a *new* array. The elements of this new array are the results of all the yield operations:

```
array = [1,2,3,4,5]
other = array.map {|n| n * 10 }
p other
```

As you'll see if you run this snippet, the `map` operation accumulates all the `n * 10` calculations from the code block and stores them in a new array. That new array is the return value of the call to `map`:

```
[10,20,30,40,50]
```

It's essentially the old array with each element laundered through the code block. That's how `map` works; and, unlike with `each`, the return value (the new array) is of primary interest.

When dealing with iterators (as you will, to a great extent), remember that two stories are being told: the story of what happens inside the code block when it's yielded to (which can happen many times), and the story of the value that gets returned at the end by the method (which only happens once per method call). To know what an iterator does, you need to know both its iterative behavior—what, and when, it yields to the block—and its eventual return value.

We'll return now to the subject of Boolean states and objects in Ruby, a topic we've dipped into already but which it pays to examine in more detail.

9.6 *Boolean states, Boolean objects, and nil*

Every expression in Ruby evaluates to an object; and every object has a Boolean value of either *true* or *false*. Furthermore, `true` and `false` are objects. This idea isn't as convoluted as it sounds. If `true` and `false` weren't objects, then a pure Boolean expression like

```
100 > 80
```

would have no object to evaluate *to*.

In many cases where you want to get at a truth/falsehood value, such as an `if` statement or a comparison between two numbers, you don't have to manipulate these special objects directly. In such situations, you can think of truth and falsehood as *states*, rather than objects.

Still, you need to be aware of the existence of the objects `true` and `false`, partly because you may need them in your own code and partly because you may see code like this usage example from the documentation for `ActiveRecord::Schema`:

```
#     create_table :authors do |t|
#        t.column :name, :string, :null => false
#     end
```

You should recognize instantly that the word *false* represents the special object `false` and isn't a variable or method name. (That snippet of code, by the way, tells you how to create a relational database table automatically with a single string column called *name* with a `NOT NULL` constraint. We won't be studying ActiveRecord schemas and migrations in this book, but they're useful as a way of manipulating the structure of your database.)

We'll look at true and false both as states and as special objects, along with the special object `nil`.

9.6.1 *True and false as states*

Every expression in Ruby is either true or false, in a logical or Boolean sense. The best way to get a handle on this is to think in terms of conditional statements. For every expression in Ruby, you can do this:

```
if expression
  # execution reaches this point only if expression is true
end
```

For lots of expressions, such code makes no sense; but it can be instructive to try it with a few of them, as listing 9.3 shows.

Listing 9.3   Testing the Boolean value of expressions using `if` constructs

```
if (class MyClass; end)        ←———❶
  puts "Empty class definition is true!"
else
  puts "Empty class definition is false!"
end

if (class MyClass; 1; end)     ←———❷
  puts "Class definition with the number 1 in it is true!"
else
  puts "Class definition with the number 1 in it is false!"
end

if (def m; "A call to this method would be 'true'!"; end)   ←———❸
  puts "Method definition is true!"
else
```

```
    puts "Method definition is false!"
end

if "string"    ◁———④
  puts "Strings appear to be true!"
else
  puts "Strings appear to be false!"
end

if 100 > 50    ◁———⑤
  puts "100 is greater than 50!"
else
  puts "100 is not greater than 50!"
end
```

As you'll see if you run the code in listing 9.3, empty class definitions ❶ are false; non-empty class definitions evaluate to the same value as the last value they contain ❷ (in this example, the number 1); method definitions are false ❸ (even if a *call* to the method would return a true value); strings are true ❹; and 100 is greater than 50 ❺. You can use this simple if technique to explore the Boolean value of any Ruby expression.

The if examples show that every expression in Ruby is either true or false, in the sense of either passing or not passing an if test. What these examples don't show you, however, is what these expressions evaluate *to*. That is what the if test is really testing: It evaluates an expression (such as class MyClass; end) and proceeds on the basis of whether the value produced by that evaluation is true.

To see what values are returned by the expressions whose truth-value we've been testing, you can print those values:

```
>> class MyClass; end    ◁———❶
=> nil
>> class MyClass; 1; end    ◁———❷
=> 1
>> def m; "A call to this method would be 'true'!"; end    ◁———❸
=> nil
>> "string literal!"    ◁———❹
=> "string literal!"
>> 100 > 50    ◁———❺
=> true
```

Some of these expressions—the empty class definition ❶ and the method definition ❸—evaluate to nil, which is a special object (discussed in section 9.6.3). All you need to know for the moment about nil is that it has a Boolean value of false (as you can detect from the behavior of the if clauses that dealt with it in listing 9.3).

The class definition with the number 1 in it ❷ evaluates to the number 1, because every class definition block evaluates to the last expression contained inside it, or `nil` if the block is empty.

The string literal ❹ evaluates to itself; it's a literal object and doesn't have to be calculated or processed into some other form when evaluated. Its value as an expression is itself.

Finally, the comparison expression `100 > 50` ❺ evaluates to `true`—not just to something that has the Boolean value true, but to the object `true`. The object `true` does have the Boolean value true. But, along with `false`, it also has a special role to play in the realm of truth and falsehood and how they're represented in Ruby.

9.6.2 *true and false as objects*

The Boolean objects `true` and `false` are special objects, each being the only instance of a class especially created for it: `TrueClass` and `FalseClass`, respectively. You can ask `true` and `false` to tell you their classes' names, and they will:

```
puts true.class      # output: TrueClass
puts false.class     # output: FalseClass
```

The terms `true` and `false` are keywords. You can't use them as variable or method names; they are reserved for Ruby's exclusive use.

You can pass the objects `true` and `false` around, assign them to variables, and examine them, just like any other object. Here's an irb session that puts `true` through its paces in its capacity as a Ruby object:

```
>> a = true
=> true
>> a = 1 unless a
=> nil
>> a
=> true
>> b = a
=> true
```

You'll often see `true` and `false` used as method arguments and values in a method-argument hash (structures similar to the `link_to` examples in chapter 3). That's the gist of the `create_table` example that started this section: For each field you create in a table, you can specify `:null => true` (if you want the field to be allowed to be null; this is also the default) or `:null => false` (if you don't).

In most cases where a method asks for a Boolean argument or a Boolean value for a key (such as `:null` in `create_table`), it will work if you send it an expression with a Boolean value of true of false:

```
:null => 100 > 50
```

The value of `100 > 50` is true, so this is like writing `:null => true`. Needless to say, this kind of trick code doesn't represent good practice. But it gives you an interesting example of how truth and falsehood can be represented in Ruby.

The relation between true/false as Boolean values and true/false as objects

As we've said, every Ruby expression is true or false in a Boolean sense (as indicated by the `if` test), and there are also objects called `true` and `false`. This double usage of the true/false terminology is sometimes a source of confusion: When you say that something is true, it's not always clear whether you mean it has a Boolean truth value or that it's the object `true`.

Remember that *every* expression has a Boolean value—*including the expression* `true` *and the expression* `false`. It may seem awkward to have to say, "The object `true` is true." But that extra step makes it possible for the model to work consistently.

Table 9.4 shows a mapping of some sample expressions to both the outcome of their evaluation and their Boolean value.

Table 9.4 Mapping sample expressions to their evaluation results and Boolean values

Expression	Object to which expression evaluates	Boolean value of expression
`1`	`1`	true
`1+1`	`2`	true
`true`	`true`	true
`false`	`false`	false
`"string"`	`"string"`	false
`puts "string"`	`nil`	false
`100 > 50`	`true`	true
`x = 10`	`10`	true
`def x; end`	`nil`	false

Like some of the earlier examples, this table uses the special object `nil`—an object it's time for us to look at more closely.

9.6.3 *The special object nil*

The special object `nil` is, indeed, an object (it's the only instance of a class called `NilClass`). But in practice, it's also a kind of non-object. The Boolean value of `nil` is false, but that's just the start of its non-object-ness.

`nil` denotes an absence of anything. You can see this graphically when you inquire into the value of, for example, an instance variable you haven't initialized:

```
puts @x
```

This command prints `nil`. (If you try this with a local variable, you'll get an error; local variables aren't automatically initialized to anything, not even `nil`.) `nil` is also the default value for nonexistent elements of container and collection objects. For example, if you create an array with three elements, and then you try to access the tenth element (at index 9; array indexing starts at 0), you'll find that it's `nil`:

```
>> ["one","two","three"][9]
=> nil
```

`nil` is sometimes a difficult object to understand. It's all about absence and nonexistence; but `nil` does exist, and it responds to method calls like other objects:

```
>> nil.to_s
=> ""
>> nil.to_i
=> 0
>> nil.object_id
=> 4
```

The `to_s` conversion of `nil` is an empty string (`""`); the integer representation of `nil` is zero; and `nil`'s object id is 4. (`nil` has no special relationship to 4; that just happens to be the number designated as its id.)

It's not accurate to say that `nil` is empty, because doing so would imply that it has characteristics and dimension (like a number or a collection), which it isn't supposed to. Trying to grasp `nil` can take you into some thorny philosophical territory. You can think of `nil` as an object that exists, and that comes equipped with a survival kit of methods, but that serves the purpose of representing absence and a state of being undetermined.

Coming full circle, remember that `nil` has a Boolean value of false. `nil` and `false` are the only two objects that do. They're not the only two *expressions* that do; `100 < 50` has a Boolean value of false, because it evaluates to the object `false`. But `nil` and `false` are the only two *objects* in Ruby with a Boolean value of false. All other Ruby objects—numbers, strings, ActiveRecord instances—have a Boolean value of true. Tested directly, they all pass the `if` test.

Boolean values and testing provide a segue into the next topic: comparisons between objects. We'll look at tests involving two objects, and ways of determining whether they're equal (and, if they aren't, which is greater, and based on what criteria).

9.7 Comparing two objects

Ruby objects are created with the capacity to compare themselves to other objects for equality, using any of several methods. Some objects can also compare themselves to each other for greater-than and less-than relationships; and you can teach objects that can't do these things how to do them.

Tests for equality are the most common comparison tests, and we'll start with them. We'll then look at a built-in Ruby module called `Comparable`, which gives you a quick way to impart knowledge of comparison operations to your classes and objects—and which also is present in a number of built-in Ruby classes.

9.7.1 Equality tests

Inside the `Object` class, all equality-test methods do the same thing: They tell you whether two objects are *exactly the same object*. Here they are in action:

```
>> a = Object.new
=> #<Object:0x401c653c>
>> b = Object.new
=> #<Object:0x401c4bd8>
>> a == a
=> true
>> a == b
=> false
>> a.eql?(a)
=> true
>> a.eql?(b)
=> false
>> a.equal?(a)
=> true
>> a.equal?(b)
=> false
```

All three of these equality test methods—`==`, `eql?`, and `equal?`—give the same results in these examples: When you test a against a, the result is `true`; and when you test a against b, the result is `false`. We appear to have three ways of establishing that a is a but not b.

There isn't much point in having three tests that do the same thing. Further down the road, in classes other than the granddaddy `Object` class, these methods are redefined to do meaningful work for different objects. Two of them, at most, are redefined; `equal?` is usually left alone so that you can always use it to check whether two objects are exactly the same object.

Furthermore, Ruby gives you a suite of tools for object comparisons, and not always just comparison for equality. We'll look next at how equality tests and their redefinitions fit into the overall comparison picture.

9.7.2 *Comparisons and the Comparable module*

The most commonly redefined equality-test method, and the one you'll see used most often, is ==. It's part of the larger family of equality-test methods, and it's also part of a family of comparison methods that includes ==, >, <, >=, and <=.

Not every class of object needs, or should have, all these methods. (It's hard to imagine what it would mean for one bicycle to be greater than or equal to another.) But for those that do need them, Ruby provides a convenient way to get them. All you have to do is the following:

1   Mix in a module called Comparable (which comes with Ruby).

2   Define a comparison method with the name <=> in your class.

The comparison method <=> (usually called the *spaceship operator* or *spaceship method*) is the heart of the matter. Inside this method, you define what you mean by *less than*, *equal to*, and *greater than*. Once you've done that, Ruby has all it needs to provide the corresponding comparison methods.

For example, let's say you're taking bids on a job and using a Ruby script to help you keep track of what bids have come in. You decide it would be handy to be able to compare any two Bid objects, based on estimate, using simple comparison operators like > and <. *Greater than* means asking for more money, and *less than* means asking for less money.

A simple first version of your Bid class might look like listing 9.4.

Listing 9.4   Example of a class that mixes in the Comparable module

```
class Bid
  include Comparable
  attr_accessor :contractor
  attr_accessor :estimate

  def <=>(other_bid)        <——❶
    if self.estimate < other_bid.estimate
      -1
    elsif self.estimate > other_bid.estimate
      1
    else
      0
    end
  end
end
```

The spaceship method ❶ consists of a cascading if/elsif/else statement. Depending on which branch is executed, the method returns -1, 1, or 0. Those three return values are predefined, prearranged signals to Ruby. Your <=> method must return one of those three values every time it's called—and they always mean less than, equal to, and greater than, in that order.

You can shorten this method. Bid estimates are either floating-point numbers or integers (the latter, if you don't bother with the cents parts of the figure). Numbers *already* know how to compare themselves to each other, including integers to floats. Bid's <=> method can therefore piggyback on the existing <=> methods of the Integer and Float classes, like this:

```
def <=>(other_bid)
  self.estimate <=> other_bid.estimate
end
```

All Ruby numerical classes include Comparable and have a definition for <=>. The same is true of the String class; you can compare strings using the full assortment of Comparable method/operators.

9.8 *Listing an object's methods*

It's important not only that you learn the details of methods available to you in the built-in classes, but also that you learn how to explore further. One way you can explore further is to ask an object to tell you about its methods.

How you do this depends on the object. When you ask Class and Module objects for their methods, you have to distinguish instance methods (methods that instances of the class, or objects with access to the module, can call) from methods the class or module can call (class methods and singleton methods of the module object).

The simplest and most common case is when you want to know what messages an object responds to—that is, what methods you can call on it. Ruby gives you a typically simple way to do this (our examples are suitable for entering into irb; we'll let irb show us the results, rather than doing an explicit printout):

```
"I am a String object".methods
```

This results in a huge array of method names. At the very least, you'll want to sort them so you can find what you're looking for:

```
"I am a String object".methods.sort
```

The `methods` method works with class and module objects, too. But remember, it shows you what the object (the class or module) responds to, not what instances of the class or objects that use the module respond to. For example, asking irb for

```
String.methods.sort
```

shows you a list of methods that the `Class` object `String` responds to. If you see an item in this list, you know you can send it directly to `String`.

One of the methods you'll see in that list is `instance_methods`. This method tells you all the instance methods that instances of `String` are endowed with:

```
String.instance_methods
```

This list corresponds exactly to what a string object tells you when you ask it for its methods (two examples back). Keep in mind, though, that an object isn't confined to the methods it gets from its class. You can add methods to an object or use `extend` to add a whole module's worth of methods. For example, say you add a method to a string:

```
>> str = "a plain old string"
=> "a plain old string"
>> def str.some_new_method; end
=> nil

>> str.methods.sort
```

The output (not shown here, for space and clutter reasons) includes the usual instance methods of a string, plus `some_new_methods`. In other words, an object's *singleton* methods show up in its methods list. And if you *only* want the singleton methods, use this approach:

```
>> str.singleton_methods.sort
=> ["some_new_method"]
```

Ruby is obliging in the matter of giving you information about the state of objects during runtime, as the next examples will also show.

9.8.1 *Generating filtered and selective method lists*

Sometimes you'll want to see the instance methods defined in a particular class without bothering with the methods every object has (those defined in the `Kernel` module). You can view a class's instance methods without those of the class's ancestors by using the slightly arcane technique of providing the argument `false` to the `instance_methods` method:

```
String.instance_methods(false).sort
```

You'll see many fewer methods this way, because you're looking at a list of only those defined in the `String` class itself. This approach gives you a restricted picture of the methods available to string objects, but it's useful for looking in a more fine-grained way at how and where the method definitions behind a given object are positioned.

Other method-listing methods include the following:

- `obj.private_methods`
- `obj.public_methods`
- `obj.protected_methods`
- `obj.singleton_methods`

The mechanisms for examining objects' methods are extensive. As always, be clear in your own mind what the object is (in particular, class/module or not) that you're querying, and what you're asking it to tell you.

9.9 *Summary*

This chapter has covered several topics that pertain to multiple built-in classes. You've seen Ruby's literal constructors, which provide a concise alternative to calling `new` on certain built-in classes. You've also seen how Ruby provides you with syntactic sugar for particular method names, including a large number of methods with names that correspond to arithmetic operators.

We looked at the significance of methods that change their own receivers, which many built-in methods do (many of them bang methods, which end with `!`). We also examined the `to_*` methods: built-in methods for performing conversions from one core class to another. The chapter also reviewed the importance of iterators, something you'll see a lot of in upcoming chapters.

You've also learned a number of important points and techniques concerning Boolean (true/false) values and comparison between objects. You've seen that every object in Ruby has a Boolean value and that Ruby also has special Boolean objects (`true` and `false`) that represent those values in their simplest form. A third special object, `nil`, represents a state of undefinedness or absence. We also discussed techniques for comparing objects using the standard comparison operator (`<=>`) and the `Comparable` module.

Finally, we looked at ways to get Ruby objects to tell you what methods they respond to—a kind of metaprogramming technique that can help you see and understand what's going on at a given point in your program.

The material in this chapter will put you in a strong position to absorb what comes later. When you read statements like, "This method has a bang alternative," you'll know what they mean. When you see documentation that tells you a particular method argument defaults to `nil`, you'll know what *that* means. And the fact that you've learned about these recurrent topics will help us economize on repetition in the upcoming chapters about built-in Ruby classes and modules, and concentrate instead on moving forward.

10

Scalar objects

The term *scalar* means *one-dimensional*. Here, it refers to objects that represent single values, as opposed to collection or container objects that hold multiple values. There are some shades of gray: Strings, for example, can be viewed as collections of characters in addition to being single units of text. *Scalar*, in other words, is to some extent in the eye of the beholder. Still, as a good first approximation, you can look at the classes discussed in this chapter as classes of one-dimensional, bite-sized objects; doing so will help you as we move in the next chapter to the matter of collections and container objects.

The built-in objects we'll look at in this chapter include the following:

- *Strings*, which are Ruby's standard way of handling textual material of any length
- *Symbols*, which are another way of representing text in Ruby
- *Numerical objects*, including integers and floating-point numbers
- *Times and dates*, which Ruby handles (as it handles everything) as objects in their own right

The upshot of this chapter will be not only that you acquire some mastery of manipulating these objects, but also that you're positioned well to explore the containers and collections—which often contain and collect scalar objects—in the next chapter.

10.1 Working with strings

Ruby gives you two built-in classes that, between them, provide all the functionality of text: the String class and the Symbol class. We'll start with strings, which are the standard way to represent bodies of text of arbitrary content and length.

10.1.1 String basics

A *string literal* is generally enclosed in quotation marks:

```
"This is a string."
```

Single quotes can also be used:

```
'This is also a string.'
```

But a single-quoted string behaves very differently, in some circumstances, than a double-quoted string. The main difference is that *string interpolation* doesn't work with single-quoted strings. Try these two snippets, and you'll see the difference:

```
puts "Two plus two is #{2 + 2}."
puts 'Two plus two is #{2 + 2}.'
```

As you'll see if you paste these lines into irb, you get two very different results:

```
Two plus two is 4.
Two plus two is #{2 + 2}.
```

Single quotes disable the #{ . . . } interpolation mechanism. If you need that mechanism, you can't use them.

 In general, single- and double-quoted strings behave differently with respect to the need to *escape* certain characters with a backslash:

```
puts "Backslashes (\\) have to be escaped in double quotes."
puts 'You can just type \ once in a single quoted string.'
puts "But whichever type of quotation mark you use..."
puts "You have to escape its quotation symbol, such as \"."
puts 'That applies to \' in single-quoted strings too.'
```

You can, if necessary, escape (and thereby disable) the string interpolation mechanism in a double-quoted string:

```
puts "Escaped interpolation: \"\#{2 + 2}\"."
```

You'll see other cases of string interpolation and character-escaping as we proceed. Meanwhile, by far the best way to get a feel for these behaviors firsthand is to experiment with strings in irb.

> **WARNING** irb ALWAYS PRINTS OUT ITS EVALUATIONS When you use irb to familiarize yourself with string-quoting behaviors, keep in mind that every time you type an expression into irb, irb evaluates the expression and displays its string representation. This result can be confusing: String representations are double-quoted strings and therefore contain a lot of backslashes, for character-escaping purposes. The best thing to do is to use the puts command, so you can see what the string will look like on output. (When you do, the return value printed by irb is nil, because that's the return value of all calls to puts.)

Other quoting mechanisms

Ruby gives you several ways to write strings in addition to single and double quotation marks. But even when you're using these other techniques, keep in mind that a string is always either fundamentally single-quoted or double-quoted—even if quotation marks aren't physically present.

 Table 10.1 summarizes Ruby's quoting mechanisms. The main reason Ruby provides mechanisms other than literal quotation marks (%q and %Q) is that they make it easier to write strings that contain quotation marks (or apostrophes, which are the same as single quotation marks).

Table 10.1   Summary of string quoting mechanisms

Token	Single- or double-quoted	Example	Print output
`'`	Single	`'You\'ll have to "escape" single quotes.'`	You'll have to "escape" single quotes.
`"`	Double	`"You'll have to \"escape\" double quotes."`	You'll have to "escape" double quotes.
`%q`	Single	`%q{'Single-quoted' example—no escape needed.}`	'Single-quoted' example—no escape needed.
`%Q`	Double	`%Q{"Double-quoted" example—no escape needed..}`	"Double-quoted" example—no escape needed.

The examples in table 10.1 use curly braces as delimiters for the strings. You can use almost any punctuation character. For example, the expression `%q.string.` represents the string "string"; the two periods serve as delimiters. As long as the second delimiter matches the first (in the sense of being the same or, in the case of braces, brackets, and parentheses, being the matching one), the delimiter pair will work. Curly braces, however, are more or less standard; unless your string contains a closing curly brace, it's just as well to stick to that practice.

Representing strings is only the first stage. There's also the matter of what you do *with* strings. We'll turn now to an exploration of some of Ruby's important string operations.

10.1.2 String operations

To put it non-technically, you can do a ton of stuff with strings. Here, we'll look at a selection of string-manipulation methods.

It's a good idea to keep the following general points in mind as we get deeper into the study of strings:

- Most of the string methods we'll look at return a new `String` object, leaving the original string itself unchanged.
- A number of these methods, however, have bang versions that perform the change on the original string instead of returning a new string.
- A few non-bang methods perform changes on the original string. The names of these methods make it clear that this is happening (such as `replace`), even though there's no `!` on the name.
- Some string methods return something other than a string—for example, the `to_i` (to integer) conversion method.

Another point to keep in mind is that discussion of several important string methods will be postponed until after we've looked at regular expressions in chapter 12. But we'll cover the bulk of the string ground here, and put strings through their paces: combining them, changing them, getting substrings from them, and more.

Combining two (or more) strings

There are several techniques for combining strings. These techniques differ as to whether the second string is permanently added to the first or whether a new, third string is created out of the first two—in other words, whether the operation changes the receiver.

To create a new string consisting of two or more strings, you can use the + operator (the syntactic sugar form of the + method) to run the original strings together. Here's what `irb --simple-prompt` has to say about adding strings:

```
>> "a" + "b"
=> "ab"
>> "a" + "b" + "c"
=> "abc"
```

The string you get back from + is always a new string. You can test this by assigning a string to a variable, using it in a + operation, and checking to see what its value is after the operation:

```
>> str = "Hi "
=> "Hi "
>> str + "there."
=> "Hi there."    <------- ❶
>> str
=> "Hi "    <------- ❷
```

The expression `str + "there."` evaluates to the new string "Hi there." ❶ but leaves `str` unchanged ❷.

To add (append) a second string permanently to an existing string, use the `<<` method, which also has a syntactic sugar, pseudo-operator form:

```
>> str = "Hi "
=> "Hi "
>> str << "there."
=> "Hi there."
>> str
=> "Hi there."    <------- ❶
```

In this example, the original string `str` has had the new string appended to it, as you can see from the evaluation of `str` at the end ❶.

Another way to combine strings is through string interpolation:

```
>> str = "Hi "
=> "Hi "
>> "#{str} there."
=> "Hi there."
```

The result is a new string: "Hi there." String interpolation is a general-purpose technique, but you can use it for this kind of simple additive purpose, among others.

Replacing a string's contents

To replace the contents of a string, you use `replace`. Again, the examples here are geared for use in irb, where you're shown the value of each expression as you enter it:

```
>> str = "Hi there."
=> "Hi there."
>> str.replace("Good-bye.")     ◀——❶
=> "Good-bye."
>> str
=> "Good-bye."     ◀——❷
```

The final value of `str` ❷ is "Good-bye.", the string with which you have replaced ❶ `str`'s original contents. Keep in mind that replacing a string's contents isn't the same as creating a completely new string. `str` still refers to the same string, which means other variables referring to that string will also reflect the change:

```
>> str = "Hi there."
=> "Hi there."
>> x = str     ◀——❶
=> "Hi there."
>> str.replace("Good-bye.")     ◀——❷
=> "Good-bye."
>> x
=> "Good-bye."
```

In this example, `str` and `x` refer to one and the same string object; that's established when you assign `str` to `x` ❶. When that one and only string object has its contents replaced via a method call on `str` ❷, the string's new contents are also reflected in `x`.

`replace` thus lets you change a string in such a way that all existing references to it (variables) still refer to the same string. It's an example of a non-bang method that changes an object in place. The name, `replace`, conveys this fact, without the need for the exclamation point. (Also, a bang method usually exists in a pair with a non-bang version, and it's impossible to imagine what "replacing the contents of a string object" without changing the string would even mean.)

We'll look next at several useful methods for manipulating and massaging strings. We won't examine everything that strings can do, but we'll discuss some of the most important string facilities and behaviors in Ruby.

Massaging strings

Ruby strings have a number of methods, all with logical names, that let you massage and tweak strings. Some of the most common are summarized in table 10.2. All of these methods have bang (!) equivalents so that you can perform the operation in place on an existing string via a variable.

Table 10.2   Miscellaneous string manipulations

Method	Example	Result
capitalize	"ruby".capitalize	"Ruby"
upcase	"cobol".upcase	"COBOL"
downcase	"UNIX".downcase	"unix"
swapcase	"rUBY".swapcase	"Ruby"
strip	" lose the outer spaces "	"lose the outer spaces"
lstrip	" lose the left spaces "	"lose the left spaces "
rstrip	" lose the right spaces "	" lose the right spaces"
chop	"remove last character"	"remove last characte"
chomp	"remove training newline\n"	"remove trailing newline"
reverse	" gnirts eht esrever"	"reverse the string"

As you'll see if you choose any of these methods and try it in irb, the non-bang version returns a new string, and the bang version modifies the old string in place. Here's an example, using reverse and its bang counterpart:

```
>> str = "Hello"
=> "Hello"
>> str.reverse        <--------●1
=> "olleH"
>> str
=> "Hello"
>> str.reverse!       <--------●2
=> "olleH"
>> str
=> "olleH"
```

The first reverse operation ❶ reverses the string; irb reports the value of the expression as "olleH". But the string is still "Hello", as you can see when you ask irb to show you the value of str. The bang version, reverse! ❷, *does* change the original string permanently—as you can see, again, by asking irb to display str.

Meanwhile, we'll look next at working with substrings and individual characters.

Grabbing characters and substrings

Strings come with a pair of get/set methods: the ubiquitous [] and [] = methods. To grab the *n*th character of a string, you use [] with an index (starting at zero). But beware: You get back a number, not a character. Specifically, you get the character's ASCII value. For example, here's how to get the ASCII value of the character "c":

```
>> "abc"[2]
=> 99
```

You can turn this number back into a character with the chr method:

```
>> "abc"[2].chr
=> "c"
```

You can also use a negative index. If you do, the index is counted from the right side of the string:

```
>> "abc"[-2].chr
=> "b"
```

(You'll see more negative, right-hand indexing when we look in detail at arrays in chapter 11.)

You can grab a substring of a string by giving two arguments to [], in which case the first argument is the starting index and the second argument is the length of the substring you want. For example, to get a four-character substring starting at the sixth character (remember, strings are zero-indexed), you do this:

```
>> "This is a string"[5,4]
=> "is a"
```

> **TIP** USING SUBSTRING SYNTAX TO GET ONE CHARACTER Because you can grab substrings of any length using the two-argument form of String#[], you can grab any one character (without having to convert it back from an ASCII value) by requesting a substring of length one: for example, "abc"[2,1] is "c".

The string set method [] = works the opposite way from []: It changes the string (in place) by inserting the substring you specify into the position you give. It also has a two-argument form. Here it is in action:

```
>> s = "This is a string."
=> "This is a string."
>> s[-1] = "!"    <——❶
=> "!"
>> s
=> "This is a string!"
>> s[2,2] = "at"    <——❷
=> "at"
>> s
=> "That is a string!"
```

This example includes two set operations; after each one, we print out the string. The first ❶ changes the string's last character from . (period) to ! (exclamation point). The second ❷ changes the third and fourth characters from *is* to *at*. The result is that evaluating s now results in "That is a string!"

These techniques give you fine-grained control over the contents of strings, enabling you to do just about any manipulation you're likely to need.

This survey has given you a good foundation in string manipulation, although by no means have we exhausted the topic. Here, as usual, irb is your friend. Test things, experiment, and see how the string methods interact with each other.

Meanwhile, we're going to move on to the matter of string comparisons.

10.1.3 Comparing strings

As you know, Ruby objects can be compared in numerous ways; what the comparisons mean, as well as which are available, varies from object to object. Strings have a full set of comparison capabilities; strings are *comparable*, in the technical sense that the class String mixes in the Comparable module.

We'll look here at the various kinds of comparisons you can perform between one string and another.

Comparing two strings for equality

Like Ruby objects in general, strings have several methods for testing equality. The most common one is == (double equals sign), which comes with syntactic sugar allowing you to use it like an operator. This method tests for equality of string content:

```
>> "string" == "string"
=> true
>> "string" == "house"
=> false
```

The two literal "string" strings are different objects, but they have the same content. Therefore, they pass the == test.

Another equality-test method, `String#eql?`, tests two strings for identical content. In practice, it usually returns the same result as `==`. (There are subtle differences in the implementations of these two methods, but you can use either. You'll find that `==` is more common.) A third method, `String#equal?`, tests whether two strings are the same object:

```
>> "a" == "a"
=> true
>> "a".equal?("a")
=> false
```

The first test succeeds because the two strings have the same contents. The second test fails, because the first string isn't the same object as the second string. This is a good reminder of the fact that strings that appear identical to the eye may, to Ruby, have different object identities.

String comparison and ordering

As officially comparable objects, strings define a `<=>` method; hanging off this method are the usual comparison pseudo-operators (the methods whose syntactic sugar representation makes them look like operators). One of these methods is the `==` method we've already encountered. The others, in a similar vein, compare strings based on alphabetical/ASCII order:

```
>> "a" <=> "b"
=> -1
>> "b" > "a"
=> true
>> "a" > "A"
=> true
>> "." > ","
=> true
```

Remember that the spaceship method/operator returns -1 if the right object is greater, 1 if the left object is greater, and 0 if the two objects are equal. In the first case in the sequence above, it returns -1, because the string "b" is greater than the string "a". However, "a" is greater than "A", because the order is done by ASCII value, and the ASCII values for "a" and "A" are 97 and 65, respectively. Similarly, the string "." is greater than "," because the ASCII value for a period is 46 and that for a comma is 44.

At this point, we'll leave strings behind—although you'll continue to see them all over the place—and turn our attention to *symbols*. Symbols, as you'll see, are a close cousin of strings.

10.2 *Symbols and their uses*

Symbols are instances of the built-in Ruby class `Symbol`. They have a literal constructor: the leading colon. You can always recognize a symbol literal (and distinguish it from a string, a variable name, a method name, or anything else) by this token:

```
:a
:book
:"Here's how to make a symbol with spaces in it."
```

You can also create a symbol programmatically, by calling the `to_sym` method (also known by the synonym `intern`) on a string, as irb shows:

```
>> "a".to_sym
=> :a
>> "Converting string to symbol with intern....".intern
=> :"Converting string to symbol with intern...."
```

Note the tell-tale leading colons on the evaluation results returned by irb.

You can also easily convert a symbol to a string:

```
>> :a.to_s
=> "a"
```

These examples illustrate how closely related symbols are to strings. Indeed they are related, in that they share responsibility for representing units of text. However, strings and symbols differ in some important ways.

10.2.1 *Key differences between symbols and strings*

One major difference between symbols and strings is that only one symbol object can exist for any given unit of text. Every time you see the notation for a particular symbol (`:a`), you're seeing *the same symbol object* represented. That differs from the situation with strings. If you see two identical-looking string literals

```
"a"
"a"
```

you're seeing two different string objects (as the string comparison examples in section 10.1.3 demonstrated). With symbols, any two that look the same *are* the same—the same object. You can test this with the `equal?` comparison method, which returns true only if both the method's receiver and its argument are the same object:

```
>> :a.equal?(:a)
=> true
>> "a".equal?("a")
=> false
```

It's true that two similar-looking *symbol* literals are the same object but false that two similar-looking *string* literals are.

Another important difference between strings and symbols is that symbols, unlike strings, are *immutable*: you can't add, remove, or change parts of a symbol. The symbol :abc is always a different symbol from :a, and you can't add :bc to :a to get :abc. Strings are different: You *can* add "bc" to "a", as we've seen.

Symbols have a reputation as "weird strings," because they're string-like in many ways but also exhibit these differences. Why do they exist? In part because they're an element of the system Ruby uses internally to store and retrieve identifiers. When you assign something to a variable—say, with x=1—Ruby creates a corresponding symbol: in this case, the symbol :x. The language uses symbols internally but also lets programmers see and use them.

This situation can lead to confusion. Ruby's use of symbols is separate from yours. In your program, the symbol :x and the variable x aren't connected. The name of the variable is, in an informal sense, a "symbol"—the letter x—but it's not a symbol object. If you're interested in how Ruby defines and uses symbol objects internally, you should find out about it. (You might start with the archives of the ruby-talk mailing list, where symbols are discussed frequently; see the appendix.) But you don't need to know the internals to use symbols; and if you do study the internals, you need to keep that knowledge separate from symbol semantics as they apply to your programs.

Think of it this way: Ruby may use the symbol :x, and you may use the symbol :x, but it's also true that Ruby may use the number 100, and so may you. You don't have to know how Ruby uses 100 internally in order to use 100 in your code. It's worth knowing, however, that symbols are efficient in terms of memory usage and processing time. Strings, on the other hand, come with an entourage of behaviors and capabilities (like being made longer than they started out, having their contents changed, and so on) that makes them more expensive to maintain and process.

You'll often see symbol literals used as arguments to methods and, especially, as hash keys. Hashes that serve as arguments to methods (a common Rails scenario) are a doubly likely candidate for symbol usage.

10.2.2 *Rails-style method arguments, revisited*

Symbols play a big role in the kind of programming-as-configuration used in Rails, which we looked at in chapter 3. In a case like this

```
class Work < ActiveRecord::Base
  belongs_to :composer
  # etc.
```

`:composer` (the thing works belong to) is represented by a symbol. This symbol is an argument to the `belongs_to` method.

As noted in chapter 3, because you can get a symbol from a string with `to_sym` or `intern`, you can theoretically write the previous method call like this:

```
belongs_to "title".intern
```

This is, of course, not recommended. But it's not as absurd a point to make as it may at first appear. You should recognize `intern` when you come across it. Also, not every Ruby programmer always opts for literal constructs (like `:title`) over programmatic ones (like `"title".intern`). You'll often see people use

```
a = Array.new
```

rather than

```
a = []
```

even though the square brackets (the literal array constructor) achieve the same goal of creating a new, empty array. (You'll learn about arrays in detail in chapter 11.)

In the case of method calls in Rails applications, a consensus exists on the syntax of method calls whose arguments are symbols. You'll probably never see `intern` or `to_sym` used in such a context. Using symbol literals is second nature in Rails development. But you should be aware of exactly what you're seeing and where it fits into the Ruby landscape.

Among other places, you'll see (and have already seen, in part 1) symbols in Rails method calls in constructs like this:

```
<%= link_to "Click here",
       :controller => "book",
       :action     => "show",
       :id         => book.id %>
```

This is an example of a method argument hash: Each of the symbols is a *key*, and each of the values to the right is a *value*. This style of method call is common in Rails application code. (We'll look further at method argument hashes in chapter 11, once we've discussed hashes.)

Symbols are fast, and they have a sleek look that adds to the cleanness of code. Rails usage favors them in many contexts, so it's a good idea (for that reason as well as for the sake of your general Ruby literacy) to become acquainted with them on an equal footing with strings.

Returning to the scalar world at large, let's move on to a realm of objects that are as fundamental to Ruby, and to programming in general, as any: numerical objects.

10.3 *Numerical objects*

In Ruby, numbers are objects. You can send messages to them, just as you can to any object:

```
n = 98.6
m = n.round
puts m          ⟵  ❶

x = 12
if x.zero?
  puts "x is zero"
else
  puts "x is not zero"   ⟵  ❷
end

puts "The ASCII character equivalent of 97 is #{97.chr}"   ⟵  ❸
```

As you'll see if you run this code, floating-point numbers know how to round themselves ❶ (up or down). Numbers in general know ❷ whether they are zero. And integers can convert themselves to the character that corresponds to their ASCII value ❸.

Numbers are objects; therefore, they have classes—a whole family tree of them.

10.3.1 *Numerical classes*

Several classes make up the numerical landscape. Figure 10.1 shows a slightly simplified view (mixed-in modules aren't shown) of those classes, illustrating the inheritance relations among them.

The top class in the hierarchy of numerical classes is `Numeric`; all the others descend from it. The first branch in the tree is between floating-point and integral numbers: the `Float` and `Integer` classes. Integers are broken into two classes: `Fixnum` and `Bignum`. (Bignums, as you may surmise, are very large integers. When you use or calculate an integer that's big enough to be a Bignum, Ruby handles the conversion automatically for you; you don't have to worry about it.)

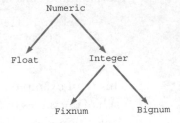

Figure 10.1
Numerical class hierarchy

10.3.2 *Performing arithmetic operations*

For the most part, numbers in Ruby behave as the rules of arithmetic and arithmetic notation lead you to expect. The examples in table 10.3 should be reassuring in their boringness.

Table 10.3 Common arithmetic expressions and their evaluative results

Expression	Result	Comments
1 + 1	2	Addition
10/5	2	Integer division
10/3	3	Integer division (no automatic floating-point conversion)
10.0/3.0	3.3333333333	Floating-point division
1.2 + 3.4	4.6	Floating-point addition
-12 - -7	-5	Subtraction
10 % 3	1	Modulo (remainder)

Note that when you divide integers, the result will always be an integer. If you want floating-point division, you have to feed Ruby floating-point numbers (even if all you're doing is adding .0 to the end of an integer).

Ruby also lets you manipulate numbers in non-decimal bases. Hexadecimal integers are indicated by a leading 0x. Here are some simple-prompt irb evaluations of hexadecimal integer expressions:

```
>> 0x12
=> 18
>> 0x12 + 12    ◁———❶
=> 30
```

The second 12 in the last expression ❶ is a decimal 12; the 0x prefix applies only to the numbers it appears on.

Integers beginning with 0 are interpreted as *octal* (base eight):

```
>> 012
=> 10
>> 012 + 12
=> 22
>> 012 + 0x12
=> 28
```

You can also use the to_i method of strings to convert numbers in any base to decimal. To perform such a conversion, you need to supply the base you want to convert *from* as an argument to to_i. The string is then interpreted as an integer in that base, and the whole expression returns the decimal equivalent. You can use any base from 2 to 36, inclusive. Here are some examples:

```
>> "10".to_i(17)
=> 17
>> "12345".to_i(13)
=> 33519
>> "ruby".to_i(35)
=> 1194794
```

Keep in mind that most of the arithmetic operators you see in Ruby are *methods*. They don't look that way because of the operator-like syntactic sugar that Ruby gives them. But they really are methods, and they can be called as methods:

```
>> 1.+(1)
=> 2
>> 12./(3)
=> 4
>> -12.-(-7)
=> -5
```

In practice, no one writes arithmetic operations that way; you'll always see the syntactic sugar equivalents (1 + 1 and so forth). But seeing examples of the method-call form is a good reminder of the fact that they *are* methods—and also of the fact that you if you define, say, a method called + in a class of your own, you can use the operator syntactic sugar. (And if you see arithmetic operators behaving weirdly, it may be that someone has redefined their underlying methods.)

We'll turn now to the next and last category of scalar objects we'll discuss in this chapter: time and date objects.

10.4 *Times and dates*

Ruby gives you lots of ways to manipulates times and dates—and Rails enhances and extends Ruby's time and date facilities with a variety of new methods. As a Rails developer, you're likely to use those added-on methods more than the raw Ruby ones. Still, you should gain some familiarity with Ruby's date and time libraries, for the sake of being able to use them when you need them as well as for the sake of understanding where the Rails methods come from.

Times and dates are manipulated through three classes: Time, Date, and DateTime. In order to reap their full benefits, you have to pull one or both of the date and time libraries into your program or irb session:

```
require 'date'
require 'time'
```

Rails automatically loads these for you, but in your own non-Rails code you have to load them yourself. (At some point in the future, all the available date- and time-related functionality may be unified into one library and made available to programs by default. But for the moment, you have to do the `require` operations.)

The full range of date and time manipulations available to you is impressive. Want to know what the day we call *April 24, 1705* would have been called in England prior to the calendar reform of 1752? Just load the `date` package, and then ask

```
>> require 'date'
=> true
>> Date.parse("April 24 1705").england.strftime("%B %d %Y")
=> "April 13 1705"
```

(Note that a successful `require` operation returns `true`. As always, irb explicitly shows the return value of every expression you type into it.)

Let that example stand in for all the fancy things the various date and/or time classes let you do. On the simpler side, here are some of the potentially useful date and time techniques you may find yourself using:

```
>> require 'date'
=> true
>> d = Date.today
=> #<Date: 4907505/2,0,2299161>
>> puts d
2006-01-17
```

This snippet outputs two different string representations of the Date object `d`. The first is the inspect string, which shows that the Date object has been successfully created and returned. The second comes from the date's `to_s` method, which is automatically called by `puts`. The `to_s` string, as you can see, is more human-readable.

Date objects respond to both a `<<` method and a `>>` method. They advance or rewind the date by a number of months; the number is indicated in the argument. For example

```
puts d << 2
puts d >> 5
```

gives you the date two months before and five months after the date stored in `d`:

```
2005-11-17
2006-06-17
```

You can also create and manipulate `Time` objects. A new `Time` object tells you, when asked, its year, month, day, minute, second, and usec (microsecond) values. Here's an irb session where a `Time` object is created and queried:

```
>> t = Time.new
=> Tue Jan 17 17:51:04 PST 2006
>> t.year
=> 2006
>> t.month
=> 1
>> t.day
=> 17
>> t.hour
=> 17
>> t.min
=> 51
>> t.sec
=> 4
>> t.usec
=> 377285
```

Time objects also let you display them or store them as strings, based on a UNIX-style format string (basically, a template that specifies how you want the date formatted). The method that does this is strftime.

```
>> t.strftime("%m-%d-%Y")
=> "01-17-2006"
```

In the example, the format specifiers used are %m (two-digit month), %d (two-digit day), and %Y (four-digit year). The hyphens between the fields are reproduced in the output as literal hyphens. Some useful format specifiers for strftime are shown in table 10.4.

Table 10.4 Common time and date format specifiers

Specifier	Description
%Y	Year (four digits)
%y	Year (last two digits)
%b, %B	Short month, full month
%m	Month (number)
%d	Day of month (left-padded with zeros)
%e	Day of month (left-padded with blanks)
%a, %A	Short day name, full day name
%H, %I	Hour (24-hour clock), hour (12-hour clock)
%M	Minute
%S	Second

Table 10.4 **Common time and date format specifiers** *(continued)*

Specifier	Description
%c	Equivalent to "%a %b %d %H:%M:%S %Y"
%x	Equivalent to "%m/%d/%y"

WARNING TIME FORMATS CAN BE LOCALE-SPECIFIC The %c and %x specifiers, which involve convenience combinations of other specifiers, may differ from one locale to another; for instance, some systems put the day before the month in the %x format. This is good, because it means a particular country's style isn't hard-coded into these formats. But you do need to be aware of it, so you don't count on specific behavior that you may not always get. When in doubt, you can use a format string made up of smaller specifiers.

Here are some more examples of time format specifiers in action:

```
>> t.strftime("Today is %x")
=> "Today is 01/17/06"
>> t.strftime("Otherwise known as %d-%b-%y")
=> "Otherwise known as 17-Jan-06"
>> t.strftime("Or even day %e of %B, %Y.")
=> "Or even day 17 of January, 2006."
>> t.strftime("The time is %H:%m.")
=> "The time is 17:01."
```

Many more date and time representations and manipulations are possible in Ruby. A third class beyond `Date` and `Time`, `DateTime`, adds more methods and facilities. It's a rich programming area, although also a vexing one; there's some sentiment among Ruby programmers that it would make sense to unify some or all of the functionality currently spread across three classes into one class, if possible. Some find it incongruous, too, that date and time facilities are split between those that are available by default and those that have to be loaded at runtime. Wherever these and other discussions lead, the functionality is there if and when you wish to explore it.

We've reached the end of our survey of scalar objects in Ruby. Next, in chapter 11, we'll look at collections and container objects.

10.5 *Summary*

In this chapter, you've seen the basics of the most common and important scalar objects in Ruby: strings, symbols, numerical objects, and time/date objects. Some of these topics involved consolidating points made earlier in the book; others were completely new in this chapter. At each point, we've examined a selection of important, common methods. We've also looked at how some of the scalar-object classes relate to each other. Strings and symbols both represent text; and though they are different kinds of objects, conversions from one to the other are easy and common. Numbers and strings interact, too. Conversions aren't automatic, as they are (for example) in Perl; but Ruby supplies conversion methods to go from string to numerical object and back, as well as ways to convert strings to integers in as many bases as the 10 digits and 26 letters of the alphabet can accommodate.

Time and date objects have a foot in both the string and numerical camps. You can perform calculations on them, such as adding *n* months to a given date; and you can also put them through their paces as strings, using techniques like the `Time#strftime` method in conjunction with output format specifiers.

The world of scalar objects in Ruby is rich and dynamic. Moreover, most of what you do with both Ruby and Rails will spring from what you have learned here about scalar objects: direct manipulation of these objects, manipulation of objects that share some of their traits (for example, CGI parameters whose contents are strings), or collections of multiple objects in these categories. Scalar objects aren't everything; but they lie at the root of virtually everything else. The tour we've taken of important scalar classes and methods in this chapter will stand you in good stead as we proceed, next, to look at collections and containers—the two- (and sometimes more) dimensional citizens of Ruby's object world.

Collections, containers, and enumerability

In programming generally, and certainly in Rails applications, you deal not only with individual objects but with *collections* of objects. You search through collections to find an object that matches certain criteria (like an Edition object containing a particular Work); you sort collections for on-screen presentation in a list; you filter collections to include or exclude particular items; and so forth. All of these operations, and similar ones, depend on objects being accessible in collections.

Ruby represents collections of objects by putting them inside *container* objects. In Ruby, two built-in classes dominate the container-object landscape: *arrays* and *hashes*. We'll start this chapter by looking at the Array and Hash classes: first in comparison with each other, to establish an overall understanding, and then separately. We'll then examine a built-in Ruby module called Enumerable, which encapsulates a great deal of the functionality of arrays, hashes, and other collection objects. Finally, we'll consider the facilities available for sorting object collections.

Keep in mind that these collections are, themselves, *objects*. You send them messages, assign them to variables, and so forth, in normal object fashion. They just have an extra dimension, beyond the scalar.

11.1 Arrays and hashes compared

An *array* is an ordered collection of objects, *ordered* meaning that you can select objects from the collection based on a consistent numerical index. You'll have noticed that we've already used arrays in some of the examples earlier in the book, going back all the way to our first Rails application walk-through. It's hard *not* to use arrays in Ruby.

Hashes are *unordered* collections, meaning that they don't have a sense of what their first or second or *n*th element is. Instead, they store objects in pairs, each pair consisting of a *key* and a *value*. You retrieve a value by means of the key. Hashes (or similar data storage types) are sometimes called *dictionaries* or *associative arrays* in other languages. They offer a tremendously—sometimes surprisingly—powerful way of storing and retrieving data.

Arrays and hashes are closely connected. An array is, in a sense, a hash, where the keys are consecutive integers. Hashes are, in a sense, arrays, where the indices are allowed to be anything, not just integers. Transformations of various kinds between the two are common. Arrays "win," in the sense that they are the more basic and fundamental of the two. Quite a few operations that you perform on hashes produce arrays. For instance, if you select key-value pairs based on some criterion (such as selecting all pairs where the value is a capitalized string), your selection operation will hand you back an *array* of the results. When you're dealing with object-collections of almost any kind, all roads lead to the array: the simple, linear, numbered collection of objects.

Still, hashes play at least two huge roles in Ruby and Rails. Some of the foundational Ruby libraries upon which Rails is built use hashes to pass data around; in particular, the Ruby CGI library makes your CGI form data available to you through a hash. To get at the values for the form-fields, you have to know how a hash works. The Rails framework, too, makes heavy use of hashes. A large number of the most common methods used in writing Rails applications take hashes *as their arguments*. (You've seen glimpses of this already, in the discussion of symbols in the previous chapter; you'll see it again here, from the hash perspective.) To call these methods correctly, you have to know how to write a hash.

In the next two sections, we'll look at arrays and hashes in depth. Let's start with arrays.

11.2 Using arrays

Arrays are the bread-and-butter way to handle collections of objects. An array is an object whose job is to store other objects.

Arrays are *ordered* collections; you can get at their contents by the use of numerical indexes. The contents of an array always remain in the same order, unless you change it.

11.2.1 Creating a new array

There are two ways to create a new array. First, you can use the new method:

```
a = Array.new
```

You can then add objects to the array (using techniques we'll look at later).

The other way to create an array is by using the *literal array constructor* [] (square brackets):

```
a = []
```

When you use the literal constructor, you can also put objects into the array at the same time you create it:

```
a = [1,2,"three",4, [] ]
```

(Notice that the last element in this array is another array. That's perfectly legitimate; you can nest arrays to as many levels as you wish.)

The advantage of using `Array.new` rather than the literal array constructor is that `Array.new` lets you specify the size of and, if you wish, initialize the contents of the array. Here's an irb exchange that illustrates both possibilities:

```
>> Array.new(3)    ◁────●
=> [nil, nil, nil]
>> Array.new(3,"abc")    ◁────②
=> ["abc", "abc", "abc"]
```

If you give one argument to `Array.new` ●, you get an array of the size you asked for, with all elements set to `nil`. If you give two arguments ②, you get an array of the size you asked for, with each element initialized to contain the second argument.

You can even supply a code block to `Array.new`. In that case, the elements of the array are initialized by repeated calls to the block:

```
>> n = 0
=> 0
>> Array.new(3) { n += 1; n * 10 }    ◁────●
=> [10, 20, 30]    ◁────②
```

In this example, the new array has a size of three. Each of the three elements is set to the return value of the code block. The code inside the block ●, executed three times, produces the values 10, 20, and 30—and those are the initial values in the array ②.

Pre-initializing arrays isn't always necessary, because your arrays will grow as you add elements to them. But if and when you need this functionality—and/or if you see it in use and want to understand it—it's there.

> **WARNING** BE CAREFUL WITH DEFAULT ARRAY ELEMENTS   When you initialize multiple elements of an array using a second argument to `Array.new`—as in `Array.new(3, "abc")`—*all the elements* of the array are initialized *to the same object*. If you do `a = Array.new(3,"abc"); a[0] << "def"; puts a[1]`, the second element of the array is changed when you add `def` to the first element, because they're the same string object. To create an array that inserts a different "abc" string into each slot, you should use `Array.new(3) { "abc" }`. The code block runs three times, each time generating a new string (same characters, different string object).

11.2.2 *Inserting, retrieving, and removing array elements*

Because an array is an ordered collection, any object you add to the array goes either at the beginning, at the end, or somewhere in the middle. The most general technique for inserting one or more items into an array is the setter method `[]=` (square brackets and equal sign). This looks odd as a method name in the middle of a paragraph like this, but thanks to its syntactic sugar equivalent, [] = works smoothly in practice.

In order to use [] =, you need to know that each item (or element) in an array occupies a numbered position. The first element is at position *zero* (not position one). The second element is at position one, and so forth.

To insert an element with the [] = method—using the syntactic sugar that allows you to avoid the usual method-calling dot—you do this:

```
a = []
a[0] = "first"
```

In this example, you end up with a one-element array whose first (and only) element is the string "first".

Once you have objects in an array, you can *retrieve* those objects by using the [] method, which is the getter equivalent of the [] = setter method:

```
a = [1,2,3,4,5]
p a[2]
```

Here, you ask for the *third* element (remember that the first element is at index 0, not index 1), which is the integer 3.

You can also perform these get-and-set methods on more than one element at a time.

Setting or getting more than one array element at a time

If you give either Array#[] or Array#[] = (the get or set method) a second argument, it's treated as a length—a number of elements to set or retrieve. In the case of retrieval, the results are returned inside a new array.

Here's some irb dialogue, illustrating the multi-element operations of the [] and [] = methods:

```
>> a = ["red","orange","yellow","purple","gray","indigo","violet"]
=> ["red", "orange", "yellow", "purple", "gray", "indigo", "violet"]
>> a[3,2]          <———❶
=> ["purple", "gray"]
>> a[3,2] = "green", "blue"    <———❷
=> ["green", "blue"]
>> a
=> ["red", "orange", "yellow", "green", "blue", "indigo", "violet"]    <—❸
```

After initializing the array a, we grab ❶ two elements, starting at index 3 (the fourth element) of a. The two elements are returned in an array. Next, we set the fourth and fifth elements, using the [3,2] notation ❷, to new values; these new values are then present in the whole array ❸ when we ask irb to display it at the end.

You can perform operations on elements anywhere in an array. However, operations affecting, specifically, the beginnings and ends of arrays crop up most often. Accordingly, a number of methods exist for the special purpose of adding items to, or removing them from, the beginning or end of an array, as we'll now see.

Special methods for manipulating the beginnings and ends of arrays

To add an object to the beginning of an array, you can use `unshift`. After this operation

```
a = [1,2,3,4]
a.unshift(0)
```

the array a now looks like this: `[0,1,2,3,4]`.

To add an object to the end of an array, you use `push`. Doing this

```
a = [1,2,3,4]
a.push(5)
```

results in the array a having a fifth element: `[1,2,3,4,5]`.

You can also use a method called `<<` (two less-than signs), which places an object on the end of the array. `<<` offers some syntactic sugar: You can use it without the usual method-calling dot. The following code adds 5 as the fifth element of a, just like the `push` operation in the last example:

```
a = [1,2,3,4]
a << 5
```

`<<` and `push` differ in that `push` can take more than one argument. This code

```
a = [1,2,3,4,5]
a.push(6,7,8)
```

adds three elements to a, resulting in: `[1,2,3,4,5,6,7,8]`.

Corresponding to `unshift` and `push` are their opposite numbers, `shift` and `pop`. `shift` removes one object from the beginning of the array (thereby shifting the remaining objects to the left by one position). `pop` removes an object from the end of the array. `shift` and `pop` both return the array element that they have removed, as this example shows:

```
a = [1,2,3,4,5]
print "The original array: "
p a
popped = a.pop
print "The popped item: "
puts popped
print "The new state of the array: "
p a
```

```
shifted = a.shift
print "The shifted item: "
puts shifted
print "The new state of the array: "
p a
```

The output is as follows:

```
The original array: [1, 2, 3, 4, 5]
The popped item: 5
The new state of the array: [1, 2, 3, 4]
The shifted item: 1
The new state of the array: [2, 3, 4]
```

As you can see from the running commentary in the output, the return value of pop and shift is the item that was removed from the array. The array is permanently changed by these operations; the elements are removed, not just referred to or captured.

We'll turn next from manipulating one array to looking at ways to combine two or more arrays.

11.2.3 *Combining arrays with other arrays*

Several methods allow you to combine multiple arrays in various ways—something that, it turns out, is common and useful when you begin manipulating lots of data in lists. Remember that in every case, even though you're dealing with two (or more) arrays, *one* array is always the receiver of the message. The other arrays involved in the operation are arguments to the method.

To add the contents of array b to array a, you can use concat:

```
>> [1,2,3].concat([4,5,6])
=> [1, 2, 3, 4, 5, 6]
```

(Note that concat differs in an important way from push. Try replacing concat with push in the example, and see what happens.)

concat permanently changes the contents of its receiver. If you want to combine two arrays into a third, new array, you can do so with the + method:

```
>> a = [1,2,3]
=> [1, 2, 3]
>> b = a + [4,5,6]
=> [1, 2, 3, 4, 5, 6]
>> a
=> [1, 2, 3]   <———❶
```

The receiver of the + message—in this case, the array a—remains unchanged by the operation (as irb tells you ❶).

Another useful array-combining method is `replace`. As the name implies, `replace` replaces the contents of one array with the contents of another:

```
>> a = [1,2,3]
=> [1, 2, 3]
>> a.replace([4,5,6])    <———❶
=> [4, 5, 6]
>> a
=> [4, 5, 6]
```

The original contents of a are gone, replaced ❶ by the contents of the argument array [4,5,6]. Note that a `replace` operation is different from reassignment. If you do this

```
a = [1,2,3]
a = [4,5,6]
```

the second assignment causes the variable a to refer to a completely different array object than the first. That's not the same as replacing the elements of the *same* array object. This starts to matter, in particular, when you have another variable that refers to the original array. It's worth looking closely at what's at stake:

```
>> a = [1,2,3]
=> [1, 2, 3]
>> b = a    <———❶
=> [1, 2, 3]
>> a.replace([4,5,6])
=> [4, 5, 6]
>> b    <———❷
=> [4, 5, 6]
>> a = [7,8,9]    <———❸
=> [7, 8, 9]
>> b
=> [4, 5, 6]    <———❹
```

Once you've performed the assignment of a to b ❶, *replacing* the contents of a means you've replaced the contents of b ❷, because the two variables refer to the same array. But when you reassign to a ❸, you break the connection; a and b now refer to different array objects: b to the same old array ❹, a to a new one.

No discussion of combining arrays would be complete without `zip`. `zip` does a kind of parallel walk-through of two arrays, producing a third array containing pairs of items taken from the original two:

```
>> [1,2,3].zip([4,5,6])
=> [[1, 4], [2, 5], [3, 6]]
```

Notice that the zipped array is *an array of arrays*. Each element in it is an array; each of these little arrays contains one item from the first array (the receiver of the `zip` message) and one from the second array (the argument to `zip`). Zipping arrays can be handy if you have, say, names in one array and phone numbers in another, and you want to print them out together. Be sure the two arrays are truly synchronized as to the order of their elements, because `zip` doesn't do any checking for you; it just marches through the arrays and grabs pairs of items.

In addition to combining multiple arrays, you can also transform individual arrays to different forms. We'll look next at techniques along these lines.

11.2.4 *Array transformations*

As you've just seen, `Array#zip` hands you back an array of arrays. Arrays of arrays are a common sight. But sometimes, what you really want is just an array. Say you have two partial arrays of numbers

```
a = [0,2,4,6]
b = [1,3,5,7]
```

and you want to zip or interweave them:

```
numbers = a.zip(b)
```

At this point, `numbers` is an array of arrays: `[[0,1],[2,3],[4,5],[6,7]]`. But what you want is an array of numbers from 0 to 7.

To achieve this, you can use `flatten`. Let's rewind and pretend we did this in the first place:

```
numbers = a.zip(b).flatten
```

`flatten` removes the nesting and leaves you with a flat array of the items that were previously inside nested arrays. `numbers` is now `[0,1,2,3,4,5,6,7]`. Note that `flatten` flattens completely, no matter how deeply nested the array is:

```
>> [1,2,[3,4,[5,6],7],[[[8,9]]]].flatten
=> [1, 2, 3, 4, 5, 6, 7, 8, 9]
```

All the nesting is removed, and only the bottom-level elements are left.

> **TIP** FLATTENING INCREMENTALLY If you want to flatten incrementally—to flatten some but not all of the levels of nesting inside an array—you can install and use the flattenx package, available on the Ruby Application Archive (see appendix).

Another array-transformation method is `reverse`, which does exactly what it says:

```
>>[1,2,3,4].reverse
=>  [4, 3, 2, 1]
```

Like its string counterpart, Array#reverse also has a bang [!] version, which permanently reverses the array that calls it.

Another important array transformation method is join. The return value of join isn't an array but a string, consisting of the string representation of all the elements of the array strung together:

```
>> ["abc", "def", 123].join
=> "abcdef123"
```

join takes an optional argument; if given, the argument is placed between each pair of elements:

```
>> ["abc", "def", 123].join(", ")
=> "abc, def, 123"
```

Joining with commas (or comma-space, as in the last example) is a fairly common operation.

You can also transform an array with uniq. uniq gives you a new array, consisting of the elements of the original array with all duplicate elements removed:

```
>> [1,2,3,1,4,3,5,1].uniq
=> [1, 2, 3, 4, 5]
```

Duplicate status is determined by testing pairs of elements with the == method: Any two elements for which the == test returns true are considered duplicates of each other. uniq also has a bang version, uniq!, which removes duplicates permanently from the original array.

The methods we've looked at in this subsection involve direct, one-step, predefined changes to arrays. You also have at your disposal a number of methods that perform transformations on arrays by means of a code block—by iterating through the array.

11.2.5 *Array iteration, filtering, and querying*

Array iterator methods generally return either a subset of the elements, information about the array, or a new array based on element-by-element transformations of the contents of the original array. In other words, they filter, query, and transform.

The basis of all these operations is the underlying method each, which iterates through the array and yields one item at a time to the code block. You're ahead of the game, having already seen each in action in simple iteration examples like this:

```
[1,2,3,4,5].each {|x| puts x * 10 }
```

As you saw in chapter 9, the action in calls to each is in the code block. The return value of the whole method call is the receiver, unchanged.

A useful variant of each is each_with_index, which yields two values to the block each time through the array: the current array element and that element's numerical index (starting with 0). Here's an example:

```
["a","b","c"].each_with_index {|x,i| puts "element #{i} is #{x}" }
```

The output of this code is as follows:

```
element 0 is a
element 1 is b
element 2 is c
```

Using each_with_index saves you the trouble of using an explicit loop variable to keep track of iterations.

Array filtering operations

It's common to want to filter a collection of objects based on some selection criterion. For example, if you have a database of people registering for a conference, and you want to send payment reminders to the people who haven't paid, you can filter a complete list based on payment status.

Ruby provides rich facilities for filtering arrays and for searching arrays to find one or more elements that match one or more criteria. We'll look at several filtering and searching methods here. All of them are iterators: They involve providing a code block. The code block is the filter; you define your selection criteria (your tests for inclusion or exclusion) inside the block. The return value of the entire method is, depending on the method and on what it finds, either one object, in cases where you specifically search for a single object; an array of objects that match your criteria (possibly an empty array); or nil, indicating that the criteria were not met.

We'll start with a one-object search: find. find locates the first element in an array for which the code block, when called with that element as an argument, returns true. For example, to find the first number greater than 5 in an array of integers, you can use find like this:

```
>> [1,2,3,4,5,6,7,8,9,10].find {|n| n > 5 }
=> 6
```

find iterates through the array, yielding each element in turn to the block. If the block returns anything with the Boolean value of true, the element yielded "wins," and find stops iterating. If find fails to find an element that passes the code-block test, it returns nil. (Try changing n > 5 to n > 100 in the example, and you'll see.)

It's interesting to ponder the case where your array has `nil` as one of its elements, and your code block looks for an element equal to `nil`:

```
[1,2,3,nil,4,5,6].find {|n| n.nil? }
```

(Note the use of the built-in `nil?` method, which returns `true` if its receiver is the object `nil`.) In these circumstances, `find` *always* returns `nil`—whether the search succeeds or fails! That means the test is useless; you can't tell whether it succeeded. You can work around this situation with other techniques, such as the `include?` method (listed in table 11.1, a little further on), with which you can find out whether an array has `nil` as an element.

Another common searching and filtering operation is `find_all`. `find_all` returns a new array containing *all* the elements of the original array that match the criteria in the code block, not just the first such element (as with `find`). If no matching elements are found, `find_all` returns an empty array:

```
>> a = [1,2,3,4,5,6,7,8,9,10]
=> [1, 2, 3, 4, 5, 6, 7, 8, 9, 10]
>> a.find_all {|item| item > 5 }
=> [6, 7, 8, 9, 10]    <——❶
>> a.find_all {|item| item > 100 }
=> []    <——❷
```

The first `find_all` operation returns an array of all the elements that pass the test in the block: all elements that are greater than 5 ❶. The second operation also returns an array, this time an array of all the elements in the original array that are greater than 10. There aren't any, so an empty array is returned ❷. (`select` is a synonym for `find_all`; the two names can be used interchangeably.)

Just as you can select items, so you can reject items: find out which elements of an array do *not* return a true value when yielded to the block. Using the `a` array from the previous example, you can do this:

```
>> a.reject {|item| item > 5 }
=> [1, 2, 3, 4, 5]
```

to get the array *minus* any and all elements that are greater than 5.

Array querying methods

Several methods allow you to gather information about an array from the array. Table 11.1 shows some useful array query methods.

With the exception of `size`, all the methods in table 11.1 return either `true` or `false`. They differ in this respect from the selecting methods like `find` and `find_all`, which return one or more elements from the array.

Table 11.1 Summary of common array query methods

Method name/sample call	Meaning
a.size (synonym: length)	Number of elements in the array
a.empty?	True if a is an empty array; false if it has any elements
a.include?(item)	True if the array includes items; false otherwise
a.any? {|item| *test* }	True if any item in the array returns true for the block; false otherwise
a.all? {|item| *test* }	True if every item in the array returns true for the block; false otherwise

Arrays are the most basic container objects in Ruby. In and of themselves, they are extremely useful. They also serve as the anchor or prototype for more complex collection objects—not only in standard Ruby (which includes array-ish classes like `Matrix` and `Set`), but also in various Ruby programs and libraries. Here, we're going to pursue the study of collections and containers by sliding over for a little while to ActiveRecord and looking at how that library's collection objects work—and what lessons in Ruby can be gleaned from their design.

11.2.6 *Ruby lessons from ActiveRecord collections*

Some programs create their own container objects or classes, endowed with capabilities that suit a special purpose. These special-purpose containers often have a lot in common with arrays; they frequently use arrays to implement their special behavior, under the hood.

For example, say you're writing a program that models a deck of cards. A deck of cards and a plain-vanilla Ruby array have a lot in common. You can add elements (cards), remove elements, search the collection on various criteria, and so forth. At the same time, however, you may want a deck of cards to do things that not every array can do:

```
deck = DeckOfCards.new
deck.jokers = 2
deck.shuffle
deck.cut
```

You can implement the `DeckOfCards` class as a subclass of `Array`, with new methods added and old ones redefined. Or you can create an array for each instance of `DeckOfCards`, held in an instance variable where the actual business of the deck is conducted:

```
class DeckOfCards
  def initialize
    @cards = []
    # etc.
  end

  def jokers=(n)
    n.times { @cards << Joker.new }    ◁──────┐    Assuming existence
  end                                         │    of Joker class
  # etc.
end
```

The point of this example isn't to steer our discussion toward modeling a deck of cards but to make the point that particular domains have particular characteristics and needs that can be addressed through creative, adroit use of basic Ruby classes.

Handling collections of objects in ActiveRecord provides an interesting case, a case where the study of an area of Rails design can shed light on the possibilities inherent in Ruby.

Automatic collections from associations

The has_many association between two ActiveRecord models is expressed through collection semantics. For example, given this

```
class Work < ActiveRecord::Base
  has_many :editions
```

every instance of class Work will have its own collection of Edition objects, available to it through the automatically created editions method. That collection is, in many respects, an array—but it's an array with strong opinions about what its role is and what sorts of operations it should be involved in. You can't add objects to it at will; it literally won't let you. The following example shows a transcript of a console session from the music store application, in which I try to do unacceptable things (with some of the verbose irb output trimmed down):

```
$ ruby script/console
Loading development environment.

>> w = Work.find(1)
=> #<Work:0x2358fec>
>> e = w.editions    ◁──────── ❶
=> [#<Edition:0x2354f78>, ...]
>> e.class
=> Array    ◁──────── ❷
>> e.push("Adding a string to the Editions collection!")
ActiveRecord::AssociationTypeMismatch: Edition expected, got String    ◁──●❸
```

The code starts by grabbing a `Work` object and getting from it the full list of its editions ❶. The editions collection reports its class as `Array` ❷. However, the collection of editions refuses to accept a string as an element: When you try to push a string onto the collection, you get a fatal error ❸.

This is a good illustration of the fact that a Ruby object (in this case, a collection of editions) isn't constrained to behave exactly the way a default or vanilla instance of its class would behave. For Ruby objects, including objects that house other objects, being created is just the beginning. What matters is how the object gets shaped and used down the road. ActiveRecord collections consider themselves instances of `Array`, but they have special knowledge and behaviors that differentiate them from arrays in general.

This is a great example of the Ruby philosophy bearing fruit with practical results.

Searching and filtering, ActiveRecord-style

ActiveRecord's approach to finding elements in collections is also instructive. At a general level, you can perform find operations on the entire existing set of records for any model you've defined. Here's an example:

```
Work.find(:all)
Work.find_by_title("Sonata")
```

You're operating at the class (and class method) level: You're looking for *all* existing objects (corresponding to database records, under the hood) of the given class.

A couple of points are noteworthy here. First, ActiveRecord uses `find(:all)` rather than `find_all`. (Actually, either will work, but `find_all` is considered old-style usage and is likely to disappear from future versions of ActiveRecord.) Second, note the call to the method `find_by_title`. That method is created automatically, because instances of `Work` have `title` attributes. This is another example of the Rails framework giving you a good return on your investment: In return for creating a database field called *title*, you get a method that lets you search specifically on that field.

`find(:all)` and its close relative `find(:first)` can both be supplied with *conditions*, which filter the results for you. These conditions are written as SQL fragments, using the kind of expression you use in an SQL query to narrow a `SELECT` operation. For example, to find all works whose titles start with the word *The* (*The Rite of Spring*, *The Lark Ascending*, and so on), you can do this:

```
Work.find(:all, :conditions => "title like 'The %'")
```

To find only the first such work, use this:

```
Work.find(:first, :conditions => "title like 'The %'")
```

It's always possible to accomplish this kind of find operation without SQL, through the use of pure Ruby array operations:

```
Work.find(:all).select {|work| /^The /.match(work.title) }
```

However, this approach is less efficient and almost certainly slower than the SQL-fragment approach, because it involves creating an array of all existing works and then filtering that array. Providing an explicit SQL fragment allows an optimization: The database engine can do the sifting and searching, presumably in a more efficient way. On the other hand, sometimes you need the ability to program a selection algorithm using Ruby's resources—or you don't mind a small slowdown in exchange for having the code be entirely in Ruby. You have to decide, based on each case, which approach is best for this kind of operation.

What you see here is the creation of a parallel universe of collection searching and filtering—parallel but not identical to the facilities provided for Ruby arrays. The syntax is different from plain Ruby syntax, but it meshes with Rails style and with the specific searching needs of ActiveRecord models.

Like arrays, hashes have popped up here and there in our discussions. Now, we'll look at them in detail.

11.3 *Hashes*

Like an array, a *hash* is a collection of objects. Unlike an array, a hash is an *unordered* collection: There is no such thing as the first or last or third-from-last item in a hash. Instead, a hash consists of *key-value pairs*. Hashes let you perform lookup operations based on keys.

A typical use of a hash is to store complete strings along with their abbreviations. Here's a hash containing a selection of names and two-letter state abbreviations, along with some code that exercises it. (The => operator connects a key on the left with the value corresponding to it on the right.)

```
state_hash = { "Connecticut" => "CT",
               "Delaware"    => "DE",
               "New Jersey"  => "NJ",
               "Virginia"    => "VA" }

print "Enter the name of a state: "
state = gets.chomp
abbr = state_hash[state]
puts "The abbreviation is #{abbr}."
```

When you run this snippet (assuming you enter one of the states defined in the hash), you see the abbreviation.

This example involves creating a hash, using hash literal syntax, and assigning it to a variable. Let's back-and-fill by looking in detail at how hashes are created.

11.3.1 *Creating a new hash*

There are three ways to create a hash. One is by means of the literal hash constructor, curly braces ({}); this is what we did in the last example. The literal hash constructor is convenient when you have values you wish to hash that aren't going to change; you're going to type them into the program file once and refer to them from the program. State abbreviations are a good example.

You can also create an empty hash with the literal constructor:

```
h = {}
```

You'd presumably want to add items to the empty hash at some point; techniques for doing so will be forthcoming in section 11.3.2.

The second way to create a hash is with the traditional `new` constructor:

```
Hash.new
```

This always creates an empty hash. However, if you provide an argument to `Hash.new`, it's treated as the default value for nonexistent hash keys. (We'll return to this point after looking at key/value insertion and retrieval.)

The third way to create a hash involves another class method of the `Hash` class: the method `[]` (square brackets). You can put key-value pairs inside the square brackets, if you want to create your hash already populated with data:

```
Hash["Connecticut" => "CT",
     "Delaware"    => "DE" ]
```

A word about `=>` is in order.

Separating keys from values in hashes

When you physically type in a key/value pair for a hash (as opposed to setting key/value pairs through a method call, as you'll learn to do shortly), you can separate the key from the value with either a comma or the special hash separator `=>` (equal-greater than). The `=>` separator makes for a more readable hash, especially when the hash includes a lot of entries, but either will work. After each complete key-value pair, you insert a comma. Look again at the state-name example, and you'll see how this syntax works.

Now, let's turn to matter of manipulating a hash's contents.

11.3.2 *Inserting, retrieving, and removing hash pairs*

As you'll see as we proceed, hashes have a lot in common with arrays, when it comes to the get- and set-style operations. However, there are differences, stemming from the underlying differences between arrays (ordered collections, indexed by number) and hashes (unordered collections, indexed by arbitrary key objects). As long as you keep this in mind, the behavior of hashes and the behavior of arrays mesh quite well.

Adding a key/value pair to a hash

To add a key/value pair to a hash, you use essentially the same technique as for adding an item to an array: the [] = method, plus syntactic sugar.

To add a state to state_hash, you do this

```
state_hash["New York"] = "NY"
```

which is the sugared version of this:

```
state_hash.[]=("New York", "NY")
```

You can also use the synonymous method store for this operation. store takes two arguments (a key and a value):

```
state_hash.store("New York", "NY")
```

When you're adding to a hash, keep in mind the important principle that *keys are unique.* You can have only one entry with a given key. If you add a key-value pair to a hash that already has an entry for the key you're adding, the old entry is overwritten. Here's an example:

```
h = Hash.new
h["a"] = 1
h["a"] = 2
puts h["a"]
```

This code assigns two values to the a key of the hash h. The second assignment clobbers the first, as the puts statement shows by outputting 2.

Note that hash *values* don't have to be unique; you can have two keys that are paired with the same value. But you can't have duplicate keys.

Retrieving values from a hash

You retrieve values from a hash with the [] method, plus the usual syntactic sugar involved with [] (no dot; the argument goes inside the brackets). For example, to get the Connecticut abbreviation from state_hash, you do this:

```
conn_abbrev = state_hash["Connecticut"]
```

Now `conn_abbrev` has "CT" assigned to it. Using a hash key is much like indexing an array—but the index (the key) can be anything, whereas in an array it's always an integer.

Hashes also have a `fetch` method, which gives you an alternative way of retrieving values by key:

```
conn_abbrev = state_hash.fetch("Connecticut")
```

`fetch` differs from `[]` in the way it behaves when you ask it to look up a nonexistent key: `fetch` raises an exception, while `[]` gives you either `nil` or a default you've specified (as discussed below).

You can also retrieve values for multiple keys in one operation, with `values_at`:

```
two_states = state_hash.values_at("New Jersey","Delaware")
```

This code returns an array consisting of `["NJ","DE"]` and assigns it to the variable `two_states`.

Now that you have a sense of the mechanics of getting information into and out of a hash, let's circle back and look at the matter of supplying a default value (or default code block) when you create a hash.

Specifying and getting a default value

By default, when you ask a hash for the value corresponding to a nonexistent key, you get `nil`:

```
>> h = Hash.new
=> {}
>> h["no such key!"]
=> nil
```

However, you can specify a *different* default value by supplying an argument to `Hash.new`:

```
>> h = Hash.new(0)
=> {}
>> h["no such key!"]
=> 0
```

Here, we get back the hash's default value, 0, when we use a nonexistent key. (You can also set the default on an already existing hash, with the `default` method.)

It's important to remember that whatever you specify as the default value is what you get when you specify a nonexistent key. This does *not* mean the key is set to that value. The key is still nonexistent. If you want a key in a hash, you have to put it there. You can, however, do this as part of a default scenario for new (nonexistent) keys—by supplying a default code block to `Hash.new`. The code block will be executed every time a nonexistent key is referenced. Furthermore, two objects will be yielded to the block: the hash and the (nonexistent) key.

This technique gives you a foot in the door when it comes to setting keys automatically when they're first used. It's not the most elegant or streamlined technique in all of Ruby, but it does work. You write a block that grabs the hash and the key, and you do a set operation.

For example, if you want every nonexistent key to be added to the hash with a value of 0, you create your hash like this:

```
h = Hash.new {|hash,key| hash[key] = 0 }
```

When the hash h is asked to match a key it doesn't have, that key is added after all, with the value 0.

Given this assignment of a new hash to h, you can trigger the block like this:

```
>> h["new key!"]    <-------- ❶
=> 0
>> h    <-------- ❷
=> {"new key!"=>0}
```

When you try to look up the key new key ❶, it's not there; it's added, with the value 0, and then that value is printed out by irb. Next, when you ask irb to show you the whole hash ❷, it contains the automatically added pair.

This technique has lots of uses. It lets you make assumptions about what's in a hash, even if nothing is there to start with. It also shows you another facet of Ruby's extensive repertoire of dynamic programming techniques, and the flexibility of hashes.

We'll turn now to ways you can combine hashes with each other, as we did with strings and arrays.

11.3.3 *Combining hashes with other hashes*

The process of combining two hashes into one comes in two flavors: the destructive flavor, where the first hash has the key/value pairs from the second hash added to it directly; and the nondestructive flavor, where a new, third hash is created that combines the elements of the original two.

The destructive operation is performed with the update method. Entries in the first hash are overwritten permanently if the second hash has a corresponding key:

```
h1 = {"Smith" => "John",
      "Jones" => "Jane" }
h2 = {"Smith" => "Jim" }
h1.update(h2)
puts h1["Smith"]    <-------- Output: Jim
```

In this example, h1's Smith entry has been changed (updated) to the value it has in h2. You're asking for a refresh of your hash, to reflect the contents of the second hash. That's the destructive version of combining hashes.

To perform nondestructive combining of two hashes, you use the merge method, which gives you a third hash and leaves the original unchanged:

```
h1 = {"Smith" => "John",
      "Jones" => "Jane" }
h2 = {"Smith" => "Jim" }
h3 = h1.merge(h2)

p h1["Smith"]   <────── Output: John
```

Here, h1's Smith/John pair isn't overwritten by h2's Smith/Jim pair. Instead, a new hash is created, with pairs from both of the other two.

Note that h3 has a decision to make: Which of the two Smith entries should it contain? The answer is that when the two hashes being merged share a key, the second hash (h2, in this example) wins. h3's value for the key Smith will be Jim.

(Incidentally, merge!—the bang version of merge—is a synonym for update. You can use either name when you want to perform that operation.)

In addition to being combined with other hashes, hashes can also be transformed in a number of ways, as you'll see next.

11.3.4 *Hash transformations*

You can perform several transformations on hashes. *Transformation*, in this case, means that the method is called on a hash, and the result of the operation (the method's return value) is a hash. The term *filtering*, in the next subsection, refers to operations where the hash undergoes entry-by-entry processing and the results are stored in an *array*. (Remember that arrays are the most common, general-purpose collection objects in Ruby; they serve as containers for results of operations that don't even involve arrays.)

Inverting a hash

Hash#invert flips the keys and the values. Values become keys, and keys become values:

```
>> h = { 1 => "one", 2 => "two" }
=> {1=>"one", 2=>"two"}
>> h.invert
=> {"two"=>2, "one"=>1}
```

Be careful when you invert hashes. Because hash keys are unique, but values aren't, when you turn duplicate values into keys, one of the pairs will be discarded:

```
>> h = { 1 => "one", 2 => "more than 1", 3 => "more than 1" }
=> {1=>"one", 2=>"more than 1", 3=>"more than 1"}
>> h.invert
=> {"one"=>1, "more than 1"=>3}
```

Only one of the two more than 1 values can survive as a key when the inversion is performed; the other is discarded. You should invert a hash only when you're certain the values as well as the keys are unique.

Clearing a hash

Hash#clear empties the hash:

```
>> {1 => "one", 2 => "two" }.clear
=> {}
```

This is an in-place operation: The empty hash is the same hash (the same object) as the one to which you send the clear message.

Replacing the contents of a hash

Hashes have a replace method:

```
>> { 1 => "one", 2 => "two" }.replace({ 10 => "ten", 20 => "twenty"})
=> {10 => "ten", 20 => "twenty"}
```

This is also an in-place operation, as the name replace implics.

11.3.5 *Hash iteration, filtering, and querying*

You can iterate over a hash several ways. Like arrays, hashes have a basic each method. On each iteration, *an entire key/value pair* is yielded to the block, in the form of a two-element array:

```
{1 => "one", 2 => "two" }.each do |key,value|
  puts "The word for #{key} is #{value}."
end
```

The output of this snippet is

```
The word for 1 is one.
The word for 2 is two.
```

Each time through the block, the variables key and value are assigned the key and value from the current pair.

The return value of Hash#each is the hash—the receiver of the "each" message.

Iterating through all the keys or values

You can also iterate through the keys or the values on their own—and you can do each of those things in one of two ways. You can grab all the keys or all the values of the hash, in the form of an array, and then do whatever you choose with that array:

```
>> h = {1 => "one", 2 => "two" }
=> {1=>"one", 2=>"two"}
>> h.keys
=> [1, 2]
>> h.values
=> ["one", "two"]
```

Or, you can iterate directly through either the keys or the values, as in this example:

```
h = {"apple" => "red", "banana" => "yellow", "orange" => "orange" }
h.each_key {|k| puts "The next key is #{key}." }
h.each_value {|v| puts "The next value is #{value}." }
```

The second approach (the each_*key_or_value* methods) saves memory by not accumulating all the keys or values in an array before iteration begins. Instead, it looks at one key or value at a time. The difference is unlikely to loom large unless you have a very big hash, but it's worth knowing about.

Let's look now at filtering methods: methods you call on a hash, but whose return value is an array.

Hash filtering operations

Arrays don't have key/value pairs; so when you filter a hash into an array, you end up with an array of two-element arrays: Each subarray corresponds to one key/value pair. You can see this by calling find_all or select (the two method names are synonymous) on a hash. Like the analogous array operation, selecting from a hash involves supplying a code block containing a test. Any key/value pair that passes the test is added to the result; any that doesn't, isn't:

```
>> { 1 => "one", 2 => "two", 3 => "three" }.select {|k,v| k > 1 }
=> [[2, "two"], [3, "three"]]
```

Here, the select operation accepts only those key/value pairs whose keys are greater than 1. Each such pair (of which there are two in the hash) ends up as a two-element array inside the final returned array.

Even with the simpler find method (which returns either one element or nil), you get back a two-element array when the test succeeds:

```
>> {1 => "un", 2 => "deux", 3 => "trois" }.find {|k,v| k == 3 }
=> [3, "trois"]
```

The test succeeds when it hits the 3 key. That key is returned, with its value, in an array.

You can also do a map operation on a hash. Like its array counterpart, Hash#map goes through the whole collection—one *pair* at a time, in this case—and yields each element (each pair) to the code block. The return value of the whole map operation is an array whose elements are all the results of all these yieldings.

Here's an example that launders each pair through a block that returns an uppercase version of the value:

```
>> { 1 => "one", 2 => "two", 3 => "three" }.map {|k,v| v.upcase }
=> ["ONE", "TWO", "THREE"]
```

The return array reflects an accumulation of the results of all three iterations through the block.

We'll turn next to hash query methods.

Hash query methods

Table 11.2 shows some common hash query methods.

Table 11.2   Common hash query methods and their meanings

Method name/sample call	Meaning
h.has_key?(1)	True if h has the key 1
h.include?(1)	Synonym for has_key?
h.key?(1)	Synonym for has_key?
h.member?(1)	Another (!) synonym for has_key?
h.has_value?("three")	True if any value in h is "three"
h.value?("three")	Synonym for has_value?
h.empty?	True if h has no key/value pairs
h.size	Number of key/value pairs in h

None of the methods in table 11.2 should offer any surprises at this point; they're similar in spirit, and in some cases in letter, to those you've seen for arrays. With the exception of size, they all return either true or false. The only surprise may be how many of them are synonyms. Four methods test for the presence of a particular key: has_key?, include?, key?, and member?. A case could be made that this is two or even three synonyms too many. has_key? seems to be the most popular of the four and is the most to-the-point with respect to what the method tests for.

The has_value? method has one synonym: value?. As with its key counterpart, has_value? seems to be more popular.

The other methods—empty? and size—tell you whether the hash is empty and what its size is. size can also be called as length.

As simple as their underlying premise may be, hashes are a powerful data structure. Among other uses, you'll see them a lot in method calls. Ruby makes special allowances for hashes in argument lists, and Rails takes full advantage of them, as you'll see next.

11.3.6 *Hashes in Ruby and Rails method calls*

In the previous chapter, you saw this example of the use of symbols as part of a method argument list:

```
<%= link_to "Click here",
        :controller => "work",
        :action    => "show",
        :id        => work.id %>
```

With a knowledge of hashes as well as symbols, you're now in a position to understand this construct—which you'll see and use frequently in Rails applications—fully.

This is a method call with two arguments: the string "Click here" and *a three-key hash.* You might expect to see curly braces around the hash, like this:

```
link_to("Click here", { :controller => "work",
                         :action    => "show",
                         :id        => work.id })
```

But as a special sugar dispensation, Ruby permits you to *end* an argument list, when you call a method, with a literal hash without the curly braces:

```
link_to("Click here", :controller => "work",
                       :action    => "show",
                       :id        => work.id )
```

If you dispense with the parentheses around the arguments, you get the original example, which has the classic Rails method-call look and feel.

Why does Ruby allow this special usage? To facilitate and "prettify" precisely the kind of labeling of method arguments by descriptive name that's so common in Rails. Passing arguments as key/value pairs allows you to indicate what the arguments are for. The elimination of the curly braces gives the idiom a clean look.

The original link_to method is defined in the ActionView library. It's complex, so for the sake of seeing something similar in operation, we'll use a scaled-down, simplified version. Let's put it in its own ERb file, together with a call to it that generates the desired HTML tag:

```
<% def mini_link_to(text, specs)
     target = "/#{specs[:controller]}/#{specs[:action]}/#{specs[:id]}"
     return "<a href=\"#{target}\">#{text}</a>"
   end
%>

<%= mini_link_to "Click here",
        :controller => "work",
        :action     => "show",
        :id         => 1
%>
```

Save this code to `minilink.erb`, and run it with ERb:

```
$ erb minilink.erb
```

ERb fills out the template, and the results look like this:

```
<a href="/work/show/1">Click here</a>
```

The method `mini_link_to` grabbed two arguments: the string "Click here" and the hash. It then did three lookups by key on the hash, interpolating them into a string that it assigned to the variable `target`. Finally, it embedded that result in a string containing the full syntax of the HTML a tag and used that final string as its return value.

You could write a method with similar functionality that doesn't use a hash argument. You'd call it like this:

```
new_link_to("Click here", "work", "show", 1)
```

On the receiving end, you'd do something like this:

```
def new_link_to(text,controller,action,id=nil)
  target = "#{controller}/#{action}/#{id}"
  return "<a href=\"#{target}\"#>#{text}</a>"
end
```

When you're writing methods and documenting the correct way to call them, should you opt for the hash approach? There's a tradeoff involved. The hash approach gives you more visual cues in the calling code as to what's what. Without the hash, you get a list of values with no indication of what role they will play in the method. You also have to make sure they're in the right order (whereas hash keys can be listed in any order).

On the other hand, it's slightly easier for the method to have the relevant values stuffed directly into the variables in its argument list, rather than having to dig them out of a hash.

Rails methods generally favor the hash calling convention. The result is that when you look at a typical Rails method call, you can tell a great deal about what it's doing just by reading the hash keys.

Hashes also show up in many Rails controller files, particularly (although by no means exclusively) in the form of the `params` hash, which is created by default and contains incoming CGI data. For example, it's common to see something like this:

```
@comment = Comment.find(params[:id])
```

You can infer that when the call came in to this controller file, it was from a form that included an `id` field that was filled in (either manually or automatically) with the database ID number of a particular `Comment`.

Hashes are powerful and adaptable collections, and you'll have a lot of contact with them as you work on Ruby and Rails projects.

Now that we've discussed arrays and hashes, Ruby's workhorse collection objects, we're going to look under the hood at the source of much of the functionality of both those classes (and many others): the `Enumerable` module. This module defines many of the searching and selecting methods you've already seen, and is mixed in by both `Hash` and `Array`.

11.4 Collections central: the Enumerable module

Ruby offers a number of predefined modules that you can mix into your own classes. You've already seen the `Comparable` module in action. Here, we're going to talk about one of the most commonly used Ruby modules: `Enumerable`. We've already encountered it indirectly: Both `Array` and `Hash` mix in `Enumerable`, and by doing so, they get methods like `select`, `reject`, `find`, and `map`. Those methods, and others, are instance methods of the `Enumerable` module.

You, too, can mix `Enumerable` into your own classes:

```
class C
  include Enumerable
end
```

By itself, that doesn't do much. To tap into the benefits of `Enumerable`, you must define an `each` instance method in your class:

```
class c
  include Enumerable
```

```
    def each
      # relevant code here
    end
  end
```

Let's look more closely at each and its role as the engine for enumerable behavior.

11.4.1 *Gaining enumerability through each*

Any class that aspires to being enumerable must have an each method; and the job of each is *to yield items to a supplied code block, one at a time.*

In the case of an array, this means yielding the first item in the array, then the second, and so forth. In the case of a hash, it means yielding a key/value pair (in the form of a two-element array), then yielding another key/value pair, and so forth. In the case of a file handle, it means yielding one line of the file at a time. Exactly what each means thus varies from one class to another. And if you define an each in a class of your own, it can mean whatever you want it to mean—as long as it yields something.

Most of the methods in the Enumerable module piggyback on these each methods, using an object's each behavior as the basis for a variety of searching, querying, and filtering operations. A number of methods we've already mentioned in looking at arrays and hashes—including find, select, reject, map, any?, and all?—are instance methods of Enumerable. They end up being methods of arrays and hashes because the Array and Hash classes use Enumerable as a mix-in. And they all work the same way: *They call the method* each. each is the key to using Enumerable. Whatever the class, if it wants to be an Enumerable, it has to define each.

You can get a good sense of how Enumerable works by writing a small, proof-of-concept class that uses it. Listing 11.1 shows such a class: Rainbow. This class has an each method that yields one color at a time. Because the class mixes in Enumerable, its instances are automatically endowed with the instance methods defined in that module.

In the example, we use the find method to pinpoint the first color whose first character is "y". find works by calling each. each yields items, and find uses the code block we've given it to test those items, one at a time, for a match. When each gets around to yielding "yellow", find runs it through the block and it passes the test. The variable r therefore receives the value "yellow".

Listing 11.1 An Enumerable class and its deployment of the each method

```
class Rainbow
  include Enumerable
  def each
```

```
      yield "red"
      yield "orange"
      yield "yellow"
      yield "green"
      yield "blue"
      yield "indigo"
      yield "violet"
    end
  end
r = Rainbow.new
y_color = r.find {|color| color[0,1] == 'y' }
puts "First color starting with 'y' is #{y_color}."
```

Output: First color starting with "y" is yellow.

Notice that there's no need to define `find`. It's part of `Enumerable`, which we've mixed in. It knows what to do and how to use `each` to do it.

`Enumerable` methods often join with each other; for example, `each` yields to `find`, and `find` yields to the block you provide. You can also get a free `each` ride from an array, instead of writing every `yield` explicitly. For example, `Rainbow` can be rewritten like this:

```
class Rainbow
  COLORS = ["red", "orange", "yellow", "green",
  "blue", "indigo", "violet"]        ◁———— ❶
  def each
    COLORS.each {|color| yield color }   ◁———— ❷
  end
end
```

In this version, we ask the `COLORS` array ❶ to iterate via its own `each` ❷, and then we yield each item as it appears in our block.

The `Enumerable` module is powerful and in common use. Much of the searching and querying functionality you see in Ruby collection objects comes directly from `Enumerable`, as you can see by asking irb:

```
>> Enumerable.instance_methods(false).sort                 ◁———— ❶
=> ["all?", "any?", "collect", "detect", "each_with_index",
"entries", "find", "find_all", "grep", "include?", "inject",
"map", "max", "member?", "min", "partition", "reject",
"select", "sort", "sort_by", "to_a", "zip"]
```

(The `false` argument to `instance_methods` ❶ suppresses instance methods defined in superclasses and other modules.) This example includes some methods you can explore on your own and some that we've discussed. The upshot is that the `Enumerable` module is the home of most of the major built-in facilities Ruby offers for collection traversal, querying, filtering, and sorting.

It's no big surprise that arrays and hashes are enumerable; after all, they are manifestly collections of objects. Slightly more surprising is the fact that strings, too, are enumerable—and their fundamental `each` behavior isn't what you might expect. Now that you know about the `Enumerable` module, you're in a position to understand the enumerability of strings, as Ruby defines it.

11.4.2 *Strings as Enumerables*

The `String` class mixes in `Enumerable`; but the behavior of strings in their capacity as enumerable objects isn't what everyone expects it to be. There's nothing you can't do, by way of filtering and manipulating strings and parts of strings. But the results you want may require techniques other than those that first occur to you.

Enumerable objects, as you now know, have an `each` method. The `each` method yields *each* item in the collection, one at a time. Strings are, in a sense, collections of individual characters. You may, then, expect `String#each` to yield the string's characters.

However, it doesn't. For purposes of their enumerable qualities, Ruby looks at strings as *collections of lines*. If you walk through a string with `each`, a new value is yielded every time there's a new line, *not* every time there's a new character:

```
s = "This is\na multiline\nstring."
s.each {|e| puts "Next value: #{e}" }
```

This snippet assigns a multiline string (with explicit newline characters (\n) embedded in it) to a variable and then iterates through the string. Inside the code block, each element of the string is printed out. The output is as follows:

```
Next value: This is
Next value: a multiline
Next value: string.
```

Going through each element in a string means going through the lines, not the characters. And because `each` is the point of reference for all the selection and filtering methods of `Enumerable`, when you perform, say, a `select` operation or a `map` operation on a string, the elements you're selecting or mapping are lines rather than characters.

However, strings have a method that lets you iterate through the characters: `each_byte`. It works like this:

```
"abc".each_byte {|b| puts "Next byte: #{b}" }
```

The output is also possibly surprising:

```
Next byte: 97
Next byte: 98
Next byte: 99
```

You get the ASCII values of the characters. If you want to turn them back into individual characters, you can call the chr method on the numbers:

```
"abc".each_byte {|b| puts "Next character: #{b.chr}" }
```

This code produces

```
Next character: a
Next character: b
Next character: c
```

There have been many discussions about the possibility of adding a method to
Ruby that would allow for direct iteration through characters, without having to
convert. If you find yourself writing a method like this:

```
class String
  def each_char
    each_byte {|b| yield b.chr }
  end
end
```

you won't be the first Rubyist to have done so.

We've searched, transformed, filtered, and queried a variety of collection
objects, using an even bigger variety of methods. The one thing we haven't done
is *sort* collections. That's what we'll do next, and last, in this chapter.

11.5 *Sorting collections*

If you have a class, and you want to be able to sort multiple instances of it, you
need to do the following:

- Define a comparison method for the class (<=>)
- Place the multiple instances in a container, probably an array

It's important to understand the separateness of these two steps. Why? Because
the ability to sort is granted by Enumerable, but this does *not* mean your class has to
mix in Enumerable. Rather, you put your objects into a container object that *does*
mix in Enumerable. That container object, as an enumerable, has two sorting
methods, sort and sort_by, which you can use to sort the collection.

In the vast majority of cases, the container into which you place objects you
want sorted will be an array. Sometimes it will be a hash, in which case the result

will be an array (an array of two-element key/value pair arrays, sorted by key or other criterion).

Normally, you don't have to create an array of items explicitly before you sort them. More often, you sort a collection that your program has already generated automatically. For instance, you may perform a `select` operation on a collection of objects and sort the ones you've selected. Or you may be manipulating a collection of ActiveRecord objects and want to sort them for display based on the values of one or more of their fields—as in the example from RCRchive in section 3.2.1. (You might find it interesting to look at that example again after reading this chapter.)

The manual stuffing of lists of objects into square brackets to create array examples in this section is, therefore, a bit contrived. But the goal is to focus directly on techniques for sorting; and that's what we'll do.

Here's a simple sorting example involving an array of integers:

```
>> [3,2,5,4,1].sort
=> [1, 2, 3, 4, 5]
```

Doing this is easy when you have numbers or even strings (where a sort gives you alphabetical order). The array you put them in has a sorting mechanism, and the integers or strings have some knowledge of what it means to be in order.

But what if you want to sort, say, an array of edition objects?

```
>> [ed1, ed2, ed3, ed4, ed5].sort
```

Yes, the five edition objects have been put into an array; and yes, arrays are enumerable and therefore sortable. But for an array to sort the things inside it, those things themselves have to have some sense of what it means to be in order. How is Ruby supposed to know which edition goes where in the sorted version of the array?

The key to sorting an array of objects is being able to sort *two* of those objects, and then doing that over and over until the sort order of the whole collection is established. That's why you have to define the `<=>` method in the class of the objects you want sorted.

For example, if you want to be able to sort an array of edition objects by price, you can define `<=>` in the `Edition` class:

```
def <=>(other_edition)
  self.price <=> other_edition.price
end
```

Once you've done that, any array of editions you sort will come out in price-sorted order:

```
price_sorted = [ed1,ed2,ed3,ed4,ed5].sort
```

Ruby applies the `<=>` test to these elements, two at a time, building up enough information to perform the complete sort.

Again, the sequence of events is as follows:

- You teach your objects how to compare themselves with each other, using `<=>`.

- You put those objects inside an enumerable object (probably an array) and tell that object to sort itself. It does this by asking the objects to compare themselves to each other with `<=>`.

If you keep this division of labor in mind, you'll understand how sorting operates and how it relates to `Enumerable`.

Getting items in order and sorting them also relates closely to the `Comparable` module, the basic workings of which you saw in chapter 9. We'll put `Comparable` in the picture, so that we can see the whole ordering and sorting landscape.

11.5.1 *Sorting and the Comparable module*

You may wonder how `<=>` defining (done for the sake of giving an assist to the sort operations of enumerable collections) relates to the `Comparable` module, which, as you'll recall, depends on the existence of a `<=>` method to perform its magical comparison operations. The `<=>` method seems to be working overtime.

It all fits together like this:

- If you don't define `<=>`, you can sort objects if you put them inside an array and provide a code block telling the array how it should rank any two of the objects. (This is discussed next, in section 11.5.2.)

- If you do define `<=>`, then your objects can be put inside an array and sorted.

- If you define `<=>` *and also include* `Comparable` *in your class*, then you get sortability inside an array *and* you can perform all the comparison operations between any two of your objects (`>`, `<`, and so on), as per the discussion of `Comparable` in chapter 9.

The `<=>` method is thus useful both for classes whose instances you wish to sort and for classes whose instances you wish to compare with each other using the full complement of comparison operators.

Back we go to sorting—and, in particular, to a variant of sorting where you provide a code block instead of a `<=>` method to specify how objects should be compared and ordered.

11.5.2 *Defining sort order in a block*

You can also tell Ruby how to sort an array by defining the sort behavior in a code block. You can do this in cases where no <=> method is defined for these objects; and if there is a <=> method, the code in the block overrides it.

Let's say, for example, that we've defined Edition#<=> in such a way that it sorts by price. But now we want to sort by year of publication. We can force a year-based sort by using a block:

```
year_sort = [ed1,ed2,ed3,ed4,ed5].sort do |a,b|
  a.year <=> b.year
end
```

The block takes two arguments, a and b. This enables Ruby to use the block as many times as needed to compare one edition with another. The code inside the block does a <=> comparison between the respective publication years of the two editions. For this call to sort, the code in the block is used instead of the code in the <=> method of the Edition class.

You can use this code-block form of sort to handle cases where your objects don't know how to compare themselves to each other. This may be the case if the objects are of a class that has no <=> method. It can also come in handy when the objects being sorted are of *different* classes and by default don't know how to compare themselves to each other. Integers and strings, for example, can't be compared directly: An expression like "2" <=> 4 causes a fatal error. But if you do a conversion first, you can pull it off:

```
>> ["2",1,5,"3",4,"6"].sort {|a,b| a.to_i <=> b.to_i }
=> [1, "2", "3", 4, 5, "6"]
```

The elements in the sorted output array are the same as those in the input array: a mixture of strings and integers. But they're ordered as they would be if they were all integers. Inside the code block, both strings and integers are normalized to integer form with to_i. As far as the sort engine is concerned, it's performing a sort based on a series of integer comparisons. It then applies the order it comes up with to the original array.

sort with a block can thus help you where the existing comparison methods won't get the job done. And there's an even more concise way to sort a collection with a code block: the sort_by method.

Concise sorting with sort_by

Like sort, sort_by is an instance method of Enumerable. The main difference is that sort_by always takes a block (the block is not optional), and it only requires that you show it how to treat one item in the collection. `sort_by` will figure out that you want to do the same thing to both items every time it compares a pair of objects.

The previous array-sorting example can be written like this, using `sort_by`:

```
>> ["2",1,5,"3",4,"6"].sort_by {|a| a.to_i }
=> [1, "2", "3", 4, 5, "6"]
```

All we have to do in the block is show (once) what action needs to be performed in order to prep each object for the sort operation. We don't have to call `to_i` on two objects; nor do we need to use the `<=>` method explicitly. The `sort_by` approach can save you a step and tighten up your code.

This brings us to the end of our survey of Ruby container and collection objects. The exploration of Ruby built-ins continues in chapter 12 with a look at regular expressions and a variety of operations that use them.

11.6 *Summary*

In this chapter, we've looked principally at Ruby's major container classes, `Array` and `Hash`. They differ primarily in that arrays are ordered (indexed numerically), whereas hashes are unordered and indexed by arbitrary objects (keys, each associated with a value). Arrays, moreover, often operate as a kind of common currency of collections: Results of sorting and filtering operations, even on non-arrays, are usually returned in array form.

We've also examined the powerful `Enumerable` module, which endows arrays, hashes, and strings with a set of methods for searching, querying, and sorting. `Enumerable` is the foundational Ruby tool for collection manipulation.

The chapter also looked at some special behaviors of ActiveRecord collections, specialized collection objects that use Ruby array behavior as a point of departure but don't restrict themselves to array functionality. These objects provide an enlightening example of the use of Ruby fundamentals as a starting point—but not an ending point—for domain-specific functionality.

As we proceed to chapter 12, we'll be moving in a widening spiral. Chapter 12 is about regular expressions, which relate chiefly to strings but which will allow us to cover some operations that combine string and collection behaviors.

*Regular expressions
and regexp-based
string operations*

In this chapter, we'll explore Ruby's facilities for pattern-matching and text processing, centering around the use of *regular expressions.*

A regular expression in Ruby serves the same purposes it does in other languages: It specifies a pattern of characters, a pattern which may or may not correctly predict (that is, match) a given string. You use these pattern-match operations for conditional branching (match/no match), pinpointing substrings (parts of a string that match parts of the pattern), and various text-filtering and -massaging operations.

Regular expressions in Ruby are objects. You send messages *to* a regular expression. Regular expressions add something to the Ruby landscape but, as objects, they also fit nicely into the landscape.

We'll start with an overview of regular expressions. From there, we'll move on to the details of how to write them and, of course, how to use them. In the latter category, we'll look both at using regular expressions in simple match operations and using them in methods where they play a role in a larger process, such as filtering a collection or repeatedly scanning a string.

As you'll see, once regular expressions are on the radar, it's possible to fill some gaps in our coverage of strings and collection objects. Regular expressions always play a helper role; you don't program *toward* them, as you might program with a string or an array as the final goal. You program *from* regular expressions *to* a result; and Ruby provides considerable facilities for doing so.

12.1 *What are regular expressions?*

Regular expressions appear in many programming languages, with minor differences among the incarnations. They have a weird reputation. Using them is a powerful, concentrated technique; they burn through text-processing problems like acid through a padlock. (Not all such problems, but a large number of them.) They are also, in the view of many people (including people who understand them well), difficult to use, difficult to read, opaque, unmaintainable, and ultimately counterproductive.

You have to judge for yourself. The one thing you should *not* do is shy away from learning at least the basics of how regular expressions work and the Ruby methods that utilize them. Even if you decide you aren't a "regular expression person," you need a reading knowledge of them. And you'll by no means be alone if you end up using them in your own programs more than you anticipated.

A number of Ruby built-in methods take regular expressions as arguments and perform selection or modification on one or more string objects. Regular expressions are used, for example, to *scan* a string for multiple occurrences of a pattern, to *substitute* a replacement string for a substring, and to *split* a string into multiple substrings based on a matching separator.

12.1.1 A word to the regex-wise

If you're familiar with regular expressions from Perl, sed, vi, Emacs, or any other source, you may want to skim or skip the expository material here and pick up in section 12.5, where we talk about Ruby methods that use regular expressions. However, note that Ruby regexes aren't identical to those in any other language. You'll almost certainly be able to read them, but you may need to study the differences (such as whether parentheses are special by default or special when escaped) if you get into writing them.

12.1.2 A further word to everyone

You may end up using only a modest number of regular expressions in your Rails applications. Becoming a regex wizard isn't a prerequisite for Rails programming.

However, regular expressions are often important in converting data from one format to another, and they often loom large in Rails-related activities like salvaging legacy data. As the Rails framework gains in popularity, there are likely to be more and more cases where data in an old format (or a text-dump version of an old format) needs to be picked apart, massaged, and put back together in the form of Rails-accessible database records. Regular expressions, and the methods that deploy them for string and text manipulation, will serve you well in such cases.

Let's turn now to writing some regular expressions.

12.2 Writing regular expressions

Regular expressions look like strings with a secret "Make hidden characters visible" switched turned on—and a "Hide some regular characters" switch turned on, too. You have to learn to read and write regular expressions as a thing unto themselves. They're not strings. They're representations of *patterns*.

A regular expression specifies a pattern. Any given string either matches that pattern or doesn't match it. The Ruby methods that use regular expressions use them either to determine whether a given string matches a given pattern or to make that determination and also take some action based on the answer.

Patterns of the kind specified by regular expressions are most easily understood, initially, in plain language. Here are several examples of patterns expressed this way:

- The letter *a*, followed by a digit
- Any uppercase letter, followed by at least one lowercase letter
- Three digits, followed by a hyphen, followed by four digits

A pattern can also include components and constraints related to positioning inside the string:

- The beginning of a line, followed by one or more whitespace characters
- The character . (period) at the end of a string
- An uppercase letter at the beginning of a word

Pattern components like "the beginning of a line", which match a condition rather than a character in a string, are nonetheless expressed with characters in the regular expression.

Regular expressions provide a language for expressing patterns. Learning to write them consists principally of learning how various things are expressed inside a regular expression. The most commonly applied rules of regular expression construction are fairly easy to learn. You just have to remember that a regular expression, although it contains characters, isn't a string. It's a special notation for expressing a pattern which may or may not correctly describe any given string.

12.2.1 *The regular expression literal constructor*

The regular expression literal constructor is a pair of forward slashes:

```
//
```

As odd as this may look, it really is a regular expression, if a skeletal one. You can verify that it gives you an instance of the `Regexp` class, in irb:

```
>> //.class
=> Regexp
```

Between the slashes, you insert the specifics of the regular expression.

A quick introduction to pattern-matching operations

Any pattern-matching operation has two main players: a regular expression and a string. The regular expression expresses predictions about the string. Either the string fulfills those predictions (matches the pattern), or it doesn't.

The simplest way to find out whether there's a match between a pattern and a string is with the `match` method. You can do this in either direction: Regular expression objects and string objects both respond to `match`.

```
puts "Match!" if /abc/.match("The alphabet starts with abc.")
puts "Match!" if "The alphabet starts with abc.".match(/abc/)
```

Ruby also features a pattern-matching operator, =~ (equal-sign tilde), which goes between a string and a regular expression:

```
puts "Match!" if /abc/ =~ "The alphabet starts with abc."
puts "Match!" if "The alphabet starts with abc." =~ /abc/
```

As you might guess, the pattern-matching "operator" is actually an instance method of both the `String` and `Regexp` classes.

The `match` method and the =~ operator are equally useful when you're after a simple yes/no answer to the question of whether there's a match between a string and a pattern. If there's no match, you get back `nil`. Where `match` and =~ differ from each other, chiefly, is in what they return when there *is* a match: =~ returns the numerical index of the character in the string where the match started, whereas `match` returns an instance of the class `MatchData`:

```
>> "The alphabet starts with abc" =~ /abc/
=> 25
>> /abc/.match("The alphabet starts with abc.")
=> #<MatchData:0x1b0d88>
```

We'll examine `MatchData` objects a little further on. For the moment, we'll be concerned mainly with getting a yes/no answer to an attempted match, so any of the techniques shown thus far will work. For the sake of consistency, and because we'll be more concerned with `MatchData` objects than numerical indices of substrings, the examples in this chapter will stick to the `Regexp#match` method.

Now, let's look in more detail at the composition of a regular expression.

12.2.2 Building a pattern

When you write a regular expression, you put the definition of your pattern between the forward slashes. Remember that what you're putting there isn't a string, but a set of predictions and constraints that you want to look for *in* a string.

The possible components of a regular expression include the following:

- *Literal characters*, meaning "match this character."
- *The dot wildcard character (.)*, meaning "match any character."
- *Character classes*, meaning "match one of these characters."

We'll discuss each of these in turn. We'll then use that knowledge to look more deeply at match operations.

Literal characters

Any literal character you put in a regular expression matches *itself* in the string. That may sound like a wordy way to put it, but even in the simplest-looking cases it's good to be reminded that the regexp and the string operate in a pattern-matching relationship:

```
/a/
```

This regular expression matches the string "a", as well as any string containing the letter "a".

Some characters have special meanings to the regexp parser (as you'll see in detail shortly). When you want to match one of these special characters *as itself*, you have to *escape* it with a backslash (\). For example, to match the character ? (question mark), you have to write this:

```
/\?/
```

The backslash means "don't treat the next character as special; treat it as itself."

The special characters include ^, $, ? , ., /, \, [,], {, }, (,), +, and *.

The wildcard character . (dot)

Sometimes you'll want to match *any character* at some point in your pattern. You do this with the special wildcard character . (dot). A dot matches any character with the exception of a newline. (There's a way to make it match newlines too, which we'll see a little later.)

This regular expression

```
/.ejected/
```

matches both "dejected" and "rejected". It also matches "%ejected" and "8ejected". The wildcard dot is handy, but sometimes it gives you more matches than you want. However, you can impose constraints on matches while still allowing for multiple possible strings, using *character classes*.

Character classes

A character class is an explicit list of characters, placed inside the regular expression in square brackets:

```
/[dr]ejected/
```

This means "match either *d* or *r*, followed by *ejected*. This new pattern matches either "dejected" or "rejected" but not "&ejected". A character class is a kind of quasi-wildcard: It allows for multiple possible characters, but only a limited number of them.

Inside a character class, you can also insert a *range* of characters. A common case is this, for lowercase letters:

```
/[a-z]/
```

To match a hexadecimal digit, you might use several ranges inside a character class:

```
/[A-Fa-f0-9]/
```

This matches any character *a* through *f* (upper- or lowercase) or any digit.

Sometimes you need to match any character *except* those on a special list. You may, for example, be looking for the first character in a string that is *not* a valid hexadecimal digit.

You perform this kind of negative search by *negating* a character class. To do so, you put a caret (^) at the beginning of the class. Here's the character class that matches any character except a valid hexadecimal digit:

```
/[^A-Fa-f0-9]/
```

Some character classes are so common that they have special abbreviations.

Special escape sequences for common character classes

To match *any digit*, you can do this:

```
/[0-9]/
```

But you can also accomplish the same thing more concisely with the special escape sequence \d:

```
/\d/
```

Two other useful escape sequences for predefined character classes are these:

- \w matches any digit, alphabetical character, or underscore (_).
- \s matches any whitespace character (space, tab, newline).

Each of these predefined character classes also has a negated form. You can match *any character that is not a digit* by doing this:

```
/\D/
```

Similarly, \W matches *any character other than an alphanumeric character or underscore,* and \S matches *any non-whitespace character.*

WARNING CHARACTER CLASSES ARE LONGER THAN WHAT THEY MATCH Even a short character class—[a]—takes up more than one space in a regular expression. But remember, each character class matches *one character* in the string. When you look at a character class like /[dr]/, it may look like it's going to match the substring "dr". But it isn't: It's going to match either *d* or *r*.

A successful match returns a `MatchData` object. Let's look at `MatchData` objects and their capabilities up close.

12.3 *More on matching and MatchData*

So far, we've looked at basic match operations:

```
regex.match(string)
string.match(regex)
```

These are essentially true/false tests: Either there's a match, or there isn't. Now we're going to examine what happens on successful and unsuccessful matches and what a match operation can do for you beyond the yes/no answer.

12.3.1 *Capturing submatches with parentheses*

One of the most important techniques of regular expression construction is the use of parentheses to specify *captures.*

The idea is this. When you test for a match between a string—say, a line from a file—and a pattern, it's usually because you want to do something with the string or, more commonly, with *part of the string*. The capture notation allows you to isolate and save substrings of the string that match particular subpatterns.

For example, let's say we have a string containing information about a person:

```
Peel,Emma,Mrs.,talented amateur
```

From this string, we need to harvest the person's last name and title. We know the fields are comma-separated, and we know what order they come in: last name, first name, title, occupation.

To construct a pattern that matches such a string, we think along the following lines:

First some alphabetical characters,
then a comma,
then some alphabetical characters,
then a comma,
then either "Mr." or "Mrs."

We're keeping it simple: no hyphenated names, no doctors or professors, no leaving off the final period on Mr. and Mrs. (which would be done in British usage). The regular expression, then, might look like this:

```
/[A-Za-z]+,[A-Za-z]+,Mrs?\./
```

That pattern matches the string, as irb attests:

```
>> /[A-Za-z]+,[A-Za-z]+,Mrs?\./.match("Peel,Emma,Mrs.,talented amateur")
=> #<MatchData:0x401f0a6c>
```

We got a `MatchData` object rather than `nil`. But now what? We don't have any way to isolate the substrings we're interested in ("Peel" and "Mrs.").

That's where parenthetical groupings come in. We want two such groupings: one around the subpattern that matches the last name, and one around the subpattern that matches the title:

```
/([A-Za-z]+),[A-Za-z]+,(Mrs?\.)/
```

Now, when we perform the match

```
/([A-Za-z]+),[A-Za-z]+,(Mrs?\.)/.match(str)
```

two things happen:

- We get a `MatchData` object that gives us access to the submatches (discussed in a moment).
- Ruby automatically populates a series of variables for us, which also give us access to those submatches.

The variables that Ruby populates are global variables, and they have numbers as names: `$1`, `$2`, and so forth. `$1` contains the substring matched by the subpattern inside the *first set of parentheses from the left* in the regular expression:

```
puts $1        ⟵——— Output: Peel
```

`$2` contains the substring matched by the *second* subpattern; and so forth. In general, the rule is this: After a successful match operation, the variable $*n* (where *n* is a number) contains the substring matched by subpattern inside the *n*th set of parentheses from the left in the regular expression.

We can deploy the match we just did as follows:

```
puts "Dear #{$2} #{$1},"     ⟵——— Output: Dear Mrs. Peel,
```

The $*n*-style variables are handy for grabbing submatches. You can, however, accomplish the same thing in a more structured, programmatic way by leveraging the fact that a successful match operation has a return value: a `MatchData` object.

12.3.2 *Match success and failure*

Every match operation either succeeds or fails. Let's start with the simpler case: failure. When you try to match a string to a pattern, and the string doesn't match, the result is always `nil`:

```
>> /a/.match("b")
=> nil
```

This `nil` stands in for the *false* or *no* answer when you treat the match as a true/false test.

Unlike `nil`, the `MatchData` object returned by a successful match has a Boolean value of true, which makes it handy for simple match/no-match tests. Beyond this, however, it also stores information about the match, which you can pry out of them with the appropriate methods: where the match began (at what character in the string), how much of the string it covered, what was captured in the parenthetical groups, and so forth.

To use the `MatchData` object, you must first save it. Consider an example where we want to pluck a phone number from a string and save the various parts of it (area code, exchange, number) in groupings. Listing 12.1 shows how we might do this.

Listing 12.1   Matching a phone number and querying the resulting `MatchData` object

```
string = "My phone number is (123) 555-1234."
phone_re = /\(((\d{3})\)\s+(\d{3})-(\d{4})/
m = phone_re.match(string)
unless m
  puts "There was no match--sorry."     ┐ exit terminates
  exit                              ←─────┘ program immediately
end
print "The whole string we started with: "
puts m.string    ←───── ❶
print "The entire part of the string that matched: "
puts m[0]    ←───── ❷
puts "The three captures: "
3.times do |index|    ←───── ❸
  puts "Capture ##{index + 1}: #{m.captures[index]}"
end
puts "Here's another way to get at the first capture:"
print "Capture #1: "
puts m[1]    ←───── ❹
```

In this code, we use the `string` method of `MatchData` ❶ to get the entire string on which the match operation was performed. To get the part of the string that matched our pattern, we address the `MatchData` object with square brackets, with an index of 0 ❷. We also use the nifty `times` method ❸ to iterate exactly three times through a code block and print out the submatches (the parenthetical captures) in succession. Inside that code block, a method called `captures` fishes out the substrings that matched the parenthesized parts of the pattern. Finally, we take another look at the first capture, this time through a different technique ❹: indexing the `MatchData` object directly with square brackets and positive integers, each integer corresponding to a capture.

Here's the output of listing 12.1:

```
The whole string we started with: My phone number is (123) 555-1234.
The entire part of the string that matched: (123) 555-1234
The three captures:
Capture #1: 123
Capture #2: 555
Capture #3: 1234
Here's another way to get at the first capture:
Capture #1: 123
```

This gives you a taste of the kinds of match data you can extract from a `MatchData` object. You can see that there are two ways of retrieving captures. We'll focus on those techniques next.

Two ways of getting the captures

One way to get the parenthetical captures from a `MatchData` object is by directly indexing the object, array-style:

```
m[0]   ◁─────── Entire match
m[1]   ◁─────── First capture (first set of parentheses from left)
m[2]   ◁─────── Second capture
#etc.
```

From 1 onward, these indices correspond to the *n* in the `$n` global variables that contain the captured substrings.

`MatchData` objects also have a method called `captures`, which returns all the captured substrings in a single array. Because this is a regular array, the first item in it—essentially, the same as the global variable `$1`—is item *zero*, not item one. In other words, the following equivalencies apply

```
m[1] == m.captures[0]
m[2] == m.captures[1]
```

and so forth.

By far the most common data extracted from a `MatchData` object consists of the captured substrings. However, the object contains other information, which you can take if you need it.

Other MatchData information

The code in listing 12.2, which is designed to be grafted onto listing 12.1, gives some quick examples of several further `MatchData` methods.

Listing 12.2   Supplemental code for phone-number matching operations

```
print "The part of the string before the part that matched was:"
puts m.pre_match
print "The part of the string after the part that matched was:"
puts m.post_match
print "The second capture began at character "
puts m.begin(2)
print "The third capture ended at character "
puts m.end(3)
```

The output from this supplemental code is as follows:

```
The string up to the part that matched was: My phone number is
The string after the part that matched was: .
The second capture began at character 25
The third capture ended at character 33
```

The `MatchData` object is a kind of clearinghouse for information about what happened when the pattern met the string. With that knowledge in place, let's continue looking at techniques you can use to build and use regular expressions.

12.4 Further regular expression techniques

This section includes coverage of a number of techniques of regular expression design and usage that will help you both with the writing of your own regular expressions and with your regular expression literacy. If matching /abc/ makes sense to you now, matching /^x?[yz]{2}.*\z/ will make sense to you shortly.

12.4.1 Quantifiers and greediness

Regular expression syntax gives you ways to specify not only what you want but also how many: exactly one of a particular character, 5 to 10 repetitions of a subpattern, and so forth.

All the quantifiers operate on either a single character or a parenthetical group. When you specify that you want to match (say) three consecutive occurrences of a particular subpattern, that subpattern can be just one character, or it can be a longer subpattern placed inside parentheses.

Zero or one

Consider a case where you want to match either "Mr" or "Mrs"—and, furthermore, you want to accommodate both the American versions, which end with periods, and the British versions, which don't.

You might describe the pattern as follows:

```
the character M, followed by the character r, followed by
zero or one of the character s, followed by
zero or one of the character '.'
```

Regular expression notation has a special character to represent the "zero or one" situation: the question mark (?). The pattern described above would be expressed in regular expression notation as follows:

```
/Mrs?\.?/
```

The question mark after the "s" means that a string with an "s" in that position will match the pattern, and so will a string without an "s". The same principle applies to the literal period (note the backslash, indicating that this is an actual period, not a special wildcard dot) followed by a question mark. The whole pattern, then, will match "Mr", "Mrs", "Mr.", or "Mrs."

Zero or more

A fairly common case is one in which a string contains whitespace, but you're not sure how much. Let's say you're trying to match closing </p> tags in an HTML document. Such a tag may or may not contain whitespace. All of these are equivalent in HTML:

```
</p>
< /p>
</    p>
</p
  >
```

In order to match the tag, you have to allow for unpredictable amounts of whitespace in your pattern—including none.

This is a case for the *zero or more* quantifier, namely the asterisk or, as it's often called, the star (*):

```
/<\s*\/\s*p\s*>/
```

Each time it appears, the sequence \s* means that the string being matched is allowed to contain zero or more whitespace characters at this point in the match. (Note too the necessity of escaping the forward slash in the pattern with a backslash.

Otherwise, it would be interpreted as the slash signaling the end of the regular expression itself.)

One or more

You can also specify a *one or more* count. It matches if the string contains at least one occurrence of the specified subpattern at the appropriate point in the match. A one-or-more count is indicated with a plus sign (+). For example, the pattern

```
/\d+/
```

matches any sequence of one or more consecutive digits.

Greedy and non-greedy quantifiers

The * (zero or more) and + (one or more) quantifiers are *greedy*. This means they match as many characters as possible, consistent with allowing the rest of the pattern to match.

Look at what .* matches in this snippet:

```
string = "abc!def!ghi!"
match = /.+!/.match(string)
puts match[0]
```

You've asked for *one or more characters* (using the wildcard dot) *followed by an exclamation point*. You might expect to get back the substring "abc!", which fits that description.

Instead, you get "abc!def!ghi!". The + quantifier greedily eats up as much of the string as it can and only stops at the *last* exclamation point, not the first.

You can make + as well as * into non-greedy quantifiers by putting a question mark after them. Watch what happens when you do that with the last example:

```
string = "abc!def!ghi!"
match = /.+?!/.match(string)
puts match[0]
```

This version says, "Give me one or more wildcard characters, but only as many as you see until you hit your first exclamation point—then give me that." Sure enough, this time you get "abc!"

The question mark comes in handy. By all means try it (along with the other techniques you're learning here) in irb, and you'll get a good sense of the difference between the greedy and non-greedy versions of the quantifiers.

Specific numbers of repetitions

You can also custom-specify how many repetitions of a subpattern you want. You do this by putting the number in curly braces ({}), as this example shows:

```
/\d{3}-\d{4}/
```

This pattern matches 555-1212 and other phone-number-like sequences. You can also specify a range inside the braces:

```
/\d{1,10}/
```

This example matches any string containing 1 to 10 consecutive digits. A single number followed by a comma is interpreted as a minimum (*n* or more repetitions). You can therefore match "three or more digits" like this:

```
/\d{3,}/
```

Ruby's regular expression engine is smart enough to let you know if your range is impossible; you'll get a fatal error if you try to match, say, {10,2} (at least 10 but no more than 2) occurrences of a subpattern.

You can specify a repetition count not only for single characters or character classes but also for any regular expression *atom*—any subexpression corresponding to a particular component of the pattern you're trying to match. Atoms include parenthetical subpatterns. Thus you can do this:

```
/([A-Z]\d){5}/
```

to match five consecutive occurrences of *uppercase letter, followed by digit*. The repetition count is understood to apply to the whole parenthesized subexpression.

We're going to look next at ways in which you can specify conditions under which you want matches to occur, rather than the content you expect the string to have.

12.4.2 Anchors and lookahead assertions

Assertions and anchors are different types of creature from characters. When you match a character (even based on a character class or wildcard), you're said to be *consuming* a character in the string you're matching. An assertion or an anchor, on the other hand, doesn't consume any characters. Instead, it expresses a *constraint*, a condition that must be met before the matching of characters is allowed to proceed.

The most common anchors are *beginning of line* (^) and *end of line* ($). You might use the beginning-of-line anchor for a task like removing all the comment lines from a Ruby program file. You'd accomplish this by going through all the lines in the file and printing out only those that do *not* start with a hash-mark (#)

or with whitespace followed by a hash-mark. To determine which lines are comment lines, you could use this regular expression:

```
/^\s*#/
```

The ^ (caret) in this pattern *anchors* the match at the beginning of a line. If the rest of the pattern matches, but *not* at the beginning of the line, that doesn't count—as you can see with a couple of tests:

```
>> comment_regexp = /^\s*#/
=> /^\s*#/
>> comment_regexp.match("  # Pure comment!")
=> #<MatchData:0x345d08>
>> comment_regexp.match("  x = 1  # Code plus comment!")
=> nil
```

Only the line that starts with some whitespace and the hash character is a match for the comment pattern. The other line doesn't match and would therefore not be deleted if you were to use this regular expression to filter comments out of a file.

Table 12.1 shows a number of anchors, including start and end of line and start and end of string.

Table 12.1 Regular expression anchors

Notation	Description	Example	Sample matching string
^	Beginning of line	/^\s*#/	" # A Ruby comment line"
$	End of line	/\.$/	"one\ntwo\nthree.\nfour"
\A	Beginning of string	/\AFour score/	"Four score"
\z	End of string	/from the earth.\z/	"from the earth."
\Z	End of string (except for final newline)	/from the earth.\Z/	"from the earth\n"
\b	Word boundary	/\b\w+\b/	"!!!word***" (matches "word")

Note that \z matches the absolute end of the string, whereas \Z matches the end of the string except for an optional trailing newline. \Z is useful in cases where you're not sure whether your string has a newline character at the end, and you don't want to have to worry about it.

Hand-in-hand with anchors go *assertions*, which, similarly, tell the regular expression processor that you want a match to count only under certain conditions.

Lookahead assertions

Let's say you want to match a sequence of numbers only if it ends with a period. But you don't want the period itself to count as part of the match.

One way to do this is with a *lookahead assertion*—or, to be complete, a *zero-width, positive lookahead assertion*. Here, followed by further explanation, is how you do it:

```
str = "123 456. 789"
m = /\d+(?=\.)/.match(str)
```

At this point, m[0] contains "456"—the one sequence of numbers that is followed by a period.

Here's a little more commentary on some of the terminology:

- *Zero-width* means it doesn't consume any characters in the string. The presence of the period is noted, but you can still match the period if your pattern continues.

- *Positive* means you want to stipulate that the period be present. There are also *negative* lookaheads; they use (?!...) rather than (?=...).

- *Lookahead assertion* means you want to know that you're specifying what *would* be next, without matching it.

Like anchors, assertions add richness and granularity to the pattern language with which you express the matches you're looking for. Also in the language-enrichment category are regular expression *modifiers*.

12.4.3 Modifiers

A regular expression modifier is a letter placed after the final, closing forward slash of the regex literal:

```
/abc/i
```

The i modifier shown here causes match operations involving this regular expression to be case-insensitive. The other most common modifier is m. The m (multi-line) modifier has the effect that the wildcard dot character, which normally matches *any character except newline*, will match *any character, including newline*. This is useful when you want to capture everything that lies between, say, an opening parenthesis and a closing one, and you don't know (or care) whether they're on the same line. Here's an example; note the embedded newline characters (\n) in the string:

```
str = "This (including\nwhat's in parens\n) takes up three lines."
m = /\(.*?\)/m.match(str)
```

The non-greedy wildcard subpattern `.*?` matches this substring:

```
(including\nwhat's in parens\n)
```

Without the `m` modifier, the dot in the subpattern wouldn't match the newline characters. The match operation would hit the first newline and, not having found a `)` character by that point, would fail.

Regular expressions aren't strings, but a close kinship exists between the two. We're going to look next at techniques for converting back and forth from one to the other, and reasons you may want to perform such conversions.

12.4.4 *Converting strings and regular expressions to each other*

The fact that regular expressions aren't strings is easy to absorb at a glance in the case of regular expressions like this:

```
/[a-c]{3}/
```

With its special character-class and repetition syntax, this pattern doesn't look much like any of the strings it matches ("aaa", "aab", "aac", and so forth).

It gets a little harder *not* to see a direct link between a regular expression and a string when faced with a regular expression like this:

```
/abc/
```

This regular expression is not the string "abc". Moreover, it matches not only "abc" but any string with the substring "abc" somewhere inside it. There's no unique relationship between a string and a similar-looking regular expression.

Still, while the visual resemblance between some strings and some regular expressions doesn't mean they're the same thing, regular expressions and strings do interact in important ways. To begin with, you can perform string (or string-style) interpolation inside a regular expression. You do so with the familiar `#{ ... }` technique, demonstrated here in an irb session:

```
>> str = "def"
=> "def"
>> /abc#{str}/
=> /abcdef/
```

The value of `str` is dropped into the regular expression and made part of it, just as it would be if you were using the same technique to interpolate it into a string.

The interpolation technique becomes more complicated when the string you're interpolating contains regular expression special characters. For example, consider a string containing a period (`.`). The period, or dot, has a special meaning in regular expressions: It matches any single character except newline. In a string, it's just a dot. When it comes to interpolating strings into regular expressions, this has the potential to cause confusion:

```
>> str = "a.c"
=> "a.c"
>> re = /#{str}/
=> /a.c/
>> re.match("a.c")
=> #<MatchData:0x32fcc4>
>> re.match("abc")
=> #<MatchData:0x32d1cc>
```

Both matches succeed; they return `MatchData` objects, rather than `nil`. The dot in the pattern matches a dot in the string "a.c". But it also matches the "b" in "abc". The dot, which started life as just a dot inside `str`, takes on special meaning when it becomes part of the regular expression.

You can, however, *escape* the special characters inside a string before you drop the string into a regular expression. You don't have to do this manually: The `Regexp` class provides a `Regexp.escape` class method that does it for you. You can see what this method does by running it on a couple of strings in isolation:

```
>> Regexp.escape("a.c")
=> "a\\.c"
>> Regexp.escape("^abc")
=> "\\^abc"
```

(irb doubles the backslashes because it's outputting double-quoted strings. If you wish, you can `puts` the expressions, and you'll see them in their real form, with single backslashes.)

As a result of this kind of escaping, you can constrain your regular expressions to match exactly the strings you interpolate into them:

```
>> str = "a.c"
=> "a.c"
>> re = /#{Regexp.escape(str)}/
=> /a\.c/
>> re.match("a.c")
=> #<MatchData:0x321dcc>
>> re.match("abc")
=> nil
```

This time, the attempt to use the dot as a wildcard match character fails; "abc" isn't a match for the escaped, interpolated string.

You can also go in the other direction: from a regular expression to a string.

Going from a regular expression to a string

Like all Ruby objects, regular expressions can represent themselves in string form. The way they do this may look odd at first:

```
>> puts /abc/
(?-mix:abc)
```

This is an alternate regular expression notation—one that rarely sees the light of day except when generated by the to_s instance method of regular expression objects. What looks like *mix* is a list of modifiers (m, i, and x) with a minus sign in front indicating that the modifiers are switched off.

You can play with putsing regular expressions in irb, and you'll see more about how this notation works. We won't pursue it here, in part because there's another way to get a string representation of a regular expression that looks more like what you probably typed: by calling inspect. You can even economize on keystrokes by using the p method, which is equivalent to calling inspect on an object and then calling puts on the result:

```
>> p /abc/
/abc/
```

Going from regular expressions to strings is useful primarily when you're studying and/or troubleshooting regular expressions. It's a good way to make sure your regexps are what you think they are.

At this point, we're going to bring regular expressions full circle by examining the roles they play in some important methods of other classes.

12.5 Common methods that use regular expressions

The payoff for gaining facility with regular expressions in Ruby is the ability to use the methods that take regular expressions as arguments and do something with them.

To begin with, you can always use a match operation as a test in, say, a find or find_all operation on a collection. For example, to find all strings longer than 10 characters and containing at least 1 digit, from an array of strings, you can do this:

```
array.find_all {|e| e.size > 10 and /\d/.match(e) }
```

However, a number of methods, mostly pertaining to strings, are based more directly on the use of regular expressions. We'll look at several of them in this section.

12.5.1 *String#scan*

The scan method goes from left to right through a string, testing repeatedly for a match with the pattern you specify. The results are returned in an array.

For example, if you want to harvest all the digits in a string, you can do this:

```
>> "testing 1 2 3 testing 4 5 6".scan(/\d/)
=> ["1", "2", "3", "4", "5", "6"]
```

Note that scan jumps over things that don't match its pattern and looks for a match later in the string. This behavior is different from that of match, which stops for good when it finishes matching the pattern completely once.

If you use parenthetical groupings in the regex you give to scan, the operation returns *an array of arrays*. Each inner array contains the results of one scan:

```
>> str = "Leopold Auer was the teacher of Jascha Heifetz."
=> "Leopold Auer was the teacher of Jascha Heifetz."
>> violinists = str.scan(/([A-Z]\w+)\s+([A-Z]\w+)/)
=> [["Leopold", "Auer"], ["Jascha", "Heifetz"]]
```

This approach buys you an array of arrays, where each inner array contains the first name and the last name of a person. Having each complete name stored in its own array makes it easy to iterate over the whole list of names, which we've conveniently stashed in the variable violinists:

```
violinists.each do |fname,lname|
  puts "#{lname}'s first name was #{fname}."
end
```

The regular expression used for names in this example is, of course, overly simple: it neglects hyphens, middle names, and so forth. But it's a good illustration of how to use captures with scan.

12.5.2 *String#split*

Another common string operation is split, which, as per its name, splits a string into multiple substrings, returning those substrings as an array.

split can take either a regular expression or a plain string as the separator for the split operation. It's commonly used to get an array consisting of all the characters in a string. To do this, you use an empty regular expression:

```
>> "Ruby".split(//)
=> ["R", "u", "b", "y"]
```

Another common use case for split is performing a conversion from a flat, text-based configuration file to a Ruby data format—array, hash, or something fancier like an ActiveRecord database entry. Usually, this involves going through a file line by line and converting each line. A single-line conversion might look like this:

```
line = "first_name=david;last_name=black;country=usa"
record = line.split(/=|;/)
```

This leaves `record` containing an array:

```
["first_name", "david", "last_name", "black", "country", "usa"]
```

With a little more work, you can populate a hash with entries of this kind:

```
data = []
record = Hash[*line.split(/=|;/)]
data.push(record)
```

If you do this for every line in a file, you'll have an array of hashes representing all the records. That array of hashes, in turn, can be used as the pivot point in converting the data to a different form.

You can provide a second argument to `split`; this argument limits the number of items returned. In this example

```
>> "a,b,c,d,e".split(/,/,3)
=> ["a", "b", "c,d,e"]
```

`split` stops splitting once it has three elements to return and puts everything that's left (commas and all) in the third string.

In addition to breaking a string into parts by scanning and splitting, you can also change parts of a string with substitution operations.

12.5.3 *sub/sub! and gsub/gsub!*

`sub` and `gsub` (along with their bang, in-place equivalents) are the most common tools for changing the contents of strings in Ruby. The difference between them is that `gsub` (*global sub*stitution) makes changes throughout a string, whereas `sub` makes at most one substitution.

sub

`sub` takes two arguments: a regular expression (or string) and a *replacement string*. Whatever part of the string matches the regular expression, if any, is removed from the string and replaced with the replacement string:

```
>> "typigraphical error".sub(/i/,"o")
=> "typographical error"
```

You can use a code block *instead of* the replacement-string argument. The block is called (yielded to) if there's a match. The call passes in the string being replaced as an argument:

```
>> "capitalize the first vowel".sub(/[aeiou]/) {|s| s.upcase }
=> "cApitalize the first vowel"
```

If you've done any parenthetical grouping, the global $n variables are set and available for use inside the block.

gsub

gsub is like sub, except it keeps substituting as long as the pattern matches anywhere in the string. For example, here's how you can replace the first letter of every word in a string with the corresponding capital letter:

```
>> "capitalize every word".gsub(/\b\w/) {|s| s.upcase }
=> "Capitalize Every Word"
```

As with sub, gsub gives you access to the $n parenthetical capture variables in the code block.

Using the captures in a replacement string

When you use the replacement-string form of sub or gsub, the $n variables aren't available inside the replacement string. However, you can access the captures by using a special notation consisting of backslash-escaped numbers. For example, you can correct an occurrence of a lowercase letter followed by an uppercase letter (assuming you're dealing with a situation where this is a mistake) like this:

```
>> "aDvid".sub(/([a-z])([A-Z])/, '\2\1')
=> "David"
```

(Note the use of single quotation marks for the replacement string. With double quotes, you'd have to double the backslashes to escape the backslash character.)
   To double every word in a string, you can do something similar, but using gsub:

```
>> "double every word".gsub(/\b(\w+)/, '\1 \1')
=> "double double every every word word"
```

We'll look next at a method of Enumerable that uses regular expressions in a filtering context.

12.5.4   grep

Unlike the previous methods discussed in this section, grep belongs to Enumerable rather than String. Like most Enumerable methods, it's used somewhat rarely on strings (which, as you'll recall, perform enumerable operations line by line rather than character by character) and much more often on arrays.
   grep does a select operation based directly on a regular expression argument. It returns all the elements in the array (or other enumerable) that match the regular expression you provide:

```
>> ["USA", "UK", "France", "Germany"].grep(/[a-z]/)
=> ["France", "Germany"]
```

You could, in fact, accomplish the same thing with `select`, but it's a bit wordier:

```
["USA", "UK", "France", "Germany"].select {|c| /[a-z]/.match(c) }
```

`grep` is a dedicated select operation, designed to make regexp-based selection operations concise and convenient.

You can also supply a code block to `grep`, in which case you get a combined select/map operation: The results of the filtering operation are yielded one at a time to the block, and the return value of the whole `grep` call is the cumulative result of those yields. For example, to select countries and then collect them in uppercase, you can do this:

```
>> ["USA", "UK", "France", "Germany"].grep(/[a-z]/) {|c| c.upcase }
=> ["FRANCE", "GERMANY"]
```

Keep in mind that `grep` only selects based on regular expression matching, so it won't select anything other than strings—and there's no automatic conversion between strings and numbers. Thus if you try this

```
[1,2,3].grep(/1/)
```

you get back an empty array; the array has no *string* element that matches the regular expression /1/.

This brings us to the end of our survey of regular expressions and some of the methods that use them. There's more to learn; pattern-matching is a sprawling subject. But this chapter has introduced you to much of what you're likely to need and see as you proceed with your study and use of Ruby.

12.6 Summary

This chapter has introduced you to the fundamentals of regular expressions in Ruby, including character classes, parenthetical captures, and anchors. You've seen that regular expressions are objects—specifically, objects of the `Regexp` class—and that they respond to messages (such as "match"). We looked at the `MatchData` class, instances of which hold information about the results of a match operation. You've also learned how to interpolate strings into regular expressions (escaped or unescaped, depending on whether you want the special characters in the string to be treated as special in the regular expression) and how to generate a string representation of a regular expression.

Methods like `String#scan`, `String#split`, `Enumerable#grep`, and the subfamily of `String` methods use regular expressions and pattern-matching as a way of determining how their actions should be applied. Gaining knowledge of regular expressions gives you access not only to relatively simple matching methods but also to a suite of string-handling tools that would otherwise not be usable.

The next chapter is the last in this part of the book and the last in the larger section of the book comprising the Ruby tutorial in parts 2 and 3. In chapter 13, we'll take things to another level by looking directly at some of the features and techniques that make Ruby dynamic.

13
Ruby dynamics

Just about everything in Ruby is dynamic. Technically, this means what's in your program files doesn't always determine what happens when the program runs. Your file may have, say, three class definitions. But it may also have a method that defines 12 *more* classes. But only if the user makes a request that requires that those classes exist....

This is an example of dynamic behavior on the part of Ruby. Things that, in other languages, would be determined before the program starts running (like how many classes will exist, what messages objects are capable of understanding, and so on) can be changed and renegotiated during runtime in a Ruby program.

The topic of this chapter, "Ruby dynamics," is almost a synonym for "Ruby programming techniques." Dynamism pervades Ruby. However, certain techniques and language constructs lie closer than others to the heart of Ruby's dynamism, providing the structure and environment on top of which all the dynamic behavior is built.

We'll survey those features of the language here. You've already seen dynamism in action; some of the first Ruby code presented in this book involved adding methods at runtime to individual objects (`def obj.talk` and similar code). This chapter shows you, in part, the underpinnings of some of these dynamic programming techniques and, in part, new programming techniques that let you take dynamism further.

These aspects of Ruby aren't always easy to absorb. But they mesh nicely with each other and with the language overall. Once you start to see how they work, a lot of concepts fall into place. Moreover (and this isn't entirely a coincidence, as you can imagine), familiarity with dynamic Ruby is indispensable for an understanding of the Rails framework. The components of Rails depend fundamentally on the ability of Ruby objects and classes to undergo all sorts of runtime modifications, changes, and interceptions. This kind of flexibility on the part of Ruby allows (for example) ActiveRecord to endow your objects with methods based on the names of the fields in your database tables. You don't have to write those methods; you just create a database, and ActiveRecord does the rest at runtime.

Nor is the deployment of Ruby's dynamism restricted to Rails. Dynamism is everywhere in Ruby, and a grasp of its key foundational techniques will put you in a good position to understand the language in many of its manifestations.

13.1 *The position and role of singleton classes*

Our first dynamics topic is the topic of the *singleton class*. The best way to understand what a singleton class is, and why it's important, is to take a running leap at it, starting with the basics.

Most of what happens in Ruby involves classes and modules, containing definitions of instance methods

```
class C
  def talk
    puts "Hi!"
  end
end
```

and, subsequently, the instantiation of classes and the calling of those instance methods:

```
c = C.new
c.talk   <——— Output: Hi!
```

However, as you saw even earlier in this book than you saw instance methods inside classes, you can also add methods directly to individual objects:

```
obj = Object.new
def obj.talk
  puts "Hi!"
end
obj.talk   <——— Output: Hi!
```

A method added to a specific object like this is called a *singleton method* of the object. When you define a singleton method on a given object, only *that object* can call that method.

As we've seen, the most common type of singleton method is the class method—a method added to a `Class` object on an individual basis:

```
class Ticket
  def Ticket.most_expensive(tickets)
  # etc.
```

But any object can have singleton methods added to it. The ability to define behavior on a per-object basis is one of the hallmarks of Ruby's design.

Instance methods—those available to any and all instances of a given class—live inside a class or module, where they can be found by the objects that are able to call them. But what about singleton methods? Where does a method live, if that method only exists to be called by a single object?

13.1.1 *Where the singleton methods live*

Ruby, as usual, has a simple answer to this tricky question: An object's singleton methods live in the object's *singleton class*. Every object really has *two* classes:

- The class of which it is an instance
- Its singleton class

The method-calling capabilities of the object amount to the sum of all the instance methods defined in these two classes (along with methods available through ancestral classes and/or mixed-in modules). An object can call instance methods from its original class, and it can also call methods from its singleton class. It has both.

You can think of an object's singleton class as an exclusive stash of methods, tailor-made for that object and not shared with other objects—not even with other instances of the object's class.

13.1.2 *Examining and modifying a singleton class directly*

Singleton classes are *anonymous*: Although they are class objects (instances of the class `Class`), they spring up automatically without being given a name. Nonetheless, you can open the class definition body of a singleton class and add instance methods, class methods, and constants to it, just as you would with a regular class.

You do this with a special form of the `class` keyword. Usually, a constant follows that keyword:

```
class C
  # method and constant definitions here
end
```

To get inside the definition body of a singleton class, you use a special notation:

```
class << object
  # method and constant definitions here
end
```

The `<< object` notation means *the anonymous, singleton class of* `object`. Once you're inside the singleton class definition body, you can define methods—and these methods will be singleton methods of the object whose singleton class you're in.

Consider this program, for example:

```
str = "I am a string"
class << str
  def twice
    self + " " + self
  end
end

puts str.twice
```

It produces the following output:

```
I am a string I am a string
```

The method `twice` is a singleton method of the string `str`. It's exactly as if we had done this:

```
def str.twice
  self + " " + self
end
```

The difference is that we've pried open the singleton class of `str` and defined the method there. (There's also a subtle difference between these two approaches to defining a singleton method, involving the scope of constants, but that's an arcane point. For the most part, you can treat them as equivalent.)

Defining class methods with class <<

By far the most frequent use of the `class <<` notation for entering a singleton method class is in connection with class method definitions. You'll see this quite often:

```
class Ticket
  class << self
    def most_expensive(tickets)
      # etc.
```

This code results in a class method `Ticket.most_expensive`. That method could also be defined like this (assuming this code comes at a point in the program where the `Ticket` class already exists):

```
class << Ticket
  def most_expensive(tickets)
    # etc.
```

Because `self` is `Ticket` inside the `class Ticket` definition body, `class << self` *inside* the body is the same as `class << Ticket` *outside* the body. (Technically, you could do `class << Ticket` even inside the body of class `Ticket`, but in practice you'll usually see `class << self` whenever the object whose singleton class needs opening is `self`.)

The fact that `class << self` shows up frequently in connection with the creation of class methods sometimes leads to the false impression that the `class <<` notation can *only* be used to create class methods, or that the only expression you can legally put on the right is `self`. In fact, `class << self` inside a class definition block is just one case of the `class << object` notation. The technique is general: It puts you in a definition block for the singleton class of `object`, whatever `object` may be. That, in turn, means you're operating in a context where whatever you do—whatever you add to the class—pertains only to that one object.

In chapter 6, we looked at the steps a process takes as it looks for a method among those defined in its class, its class's class, and so forth. Now we have a new item on the radar: the singleton class. What's the effect of this extra class on the method lookup process?

13.1.3 *Singleton classes on the method lookup path*

Recall that method searching goes up the class inheritance chain, with detours for any modules that have been mixed in. When we first discussed this process, we hadn't talked about singleton methods, and they were not present in the diagram. Now we can revise the diagram to encompass them, as shown in figure 13.1.

An object's singleton class comes *first* in the method lookup path. The singleton class is the object's personal method-storage area, so it takes precedence. After the singleton class come any modules mixed into it. Next comes the object's original class, and so forth.

There are two ways to insert a module just above an object's singleton class in the method lookup path. First, you can mix the module into the singleton class:

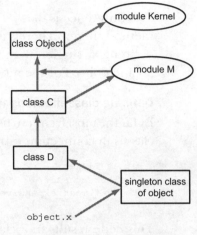

Figure 13.1   Method search order, revised to include singleton classes

```
class C
end

module M
  def talk
    puts "Hello."
  end
end

obj = C.new
class << obj
  include M
end

obj.talk        ◁——————  Output: Hello.
```

The second way is to use `extend`. As you'll recall, `extend` is a sort of per-object variant of `include`. Instead of mixing the module into an entire class, `extend` endows a single object with access to the module's instance methods. Given the same class `C` and module `M` from the previous example, you can extend an object like this:

```
obj = C.new
obj.extend(M)
obj.talk        ◁——————  Output: Hello.
```

The effect is almost identical to the effect of including the module M in the object's singleton class. (The only differences are obscure and have to do with the visibility and scope of constants at the time of the extend or include operation. You can generally treat these two techniques as equivalent.) They both interpose a module in the object's method lookup path, after the object's singleton class but before the object's original class.

Singleton module inclusion vs. original-class module inclusion

When you mix a module into an object's singleton class (or extend the object with the module), you're dealing with that object specifically; the methods it learns from the module take precedence over any methods of the same name in its original class. Listing 13.1 shows the mechanics and outcome of doing this kind of include operation.

Listing 13.1   Including a module in a singleton class

```
class C
  def talk
    puts "Hi from original class!"
  end
end

module M
  def talk
    puts "Hello from module!"
  end
end

c = C.new
c.talk     <———1
class << c
  include M   <———2
end
c.talk     <———3
```

The output from listing 13.1 is as follows:

```
Hi from original class!
Hello from module!
```

The first call to talk ❶ executes the talk instance method defined in c's class, C. Then we mix in the module M, which also defines a method called talk, into c's singleton class ❷. As a result, the next time we call talk on c ❸, the talk that gets executed (the one that c sees first) is the one defined in M.

It's all a matter of how the classes and modules on the object's method lookup path are stacked. Modules included in the singleton class are encountered before the original class and before any modules included in the original class.

You can see this graphically by using the `ancestors` method, which gives you a list of the classes and modules in the inheritance and inclusion hierarchy of any class or module. Starting from after the class and module definitions in the previous example, try using `ancestors` to see what the hierarchy looks like:

```
c = C.new
class << c
  include M
  p ancestors
end
```

You'll get an array of ancestors—essentially, the method lookup path for instances of this class. Because this is the singleton class of `c`, that means the method lookup path for `c`:

```
[M, C, Object, Kernel]
```

(Singleton classes aren't reported by `ancestors`. If they were, they would come first.)

Now, look what happens when you not only mix `M` into the singleton class of `c` but *also* mix it into `c`'s class (`C`). Picking up after the previous example:

```
class C
  include M
end

class << c
  p ancestors
end
```

This time, you see the following result:

```
[M, C, M, Object, Kernel]
```

The module `M` appears twice! Two different classes—the singleton class of `c` and the class `C`—have mixed it in. Each mix-in is a separate transaction. It's the private business of each class; the classes don't consult with each other. (You could even mix `M` into `Object`, and you'd get it three times in the ancestors list.)

You're encouraged to take these examples, modify them, turn them this way and that, and examine the results. Classes are objects too—so see what happens when you take the singleton class of an object's singleton class. What about mixing modules into other modules? There are many possible permutations; you can learn a lot through experimentation, using what we've covered here as a starting point.

The main lesson is that per-object behavior in Ruby is based on the same principles as "regular," class-derived object behavior: definition of instance methods in classes and modules, mixing in of modules to classes, and a method lookup path consisting of classes and modules. If you master these concepts and revert to them whenever something seems fuzzy, your understanding will scale upward successfully.

Equipped with this knowledge, let's go back and look at a special case within the world of singleton methods (special, because it's common and useful): class methods.

13.1.4   *Class methods in (even more) depth*

Class methods are singleton methods defined on objects of class `Class`. In many ways, they behave like any other singleton method:

```
class C
end

def C.a_class_method
  puts "Singleton method defined on C"
end

C.a_class_method    <———  Output: Singleton
                          method defined on C
```

However, class methods also exhibit special behavior. Normally, when you define a singleton method on an object, *no other object* can serve as the receiver in a call to that method. (That's what makes singleton methods singleton, or per-object.) Class methods are slightly different: A method defined as a singleton method of a class object can also be called on *subclasses* of that class. Given the previous example, with C, you can do this:

```
class D < C
end

D.a_class_method
```

Here's the rather confusing output (confusing because the class object we sent the message to is D, rather than C):

```
Singleton method defined on C
```

You're allowed to call C's singleton *methods* on a subclass of C, in addition to C, because of a special setup involving the singleton *classes* of class objects. In our example, the singleton class of C (where the method a_class_method lives) is considered *the superclass of the singleton class of D*.

When you send a message to the class object D, the usual lookup path is followed—except that after D's singleton class, the superclass of D's singleton class is searched. That's defined as the singleton class of C, D's superclass. And there's the method.

Figure 13.2 shows the relationships among classes in an inheritance relationship and their singleton classes. As you can see from figure 13.2, the singleton class of C's child, D, is considered a child (a subclass) of the singleton class of C.

Singleton classes of class objects are sometimes called *metaclasses*. (You'll sometimes hear the term *metaclass* applied to singleton classes in general, but there's nothing particularly meta about them and *singleton class* is a more descriptive term.)

You can treat this explanation as a bonus topic. It's unlikely that an urgent need to understand it will arise very often. Still, it's a great example of how Ruby's design is based on a relatively small number of rules (such as every object having a singleton class, and the way methods are looked up). Classes are special-cased objects; after all, they're object factories as well as objects in their own right. But there's little in Ruby that doesn't arise naturally from the basic principles of the language's design—even the special cases.

At this point, we've covered what we need to, regarding singleton methods and classes. Next stop on the tour of dynamic Ruby: the *eval* family of methods. These methods let you hand the interpreter chunks of code in the form of strings or code blocks for evaluation based on content determined at runtime (rather than based on what's already typed into the program file). As you'll see, this kind of dynamic evaluation of code comes in several varieties.

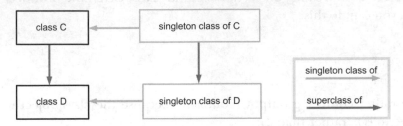

Figure 13.2   Relationships among classes in an inheritance relationship, and their singleton classes

13.2 *The eval family of methods*

Like many languages, Ruby has a facility for executing code stored in the form of strings at runtime. In fact, Ruby has a cluster of techniques to do this, each of which serves a particular purpose but all of which operate on a similar principle: that of saying in the middle of a program, "Whatever you read from the program file before starting to execute this program, execute *this* right now."

The most straightforward method for evaluating a string as code, and also the most dangerous, is the method `eval`. Other eval-family methods are a little softer, not because they don't also evaluate strings as code, but because that's not all they do. `instance_eval` brings about a temporary shift in the value of self, and `class_eval` (also known by the synonym `module_eval`) takes you on an ad hoc side-trip into the context of a class definition block. These eval-family methods can be called with a code block; they don't always operate as bluntly as `eval`, which just executes strings.

Let's unpack this description with a closer look at `eval` and the other eval methods.

13.2.1 *eval*

`eval` executes the string you give it:

```
>> eval("2+2")
=> 4
```

`eval` is the answer, or at least one answer, to a number of frequently asked questions, such as, "How do I write a method and give it a name someone types in?" You can do so like this:

```
print "Method name: "
m = gets.chomp
eval("def #{m}; puts 'Hi!'; end")
eval(m)
```

This code outputs the following:

```
Hi!
```

A new method is being written. Let's say you run the code and type in `abc`. The string you subsequently use `eval` on is

```
def abc; puts 'Hi!'; end
```

After you apply `eval` to that string, a method called `abc` exists. The second `eval` executes the string "abc"—which, given the creation of the method in the previous line, constitutes a call to abc. When abc is called, the string "Inside new method!" is printed out.

The dangers of eval

eval gives you a lot of power, but it also harbors dangers—in some people's opinion, enough dangers to rule it out as a usable technique. What would happen, for example, if you entered this instead of abc?

```
abc; end; system("rm -rf /*"); #   ◁——— !! DO NOT DO THIS !!
```

You'd end up running eval on this string:

```
def abc; end; system("rm -rf /*"); # puts 'Hi!'; end
```

Everything to the right of the # would be treated as a comment when eval ran on it and would therefore be discarded. The code that was executed would create a method called abc (a method that does nothing) and then attempt to remove all the files on the system, courtesy of the system command. (system sends a command to the system, as its name implies.)

In other words, *what* string you run eval on can make a *big* difference.

eval can be seductive. It's about as dynamic as a dynamic programming technique can get: You're evaluating strings of code that probably didn't even exist when you wrote the program. Anywhere that Ruby puts up a kind of barrier to absolute, easy manipulation of the state of things during the run of a program, eval seems to offer a way to cut through the red tape and do whatever you want.

But, as you can see, eval isn't a panacea. If you're running eval on a string you've written, it's generally no worse than running a program file you've written. But any time an uncertain, dynamically generated string is involved, the dangers mushroom.

In particular, it's very difficult to clean up user input (including input from Web forms and files) to the point that you can feel safe about running eval on it. Ruby maintains a global variable called $SAFE, which you can set to a high number (on a scale of 0 to 4) to gain protection from dangers like rogue file-writing requests. $SAFE makes life with eval a lot safer. Still, the best habit to get into is the habit of not using eval.

It isn't hard to find experienced and expert Ruby programmers (as well as programmers in other languages) who never use eval and never will. You have to decide how you feel about it, based on your knowledge of the pitfalls.

Let's move now to the wider eval family of methods. These methods can do the same kind of brute-force string evaluation that eval does; but they also have kindler, gentler behaviors that make them usable and useful.

13.2.2 *instance_eval*

instance_eval is a specialized cousin of eval. It evaluates the string *or code block* you give it, changing self to be the receiver of the call to instance_eval.

This code

```
p self
a = []
a.instance_eval { p self }
```

outputs two different selfs:

```
main
[]
```

instance_eval is mostly useful for breaking in to what would normally be another object's private data—particularly instance variables. Here's how to see the value of an instance variable belonging to any old object (in this case, the instance variable of @x of a C object):

```
class C
  def initialize
    @x = 1
  end
end

c = C.new
c.instance_eval { puts @x }
```

This kind of prying into another object's state is generally considered impolite; if an object wants you to know something about its state, it provides methods through which you can inquire. Nevertheless, because Ruby dynamics are based on the changing identity of self, it's not a bad idea for the language to give us a technique for manipulating self directly.

We've saved the most useful of the eval family of methods for last: class_eval (synonym: module_eval).

13.2.3 *The most useful eval: class_eval (a.k.a. module_eval)*

In essence, class_eval puts you inside a class definition body:

```
c = Class.new
c.class_eval do
  def some_method
    puts "Created in class_eval"
  end
end
c = C.new
c.some_method   ⟵——— Output: Created in class_eval
```

However, you can do some things with `class_eval` that you can't do with the regular `class` keyword:

- Evaluate a string in class-definition context
- Open the class definition of an anonymous class (other than a singleton class)
- Gain access to variables in the surrounding scope

The third item on this list is particularly worthy of note.

When you open a class with the `class` keyword, you start a new local variable scope. The block you use with `class_eval`, however, can see the variables created in the scope surrounding it. Look at the difference between the treatment of `var`, an outer-scope local variable, as between a regular class definition body and a block given to `class_eval`:

```
>> var = "initialized variable"
=> "initialized variable"
>> class C
>> puts var
>> end
NameError: undefined local variable or method `var' for C:Class
        from (irb):3
>> C.class_eval { puts var }
initialized variable
```

The variable `var` is out of scope inside the standard class definition block, but still in scope in the code block passed to `class_eval`.

The plot thickens a little when you define an instance method inside the `class_eval` block:

```
>> C.class_eval { def talk; puts var; end }
=> nil
>> C.new.talk
NameError: undefined local variable or method `var' for #<C:0x350ba4>
```

Like any `def`, the `def` inside the block starts a new scope—so the variable `var` is no longer visible.

If you want to shoehorn an outer-scope variable into an instance method, you have to use a different technique for creating the method: the method `define_method`. You hand `define_method` the name of the method you want to create (as a symbol or a string) and provide a code block; the code block serves as the body of the method.

To get the outer variable `var` into an instance method of class C, you therefore do this:

```
>> C.class_eval { define_method("talk") { puts var }  }
=> #<Proc:0x003452f4@(irb):8>
```

(The return value you're seeing is a Proc object created from the code block given to `define_method`.)

At this point, the `talk` instance method of C will, indeed, have access to the outer-scope variable `var`:

```
>> C.new.talk
initialized variable
```

You won't see techniques like this used as frequently as the standard class- and method-definition techniques. But when you see them, you'll know that they imply a flattened scope for local variables rather than the new scope triggered by the more common `class` and `def` keywords.

`define_method` is an instance method of the class `Module`, so you can call it on any instance of `Module` or `Class`. You can thus use it inside a regular `class` definition body (where the default receiver `self` is the class object) if there's a variable local to the body that you want to sneak into an instance method. That's not a frequently encountered scenario, but it's not unheard of.

We're going to turn next to a broad but unified category: callable objects.

13.3 Callable objects

A *callable object* is an object to which you can send the message `call`, with the expectation that some code defined in the object (usually in a code block) will be executed. The main callable objects in Ruby are methods (which you've already seen), Proc objects, and lambdas. Proc objects are self-contained code sequences that you can create, store, pass around as method arguments, and, when you wish, execute with the `call` method. Lambdas are similar to Proc objects. The differences will emerge as we examine each in turn.

13.3.1 Proc objects

You create a Proc object by instantiating the `Proc` class, including a code block:

```
pr = Proc.new { puts "Inside a Proc's block" }
```

Note that the code block isn't executed at this point. Instead, it's saved as the body of the Proc object. If you want to execute the block (the Proc object), you must call it explicitly:

```
pr.call
```

It will report:

```
Inside a Proc's block
```

That's the basic scenario: A code block, supplied to a call to `Proc.new`, becomes the body of the Proc object and gets executed when you `call` that object. Everything else that happens, or that can happen, involves additions to and variations on this theme.

Proc objects as closures

You've already seen that the local variables you use inside a method body aren't the same as the local variables you use in the scope of the method call:

```
def talk
  a = "Hello"
  puts a
end

a = "Goodbye"
talk
puts a    <————    Output: Goodbye
```

The identifier a has been assigned to twice, but the two assignments (the two a variables) are unrelated to each other.

Proc objects put a slightly different spin on scope. When you construct the code block for a call to `Proc.new`, the local variables you've created are still in scope (as with any code block). Furthermore, *those* variables *remain* in scope inside the Proc object, no matter where or when you call it.

Look at listing 13.2, and keep your eye on the two variables called a.

Listing 13.2 Example of preservation of local context by a Proc object

```
def call_some_proc(pr)
  a = "irrelevant 'a' in method scope"    <————①
  puts a
  pr.call    <————②
end

a = "'a' to be used in Proc block"    <————③
pr = Proc.new { puts a }
pr.call
call_some_proc(pr)
```

As in the previous example, there's an a in the method definition ① and an a in the outer (calling) scope ③. Inside the method is a call to a Proc object. The code for that Proc object, we happen to know, consists of `puts a`. Notice that when the Proc is called *from inside the method* ②, the a that is printed out isn't the a defined in the method; it's the a from the scope *where the Proc object was originally created*:

```
'a' to be used in Proc block
irrelevant 'a' in method scope
'a' to be used in Proc block
```

The Proc object carries its *context* around with it. Part of that context is a variable called a, to which particular string is assigned. That variable lives on inside the Proc.

A piece of code that carries its creation context around with it like this is called a *closure*. Creating a closure is like packing a suitcase: Wherever you open the suitcase, it contains what you put in when you packed it. When you open a closure (by calling it), it contains what you put into it when it was created.

Arguments for Proc objects

Like any code block, the block you provide when you create a Proc object can take arguments:

```
pr = Proc.new {|x| puts "Called with argument #{x}" }
pr.call(100)   <——— Output: Called with argument 100
```

Proc objects handle their arguments in a subtle (some might say complicated) way. If the Proc takes only one argument, as in the previous example, and you send it some number of arguments other than one, you get a warning. If you give it no arguments, the single variable is initialized to nil, and you get a warning:

```
>> pr = Proc.new {|x| p x }
=> #<Proc:0x401f326c@(irb):1>
>> pr.call
(irb):1: warning: multiple values for a block parameter (0 for 1)
        from (irb):2
nil
```

If you call the one-argument Proc with more than one argument, you get a warning, and the arguments are all put into an array:

```
>> pr.call(1,2,3)
(irb):1: warning: multiple values for a block parameter (3 for 1)
        from (irb):3
[1, 2, 3]
```

If your Proc takes more than one argument, the arguments you call it with are assigned to the variables in its argument list. Extra arguments on either end of the transaction are ignored:

```
>> pr = Proc.new {|x,y,z| p x,y,z }
=> #<Proc:0x001b5598@(irb):1>
>> pr.call(1,2)
1
2
nil   <———❶
```

```
=> nil
>> pr.call(1,2,3,4)
1
2
3
=> nil
```

The first time we call pr, we provide three arguments; inside pr, the third argument, z, gets nothing assigned to it and defaults to nil ❶. (Note that the *second* nil that irb prints out is the return value of the execution of pr, which returns nil because it ends with a puts statement!) The second time we call pr, all three variables are assigned values; the fourth value, 4, is discarded, because there's no variable left to assign it to.

You can also sponge up all the arguments into a single argument, with the star (*) operator:

```
pr = Proc.new {|*x| p x }
pr.call
pr.call(1)
pr.call(1,2)
```

As you'll see if you run this snippet, x is set to an array on each call to the Proc. Each time, the array contains all the arguments you've called the Proc with:

```
[]
[1]
[1, 2]
```

If you have multiple arguments and put the sponge last, it's assigned an array of all the arguments that haven't been assigned to other variables already. Here's an example:

```
pr = Proc.new {|x,*y| p x, y }
pr.call(1,2,3)
```

The output

```
1
[2, 3]
```

represents x, which was assigned the 1, and y, which was assigned the remaining arguments (2,3) as an array.

The bottom line is that Procs are a little less fussy than methods about their argument count—their *arity*.

Ruby offers several variations on the callable method-or-function theme. We'll look next at another form of anonymous function: the *lambda*.

13.3.2 *Creating anonymous functions with the lambda keyword*

The `lambda` keyword lets you create an anonymous function. All you have to do is provide `lambda` with a code block; that block becomes the function. You can then send it a "call" message, and the function executes:

```
>> lam = lambda { puts "A lambda!" }
=> #<Proc:0x00330cb4@(irb):31>   <———①
>> lam.call
A lambda!
```

Lambdas, as you can see from irb's evaluative printout ①, aren't objects of a class called `Lambda`; rather, they're objects of class `Proc`:

```
>> lam.class
=> Proc
```

Like all Proc objects, they are closures; they carry the local context of their creation around with them.

However, there's a difference between Procs you create with `lambda` and those you created with `Proc.new`. It's a subtle difference, but one you may need to be aware of at some point. It involves the `return` keyword. `return` inside a lambda returns from the lambda. `return` inside a Proc returns from the surrounding method.

> **NOTE**   THE PROC/LAMBDA/BLOCK REALM IN FLUX   In recent versions of Ruby—and in future versions, judging by discussions on various mailing lists and forums—the matter of how Proc objects, code blocks, and lambdas relate to each other has been, and still is, in a certain amount of flux. Don't be surprised if you see other differences, or even the elimination of differences, from one version of Ruby to another.

Here's an illustration of the difference:

```
def return_test
  l = lambda { return }
  l.call   <———①
  puts "Still here!"
  p = Proc.new { return }
  p.call   <———②
  puts "You won't see this message!"   <———③
end

return_test
```

The output of this snippet is "Still here!" You'll never see the second message ③ printed out because the call to the Proc object ② triggers a return from the method. The call to the lambda ❶, however, triggers a return from the lambda; execution of the method continues where it left off.

Before we leave lambda, it's worth mentioning that lambda has a synonym: proc. However, because proc and Proc.new look and sound so similar, but don't do exactly the same thing, Matz has agreed in principle to phase out proc, leaving just Proc.new and lambda as the techniques for creating anonymous functions. You'll probably continue to see the proc keyword in use for a while; just remember that it's a synonym for lambda.

We're now going to take another look at *code blocks*, in light of what we've discussed about anonymous functions.

13.3.3 *Code blocks, revisited*

A code block (the thing you type after a method call and to which the method yields) exists only in the syntax of Ruby. There is no such thing as a Block class or Block object. The block is just some code that floats in front of the method inside curly braces (or do/end), waiting to be used.

However, you can *convert* a code block into a Proc object, inside the method. You do this by capturing the block in a variable. This variable is part of the argument list of the method, but it has an ampersand (&) at the beginning:

```
def grab_block(&block)
  block.call
end

grab_block { puts "This block will end up in the variable 'block'" }
```

The &var variable must be the last item in the argument list:

```
def grab_block(x,y,*z,&block)
```

You can also convert a Proc object or lambda *to* a code block. You do this with the ampersand:

```
lam = lambda { puts "This lambda will serve as a code block" }
grab_block &lam
```

Here's another example:

```
grab_block &lambda { puts "This lambda will serve as a code block" }
```

The & symbol serves in all of these cases as a signal that conversion back and forth is going on, as between lambda/Proc on the one hand and code blocks on the other.

13.3.4 *Methods as objects*

In practice, the things you call most often in Ruby aren't Procs or lambdas but methods. So far, we've viewed the calling of methods as something we do at one level of remove: We send messages to objects, and the objects execute the appropriately named method. But it's possible to handle methods as objects. You're not likely to need this technique often, but it's interesting to know that it's possible.

You get hold of a method object by using the `method` method, with the name of the method as an argument (in string or symbol form):

```
class C
  def talk
    puts "Method-grabbing test!  self is #{self}."
  end
end

c = C.new
meth = c.method(:talk)
```

At this point, you have a method object. In this case, it's a *bound* method object; it isn't the method talk in the abstract, but rather the method talk specifically bound to the object c. If you send a "call" message to meth, it knows to call itself with c in the role of self:

```
meth.call
```

Here's the output:

```
Method-grabbing test!  self is #<C:0x353854>.
```

You can also *unbind* the method from its object and then *bind* it to another object, as long as that other object is of the same class as the original object (or a subclass):

```
class D < C
end

d = D.new
unbound = meth.unbind
unbound.bind(d).call
```

Here, the output tells you that the method was, indeed, bound to a D object (d) at the time it was executed:

```
Method-grabbing test!  self is #<D:0x32d7bc>.
```

To get hold of an unbound method object directly, without having to call `unbind` on a bound method, you can get it from the class rather than from a specific instance of the class, using the `instance_method` method. This single line is equivalent to a `method` call plus an `unbind` call:

```
unbound = C.instance_method(:talk)
```

Once you have the unbound method in captivity, so to speak, you can use `bind` to bind it to any instance of either `C` or a `C` subclass like `D`.

But why?

There's no doubt that unbinding and binding methods is a specialized technique, and you're not likely to need more than a reading knowledge of it. However, aside from the principle that at least a reading knowledge of anything in Ruby can't be a bad idea, on some occasions the best answer to a "how to" question is, "With unbound methods."

Here's an example. The following question comes up periodically in Ruby forums: "Suppose I've got a class hierarchy where a method gets redefined:

```
class A
  def a_method
    puts "Definition in class A"
  end
end

class B < A
  def a_method
    puts "Definition in class B (subclass of A)"
  end
end

class C < B
end
```

"And I've got an instance of the subclass:

```
c = C.new
```

"Is there any way to get that instance of the lowest class to respond to the message ('a_method') by executing the version of the method in the class two classes up the chain?"

By default, of course, the instance doesn't do that; it executes the first matching method it finds as it traverses the method search path:

```
c.a_method    ◁─────── Output: Definition in class B (subclass of A)
```

You can, however, force the issue through an unbind and bind operation:

```
A.instance_method(:a_method).bind(c).call    ◁─────── Output: Definition in class A
```

You can even stash this behavior inside a method in class C

```
class C
  def call_original
    A.instance_method(:a_method).bind(self).call
  end
end
```

and then call `call_original` directly on c.

This is an example of a Ruby technique with a paradoxical status: It's within the realm of things you should understand, as someone gaining mastery of Ruby's dynamics; but it's outside the realm of anything you should probably be doing. If you find yourself coercing Ruby objects to respond to methods you've already redefined, you should review the design of your program and find a way to get objects to do what you want *as a result of*, and not *in spite of*, the class/module hierarchy you've created.

Still, methods are callable objects, and they can be detached (unbound) from their instances. As a Ruby dynamics inductee, you should at least have recognition-level knowledge of this kind of operation.

We'll descend from the dynamic stratosphere next, and look at some of the ways you can deploy Ruby methods strategically during runtime in the form of callbacks and hooks.

13.4 *Callbacks and hooks*

The use of *callbacks* and *hooks* is a fairly common meta-programming technique. These methods are called when a particular event takes place during the run of a Ruby program. An event is something like

- A nonexistent method being called on an object
- A class mixing in a module
- The subclassing of a class
- An instance method being added to a class
- A singleton method being added to an object
- A reference to a nonexistent constant

For every event in that list, you can (if you choose) write a callback method that will be executed when the event happens. These callback methods are per-object or per-class, not global; if you want a method called when the class `Ticket` gets subclassed, you have to write the appropriate method specifically for class `Ticket`.

What follows are descriptions of each of these runtime event hooks. The Rails framework uses several of them; we'll see a couple of examples from the Rails source here and examine Rails hooks in more detail later.

13.4.1 *Intercepting unrecognized messages with method_missing*

When you send a message to an object, the object executes the first method it finds on its method lookup path with the same name as the message. If it fails to find any such method, it raises a NoMethodError exception—*unless* you have provided the object with a method called method_missing.

method_missing is in part a safety net: It gives you a way to intercept unanswerable messages and handle them gracefully:

```
class C
  def method_missing(m)
    puts "There's no method called #{m} here -- please try again."
  end
end

C.new.anything
```

You can also use method_missing to bring about an automatic extension of the way your object behaves. For example, let's say you're modeling an object that in some respects is a container but also has other characteristics—perhaps, just for the sake of variety, a cookbook. You want to be able to program your cookbook as a collection of recipes, but it also has certain characteristics (title, author, perhaps a list of people with whom you've shared it or who have contributed to it) that need to be stored and handled separately from the recipes. Thus the cookbook is both a collection and the repository of metadata about the collection.

One way to do this would be to maintain an array of recipes and then forward any unrecognized messages to that array. A simple implementation might look like this:

```
class Cookbook
  attr_accessor :title, :author

  def initialize
    @recipes = []
  end

  def method_missing(m,*args,&block)
    @recipes.send(m,*args,&block)
  end
end
```

Now we can perform manipulations on the collection of recipes, taking advantage of any array methods we wish. (Let's assume there's a `Recipe` class, separate from the `Cookbook` class, and we've already created some recipe objects.)

```
cb = Cookbook.new
cb << recipe_for_cake
cb << recipe_for_chicken
beef_dishes = cb.find_all {|recipes| recipe.main_ingredient ==
  "beef" }
```

The cookbook instance, `cb`, doesn't have methods called `<<` and `find_all`, so those messages are passed along to the `@recipes` array, courtesy of `method_missing`. We can still define any methods we want directly in the `Cookbook` class—we can even override array methods, if we want a more cookbook-specific behavior for any of those methods—but `method_missing` has saved us from having to define a whole parallel set of methods for handling pages as an ordered collection.

> **TIP**   RUBY HAS LOTS OF METHOD-DELEGATING TECHNIQUES   In this `method_missing` example, we've *delegated* the processing of messages (the unknown ones) to the array `@pages`. Ruby has several mechanisms for delegating actions from one object to another. We won't go into them here, but you may come across both the `Delegator` class and the `SimpleDelegator` class in your further encounters with Ruby.

`method_missing` looms large in the Rails framework. Much of what you do in Rails involves making calls to nonexistent methods and then having those calls interpreted by Rails in the light of the structure of your database. (Examining the `method_missing` code, especially in the `ActiveRecord::Base` class, is worthwhile, although you may want to hold off until we've looked a little more systematically at how to explore the Rails framework source in chapter 17.) In general, `method_missing` is a useful tool—perhaps the most widely used among all the standard Ruby hooks and callbacks.

13.4.2 *Trapping include operations with Module#included*

When a module is included (mixed in) to a class, *if* a method called `included` is defined for that module, then that method is called. The method receives the name of the class as its single argument.

You can do a quick test of `included` by having it trigger a message printout and then perform an include operation:

```
module M
  def self.included(c)
    puts "I have just been mixed into #{c}."
```

```
      end
    end

    class C
      include M
    end
```

You'll see the message "I have just been mixed into C." printed out as a result of the execution of M.included when M gets included by (mixed into) C. (Because you can also mix modules into modules, the example would also work if C were another module.)

When would it be useful for a module to intercept its own inclusion like this? One commonly discussed case revolves around the difference between instance and class methods. When you mix a module into a class, you're ensuring that all the *instance methods* defined in the module become available to instances of the class. But the class object isn't affected. The following question often arises: What if you want to add *class methods* to the class by mixing in the module along with adding the instance methods?

Courtesy of included, you can trap the include operation and use the occasion to add class methods to the class that's doing the including. Listing 13.3 shows an example.

Listing 13.3   Using the included callback to add a class method as part of a mix-in operation

```
module M
  def self.included(cl)
    def cl.a_class_method
      puts "Now the class has a new class method."
    end
  end

  def an_inst_method
    puts "This module supplies this instance method."
  end
end

class C
  include M
end

c = C.new
c.an_inst_method
C.a_class_method
```

The output from listing 13.3 is as follows:

```
This module supplies this instance method.
Now the class has a new class method.
```

When class C included module M, two things happened. First, an *instance method* called an_inst_method appeared in the lookup path of its instances (such as c). Second, thanks to M's included callback, a *class* method called a_class_method was defined for the class object C.

NOTE append_features IS A (DEPRECATED) SYNONYM FOR included   The method name included is being phased in to replace the name append_features. In the Rails framework (at the time of this writing), the latter name occurs rather than the former. It's best to get used to the new name, but you should recognize them both.

Module#included is a useful way to hook into the class/module engineering of your program. We'll see some usage of it in the Rails source code in part 4. Meanwhile, let's look at another callback in the same general area of interest: Class#inherited.

13.4.3 *Intercepting inheritance with Class#inherited*

You can also hook into the subclassing of a class, by defining a special class method called inherited for that class. If inherited has been defined for a given class, then when you subclass the class, inherited is called with the name of the new class as its single argument:

```
class C
  def self.inherited(subclass)
    puts "#{self} just got subclassed by #{subclass}"
  end
end

class D < C
end
```

The subclassing of C by D automatically triggers a call to inherited and therefore produces the following output:

```
C just got subclassed by D
```

inherited is a class method, so descendants of the class that defines it are also able to call it. The actions you define in inherited cascade: If you inherit from a subclass, that subclass triggers the inherited method, and similarly down the chain of inheritance. If you do this

```
class E < D
end
```

you're informed that D just got subclassed by E. You get similar results if you subclass E, and so forth.

Using inherited in ActiveRecord

When we return to the music store application in part 4 of the book, we'll look closely at some key aspects of how the Rails libraries organize their classes and modules using inheritance and other techniques. But here's a preview: the use of inherited in the ActiveRecord library (slightly rearranged and edited for illustration purposes).

The back story to this example is that every time you define a *model* in your Rails application, you inherit from a class called ActiveRecord::Base. For example, a Work model definition file might start like this:

```
class Work < ActiveRecord::Base
```

That's an inheritance event, suitable for being intercepted or hooked by the inherited method. Sure enough, the file base.rb in the ActiveRecord source contains a definition for inherited. This snippet of code also gives you a glimpse of *class variables*, which are recognizable by the two at-signs (@@) with which their names start:

```
module ActiveRecord
  class Base
    @@subclasses = {}
    def self.inherited(child)
      @@subclasses[self] ||= []
      @@subclasses[self] << child    ◁━━━━━━━━❶
      super
    end
# etc.
```

Every time you inherit from ActiveRecord::Base—essentially, every time you create a new model definition—the name of your new class (child, in the code ❶) gets added to an array. That array is stored inside the hash @@subclasses.

> **NOTE** CLASS VARIABLES Class variables, like @@subclasses in the example from the base.rb source file, are scoped in such a way that they are visible when self is the class to which they belong, a descendant (to any level) of that class, or an instance of the class or its descendants. Despite their name, they're not really class scoped; they're more like hierarchy scoped. Matz

has mentioned plans to change the scoping of class variables in future versions of Ruby so that their visibility is more confined to the class (or module; modules can have class variables too) where they're defined.

ActiveRecord thus uses the `inherited` hook to log information internally about the models you've created. This kind of behind-the-scenes interception of information, generally without impact on (or even the knowledge of) the programmer using a library, is typical of the use of callbacks and typical of the kind of technique Rails uses to manage the universe of your domain in Ruby terms as you create it.

13.4.4 Module#const_missing

`Module#const_missing` is another commonly used callback. As the name implies, this method is called whenever an unidentifiable constant is referred to inside a given module or class:

```
class C
  def self.const_missing(const)
    puts "#{const} is undefined—setting it to 1."
    const_set(const,1)
  end
end

puts C::A
puts C::A
```

The output of this code is as follows:

```
A is undefined—setting it to 1.
1
1
```

Thanks to the callback, `C::A` is defined automatically when you use it without defining it. This is taken care of in such a way that `puts` can print the value of the constant; `puts` never has to know that the constant wasn't defined in the first place. Then, on the second call to `puts`, the constant is already defined, and `const_missing` isn't called.

13.5 Overriding and adding to core functionality

One of Ruby's most powerful features is the ability to change and augment the language's core functionality. You can open up core classes just as easily as you can open up your own classes. And you can add new methods and override old ones to your heart's content. Want arrays to know how to shuffle themselves? Here's how to teach them:

```
class Array
  def shuffle
    sort_by { rand }
  end
end
```

There are reasons, however, to be very, very cautious about making changes to the Ruby core in your own programs. In particular, if you're writing a code library that you expect other people to use, and that library contains code that changes the behavior of core objects and classes, you're in essence changing the rules of the game for everyone who uses your code. That means *their* code may fail to work.

13.5.1 A cautionary tale

Here's an example involving MatchData. It's notoriously annoying that when a match operation fails, you get back nil, and when it succeeds, you get back a MatchData object. This result is irritating because you can't do the same things with nil that you can with a MatchData object. This code, for example, succeeds if there's a first capture created by the match:

```
some_regexp.match(some_string)[1]
```

But if there's no match, you get back nil—and because nil has no [] method, you get a fatal NoMethodError exception when you try the [1] operation.

It may be tempting to do something like this:

```
class Regexp
  alias :old_match :match       ◁———❶
  def match(string)
    old_match(string) || []
  end
end
```

This code first sets up an *alias* for match, courtesy of the alias keyword ❶. The alias means you can now call the method using either of two names. Then, the code redefines match. The new match hooks into the original version of match (through the alias) and then returns *either* the result of calling the original version, *or* (if that call returns nil) an empty array.

You can now do this:

```
/abc/.match("X")[1]
```

Even though the match fails, the program won't blow up, because the failed match now returns an empty array rather than nil. The worst you can do with the new match is try to index an empty array, which is legal. (The value you'll get is nil, but at least you're not trying to *index* nil.)

The problem is that the person using your code may be depending on the match operation to return `nil` on failure:

```
if regexp.match(string)
  do something
else
  do something else
end
```

Because an array (even an empty one) is true, whereas `nil` is false, returning an array for a failed match operation means that the true/false test (as embodied in an `if/else` statement) always returns true.

The moral of the story is that you have to be *very* careful about changing core behaviors. Even adding new methods to `Array`, `String`, and the other built-in classes is risky. What if someone else adds a method with the same name that behaves differently? The only way to be safe is to leave the core methods alone.

This cautionary tale brings us to the end of our survey of callbacks and hooks and of Ruby dynamics in general. The techniques in this chapter are powerful and inventive. Used knowledgeably, they can buy you a lot of programming functionality. A good sense of Ruby's repertoire of dynamic behaviors will put you in a new bracket when it comes to understanding and analyzing what Ruby code is doing—including, but by no means limited to, the Rails framework source and specific Rails applications.

13.6 Summary

This chapter has given you a guided tour of some of the more meta aspects of Ruby: techniques for manipulating not only your program's data but also the programming environment. We've looked at singleton classes, Ruby's mechanism for making per-object behaviors a reality. We've discussed callable objects (Procs, blocks, and their relatives); runtime evaluation of strings with `eval`, as well as the operations of the `*_eval` family; and hooks you can use to make things happen at predefined junctures (subclassing, calls to nonexistent methods, and so on).

You've also seen some of the power, as well as the risks, of the ability Ruby gives you to pry open not only your own classes but also Ruby's core classes. This is something you should do sparingly, if at all—and it's also something you should be aware of other people doing.

We've reached the end of the parts of the book containing concentrated Ruby-language tutorial material. We're now in a good position to return to the R4RMusic application and take it to the next level.

Part 4

Rails through Ruby, Ruby through Rails

The purpose of this part of the book is to bring to full fruition the book's overall plan: helping you get more out of Rails by knowing more about Ruby. The goals here are the goals of the book itself:

- Learning the Ruby foundations of specific Rails techniques
- Using your Ruby knowledge to add programming value and power to your Rails applications by writing your own custom code
- Gaining skill and experience in examining the Rails source code

Over the course of the four chapters that make up part 4, we'll revisit and revise R4RMusic, the music store application from chapter 2. Along the way, we'll use selected features and components of the application as windows onto the inner workings of both Ruby and Rails—and, of course, Ruby and Rails together. The new version of R4RMusic will include a Customer model and rudimentary but operational shopping-cart capabilities. We'll also implement more fine-tuned facilities for handling musical works and published editions, along with the composers, instruments, and publishers associated with them.

The sequence of the first three chapters is guided by the development of the phases of the application revision process. Domain model and database (re)design come first, in chapter 14; then, in chapter 15, we'll add custom-written Ruby code to the model files, by way of enhancing and augmenting model functionality. Chapter 16 covers the updates and changes to the controller and view files, bringing to a close the revision of the application.

Chapter 17 is devoted to demonstrating a variety of techniques for finding your way around the Rails framework source code and starting to familiarize yourself with it. We can't walk through all of it in this book; but once you get a sense of how to negotiate the source, you'll be in a position to do as much of it as you wish.

The spotlight is on developing the application in ways that wouldn't have been possible before parts 2 and 3 of the book, and that point the way to further Ruby mastery.

14

(Re)modeling the R4RMusic application universe

371

The province of this chapter, together with chapter 15, is everything on the domain-modeling, database-designing, and ActiveRecord-modeling side of the music store application revision process—in other words, everything pertaining to the *what* of the R4RMusic universe.

In the course of refining and expanding that universe, we'll be doing several things, all of them parallel to what we did on the first iteration of the application:

- Adding new entities to the domain model
- Revising and tweaking old entities
- Creating and/or modifying the SQL database table definitions to reflect the changes
- Creating and/or modifying ActiveRecord model files to reflect the changes

The first three items on this list are covered in this chapter. The fourth item—creating and/or modifying model files—is split between this chapter and chapter 15. (Chapter 15, specifically, covers the process of adding new methods manually to your model class files.)

Although the steps we'll go through here are similar to those we went through in chapter 2, the scenery has changed. The days of black-box, just-trust-me code are over, and the glass ceiling separating the "Rails person" from the "Ruby person" is gone. This is where we bring the threads together: knowing what's *really* happening when you use standard Rails techniques, and devising ways to go beyond those techniques—all thanks to your knowledge of Ruby.

The first section of this chapter provides a roadmap of how to understand Rails entity models in Ruby terms. From there, we'll proceed to a detailed reassessment and upgrading of the domain database. In addition to illustrating some important language and framework techniques, that section will anchor the next chapter, which is devoted to the process of using Ruby code to enhance ActiveRecord model functionality.

This chapter doesn't draw a sharp line between developing the application, learning Rails techniques, and bringing Ruby techniques to bear on the Rails application for the sake of added value. The point is that it's all one process.

14.1 *Tracking the capabilities of an ActiveRecord model instance*

Rails entity models are Ruby classes. When you do things with Rails data—create a composer, give a work a title—you're dealing with *instances* of those model classes on the same terms as you would deal with any Ruby class and its instances. Everything else flows from that fact. If you understand how Ruby classes and their instances work, there's nothing about a Rails model instance you can't understand. And if you know how to write class and instance methods that add programming value to a class, you can add value to your Rails models.

Let's look in detail at how an ActiveRecord model instance comes to be able to do the things it can do.

14.1.1 *An overview of model instance capabilities*

Like any Ruby object, an instance of a model class—Composer, Work, and so on—has certain methods you can ask it to execute. The capabilities of a Rails model instance come from four places:

- *Inheritance* on the part of its class, through which the instance gains the ability to call the instance methods of its class's superclass (ActiveRecord::Base or another descendant of that class)
- *Automatic creation of accessor and other methods,* based on the *field names* in the relevant database table (Composer objects have a title and a title= method, thanks to the presence of the *title* field in the *composers* database table)
- *Semi-automatic creation of accessor and other methods,* when prompted with an *association* directive (such as has_one :composer, in the case of the Work class)
- *Programmatic addition of arbitrarily many instance methods,* added to the model definition file as needed and desired

The open-ended programming power lies in the fourth item. But it's rooted firmly in the programming context, already rich with functionality on the part of the objects, provided by the first three items in the list.

In the next two subsections, we'll look more closely the first three of the four sources of object capability. We'll examine inheritance and automatic creation of instance methods together. We'll consider semi-automatic creation of methods via associations separately, taking the opportunity to examine more closely the matter of what an ActiveRecord association is.

The fourth item on the list, programmatic enhancement of model classes, we'll save until chapter 15, which is entirely devoted to it.

Let's turn now to a combined discussion of the first two items: behaviors bestowed upon ActiveRecord model instances automatically or through inheritance.

14.1.2 *Inherited and automatic ActiveRecord model behaviors*

An ActiveRecord model object, such as an instance of the `Composer` class, already has a good deal of functionality when it's created. As with Ruby built-in classes, you can get a quick sense of how many methods an instance of `ActiveRecord::Base` (or one of its subclasses) has by default; just ask the application irb console:

```
$ ruby script/console
Loading development environment.
>> ActiveRecord::Base.instance_methods.size
=> 180
```

With almost 200 methods present at birth, a `Composer` or `Work` or `Edition` object can already do a lot. Some of these capabilities are more important than others for the typical Rails developer, and we are by no means going to talk about all of them here. A handful of them, though, are particularly useful and worth discussing.

Accordingly, we're going to zero in on a small cluster of instance methods, all pertaining to the overall lifecycle of ActiveRecord objects: `save`, `update`, and `destroy`. To get the full picture of this sector of ActiveRecord behavior, we'll also look at some related class methods: `new`, `create`, `find`, and `delete`. (If it seems strange to you that a discussion of the capabilities of instances involves four *class* methods but only three instance methods, keep in mind that some of the class methods call the underlying instance methods; the two method levels are closely intertwined.)

> **TIP**   LOOK AT THE ONLINE RAILS API DOCUMENTATION   Chapter 17 includes detailed discussion of navigating the online Rails API documentation at http://api.rubyonrails.org. But even now, don't hesitate to look at that site at any time—especially the links (on the left side of the screen) to information about specific method in the Rails framework.

The two lives of the ActiveRecord object

We're looking at methods that pertain to object creation, persistence (saving to and retrieving from the database), and destruction. Let's jumpstart the analysis of these methods by going briefly back to basics.

In the vast majority of cases, when you want to create a new object from a Ruby class, you do this:

```
b = Bicycle.new
```

ActiveRecord objects allow for the same treatment. You can create a new `Composer` instance like this

```
c = Composer.new
```

and then call methods on the object you've created:

```
c.first_name = "Johannes"
c.last_name = "Brahms"
```

The difference between an ActiveRecord object and a typical Ruby object, how-ever, is that the ActiveRecord object lives two lives. On the one hand, it's a Ruby object. On the other hand, it's a handle with which you can directly manipulate a database record.

Similarly, the model classes, in their role as object factories, do more than the standard new of the typical Ruby class. They also have the power to do things that have a direct impact on the contents of a database.

This double-life aspect of ActiveRecord objects is directly embodied in the meth-ods available for creating, changing, saving, and destroying them. You can think of these methods as an extended, super-charged family branching off from the lowly new method. These objects need to do more than just spring into existence.

Some of ActiveRecord's class-level functionality performs actions on the data-base without creating a corresponding Ruby object. For example, if you have the ID number of a record in the *composer* table, and you do this

```
Composer.delete(id)
```

that record is removed from the database directly. You don't even have to create a corresponding instance of `Composer` (although you could, with `Composer.find(id)`).

A traditional new operation marks a transition from a state where an instance doesn't exist to a state where it does. With the ActiveRecord family of creation methods, there are not one but two criteria of existence:

- The existence of an instance of the class
- The existence of a directly corresponding record in the database

These two criteria can vary independently and be manipulated independently.

Therein lies the complexity of the world of creating ActiveRecord objects. But if you think of the whole cluster of methods as variations on new—or as members of new's extended family—the concept falls into place.

Table 14.1 shows the permutations that the methods exhibit. Note that some of these methods have both instance and class versions, and some are class-only.

Table 14.1 ActiveRecord class and instance methods and their relation to object and/or database-record existence

	new	create (new + save)	find	save	update	delete (find + destroy)	destroy
Before method is called:							
Is there a Ruby object?	No	No	No	Yes	Yes	No	Yes
Is there a database record?	No	No	Yes	Yes	Yes	Yes	Yes
After method is called:							
Is there a Ruby object?	Yes	Yes	Yes	Yes	Yes	Yes (frozen)	Yes (frozen)
Is there a database record?	No	Yes	Yes	Yes	Yes	No	No

- The methods where there is no object in existence before the method is called are class methods (which you can deduce from the fact that there's no instance on which to call them).

- The designation "(frozen)" means that the instance has been frozen via the Ruby `freeze` method. This ensures that the object can't be altered; its instance variables can't be reassigned. This is done after destruction of an ActiveRecord object. Although a record can be obliterated from the database, there's no equivalent operation on the Ruby side to destroy all traces of an instance. Therefore, freezing it is the best way to indicate that its lifecycle is over.

- `update`, `delete`, and `destroy` have variants ending in `_all` (`update_all`, and so on), which perform the given operation on all existing database records and/or corresponding Ruby instances. As always, for complete details on all available methods, see the Rails API documentation Web site.

The two-life nature of ActiveRecord model objects means you need to be both Ruby-aware and database-aware when you're manipulating those objects, either by themselves or via the class methods of their classes. Much of the point of Rails is to let you manipulate database records *as* Ruby objects so you don't have to concern yourself with the details of database operations while manipulating objects in your application's universe. However, you need to be aware of the dual nature of the objects: Specifically, you must understand that some of the manipulations you perform are strictly in Ruby space, whereas other manipulations trigger a change to the database—and some do both.

Methods created automatically from database field names

In addition to the methods that every ActiveRecord object has by inheritance, these objects are also endowed with methods based on the field names of the database tables to which they correspond. Thus, given a *composer* table with a *first_name* field, every instance of the Composer class responds to the message "first_name".

Moreover, these instances also respond to "first_name="—they have a setter method as well as a getter method for each property they derive from their database table. All this is arranged automatically by ActiveRecord; you don't need to define these methods.

ActiveRecord maps the database structure and naming onto Ruby, turning table names into classes and field names into instance methods. The former requires some programmer intervention: You have to create a model file (using the generate script) to prompt ActiveRecord to see what your classes are (composer, edition, and so on). But once you've done that, ActiveRecord can connect the dots. The field names in the relevant database tables are automatically transferred to the Ruby side as instance methods of the objects you create.

Rails is by no means the only system to provide this kind of bridge from database to programming language, or *object/relational mapping* (ORM). It's not even the only one written in Ruby. Relational databases generally do real-world modeling by table and field name; and object-oriented languages *also* do real-world modeling, via class naming (and module naming, in Ruby's case) and inheritance structures. The challenge of getting the two to talk to each other—of coming up with programming-language idioms that fit into the language but also give you leverage over the database—has been faced and met many times.

You don't have to master ORM systems other than Rails unless you're interested in doing so. The point is that Rails is creating a bridge between one modeling system (the relational database) and another (the classes and instances and method-calls of Ruby). The automatic creation of methods based on the names of database fields is the Rails (or ActiveRecord, strictly speaking) way of giving you a familiar Ruby idiom—getter and setter methods, in pairs—for manipulating database properties.

(If you get lulled into forgetting you're dealing with a database as well as a bunch of in-memory Ruby Composer and Edition objects, you'll be reminded when you forget to perform an explicit `save` operation and all your attribute settings disappear! In some respects, despite the Ruby orientation of Rails, you still have to be database-aware.)

We've now looked at inherited behaviors and automatically assigned behaviors. Moving up the scale of programmer presence (or down the scale of Rails automation, if you prefer) we'll next examine the way Rails performs semi-automatic creation of methods, based on what you've specified in the form of ActiveRecord *associations*.

14.1.3 *Semi-automatic behaviors via associations*

ActiveRecord associations give you a semi-automatic way to add instance methods to your model entity classes. They're semi-automatic in the sense that Rails creates them based on a combination of the naming scheme it finds in the database and the explicit directives you put in the model file. Thus they're not as automatic as the accessor methods that spring into being automatically based on the names of the fields in the database tables, but they're more automatic than methods you write from scratch.

What is an association?

The term *association* vividly and accurately describes the *has* and *belongs to* relations between Rails entity models. When we say, "There's a one-to-many association between the Composer and Work models," we're using shorthand for saying that the `Composer` class definition includes this

```
has_many :works
```

and the `Work` class definition includes this:

```
belongs_to :composer
```

One-to-many also implies that the *works* table in the database has a *composer_id* field, which serves the purpose of labeling each work with the ID number of a particular composer record.

Associations are the prime example of a Rails idiom that looks like a line in a configuration file or a directive in a simple declarative language. It's not uncommon for newcomers to Rails to ask, "When I do that 'has_many :somethings' thing, what *exactly* am I doing?"

The answer isn't hard to come by, if you apply the principles for orienting yourself in a Ruby program that we've already covered. In this code

```
class Composer < ActiveRecord::Base
```

```
has_many :works
# etc.
```

has_many is a class method call. You know this because

- It's at the top level of a class definition body, so self is the class object (Composer).

- It's a bareword, but neither a keyword nor a local variable—which means it's a method call, a message being sent to the implied receiver self.

You also know that you didn't define has_many yourself, so it must be a class method of the parent class, ActiveRecord::Base. The same is true of the other associations: belongs_to, has_one, and has_and_belongs_to_many.

The association directives are class methods of the model classes you create, which means they're class methods of ActiveRecord::Base, because they appear in your classes courtesy of inheriting from that preexisting class. When you call these methods, they bring about the creation of one or more *instance* methods, based on what you've specified both in the call to the association method and in the database. Thus, for example,

```
class Work < ActiveRecord::Base
  belongs_to :composer
```

causes all instances of Work to have an instance method called composer. That composer method returns the Composer object whose *id* field matches the *composer_id* field of the Work object.

It's as if you'd written this

```
class Work < ActiveRecord::Base
  def composer
    Composer.find(composer_id)
  end
```

where composer_id directly pulls up the value of the Work object's *composer_id* field. (just as title pulls up the value of its *title* field, and so forth). Calling belongs_to at the class level saves you the trouble of having to write the composer method manually.

The association methods are analogous to Ruby's attr family of methods. In both of these method families, you use class-method calls to automate the creation of one or more instance methods. The specifics of what happens are different, as between, say, attr_writer and has_and_belongs_to_many. But the basic contours of how they work (and even how they look) are similar.

Onward, in two directions

The next level of model enhancement is the level of programmatic enhancement—the writing of methods, with names of your choice and with functionality designed by you, in your model files. You saw some of this in chapter 3, and you'll be seeing more in chapter 15, which will be devoted entirely to programmatic model enhancement.

Meanwhile, by way of setting the stage, we're going to turn now to the music store domain model and make some changes to it. These changes will take the music store to the next level of functionality and will also lead in to the model-programming coming up in chapter 15.

14.2 Advancing the domain model

Advancing the music store domain model will involve adding new entities and fine-tuning some old ones.

We'll start with domain and database (re)design. From there, we'll proceed to look at all the model files: those we have to create and those we need to change. As was the case in the earlier iteration of the music store, the SQL will be Rails-friendly and will anticipate certain aspects of the model files.

As we go through these domain model revisions, the discussion will include important techniques and points about how things work and what's involved in choosing a design, from the combined Ruby/Rails perspective. Understanding these subtopics will give you a firm footing when we proceed to the matter of programmatically altering entity models.

We're going to make various changes to the domain model. Some will promote *properties* to *entities*—essentially, turning certain fields into tables. Some will be new entities. Throughout, they will involve the creation of new associations.

14.2.1 Abstracting and adding models (publisher and edition)

In the first iteration of the music store application, publishers were attached to editions as simple text fields; the *editions* table had a field called *publisher*, into which the name went. In this second iteration, we'll put publishers in their own model.

This approach will allow more detail to be stored: not only the name of the publisher, but also the country. It will also make it easier to associate publishers directly or indirectly with other entities, should that become necessary. It's also less likely, when the publishers are stored as separate records rather than text strings, that a given publisher's name will inadvertently be spelled two different ways, creating the appearance of two publishers where there is only one.

The goal, then, is to extract a Publisher model from the Edition model. One model must be created, and one must be modified in place. As with all the other models, you create the Publisher model as follows:

```
$ ruby script/generate model publisher
```

This gives you, among other things, the file app/models/publisher.rb. In this file, you can establish the publisher's end of the association between publisher and edition:

```
class Publisher < ActiveRecord::Base
  has_many :editions
end
```

On the database side, you need to create a new *publishers* table. It can have as many fields as you want. In this case, we'll keep it small, but remember that you can add other fields (address, phone number, and so on). Note that the *name* field of the new *publishers* table is identical to the *publisher* field in the *editions* table:

```
CREATE TABLE publishers (
  id INT(11) NOT NULL AUTO_INCREMENT,
  name VARCHAR(60),
  city VARCHAR(30),
  country CHAR(2),
  PRIMARY KEY (id)
);
```

To keep all the database tables in sync, you should remove the *publisher* field from the *editions* table and add a *publisher_id* field. That field's contents will match the *id* field from the record for the edition's publisher.

Corresponding to the new *publisher_id* field in the *edition* table, you'll need to add this:

```
belongs_to :publisher
```

to the class definition in the edition.rb model file. At this point, the Edition model has most of what it needs.

But to make the model complete, it would make sense to add a *title* field. Why bother giving titles to editions, when the musical works inside them already have titles? Because an edition can contain more than one work. In such a case, the edition has a name—like *The Complete String Quartets*, or *The Late Piano Sonatas*—that refers to the individual works collectively. Musicians shop for these collections, so they should have their own presence by title in the online catalogue.

Figure 14.1 gives you a graphic view of the changes to the *editions* table along with the creation of the *publishers* table.

```
CREATE TABLE editions (
  id INT(11) NOT NULL AUTO_INCRIMENT,
  description VARCHAR(30),              CREATE TABLE publishers (
  work_id INT(11) NOT NULL,              id INT(11) NOT NULL AUTO_INCREMENT,
  publisher_id INT(11) NOT NULL,         name VARCHAR(60),
  title VARCHAR(100)                     city VARCHAR(30),
  publisher VARCHAR(60),                 country CHAR(2),
  year INT(4),                           PRIMARY KEY (id)
  PRIMARY KEY (id)                     );
);
```

Figure 14.1   Creation of the *publishers* table and changes to the *editions* table

The new fields in *editions* are shown in *italics*. An arrow shows you the connection, as Rails will see it, between *publisher_id* in *editions*, and *id* in *publishers*. Another arrow (the lighter one) shows that the ghost of the old *publisher* field (which isn't present in the new version of the *editions* table) lives on as the *name* field in the new *publishers* table.

We have some more table and model creation to do, in the course of which we'll establish some many-to-many associations.

14.2.2   *The instruments model and many-to-many relations*

The next new model we'll create is the *instrument* model. This model was conspicuous by its absence from the first iteration of the music store—after all, it's common to want to browse sheet music inventory by instrument. It's possible to do that by fishing instrument names out of the titles of works, but it's cleaner and more accurate to do it by having a separate database table (and ActiveRecord model) for instruments.

As usual when a new model comes onto the scene, we generate it

```
$ ruby script/generate model instrument
```

and add the new entity to the database.

The Instrument model has two properties: *name* and *family*. Examples of instrument names are *violin*, *piano*, and *trumpet*; examples of instrument families are *strings*, *keyboard*, and *brass*. The SQL looks like this:

```
CREATE TABLE instruments (
  id INT(11) NOT NULL AUTO_INCREMENT,
  name VARCHAR(20),
  family VARCHAR(15),
  PRIMARY KEY (id)
);
```

Instruments relate to musical works in a *many-to-many* relationship: Any work can be for any number of instruments, and any instrument can have any number of works written for it. This contrasts with the typical *one-to-many* relationship, as exemplified by the association between a work and its composer. Each work has one composer; in practical terms, each database record for a work is stamped with the ID of a particular composer record. We've seen this in the SQL table definition for works:

```
composer_id INT(11),
```

and in the corresponding association declarations in the model files:

```
class Work < ActiveRecord::Base
  belongs_to :composer
  # etc.
end

class Composer < ActiveRecord::Base
  has_many :works
  # etc.
end
```

This mechanism—the *entity_id* field, coupled with the appropriate associations— drives the one-to-many relationships. Something similar (but not identical) drives the many-to-many relationships. If *instruments* and *works* stand in a many-to-many relation to each other, then an instrument record can't have one *work_id* field. That would imply that for every instrument, there is one and only one work to which it belongs. Nor can the *works* table have an *instrument_id* field. That would make sense only if we were dealing with works that were never written for more than one instrument.

Instead, we need a way to keep track of any number of instruments related to any number of musical works, all at the same time.

Expressing many-to-many in Rails-friendly SQL

A many-to-many relationship is expressed in Rails-friendly SQL with a special, separate table. Unlike most other tables, this table doesn't correspond directly to a Rails model or Ruby class. Instead, it provides a way for Rails to track and record each case of a relationship between an edition and an author.

We'll use standard Rails-compliant naming for this table: It's called *instruments_works*. It has two fields: one for the ID field of a particular instrument record and one for a work's ID. The table's role is to record the associations between authors and books. It has no fields other than those that serve this purpose:

```
CREATE TABLE instruments_works (
  instrument_id int(11),
  work_id int(11)
);
```

Rails is engineered to glean from this table the fact that instruments and works can relate in a many-to-many way and to provide a number of programming techniques for maintaining those relationships. All you have to do is design the table according to the right naming scheme (as we're doing here) and prompt Rails with the appropriate association instructions in the relevant model files.

The has_and_belongs_to_many association

Corresponding to the table is the following association instruction in `instrument.rb`:

```
class Instrument < ActiveRecord::Base
  has_and_belongs_to_many :works
  # etc.
end
```

And here's the mirror-image instruction in `work.rb`:

```
class Work < ActiveRecord::Base
  has_and_belongs_to_many :instruments
  # etc.
end
```

With this code in place, it's now possible to query `Instrument` objects as to their works and `Work` objects as to their instruments. When Rails sees something like this

```
v = Instrument.find(:first,:conditions => "name = 'violin'")
works_for_violin = v.works
```

it places in `works_for_violin` a collection of all the `Work` objects associated (via entries in the *instruments_works* table) with the instrument whose *name* field value is violin—all the pieces for violin, whether solo or multi-instrument music.

Implications of the instrument model for the work model

In its original incarnation, the Work model had a *title* field that contained not only the title of the work but also the instrumentation and the key. Now we've pulled out the instruments. That suggests we could do the same with the key and the opus number.

A *key* table would be overkill; instead, it's enough to create a *key* field for the *work* table. However, `key` is a reserved work in SQL. Let's call the field *kee*.

We'll also add a field for the opus number. This field will be set to accommodate up to 20 characters. Most opus numbers are shorter, but the works of some composers are indexed in ways that don't correspond to the standard opus-numbering scheme. (The works of Mozart, for instance, were catalogued by Ludwig Ritter von Köchel in the nineteenth century and are referred to by K numbers rather than opus numbers. Similarly, Bach's works are referred to with the designation BWV [from the German for *Index of Bach's Works*].)

The *opus* field in the *works* table must be able to accommodate strings like "BMV 1006" and "K.85" as well as numbers. Many works also have a number designation as well as an opus designation—for example, "Opus 1, no. 3."

The SQL for the *works* table now looks like this:

```
CREATE TABLE works (
  id INT(11) NOT NULL AUTO_INCREMENT,
  composer_id INT(11),
  title VARCHAR(100),
  year INT(4),
  kee CHAR(9),
  opus VARCHAR(20),
  PRIMARY KEY (id)
);
```

This table definition should be equal to the task of handling any unconventional opus designations we throw at it.

Next, we'll revisit an existing relationship in a new light.

Editions-to-works many-to-many mapping

In the first iteration of the music store, every edition belonged to a work, and every work had many editions. That way of modeling the relationship is workable only up to a point. In the field of music publishing, it's common for one edition—one publication—to include multiple works, possibly by different composers (although most often by the same composer).

That means that every work can appear in multiple editions, and any one edition can be an edition of multiple works. Editions and works stand in a many-to-many relation.

On the SQL side, this situation isn't hard to implement. In the *editions* table, you remove the *work_id* field, because the edition no longer belongs to a particular work. Then, you add a table to store the relationships between works and editions:

```
CREATE TABLE editions_works (
  edition_id int(11),
  work_id int(11)
);
```

On the ActiveRecord side, you modify the model files appropriately. In `edition.rb`, you remove the `belongs_to :work` directive and insert the following:

```
has_and_belongs_to_many :works
```

In `work.rb`, add this:

```
has_and_belongs_to_many :editions,
                        :order => "year ASC"
```

(The `:order` argument is an SQL fragment that tells ActiveRecord to return editions in ascending order by year—a rough-and-ready way to sort them, but one that provides a basically chronological listing of multiple editions.)

The ultimate goal of any online store is to have customers who order things. Next, we'll round out the R4RMusic model universe by adding the customer and order models.

14.2.3 *Modeling for use: customer and order*

The addition of the Customer entity is the biggest change we'll make to the R4RMusic domain model in the course of the application revision process. The Order entity, also on the creation agenda in this section, is closely related to Customer.

Modeling the customer

The customer will be expected to do the following:

- Sign up
- Log in
- Select items to put in a shopping cart
- Check out (purchase the items)

As with the other aspects of the application, the goals for Customer will be to create an adequately "thick" (detailed) model in support of the planned actions, and to give you a basis for experimentation and learning. And as with the rest of the application, if you want to take the underdeveloped parts of the customer and experiment with developing them further, you can and should.

On the Rails side, you need to create model and controller files for the *customer* model:

```
$ ruby script/generate model customer
$ ruby script/generate controller customer
```

On the database side, the relatively simple customer looks like this in SQL form:

```
CREATE TABLE customers (
  id INT(11) NOT NULL AUTO_INCREMENT,
  first_name VARCHAR(30),
  last_name VARCHAR(30),
  nick VARCHAR(15),
  password VARCHAR(40),
  email VARCHAR(50),
  PRIMARY KEY (id)
);
```

(The *nick* is the name under which the customer logs in. It will be created when the customer signs up for an account.)

Modeling the order

The Customer model is accompanied by an Order model. (You need to generate a model, but not a controller, for order, using the `generate` script.) The order records in the database connect a customer with an edition via their respective ID fields. The Order model also contains a *status* field, which can (for example) be set to "paid" once the order has been paid for, "shipped" when the order has been shipped, and so forth.

In order to track orders chronologically, we'll also equip the *orders* table with a special field called *created_at*. This fieldname is special to Rails: When an order object is saved, Rails automatically saves the time and date that the save took place to this field. When the record is retrieved, the date is available via the new object's `created_at` method.

The whole *orders* table looks like this:

```
CREATE TABLE orders (
  id INT(11) NOT NULL AUTO_INCREMENT,
  edition_id INT(11),
  customer_id INT(11),
  status CHAR(4),
  created_at DATETIME,
  PRIMARY KEY (id)
);
```

The *orders* table is stamped with the ID of an edition and a customer, which means it belongs to those two entities. Let's deal with the associations pertaining to orders.

Associating orders with customers and editions

Every order belongs to a customer; and every order also belongs to an edition. Therefore, the model file `app/models/order.rb` includes two `belongs_to` association directives. Here are the first three lines of that file:

```
class Order < ActiveRecord::Base
  belongs_to :customer
  belongs_to :edition
```

On the other side of the *has/belongs to* balance sheet, customers and editions both have orders. A customer's orders consist of all the orders placed by that customer. (Remember that orders have a *status* property, so you can track which orders are still pending, which have been completed, and so on). An edition's orders are all orders placed for that edition.

We want `Customer` and `Edition` objects to have an `orders` instance method, returning a collection of all the object's orders. For instance, we can do this as part of the process of preparing a view of a customer's shopping cart:

```
c = Customer.find(params[:id])
orders = c.orders
```

To ensure that `Customer` objects have an `orders` method, we need to put an association directive in the Customer model file. A first pass at creating that association looks like this:

```
class Customer < ActiveRecord::Base
  has_many :orders
end
```

Another subtlety wouldn't be amiss here: establishing *dependence* between the customer and its orders. Dependence, in this context, means that if the customer record in the database is ever deleted, all of its orders will be deleted along with it. It's a handy way of making sure you don't end up with a lot of orphaned records that serve no purpose once the record they pertained to no longer exists.

The next iteration of the association looks like this:

```
class Customer < ActiveRecord::Base
  has_many :orders,
           :dependent => true
end
```

The association can benefit from one more little tweak. Let's specify the order in which you want the orders listed. We can do this with an SQL fragment, much as we did for the association between works and editions in section 14.2.2. Here's the final version of the `has_many` association between customers and orders:

```
class Customer < ActiveRecord::Base
  has_many :orders,
           :dependent => true,
           :order     => "created_at ASC"
end
```

We're asking that the customer's orders be returned, when requested, in ascending order based the *created_at* field. As you'll recall, *created_at* is a special field; if a table has a field of that name, ActiveRecord automatically inserts a creation timestamp into that field for each newly created record.

We'll add an *orders* association to the *edition* model, too, so we can query editions as to their order history:

```
class Edition < ActiveRecord::Base
  has_many :orders
end
```

It would be possible to make an edition's orders dependent on the edition object, as we did in the case of customers. If a given edition was ever removed from the database, all orders for that edition would also disappear. That may not be a good idea, though. True, an edition might go out of print; but you'd probably want to do something more graceful than just deleting all its orders (like flagging them so the customers who placed the orders could be notified). So we won't make order records dependent on the corresponding edition records.

We'll add methods to both the *customer* and *edition* models in chapter 15. Meanwhile, let's go back briefly to the Order class and make another important provision: arranging for every newly created order to be given a default status of "open".

The default status can be arranged via the ActiveRecord callback method before_create.

Setting a default status for orders

If you provide a definition for the special method before_create in an ActiveRecord model class, then that method is called automatically every time a new instance of the model is saved to the database. You don't have to define before_create; but if you do, ActiveRecord will recognize the name and execute it the first time a new record is created.

Define before_create in the Order class as follows:

```
def before_create
  self.status = "open"
end
```

(Note that the explicit receiver self is necessary so that the Ruby parser interprets status as a method call and not a local variable on the left side of an assignment.)

Without any further intervention, ActiveRecord will now set the *status* field of every newly created order object to "open". Order objects are also automatically endowed with a status method, which returns the object's status, and a status= method, with which the order's status can be set. You aren't stuck with "open"; it's just the default, and setting it will be taken care of automatically thanks to ActiveRecord's callback facilities.

Viewing the new domain graphically

Figure 14.2 shows a simple graphical representation of the new look of the R4RMusic domain.

Keep in mind that figure 14.2 is intended to illustrate the domain itself—the universe of the music store and its inventory—not to replicate the names of the database tables and fields. (There's a close correspondence, of course; but the illustration is a little more abstract in its property-naming than the tables.) The

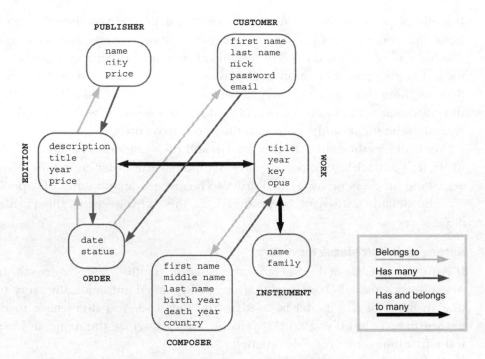

Figure 14.2 Diagram of the revised R4RMusic domain, with ActiveRecord associations indicated by arrows

arrows in figure 14.2 relate directly to the associations among the models in the domain; as the key indicates, different arrows represent different associations. These associations are implemented, as we've seen, through *_id field names in the database, association directives in the model files, and/or many-to-many join tables in the database, as appropriate in each case. The illustration thus gives you both an overview of entities and their properties, and Rails-specific indications of how they're interconnected.

With the database, the models, and the basic associations in place, we're ready to launch into further, programmatic enhancement of the models—the subject of chapter 15.

14.3 Summary

We've worked on two fronts in this chapter: looking at three of the four ways in which ActiveRecord model classes and objects come by their methods and capabilities, and revisiting and expanding our music store domain. All of this has been in the service of going more deeply into the *what* side of things: the programming and design tasks associated with pinning down the specifics of an application's universe, and expressing the structure of that universe both in database form and in Ruby form.

We looked at inheritance (from `ActiveRecord::Base`), automatic creation of methods (based on the names of database fields), and semi-automatic creation of methods (via ActiveRecord associations). The fourth source of ActiveRecord object capability—the addition of methods custom-written by the programmer—will be the topic of chapter 15.

On the domain-modeling and database side, we added entities to the domain and made changes and enhancements to existing entities. These changes give more contour to the domain and put us in a good position to get more deeply into the programmatic enhancement of models in the next chapter.

15 *Programmatically enhancing ActiveRecord models*

In the previous chapter, we looked at some of the ways in which ActiveRecord objects gain their functionalities (inheritance, methods based on table-field names, and methods based on associations), and we also revisited the domain and database modeling for the music store—the foundations of the ActiveRecord models for that domain. In this chapter, we'll build on this foundation by looking at the process of extending and enhancing ActiveRecord models *programmatically.*

Enhancing a model programmatically basically means going into the model file and writing whatever methods you want inside the class definition body of the model class. Even without this kind of added functionality, ActiveRecord models are already powerful and versatile. And when you start identifying what *more* they might do—and scripting those capabilities yourself, in Ruby—the power and versatility become truly open-ended. Programmatic enhancement of models brings together your Ruby skills and your Rails knowledge in a particularly dynamic way.

Naturally, this isn't something to be done haphazardly. You don't want to duplicate the functionality that ActiveRecord already gives your objects, and you don't want to endow your objects with behaviors that don't fit their domain. But used skillfully and in the right places, this kind of pure-Ruby extension of model functionality can add considerably to your applications.

In this chapter, we're going to make a distinction between two different kinds of programmatic model enhancement: *soft enhancement* and *hard enhancement.* We'll start with a look at what this distinction means; then, we'll proceed to a series of examples of each kind, with explanations and discussion of how Ruby is deployed to achieve the desired extension of model functionality. We'll also examine the creation of class methods for ActiveRecord model classes.

The examples will be taken directly from—or, more accurately, inserted into—the music store application. By the end of this chapter, the entire model side (the *what* of the music store universe) will be in place. At that point we'll move on to the process of enhancing the controllers and views, in chapter 16.

15.1 Soft vs. hard model enhancement

In chapter 14, we identified four sources from which an ActiveRecord model can gain capabilities: inheritance, automatically created methods, semi-automatically created methods, and open-ended programming. This chapter is about the fourth of these sources: methods you yourself write, for your own reasons and purposes, in your model files: *programmatic enhancement* of models.

We're going to divide programmatic enhancement into two categories. The division we'll make is descriptive, not official. Its purpose is to help you organize your understanding of what's involved in adding your own program code to ActiveRecord model classes, and also to strengthen your insights into how ActiveRecord classes and objects work.

We'll call the two types of programmatic model enhancement *soft enhancement* and *hard enhancement*. The difference between them is best illustrated by example. We'll look at an example of each type here, to lay the groundwork, and then spend most of the rest of the chapter exploring further examples as we delve more deeply into programming the music store model classes.

15.1.1 *An example of model-enhancement contrast*

When you write a new method in an ActiveRecord model class, that method does one of two things:

- Searches for and returns one or more ActiveRecord objects based on existing data
- Manipulates available data into a new, previously nonexistent form

You might say that there are *passive methods*—those that just unearth information for you and return it—and *active methods*—those that bring new data structures into existence. The difference can be seen by looking at a new version of the Composer class (which you can put in the `composer.rb` model file for this version of R4RMusic). Note the two new methods in listing 15.1.

Listing 15.1 One example each of soft and hard programmatic model enhancement

```
class Composer < ActiveRecord::Base
  has_many :works

  def editions
    works.map {|work| work.editions }.flatten.uniq      ←———❶
  end

  def whole_name      ←———❷
    first_name + " " +
    (if middle_name then middle_name + " " else "" end) +
    last_name
  end
end
```

The first of the two new methods, `editions`, is the passive or *soft* one. It returns an array of all the editions of all the works by this composer. These editions already exist; all `editions` does is gather them together. To do so, it walks one by one through the composer's works, using map ❶. For each work, it grabs an array of editions. The entire mapping operation results in an array of arrays: one array for each work, one entry for each edition.

We then flatten this array of arrays so it's just one array of edition objects. Finally, we uniq it; doing so removes duplicate editions if, say, two works by the same composer appear in one publication (which happens frequently).

From now on, our composer objects will respond to the "editions" message by handing back an array containing all editions with works by the composer. Composers now can tell us what their works are (thanks to the has_many association with the Work model) and can also tell us what editions contain one or more of their works (thanks to the method we just wrote).

From the perspective of any code that might use this new method, there won't be any noticeable difference in syntax (given a composer object comp) between this

```
eds = c.editions
```

and this:

```
works = c.works
```

When you add an instance method to an ActiveRecord model class, that instance method is just as real and has just as much programming status as the methods that the objects of that class derive automatically or semi-automatically from ActiveRecord.

The second of the two new methods in this revision of the Composer class is whole_name ❷—and you'll recognize it as closely related to an example from chapter 2, where we took a sneak peek at writing methods for model classes. The whole_name method uses information available from the composer object's existing methods, methods the object has been given based on field names in the *composers* database table.

whole_name creates a new object out of this information: a string that contains existing data but that doesn't directly correspond to any single property of the object or to any single or collective existing ActiveRecord object. That's what makes whole_name an example of hard programmatic enhancement.

Soft vs. hard model enhancement: the bottom line

The bottom line is that the term *soft enhancement* describes cases where you're giving ActiveRecord an assist, so to speak. Our editions method doesn't do much *with* the data it finds; its job is to extend the reach of the composer's access to other existing information. Informally, you might say, "Well, a composer really already *has* editions—I just need to give a little boost to make them available."

Hard enhancement, on the other hand, involves generating new data, like a full name. Doing such things isn't better or worse than doing soft enhancements. It all depends on what you need.

Being aware of this distinction is a good way to get yourself thinking about why and when you might add an enhancement, and to what effect. For example, if you find yourself doing tons of soft enhancements—programming many ways for a given model to come up with arrays of properties at one or more levels of remove (the way editions are at a level of remove from composers, via the composers' *works* property)—that may be a sign that your domain model needs revision. ActiveRecord is engineered to give your model classes *most* of the functionality they need. Maybe you should be engineering some associations and letting them generate the methods, rather than manually writing methods yourself.

In addition, the soft/hard enhancement dichotomy is an excellent way to organize an exploration of examples of programmatic enhancement of ActiveRecord models. And that's where we're going next. We'll look first at soft enhancements and then at hard enhancements pertaining to the music store application. These enhancements will mesh with the changes to the domain model and database design carried out in chapter 14.

The examples in this chapter will also feed into the controller and view enhancements in chapter 16. (If the choice of example methods seems arbitrary at times, keep that in mind!) The goal is to have the *what*—the things of the music store universe—have all the functionality they need to live up to what's expected of them when they're picked up and used by the running application.

15.2   *Soft programmatic extension of models*

In this section, we'll write methods in several of the R4RMusic model files that extend what the models can do by reaching along the path already established by the model's existing properties. For a change of pace, this section is organized as a series of questions; the answers involve Ruby code that extends the model's capabilities.

The adoption of the "Q&A" format serves several purposes. For one thing, it's close to what happens during a typical development cycle: You realize that you need access to some information, and you write code that gives you that access. It also points the way toward doing more. The examples here aren't magical or sacred. They represent a good-sized sampling of things you might want to do with these particular models, and they've been chosen to represent a broad range of possibilities. But the point is that the door is open. As you become increasingly familiar and comfortable with Ruby, writing this kind of code will come more and more naturally.

We'll work model by model, adding soft programmatic enhancement to the Work, Customer, and Composer models. To give you an overview, here's a list of all the questions that we'll ask and answer by writing methods in this section:

- The Work model
  - Which publishers have published editions of this work?
  - What country is this work from?
  - What key is this work in?
- The Customer model
  - Which customers have ordered this work?
  - What open orders does this customer have?
  - What editions does this customer have on order?
  - What editions has this customer ever ordered?
  - What works does this customer have on order?
  - What works has this customer ever ordered?
- The Composer model
  - What editions of this composer's works exist?
  - What publishers have editions of this composer's works?

As you'll see, all of these methods involve giving the models a boost—a way to unearth and collect existing information that isn't available already in the form we want it through an existing method.

> **NOTE**   PLAIN ARRAYS VS. MAGIC COLLECTIONS   You should keep one important point in mind as you look at, and eventually write, soft enhancements to your models. When you gather together, say, an array of Edition objects by traversing a collection of Work objects and accumulating their editions, you end up with a plain Ruby array. You *don't* end up with a magic ActiveRecord collection. You'll recall that in discussing arrays in chapter 11, we looked at ActiveRecord collections as an example of something array-like that is also endowed with methods and behaviors that go beyond those of the normal array. Those extra powers aren't added to arrays that you create, even if they contain ActiveRecord objects.

15.2.1 *Honing the Work model through soft enhancements*

The soft programmatic extensions to the Work model involve mining the model and its associated entities for a next level of information. This information, in turn, might be used for in-house reports, richer on-screen information displays, or sales profiling.

All these Work enhancements belong in the work model file, `work.rb`.

Which publishers have published editions of this work?

This method uses the same basic approach as the `editions` method that served as an introductory example in section 15.1. In fact, it builds on that method: It calls `editions` and uses `map` on the resulting array to extract the publisher of each edition. It then performs a `uniq` operation, resulting in a nonduplicative list of all publishers who have published this work:

```
def publishers
  editions.map {|e| e.publisher}.uniq
end
```

This technique skims the publishers from the editions, producing a list of the latter.

What country is this work from?

A case could be made for assigning the work either to the native country of the composer or to the country of first publication. Because we're dealing with a sheet-music store and not a library, we don't necessarily know what the first publication was. That means if we want to assign a country to a work, it's best to echo the composer's country. This is an easy soft enhancement to the Work model:

```
def country
  composer.country
end
```

The enhancement qualifies as soft because it's passive: It reaches out one level, from the work to its composer, and gathers information, which it returns unchanged.

Which customers have ordered this work?

A method like this could conceivably be of interest in calculating sales figures and trends. Once again, we use the `editions` method as a point of entry for gathering further information. In this case, we map all the existing orders for all editions of this work—and from that mapping, we harvest the customers of the orders:

```
def ordered_by
  editions.orders.map {|o| o.customer }.uniq
end
```

We then make the resulting array unique, in case any customer has purchased two different editions of the work or purchased one edition twice. For some purposes, you may want to keep such duplicates—for example, if you're trying to determine a work's popularity (in which case someone who bought every edition of it might legitimately be counted multiple times). But assuming that you're interested simply in a list of customers who have bought this work, there's no point saving the duplicates.

What key is this work in?

You might not have been expecting this to be one of the enhancements, because the work's key is already stored directly in the database. But remember: *key* is a reserved word in SQL, so we named the field containing the key *kee*. The enhancement we need is one that will let us use `key` as a method name to get the key of a work.

It's simple:

```
def key
  kee
end
```

Now, when we ask a work for its key, it will tell us its *kee*, which is what we really want to know.

15.2.2 Modeling the customer's business

In the case of the customer, we want to know a number of things. Some of these methods are layered on, or embedded into, others. Some will be of direct use at the controller/view stage.

What open orders does this customer have?

We'll write `open_orders` to return an ActiveRecord collection:

```
def open_orders
  orders.find(:all, :conditions => "status = 'open'")
end
```

Although we may treat the resulting collection in most contexts as a normal array, having it be an ActiveRecord collection means that, if the occasion arises, we'll be able to query it using the hybrid Ruby/SQL semantics that such collection objects allow.

What editions does this customer have on order?

Here, we use standard Ruby array methods to grab all the editions this customer has ordered:

```
def editions_on_order
  open_orders.map {|order| order.edition }.uniq
end
```

First, wc generate an array of editions by iterating through the customer's orders and skimming off each order's edition object (courtesy of `map`, which will return a new array). Then, we run the results through `uniq`, producing a list of editions without regard to how many copies of each have been ordered.

What editions has this customer ever ordered?

This method is a superset of `editions_on_order`, returning a list of all the editions this customer has ever ordered. This information will be useful in calculating a customer's favorites (favorite composers and/or instruments):

```
def edition_history
  orders.map {|order| order.edition }.uniq
end
```

We'll now do for works what we've already done for editions: provide a way to grab the works that are on order (regardless of what edition each one is in) and a way to generate a list of every work the customer has ever ordered.

What works does this customer have on order?

Here, we start with `editions_on_order` and then dig into the contents of the edition (its list of works):

```
def works_on_order
  editions_on_order.map {|edition| edition.works }.flatten.uniq
end
```

Mapping that operation across all the editions on order returns one array of works for each edition—overall, an array of arrays. We want a flat array of works, so we flatten it and then run it through `uniq` to get rid of duplicate works.

What works has this customer ever ordered?

This method is like the previous one, but it gathers works from all editions, not just those on order:

```
def work_history
  edition_history.map {|edition| edition.works }.flatten.uniq
end
```

All the methods you've now added to the `Customer` class involve looking through lists of entity model instances (ActiveRecord objects) and returning transformed lists. The remaining `Customer` methods fall into the category of hard model enhancement; they involve calculating a new value from existing data. We'll leave those for the next section, and turn briefly to the composer.

15.2.3 *Fleshing out the Composer*

Composers are a fairly inactive element in the universe of our domain. They don't change much, and most of them have stopped composing, so there's not as much need to provide them with a data-manipulation toolset as there is with some of the other models. We'll define only two composer instance methods; they go in the `Composer` class, in `composer.rb`.

What editions of this composer's works exist?

This is the method that served as the preliminary example of a soft model enhancement:

```
def editions
  works.map {|work| work.editions }.flatten.uniq
end
```

This method is used for the purpose of generating a list of editions to be embedded in a clickable list—something we'll include among the new and enhanced music store views in the next chapter.

What publishers have editions of this composer's works?

This method may possibly be of use only for internal accounting purposes—but we'll throw it in for good measure and as a lesson in how easy it is to expand your application's repertoire of methods:

```
def publishers
  editions.map{|edition| edition.publisher }.uniq
end
```

That brings us to the end of our list of questions and the corresponding soft enhancements of the R4RMusic models. Our next big topic is hard programmatic enhancements: methods that go as far as you want them to in manipulating data and creating new objects and data structures.

First, by way of final reflection on soft enhancements, a few words are in order about the relationship between Ruby code and SQL—or, more accurately, the process of choosing between Ruby and SQL—in the writing of soft enhancements.

15.2.4 *Ruby vs. SQL in the development of soft enhancements*

When you write code whose main purpose is to pull records out of a relational database, the most efficient, fastest code you can write is SQL code. As you probably know, much of what ActiveRecord does for you under the hood is to translate your Ruby code into SQL statements and then query your application's databases with those statements.

In the interest of increasing execution speed, ActiveRecord lets you feed it pure SQL almost whenever you want. You lose the nice Ruby-wrapped look-and-feel, but you gain efficiency.

As a study in Ruby/SQL contrast, take the `Composer#editions` method from section 15.2.3:

```
def editions
  works.map {|work| work.editions }.flatten.uniq
end
```

This method starts by unconditionally gathering all the works by this composer, which it does by calling `works`. At this point, ActiveRecord is finished; the one and only database query required here returns all the works for this composer. What remains is pure Ruby: harvesting the editions of the works (courtesy of `map`) and massaging the resulting array-of-arrays of editions with `flatten` and `uniq`. Each of these operations creates a new array—potentially a large one, if we're dealing with a well-stocked music store.

Here's an alternative `editions` method, written using SQL instead of Ruby to narrow the selection of Edition objects:

```
def editions
    Edition.find_by_sql("SELECT edition_id from editions_works
    LEFT JOIN works ON editions_works.work_id = works.id
    LEFT JOIN composers ON works.composer_id = composers.id
    WHERE (composers.id = #{id})")
end
```

This method asks the database engine to do the work. By the time the single call to `find_by_sql` is finished, we have all the editions we need; no further Ruby commands are required.

Database engines such as MySQL tend to be efficient (at least, ideally). Asking for the right records in the first place, rather than asking for more records than you need and then pruning them in Ruby, is faster and more efficient.

But it also means you have to write everything in SQL—which is not necessarily a hardship from the point of view of programming but does destroy your program's consistent look and feel. Nor is this issue entirely cosmetic. The consistent "Rubyness" of a Rails application makes for a consistent development experience: It's easier to think in Ruby the whole time than it is to switch back and forth. (You have to do some switching anyway, if you're writing the database; but the ideal is to keep that process as separate as possible from the higher-level coding.)

Because it involves hard-coding table and field names into your Ruby methods, doing soft enhancements in SQL has the potential to make the application code harder to maintain later on. True, you can't write a Rails application without knowing the table and field names; but having them physically present in your model code takes the coupling of database and code a step further. But it will make your application faster, as well as giving you "magic" ActiveRecord collections rather than standard Ruby arrays as containers for your objects.

What's the right choice? Not surprisingly, it all depends. Luckily, you don't have to make an all-or-nothing, winner-take-all choice between Ruby and SQL as model enhancement languages. Rails is designed in full knowledge of the pros and cons of SQL versus pure Ruby. The existence of the `find_by_sql` method attests to this fact; so does the use of SQL fragments to specify record order (as in `:order => "created_at, ASC"`, an SQL hint used in the customer's `has_many` `:orders` association). The reality of relational database programming is that you should know some SQL if you're going to do it, even at one level of remove—and Rails facilitates your using SQL when you want to.

The philosophy of this book is that it's good to use Ruby to enhance the functionality of models until you hit a performance wall and have to use raw SQL. The relationship between Ruby and SQL, in this context, isn't unlike the relationship between Ruby and C in the general Ruby-programming context: Ruby programmers write in Ruby, *knowing* that it isn't a terribly fast language; when they hit serious performance bottlenecks, they write parts of their programs as C extensions, so that those parts will speed up and the whole program will run faster.

SQL can play a similar role for you in your Rails application development. Think of Rails applications as Ruby programs, first and foremost. But by all means take advantage of the options that ActiveRecord gives you, by way of using SQL, when you spot something you've written in Ruby that seems to be seriously slowing your program.

This meditation on SQL and Ruby truly brings us to the end of our soft programmatic enhancement discussion and to our next major topic: hard programmatic enhancements of ActiveRecord models.

15.3 *Hard programmatic enhancement of model functionality*

In this section, we're going to pull out the Ruby stops and show how you can add new functionality to your models that may not have any direct relation to the models' basic properties and capabilities. Basically, you can define any method for your models to respond to. The idea isn't to create chaos, but to come up with things you might want to know.

The examples here are clustered by type of example rather than in a question-and-answer format. This reflects the fact that hard enhancements tend to have a purpose other than straightforward querying of an object for information; they entail the creation of a new object or data structure rather than a culling of existing objects.

In the sections that follow, we'll develop hard programmatic enhancements of several of the R4RMusic models. The enhancements fall into three categories:

- Prettification of string properties
- Calculating a work's period
- Providing the customer with more functionality

Your Ruby skills will get a workout here, and you'll learn a few new techniques along the way.

15.3.1 *Prettification of string properties*

A common use for hard model enhancements is the *prettification* of string properties—the generation of a new string in which existing string information is embedded and which looks better, for presentation, than the raw string data available through the object would look.

We've already seen one example of prettification of strings: the `Composer#whole_name` method defined for the purpose of easily displaying all the components of a composer's name together. This kind of thing can come in handy frequently and can involve greater complexity and planning than just stringing strings together. We'll look at some examples here.

Formatting the names of the work's instruments

The `Work` model is a good candidate for some pretty-formatting operations. It has a title, an opus number, and a list of instruments, all of which are stored in raw form and are in need of massaging on the way to public viewing.

We'll begin with the instruments, because the resulting list will be of use in the title.

Let's start with the `nice_instruments` method, an instance method of the `Work` class in `work.rb`, like this:

```
def nice_instruments
    instrs = instruments.map {|inst| inst.name }
```

This `map` operation skims the *name* values from the list of instrument objects and stores them in a new array, which we save to the variable `instrs`.

The next step (almost) is to format these names into a nice string. There's one intermediate tweak, though. It has to do with the order of instruments: cello and piano, or piano and cello?

We'll handle this in the following way. First, we create an array of instrument names in what we consider the canonical (or at least likely to be correct almost every time) order. Incidentally, you'll encounter a new technique in this line of code: the `%wf{...}` construct, which generates an array whose elements are the individual words inside the curly braces.

```
ordered = %w{ flute oboe violin viola cello piano orchestra }
```

Next, we sort `instrs` according to where in this array (at what numbered index) each instrument occurs. Because it's possible that we'll encounter an instrument that isn't on this list, if no index is found we return 0, which in a sorting context means *equal to*:

```
instrs = instrs.sort_by {|i| ordered.index(i) || 0 }
```

We can also put the list of ordered instruments in a constant at the top of the model file and then refer to that constant in the method. That would probably make the list easier to maintain. It still has the disadvantage of having to be updated manually, but in a production environment you could ensure that every time a new instrument was introduced into the universe, a decision would have to be made about where it fitted into the list. (You could also start with a much bigger list, of course.)

We now have a list of instrument names sorted according to conventional instrument-listing semantics. What we now do with those names, for purposes of inserting them into the nice title of the work, depends on how many there are:

- If there are none, we want `nil` (not an empty string, for reasons that will become apparent when we put together the whole title).
- If there's just one, we want it by itself (*Partita for Violin*).

■ If there are two, we want them joined by the word *and* (*Sonata for Violin and Piano*).

■ If there are three or more, we want to join them with commas—except the last two, which are additionally joined by *and* (*Trio for Violin, Cello, and Piano*).

It will be a matter of testing the size of `instrs` and proceeding accordingly. We can do this with a `case` statement, with separate branches for each of the four possibilities:

```
case instrs.size
when 0
  nil
when 1
  instrs[0]
when 2
  instrs.join(" and ")
else
  instrs[0..-2].join(", ") + ", and " + instrs[-1]
end
end
```

(You can see the code grow in length, as well as complexity, as the number of instruments in the work increases!)

The last case—more than two names—is worth examining up close. It uses the trick of grabbing all elements of the array *except* the last:

```
instrs[0..-2]
```

Negative array indices are counted from the right, so `instrs[-2]` is the second-to-last item in the array. All of the items thus selected then get joined with commas. To the resulting substring, we add the string ", and " followed by the last item in the array (`instrs[-1]`).

Because we've built it in fragments, here's the full `nice_instruments` method in one place:

```
def nice_instruments
  instrs = instruments.map {|inst| inst.name }
  ordered = %w{ flute oboe violin viola cello piano orchestra }
  instrs = instrs.sort_by {|i| ordered.index(i) || 0 }
  case instrs.size
  when 0
    nil
  when 1
    instrs[0]
  when 2
    instrs.join(" and ")
  else
```

```
        instrs[0...-1].join(", ") + ", and " + instrs[-1]
    end
end
```

That should give us a reasonably well-formatted, descriptive string for later insertion into the nice title.

Formatting a work's opus number

Let's prettify the opus number next. As you'll recall, the *opus* field in the database
holds a string. Due to the vagaries of indexing systems, several formats are possible for entries in this field:

- Plain opus number ("129")
- Opus number plus number designation ("129 no.4")
- Special catalogue designation, plus number ("K.84", "BWV1005", and so on)

Plain opus numbers, and those with a number designation, should be rendered as
they are but with "op." in front of them. The more specialized designations
should be rendered exactly as we find them.

To accomplish this, we have to know whether the string in the opus field begins
with a series of digits. If it does, we can assume that it's in one of the first two categories. If it doesn't, we can assume that it's a specialized index like K. or BWV.

We can use a simple regular-expression match operation to test for a digit at the
beginning of the opus string and determine the correct return string accordingly:

```
def nice_opus
    if /^\d/.match(opus)      <———❶
        "op. #{opus}"          <———❷
    else
        opus       <———❸
    end
end
```

Based on the test for a digit at the beginning of the opus ❶, we get back either
the number with "op. " in front of it ❷ or the whole original opus string ❸.

Now that we have nice-looking instrument and opus strings available, we can
put together a full-featured title string.

The work's prettified title

Creating a nice title is a matter of putting the nice components in place, with a
couple of connector words. The format is represented by this example:

```
Sonata in F Major, op. 99, for cello and piano
```

More is going on here than retrieving the parts. We're also connecting them with a mixture of commas, spaces, and the word *for*. The elements of the title are as follows:

- Title
- If there's a key, then the phrase "in " + *key*
- If there's an opus number, then the sequence ", " + *nice_opus*
- If there are instruments, then the sequence ", for " + *nice_instruments*

The main thing is that if no key is indicated, we don't want the word *in*, and likewise for the connecting strings for opus and instruments. We therefore have to put the nice title string together *conditionally*.

We do this as follows:

```
def nice_title
  t,k,o,i = title, key, nice_opus, nice_instruments
  "#{t} #{"in #{k}" if k}#{", #{o}" if o}#{", for #{i}" if i}"
end
```

First, the four pieces of information are retrieved and saved to variables with short names. There are two reasons to do this. First, it saves us from calling methods more than once. If we used expressions like

```
#{nice_opus} if nice_opus
```

we'd be calling `nice_opus` twice. Also, assigning the values to one-letter variables makes for a shorter (if somewhat peculiar-looking) final string.

Next, we create the string—with much of it included conditionally. There's double interpolation going on. First, we interpolated the title. Then, we interpolate this entire expression:

```
" in #{k}" if k
```

This expression returns, for example, "in F major" if there's a key. If there's no key (if k is nil) then the expression returns `nil` (the return value of a failed `if` statement). That `nil`, in turn, is interpolated in the outer string. The string representation of nil is "", the empty string. Therefore, if there's no key, the whole `"in #{k}"` `if k` expression is rendered as an empty string and has no impact on the final string.

(The need to test truth-value with `if`, by the way, is why we have `nice_instruments` return `nil` rather than an empty string if the work has no instruments. Empty strings evaluate to true in a Boolean context; `nil` evaluates to false. It's possible to test a string for emptiness with `empty?`, but using `nil` allows for a quick Boolean check.)

All told, you can get quite a bit of prettification mileage out of a decent knowledge of how to manipulate, test, and combine strings in Ruby.

A nice title for the Edition model

When it comes to titles of editions, there are two possibilities. Some editions' titles are the titles of the one work they contain. Other editions—collections of works, such as a volume of piano sonatas or string quartets—have one title encompassing the whole collection: *The Late String Quartets*, for example, or *Suites for Unaccompanied Cello.*

The steps we'll take to define a nice title for an edition are as follows:

- If the edition object has its own title, use that.
- If not, use the nice title of its first work (which is probably its only work—but for anomalous cases, this is a reasonable fallback).
- In either case, add the publisher and year, in parentheses, after the title.

We'll do an "or" operation, using the Boolean operator ||, to handle the first two steps. This operator returns the value of the expression to its left if that expression has a Boolean value of true (like, for example, a non-nil title); otherwise, it returns the value of the expression to its right. We'll then use a string addition operation to handle the third step:

```
def nice_title
  (title || works[0].nice_title) +
  " (#{publisher.name}, #{year})"
end
```

Having this method saves us from worrying later about the edition's title if it doesn't have one that's different from the name of the work it contains.

15.3.2 Calculating a work's period

Let's look at a more involved example: getting musical works to know what period they come from—not just by date, but by name or description.

Teaching a work what its century is

One fairly easy way to do this is by century. Here's a method you can add to work.rb that causes each work to report what century it was written in:

```
def century
  c = (year - 1).to_s[0,2].succ
  c += case c
       when "21" then "st"
       else "th"
```

```
      end
  c + " century"
end
```

This method first determines a two-digit century equivalent of the year. To do this, it subtracts 1 from the year (so that the zero years, like 2000, land in the right century). It then converts the year to a string and grabs the first two characters of the string. It increments the string with a `succ` (successor) so that 19, for example, ends up as 20, which is the correct century designation.

Next comes an algorithm for adding the correct suffix to the century. This algorithm only works as far back as the fourth century; it won't hand the *rd* suffix of *3rd* correctly. Because the music we're selling tends to date from a lot later than the third century, that shouldn't be a problem.

Centuries are fine, although they're easy to glean by looking at the year. You can also get musical works to give you descriptive information about their period.

A more descriptive periodization of a work

Like painting, literature, architecture, and other arts, musical works are often described not just by year or century but by terms referring descriptively to a period: *baroque, classical, romantic,* and so forth. With a little ingenuity, it's possible to get musical works to tell you what period they're from and to do so programmatically.

The first step is to make a set of decisions about the period descriptions. It's possible to associate a given time period with a description. However, and in spite of the fact that it involves a bit more work up front, a more scalable approach is to define each period as a combination of *time* and *place*. For example, we might want British music of the nineteenth century (at least, most of it) to be described as *Victorian,* whereas that term wouldn't make sense for music from Italy or France.

We're looking for a Ruby data structure that lets us make connections among time spans, countries, and descriptive period names.

There are a couple of tools we can reach for. One possibility is to create a new class, encapsulating periods, along these lines:

```
class Period
  attr_accessor :name, :start_date, :end_date
  attr_reader :countries
  def initialize
    self.countries = []
  end
end
```

We could then write the time and country specifications for, say, the Baroque period. Music historians might argue one way or the other about the details, but we'll go ahead and define it like this:

```
period = Period.new
period.name = "Baroque"
period.start_date = 1650
period.end_data = 1750
period.countries = %w{ EN DE FR IT ES NL }
```

If you put this code in a file in the lib subdirectory of the music application, it will be visible from the model files at runtime. You could then write a method that culled all the existing periods and searched them on certain criteria.

Nothing is wrong with this code in principle, and it would be feasible in practice. But there's another valid approach to the problem: storing the period information in a hash. This hash can live inside work.rb or in a separately loaded file in the lib directory. We'll take the former approach here.

A period hash can be constructed in any of several ways. One way or another, you must include a range of dates, a list of countries, and a descriptive tag (like "Baroque"). Something has to be the key, and something has to be the value, for each entry.

Because we have three pieces of information to record for each period, and hashes are fundamentally based on pairs rather than triples, we need to combine two of the items into one object—presumably an array. The most logical choice is for each hash entry to have an array containing the time span of the period along with the countries. Such an array looks like this:

```
[1650..1750, %w{ EN DE FR IT ES NL }]
```

This array contains two elements:

- A *range*, bracketing the years covered by the period
- An inner *array* of country designations (England, Germany, France, Italy, Spain, the Netherlands)

NOTE   RANGE OBJECTS   A *range* is an object with a starting point and an ending point and the ability to be queried as to whether it does or doesn't include a particular value. The range 1650..1750, for example, includes 1697 but doesn't include 1811. The two numbers with two dots between them are a range *literal*. If you use three dots, the range excludes its own endpoint; with two, it includes the endpoint. Some ranges, but not all, can also be iterated through, like arrays. For purposes of dating music, we're only interested in being able to determine whether a given year falls inside the range.

The primary remaining task is to link this array (and several others like it) to descriptive period tags—"Baroque", in the case of the example.

But should the arrays serve as hash keys, or hash values? In other words, do we want a typical pair in the period hash to look like this

```
"Baroque" => [1650..1750,  %w{ EN DE FR IT ES NL }]
```

or like this

```
[1650..1750,  %w{ EN DE FR IT ES NL }] => "Baroque"
```

Either form could serve the purpose of matching a work with a period by searching the range of years and the countries and returning the descriptive name. We'll use the second version, where the array of match criteria is the key and the name of the period is the key. Because we're going *from* the match criteria *to* the name, the left-to-right orientation makes a good visual fit.

We'll put the period criteria in a hash. Let's make it a constant in the Work class:

```
PERIODS = { [1650..1750, %w{ EN DE FR IT ES NL}] => "Baroque",
            [1751..1810, %w{ EN IT DE NL }]      => "Classical",
            [1751..1830, %w{ FR }]               => "Classical",
            [1837..1901, %w{ EN }]               => "Victorian",
            [1820..1897, %w{ DE FR }]            => "Romantic" }
```

There's nothing definitive about the scholarship reflected in these choices and certainly nothing comprehensive about the data, but this data structure has the benefit of being quite pliable. Notice how the Classical period is defined differently in France from the other countries. Because the logic depends on both a time match and a country match, French works of the given period will find the right match. It's also easy to change the data in the hash, in the event that scholarship advances or works that aren't represented here are added to the inventory.

We now need to write an instance method for the Work class that searches this hash and finds a match based on the work's year and country. In the event that no match is found for a given work, we'll fall back on the default of providing the work's century.

Here is the period method:

```
def period
  pkey = PERIODS.keys.find do |yrange,countries|    ◁———❶
    yrange.include?(year) && countries.include?(country)
  end
  PERIODS[pkey] || century    ◁———❷
end
```

This method uses two Boolean operators: the Boolean *or* operator (||), which you saw in action in the nice_title method for editions, and the *and* operator (&&).

The `&&` operator tests the expression to its left for truth-value, returning the value of the expression on the *right* if the expression on the left has a Boolean value of true. If the expression on the right isn't true—if it evaluates to `false` or `nil`—the whole expression returns `false` or `nil`.

Starting at the end of the method ❷, you can see that it uses an *or* test to return either a value from the `PERIODS` hash or the work's century. If `PERIODS[pkey]` returns something true, which it will if `pkey` is an existing key of `PERIODS` (remember that strings like "Classical" are true in the Boolean sense), then the method returns that value. If not (in other words, if `pkey` isn't an existing key, and specifically if `pkey` is `nil`), the method returns the work's century.

`pkey` is calculated by iterating through the keys of the `PERIODS` hash ❶. Each key, as you'll recall, is an array consisting of a range of years (assigned to `yrange`) and an array of countries (assigned to `countries`). If there's a hash key whose year-range includes `year` *and* whose country-array includes `country`, that hash key is assigned to `pkey`. The *and* test is performed with the `&&` operator. If no key is found that passes the double test, `pkey` is `nil` and, subsequently, `PERIODS[pkey]` is also `nil`. If a key passes the tests, you get the corresponding value when you ask for it ❶.

We now have a programmatic way to get a work to report its artistic period. We also have a good example of a case where doing something programmatically has distinct advantages over just putting data in a database. Yes, we could just create a field in the *works* table that contained the period. But by calculating the period dynamically, we've made it a lot easier to make additions and changes. An entire chart of periods is available at a glance and can be modified and augmented as needed.

On the other side of the convenience equation, if you were migrating the database to another application, you'd have to reconstruct a way to get at the period information, since it wouldn't be in the database—or you'd have to redesign the database and write a script that determined each work's period and put it in a database field after all. And in making real-world decisions about data storage versus programmatic calculation of values, you do have to weigh considerations of that kind.

We'll settle on doing periods programmatically, on the theory that the music store application will be stable and fairly permanent.

Now we'll return to a strong candidate for a considerable amount of hard model enhancement: the `Customer`.

15.3.3 *The remaining business of the Customer*

The Customer model can be enhanced in a number of ways, and we're going to do several. We'll start by developing code to determine various *rankings*—the customer's favorites in various categories. We'll then move from rankings to business calculations, including the customer's order history and outstanding balance. Finally, we'll teach the customer how to check out (complete all pending orders).

Rankings per customer

It's popular for online shopping sites to put links and special offers on the screen based on a customer's known favorite items. Some of this information may be stored on the server or on the customer's computer in the form of cookies. Some of it (if there isn't too much to do reasonably quickly) can be calculated in real time based on the customer's searching and/or ordering history.

We'll perform a couple of calculations of this type: determining this customer's favorite composers and instruments. (Both of these methods are instance methods of the Customer class and therefore belong in the customer.rb model file; but they'll undergo some revision before they're final.)

The two methods work in similar ways. First, they create an array of the item's history (composer or instrument) by traversing either the edition history or the work history. This array is in chronological order; the most recently ordered composers or instruments are *last*. (This happens automatically, because of the way we've specified the ordering of order objects. That order propagates to edition_history and work_history.)

Next, we run uniq on the array, because we only want to rank each item once. The rank is based on how many times the item occurs in the complete array. Finally, we reverse the result. Because the number of occurrences is higher for the favorites, they're at the end of the array—so we reverse it, to put them at the beginning:

```
def composer_rankings
  history = edition_history.map {|ed| ed.composers }.flatten
  history.uniq.sort_by do |c|
    history.select {|comp| comp == c}.size
  end.reverse
end

def instrument_rankings
  history = work_history.map {|work| work.instruments }.flatten
  history.uniq.sort_by do |i|
    history.select {|instr| instr == i}.size
  end.reverse
end
```

These two methods will work, but even a glance at them glaringly reveals the fact that they're almost identical. You can trim them down a lot by extracting their common code into a separate method and calling that method where it's needed:

```
def rank(list)
  list.uniq.sort_by do |a|
    list.select {|b| a == b }.size
  end.reverse
end

def composer_rankings
  rank(edition_history.map {|ed| ed.composers }.flatten)
end

def instrument_rankings
  rank(work_history.map {|work| work.instruments }.flatten)
end
```

Here's a walk-through of how these methods work. We'll use instruments for this example and refer to them by name for simplicity.

Let's say someone orders:

- A work for cello and piano
- A work for cello and orchestra
- A work for orchestra

That means our pre-flattened instrument history is

```
[["cello", "piano"], ["cello", "orchestra"], ["orchestra"]]
```

and the flattened version is

```
["cello","piano","cello","orchestra","orchestra"]
```

We then send this array to the rank method. Going through these one at a time, and never repeating an item (thanks to uniq), rank sorts them by how often they occur in the non-uniqued list. The statistics are as follows:

- *cello* => 2
- *piano* => 1
- *orchestra* => 2

We sort them by this order. When there's a tie, as between *cello* and *orchestra*, the first one encountered (*cello*) ends up earlier in the final list—which is what we want, because it means the instruments from more recently ordered works land further toward the end of the list.

The almost-final order, then, is *piano, cello, orchestra*. Because we want the list in descending order of favoriteness (most favorite first in the array; least favorite last), we reverse it: *orchestra, cello, piano*. That gives us a reasonable representation of this customer's most- and/or most-recently ordered instruments.

NOTE   ALGORITHM GRANULARITY The algorithm we're using to determine favorites is reasonably fine-grained. It's slightly vulnerable, however, to the ordering of instruments *within* a work or composers within an edition. If works for cello and piano are listed with *piano* first, and *cello* and *piano* are tied, *piano* will come out ahead. If they're listed the other way around, *cello* will. (You can try this in irb. Paste the `rank` method directly into the irb session—it can operate as a standalone, top-level method inside irb—and then look at the difference between `rank(%w{c p c p})` and `rank(%w{p c p c})`.) It would be possible to store items in a hash that kept closer track of ties, but it's questionable whether the effort to do this would pay off. After all, when it comes to displaying favorite items on the screen, you'd probably end up choosing among the tied items anyway. Moreover, if you wanted to be more nuanced, you could do something along the lines of the instrument-ordering we did for the `nice_instruments` method—perhaps write a `weighted_instruments` method and then call that instead of `instruments`. It would still be no more than a calculated guess. With instruments, this kind of pre-rank weighting would be hard to justify; with composers, impossible. Determining customer favorites is a fuzzy process (as anyone knows who has seen his or her own favorites page on a shopping site populated with suggestions based on items ordered as gifts for other people).

We now have a way to determine customer favorites—and we'll come back to it and complete the picture, when we get to controllers and views in the next chapter. Meanwhile, let's turn now to the business end of the customer: the methods we'll need as a foundation for accepting orders and calculating costs.

Calculating the number of copies ordered

We need a way to know how many copies of a given edition a customer has ordered. It would be possible, and plausible, to design the application and the database so that this number was stored in the database and incremented when the customer changed the number of copies of an edition or ordered another copy. However, order counting is also a good example of a case where you might calculate a value on the fly, programmatically; and that's how we'll do it here.

The following method, an instance method of `Customer`, tells us how many copies of a given edition the customer has ordered:

```
def copies_of(edition)
  orders.find(:all, :conditions => "edition_id = #{edition.id}").size
end
```

The call to the `orders` method returns an ActiveRecord collection, rather than a plain array, of all of the customer's orders. This enables us to use the ActiveRecord flavor of `find` to zero in on all the orders for this edition, by matching the edition's ID field with the *edition_id* field in the database records for the customer's orders. (Note the use of SQL, and in particular the single equal-sign for comparison where you would use `==` in Ruby.) Finally, we take the size of this subset of the customer's orders; this tells us how many copies of this edition the customer has ordered.

Remaining unpaid balance

At some point, we'll need to be able to calculate how much the customer owes for unpaid orders (their unpaid balance). We already have a method that returns an array of all the customer's open orders. All we need to do is add up the prices of the items in that array.

Let's look at two ways to do this: one by hand and one using the `Array#inject` method. The first version of the method looks like this:

```
def balance
  acc = 0
  open_orders.each do |order|
    acc += order.edition.price
  end
  "%.2f" % acc
end
```

First, we set up an accumulator, initialized to zero. We then cycle through all the open orders of this customer, adding the price associated with that order (the price of the edition to which the order pertains) to the accumulator. Finally, we format the accumulator in a string with two decimal points, corresponding to the canonical dollars-and-cents format.

This kind of operation—iterating through a collection and accumulating the results of some calculation incrementally—can be done automatically with the `inject` method. This method initializes an accumulator (in this case, zero) and then iterates through the array. On the first iteration, `inject` yields two values to the block: the accumulator object and the first element of the array. On the second and subsequent iterations, it also yields two values: the return value of the previous call to the block and the current element of the array.

The `inject`-based version of the balance method looks like this:

```
def balance
  "%.2f" % open_orders.inject(0) do |acc,order|
    acc + order.edition.price
  end
end
```

The two versions produce exactly the same result. Which you use is up to you, although it's a good idea to make sure you understand both of them.

Customer check-out

Checking out—paying for all purchases and emptying the shopping cart—is a two-pronged process. On the one hand, it's a controller action with an associated view (a "Thank you" screen or something along those lines). On the other hand, it's the business of the customer entity model to do the housekeeping associated with checking out.

We'll write the controller action in the next chapter. Here, let's specify what the customer object has to do with regard to the state of its own data when it checks out. It needs to change the status of every order to "paid":

```
def check_out
  orders.each do |order|
    order.status = "paid"
    order.update
  end
end
```

This method sets the `status` property of each order to "paid" and then updates the database record to reflect the new value.

ActiveRecord lets you do this in one command: `update_attribute`. We could rewrite the `check_out` method to use this command:

```
def check_out
  orders.each do |order|
    order.update_attribute(:status, "paid")
  end
end
```

Either of these techniques is acceptable.

We've now added a considerable amount of functionality to the composer, work, and customer models in the form of both soft and hard programmatic enhancement. This draws us closer to a reasonably functional music store; and, most important, it provides a display of the *kinds* of things you can do to, and with, your ActiveRecord models when you know how to add programmatic value to them.

So far, all the enhancements have involved instance methods. To round out the chapter, we'll look next at a few examples of how you can enhance an ActiveRecord model at the *class* method level.

15.4 Extending model functionality with class methods

Class methods, in general, are an appropriate choice when you want to calculate something that pertains generally to a class's domain, its field of expertise. That's true in the case of ActiveRecord model classes too. Although instance methods make sense when what you want to achieve is at the level of a particular instance (like determining a work's century), class methods make sense when you want to do something at a more abstract level—or, as is often the case, something that involves searching and manipulation of *all* the existing records for a given class.

15.4.1 Soft and hard class methods

Class methods written for model classes, like instance methods, can be categorized as *soft* or *hard*, depending on whether they search and retrieve existing data in a relatively passive, low-impact way, or construct entirely new data structures out of the data they find. Don't forget that a number of the class methods your model classes have by default are even more active than this—methods like `delete_all`, which clears the database table corresponding to the class of all its entries. You probably won't need to write class methods that do database housekeeping at that level (ActiveRecord supplies a pretty full toolkit for those operations). Still, some of the class methods you write for your model classes will be more active than others.

Determining all editions for a list of works

This is a specialized method, but it will come in handy at least once when we get to view and controller enhancement in chapter 16. It's a class method on the `Edition` class, and therefore it belongs in `edition.rb` in the `app/models` subdirectory:

```
def Edition.of_works(works)
  works.map {|work| work.editions }.flatten.uniq
end
```

This method starts with a list of works—say, all the works by Bach, or all works written in 1830, or whatever you want to sent it—and returns a list of editions of all those works. It's a useful method for crossing over from a works list to a corresponding editions list.

Determining all periods represented in the stock

The following soft class method finds all periods represented by all the works in the database:

```
def Work.all_periods
  find(:all).map {|c| c.period }.flatten.uniq.sort
end
```

This method uses `find(:all)` to create an array of all the available `Work` objects. It then maps through that array, creating a new array consisting of the objects' periods. That array, in turn, gets flattened, made unique, and sorted. The result is an array that might be used, say, to show the visitor a list of all periods represented by music available in the store.

Determining sales rankings for works

Here we'll do something parallel to the rankings instance methods we added to the `Customer` class. This is an example of hard programmatic enhancement at the class level: The method creates and returns a new data structure.

We want a ranking, contained in a hash, of all works by sales order. The keys of the hash are the database ID fields of the works; the value corresponding to each key is the number of copies of that work (in any edition) that have been ordered.

This can be achieved by cycling through all the existing work records and then doing an inner iteration through all of that work's editions. For each edition, the number of orders (equivalent to the size of the edition's `orders` collection) is added to the hash entry for that work. At the end, the hash is returned from the method:

```
def Work.sales_rankings
  r = Hash.new(0)      ◁——— Gives hash default value of zero
  find(:all).each do |work|
    work.editions.each do |ed|
      r[work.id] += ed.orders.size
    end
  end
  r
end
```

To use this hash, we need to do some sorting, because hashes are unordered:

```
rankings = Work.sales_rankings
r_sorted = rankings.sort_by {|key,value| value }
```

This results in an array of arrays, each inner array containing one key-value pair from the hash, in ascending order by value.

We can do something similar for composers.

Determining sales rankings for composers

We can use `Work.sales_rankings` as the basis for calculating sales rankings for composers. This method goes in `app/models/composer.rb`:

```
def Composer.sales_rankings
  r = Hash.new(0)
  Work.sales_rankings.map do |work,sales|
    r[work.composer.id] += sales
  end
  r
end
```

For each work in the sales rankings hash, we add the sales figure to the hash entry for the work's composer. The sales ranking hash provides the information we need, courtesy of the class method we added to `Work`.

This brings us to the end of our model-enhancement workshop (except for one method sneaked into chapter 16—but that can wait). We'll turn next to the controller and view realm, where we'll make our newly intelligent models do things.

15.5 Summary

This chapter has taken you on a guided tour of a selection of programmatic enhancements to the ActiveRecord model files from the music store application. You've seen examples of both soft and hard enhancements—enhancements that return instances or collections based on existing data, and enhancements that manipulate data more actively to produce new representations in new data structures. We've examined this at both the instance-method and class-method levels.

Along the way, we've also noted some of the factors, pro and con, that may influence you when you're deciding whether to write a new method for a model or carry out a database redesign that creates a new table or field. In the case of determining the period of a work, for example, putting a tag like "Classical" in a database field is possible and probably faster than calculating a work's period on the fly—but this approach is also less flexible and scalable, in the event that you want to make changes, than maintaining a single hash of period information. These and other factors are always present, and you need to make the best decision you can in each case.

This brings us to the end of our work on the domain-database-model side of the music store universe. Next, we'll turn to the realm of ActionPack: the view templates, and the controllers that feed data to them. This is literally where the action is and where the work we've put into enhancing the models bears visible fruit.

16

Enhancing the controllers and views

In this chapter

- Built-in and custom helper methods
- Using partial view templates
- Login and authentication
- Maintaining session state
- Dynamic determination of method branching

In this chapter, we'll round out the music store application by adding new controller actions and the corresponding views. These actions and views will use the programmatic model enhancements we completed in chapter 15 as well as the refinements we made to the music store domain and database in both chapters 14 and 15. They'll also use a variety of Ruby techniques that were not on our radar back in chapter 2.

The actions available in the second version of R4RMusic are summarized in table 16.1.

Table 16.1 Summary of controller actions and corresponding templates in the second version of R4RMusic

Controller	Description	Action method name	Master template rendered
Customer	Log in	`login`	`main/welcome.rhtml`
	Log out	`logout`	`main/welcome.rhtml`
	Sign up for a new account	`signup`	`main/welcome.rhtml`
	Add an edition to the shopping cart	`add_to_cart`	`customer/view_cart.rhtml`
	View the shopping cart	`view_cart`	`customer/view_cart.rhtml`
	Check out (complete purchases)	`check_out`	`customer/check_out.rhtml`
Main	Welcome the visitor	`welcome`	`main/welcome.rhtml`
	Show all works from a given period	`show_period`	`main/show_period.rhtml`
Composer	Show all editions of a composer's works	`show`	`composer/show.rhtml`
Edition	Show publication details for an edition	`show`	`edition/show.rhtml`
Instrument	Show all works for a given instrument	`show`	`instrument/show.rhtml`
Work	Show all editions of a given work	`show`	`work/show.rhtml`

A few of these actions haven't changed since the chapter 2 version of R4RMusic. The rest we'll rewrite (or just *write*, in the case of the new ones) in this chapter. As always, you're encouraged to download the complete application code from the *Ruby for Rails* Web site, so that you can see every aspect of how the pieces fit together.

We'll proceed as follows. In the first two sections of the chapter, we'll look at two important facilities that ActionPack (the combined controller/view subsystem of Rails) provides to help you organize and extend the functionality of your application. The first of these is the *helper file* facility; the second is the *partials* mechanism, which lets you split large view templates into smaller files. Many new and modified views and controller actions necessary for this phase of the application will be introduced as examples in the course of the exploration of these Action-Pack facilities.

Then, in section 16.3, we'll take a close look at the revisions to the main controller, which handles the main welcome view. The remaining sections of the chapter will address the views and controller actions associated with the most important completely new figure in this second version of the application: the customer. We'll look at signing up, logging in and out, and ordering items; and we'll conclude by programming the display of the customer's favorites, based on the ranking methods we developed in chapter 15.

16.1 *Defining helper methods for view templates*

The view and controller phases of the Model/View/Controller framework work closely together. The basic contract between the controllers and the views is that the controllers gather, sort, sift, and prepare data, which they store in instance variables; and the views use those instance variables in ERb templates. Sometimes, however, you'll need to manipulate data or make calculations in ways that can't be done in advance by the controller, but have to be done in the template. For example—really a whole category of examples—it's convenient to have access in the templates to shortcut methods that write out repetitive sequences of HTML.

ActionPack, the parent package of both ActionController and ActionView, provides two forms of help in the realm of shortcut methods available for use in your templates. First, you can use any of a large number of predefined helper methods; we've already seen an example of such a method: `link_to`. Like many of the other built-in ActionPack helper methods, `link_to` gives you a programmatic (method call–based) alternative to writing out HTML markup manually. (We're not going to discuss the built-in helper methods extensively here; but you'll come across not only `link_to` but `form_tag`, `text_field`, and others in R4RMusic and in the majority of Rails applications you write or see.)

The second way in which ActionPack provides you with helper-method facilities, and the one we'll focus on in this section, is through the *helper file* facility, which gives you a structured way to define methods of your own that extend the functionality of your templates. The helper files exist for the purpose of storing any and all helper methods you wish to write; those methods, once defined, can be called from your templates just like the built-in Rails helper methods (`link_to` and so on).

We toured helper files briefly way back in section 3.2.2, as an example of one of the ways in which Rails supports and encourages the writing of customized code for your application. In this section, we'll examine the helper file mechanism closely, and we'll also add some helper methods to the R4RMusic application.

16.1.1 *Organizing and accessing custom helper methods*

The helper file mechanism kicks in whenever you create a controller with the `script/generate` utility: As part of the controller creation process, a file with the name *controller*`_helper.rb` is created in your application's `app/helpers` directory. That's where you put helper methods you want to be able to call from your templates.

Inside each *controller*`_helper.rb` file is an empty module definition; the module is named after the controller. For example, `composer_helper.rb` contains this:

```
module ComposerHelper
end
```

During the rendering of any template inside the `app/views/composer` directory, any instance methods you add to the body of this module are directly callable.

Defining methods in helper files can help you economize on repeated code. For example, you may find that you frequently want to create a link to the `composer/show` action for one composer or another. In such a case, you can write a helper method that automatically creates a link—such as the following method, `link_to_composer`, which piggy-backs on the built-in `link_to` method:

```
module ComposerHelper
  def link_to_composer(composer)
    link_to(composer.whole_name,
            :controller => "composer",
            :action     => "show",
            :id         => composer.id)
  end
end
```

And here's an example of how you might use the new `link_to_composer` method in a template:

```
<ul>
  <% @composers.each do |composer| %>
    <li><%= link_to_composer(composer) %></li>
```

```
    <% end %>
  </ul>
```

Every time through the `each` loop, the string that's returned from the call to `link_to_composer`, containing a link to a composer object, is interpolated into the template, courtesy of the `<%= ... %>` ERb notation. You end up with a list of links to composers, as defined by the custom method.

Using methods from a different helper file

By default, templates in the `views/composer` directory have automatic access to the methods defined in the `ComposerHelper` module in the file `helpers/composer_helper.rb`. Sometimes, though, you may want to use a composer-related helper method in a template from another directory. A case in point is the `link_to_composer` method, which is used by a number of templates from a number of directories.

There are two ways to make a method like `link_to_composer` available not just to composer templates, but to others as well:

- Declare `:composer` to be a helper in the controller file whose templates need access to it

- Define the method in the generic `application_helper.rb` helper file rather than the `composer_helper.rb` file

The first of these options, translated into code, means (for example) doing this in `main_controller.rb`:

```
class MainController < ApplicationController

  helper :composer
  # etc.
end
```

`helper` is a class method of `ActionController::Base` (hence inherited via `ApplicationController`). It establishes a crossover helper relationship; the templates in `views/main` now have access to the helper code in `composer_helper.rb`.

Then there's the second approach to making helper methods available across different controllers and templates: put them all in the generic helper file `application_helper.rb`, where they're visible to and callable from all your controllers and templates.

Which of the two approaches is best? It's certainly easier to stash all the helper methods you may need in `application_helper.rb`. On the other hand, if you put each helper method in the most suitable file (for example, the `link_to_composer` method in `composer_helper.rb`) and then use explicit `helper` declarations to make helper methods visible across controllers, you end up with more explicit information about what's being used where.

As often happens, there's a tradeoff. Here, we'll use the first method: distributing helper methods into different files, and using calls to `helper` to prompt their inclusion as needed.

16.1.2 *The custom helper methods for R4RMusic*

R4RMusic uses some of the built-in helper methods (including `link_to`). In addition, we'll write some custom helper methods for it, thus taking advantage not only of the predefined helpers but also of the helper file mechanism. We'll write a total of six helper methods. This isn't a huge number, but it will be enough to illustrate the helper file facility in practice and to help with the organization of the application's code.

The six methods are summarized in table 16.2.

Table 16.2 Summary of helper methods, their locations, and the controllers that need them

Method	Defined in	Included with `helper` call in these controller files
`link_to_composer`	`composer_helper.rb`	customer, edition, main
`link_to_work`	`work_helper.rb`	composer, customer, edition, instrument, main
`link_to_edition`	`edition_helper.rb`	customer, work
`link_to_edition_title`	`edition_helper.rb`	composer, instrument
`link_to_instrument`	`instrument_helper.rb`	main
`two_dec`	`application_helper.rb`	*Automatically available to all*

Five of them are automatic link generators; the sixth formats currency figures (dollars and cents) as strings to exactly two decimal places. In each case, the method should be written as an instance method in the file specified in the *Defined in* column of table 16.2. In addition, you should insert a helper directive into the controller files indicated in the third column. For instance, because "edition" appears in the third column for helper methods in both the composer and work helper files, `edition_controller.rb` will contain this line:

```
helper :composer, :work
```

Here are the first five helper methods:

```
def link_to_composer(composer)
  link_to(composer.whole_name,
        :controller => "composer",
        :action     => "show",
        :id         => composer.id)
end

def link_to_edition(edition)
  link_to edition.description,
        :controller => "edition",
        :action     => "show",
        :id         => edition.id
end

def link_to_edition_title(edition)
  link_to edition.nice_title,
        :controller => "edition",
        :action     => "show",
        :id         => edition.id
end

def link_to_work(work)
  link_to(work.nice_title,
        :controller => "work",
        :action     => "show",
        :id         => work.id)
end

def link_to_instrument(instrument)
  link_to instrument.name,
        :controller => "instrument",
        :action     => "show",
        :id         => instrument.id
end
```

The sixth helper method, two_dec, formats a floating-point number as a string to exactly two decimal places. Its purpose is to make sure prices are displayed in correct dollars-and-cents format. To achieve this, we use the built-in Ruby utility method sprintf; like the C method of the same name, sprintf interpolates values into a string, using format specifiers in the string to format the values correctly. The format specifier we want is %.2f (floating point to two decimal points), and the value we want formatted is whatever argument is passed to two_dec.

two_dec goes in application_helper.rb, which now looks like this:

```
module ApplicationHelper
  def two_dec(n)
    sprintf("%.2f", n)
  end
end
```

We don't need to declare a helper connection in any controller for this method; it's in the generic helper file and therefore already visible to all controllers and templates.

That's pretty much it for helper methods in the music store application. We'll turn next to another tool provided by ActionPack to help you produce and organize efficient templating code: the facility for splitting your views into main templates and *partials*—modular, reusable template fragments that live in separate files.

16.2 Coding and deploying partial view templates

To get Rails to display a view called `composer/show.rhtml`, we put a file of that name beneath the `app/views` directory, and we request `composer/show` as the action in our URL. The file contains template code, which is filled in based on variables handed over from the controller (`@composer`, for example).

Meanwhile, inside `composer/show.rhtml`, we can trigger the automatic inclusion of one or more *partial* views. We summon up the partial view at a particular place in the main or master template with a call to `render`.

16.2.1 Anatomy of a master template

The best way to see how partial templates fit into the overall template landscape is by looking at an entire template file, such as the one shown in listing 16.1.

Listing 16.1   The `composer/show.rhtml` template file

```
<% @page_title = "Editions of works by #{@composer.whole_name}" %>

<h2 class="info"><%= @page_title %></h2>
<p>Click on any edition to see details.</p>
<%= render :partial => "editions" %>
```

The `render` method examines the name of the partial (`editions`, in this case), adds an underscore at the beginning and the `.rhtml` suffix at the end, and then looks for the file of the resulting name: `_editions.rhtml`.

The `_editions.rhtml` partial template file is also in the `composer` view directory. It's shown in listing 16.2.

Listing 16.2   The `composer/_editions.rhtml` partial template

```
<ul>
  <% @composer.editions.map do |edition| %>
```

```
<li><%= link_to_edition_title(edition) %>
(<%= edition.publisher.name %>, <%= edition.year %>)</li>
<% end %>
```

The template code in `_editions.rhtml` creates a list (a `<ul>` HTML element) of links to editions. When you click such a link, you trigger the `show` action for that edition. (*Showing* an edition means showing its publication and price details.)

The HTML for the list of edition links is dropped into the master template in listing 16.1 at the point where the master template makes the call to `render`. In terms of application design, all that's happened is that we've split what might otherwise be one template file into a master file and a partial. It's never mandatory that you do this, but it can help keep your template code organized and clear.

The new version of the master template for the application's welcome screen, `main/welcome.rhtml`, will use quite a few partials. And we, in turn, will use *it* as a point of departure for further examination of partials and how templates fit together.

16.2.2 *Using partials in the welcome view template*

Figure 16.1 shows a screenshot of the R4RMusic application's welcome screen. The figure shows things at a point where I've already logged in, so you don't see the login or signup forms. But that's OK, because our focus in this section is on three of the lists: composers, instruments, and musical periods. (We'll deal with the favorites list separately, in section 16.6.) These three lists are the portals to browsing the music store's inventory—and each of them also happens to be generated by a partial template.

Let's start with the composers.

Creating the list of composer links

We've already seen the partial that creates the list of composer links; in section 16.1.1, it served as the example of how to use `link_to_composer` in a template. It's shown again, now officially a partial template called `_list.rhtml`, in listing 16.3.

Listing 16.3 The `composers/_list.rhtml` partial template

```
<ul>
  <% @composers.each do |composer| %>
    <li><%= link_to_composer(composer) %></li>
  <% end %>
</ul>
```

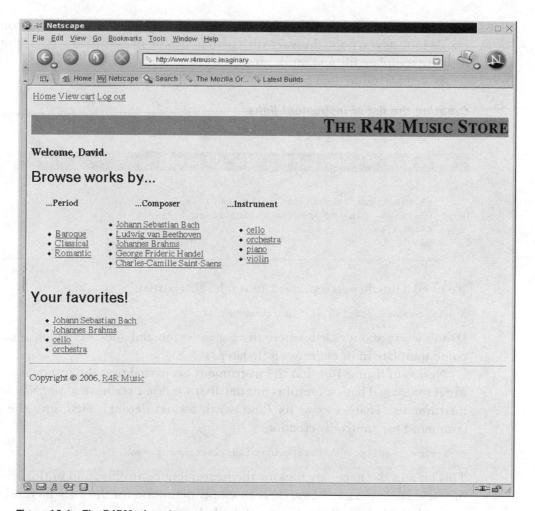

Figure 16.1   The R4RMusic welcome screen

To use this partial, put the following line in the master template main/
welcome.rhtml:

```
<%= render :partial => "composer/list" %>
```

Notice that the name of the partial is double-barreled: composer/list. The significance of this is that the partial template _list.rhtml is retrieved from the views/
composer directory, which isn't the same as the directory where the master template
resides (view/main). You *could* store the composer list partial in the main view directory, alongside welcome.rhtml. The decision *not* to do so is semantic or aesthetic:

The `composer` directory is a better fit for a template that generates a list of composers. As long as you point the way with a path indicator, like `composer/list`, Rails will find the template file and render it.

As we have done unto composers, let us now do unto instruments.

Creating the list of instrument links

Listing 16.4 shows the partial template `instrument/_list.rhtml`.

Listing 16.4   The `instrument/_list.rhtml` partial template

```
<ul>
  <% @instruments.each do |instrument| %>
    <li><%= link_to_instrument(instrument) %></li>
  <% end %>
</ul>
```

We need a line in `welcome.rhtml` to render this partial:

```
<%= render :partial => "instrument/list" %>
```

(Don't worry about exactly where this `render` command goes; we'll look at the welcome template in its entirety a little later.)

Notice in listing 16.4 that the instrument list partial uses the instance variable `@instruments`. That's a useful reminder that we don't yet have a *controller* file for instruments. That's easy to fix (and worth a brief detour). First, give the usual command for controller creation:

```
$ ruby ./script/generate controller instrument show
```

This creates the necessary files for the instrument controller; and in the principal file, `instrument_controller.rb`, is an empty definition for the `show` method. That method needs to be fleshed out and the helper directive inserted.

Listing 16.5 shows the completed file.

Listing 16.5   Completed `instrument_controller.rb` file

```
class InstrumentController < ApplicationController
  helper :work, :edition
  def show
    @instrument = Instrument.find(params[:id])
  end
end
```

The initialization of the `@instrument` instance variable, necessary for rendering of the `instrument/_list.rhtml` partial, is now taken care of.

On we go, to the third of the three lists on the welcome page: the list of musical periods.

Creating the list of links to musical periods

Listing 16.6 shows the partial template that generates the list of links to musical periods.

Listing 16.6 The `main/_period_list.rhtml` partial template

```
<ul>
  <% @periods.each do |period| %>
  <li><%= link_to period,
                :controller => "main",
                :action     => "show_period",
                :id         => period %>
  <% end %>
  </li>
</ul>
```

As per the designation `main/_period_list.rhtml`, this file is stored directly in the `main` views subdirectory. There's nowhere else to put it; a list of periods is a high-level concept, not uniquely associated with any of the application models or controllers (composer, instrument, and so on).

We also need to add the traditional line to the welcome template:

```
<%= render :partial => "period_list" %>
```

Like its composer and instrument counterparts, this line causes the insertion of the list of musical periods into the main welcome screen. (You'll see exactly where this line fits into the template shortly.)

Let's bring the discussion full circle by looking at the `welcome.rhtml` template, also in its entirety.

The complete welcome template

We've added enough lines to `welcome.rhtml` that it's worthwhile looking at that file all in one place. You can see the entire welcome template, with its references to partial templates, in listing 16.7. (Any partials mentioned in the template but not yet discussed will be covered when we develop the views related to the customer.)

Listing 16.7 `views/main/welcome.rhtml`

```
<% if @c %>
  <h3>Welcome, <%= @c.first_name %>.</h3>
<% end %>
<h2 class="info">Browse works by...</h2>

<table>
  <tr>
    <th>...Period</th>
    <th>...Composer</th>
    <th>...Instrument</th>
  </tr>
  <tr>
    <td>
      <%= render :partial => "period_list" %>
    </td>
    <td>
      <%= render :partial => "composer/list" %>
    </td>
    <td>
      <%= render :partial => "instrument/list" %>
    </td>
  </tr>
</table>

<% if @c %>
  <%= render :partial => "favorites" %>
<% else %>
  <h2 class="info">Log in or create an account</h2>
  <table border="1">
    <tr>
      <th>Log in to your account</th>
      <th>Sign up for an account</th>
    </tr>
    <tr>
      <td><%= render :partial => "customer/login" %></td>
      <td><%= render :partial => "customer/signup" %></td>
    </tr>
  </table>
<% end %>
```

The use of partials keeps the welcome template file of reasonable size while incorporating enough semantic information—the names of the partials, primarily—to make it fully informative as to its content. Rather than a spaghetti-style unrolling of lists and forms, the master template contains a series of references to subdocuments to be included.

We'll leave the subject of partials with a summary, in table 16.3, of all the partials used in the music store application.

Table 16.3 Summary of partials used in the music store application views

Partial file directory/filename	Description	Master template(s) using
`composer/_list.rhtml`	Clickable list of composers' names	`main/welcome.rhtml`
`composer/_editions.rhtml`	Clickable list of editions of the composer's works	`composer/show.rhtml`
`customer/_cart.rhtml`	Table of the customer's open orders	`customer/view_cart.rhtml`
`customer/_login.rhtml`	Login form	`main/welcome.rhtml`
`customer/_signup.rhtml`	Signup form	`main/welcome.rhtml`
`edition/_details.rhtml`	Table with edition details and a link to the shopping cart	`edition/show.rhtml`
`instrument/_list.rhtml`	Clickable list of all instruments	`main/welcome.rhtml`
`instrument/_works.rhtml`	Clickable list of all works for this instrument	`instrument/show.rhtml`
`work/_editions.rhtml`	Clickable list of editions of this work	`work/show.rhtml`
`main/_period_list.rhtml`	Clickable list of periods (baroque, and so on)	`main/welcome.rhtml`
`main/_period.rhtml`	Display of editions of works from a given period	`main/show_period.rhtml`
`main/_favorites.shtml`	Customer's favorite composers and instruments	`main/welcome.rhtml`

Our examination of partials has revealed some organizational techniques for template files. But it's also left us with a couple of loose ends. In particular, the main controller file is lagging behind; we have nice lists in the views but not much indication of where those lists get their data. Let's look at `main_controller.rb` and bring it into alignment with the new look of the views.

16.3 *Updating the main controller*

This time around, we'll start with the finished product and then account for how it got that way. Listing 16.8 shows the entire `main_controller.rb` file for this version of the application.

Listing 16.8   The file `main_controller.rb`

```ruby
class MainController < ApplicationController

  helper :work, :composer, :instrument
  def welcome
    @composers = Composer.find(:all).sort_by do |composer|
      [composer.last_name, composer.first_name, composer.middle_name]
    end
    @periods = Work.all_periods
    @instruments = Instrument.find(:all, :order => "name ASC" )
  end

  def show_period
    @period = params[:id]
    works = Work.find(:all).select do |work|
      (work.period == @period) || (work.century == @period)
    end
    @editions = Edition.of_works(works)
  end
end
```

There are only two methods (actions) defined in this file; but they're both worth a look.

16.3.1 *The new face of the welcome action*

In case you don't remember (and don't feel like looking it up), the main controller file in the previous version of R4RMusic looked like this:

```ruby
class MainController < ApplicationController
  def welcome
    @composers = Composer.find(:all).sort_by {|c|
      [c.last_name, c.first_name]
    }
  end
end
```

The new `welcome` action is bit more involved—but not much more than a bit. Where the old `welcome` stored data in one instance variable (a sorted list of composers stored in @composers), the new welcome, as listing 16.8 showed, stores data in three: @composers, @instruments, and @periods.

The composers are still stored in @composers, and the new *middle_name* field is used in the sort. @composers is used by the composer/_list.rhtml partial.

The variable @periods is assigned a list of all the musical periods represented in the inventory of the music store. This information is available via the all_periods class method of Work, a method we wrote in chapter 15. (This is a good example of how the customization of models at both the instance- and class-method levels can pay off in simplicity later.) @periods is used in main/_period_list.rhtml.

Finally, @instruments contains a list of instruments, sorted in ascending order by name. @instruments is used in the instrument/_list.rhtml partial.

The new welcome method primes the pump, so to speak, for the views—which is what controllers do in general. Here, the three instance variables initialized in the controller happen to appear in the three list partials we've already examined.

Then there's the new action, show_period. You'll recall from listing 16.6 that the partial template for the list of musical periods includes a reference to this action. Every link in the list of periods is a link *to* the show_period action for that period. The action is specified in a link_to call, as per listing 16.6, with:

```
:controller => "main",
:action      => "show_period"
```

And *which* period is shown when you click one of the links to show_period? The answer is in show_period:

```
@period = params[:id]
```

The id parameter tells show_period which period to show.

Going back to listing 16.6 and its link_to command, the period is stored in the id parameter like this:

```
:id       => period
```

For the link to the Baroque period, the id parameter is "Baroque"; for the Classical period, it's "Classical", and so on. show_period extracts the period and stores it in @period.

Next, show_period searches through all the works in the database, selecting only those whose period matches the period in question. Two tests are performed: one to match the period and one to match the century. The latter serves as a fallback in case a century rather than a period has been specified:

```
works = Work.find(:all).select do |work|
  (work.period == @period) || (work.century == @period)
end
```

Finally, the `@editions` variable is assigned all the editions of all the works for this period, using the `of_works` class method written in chapter 15. `@editions` and `@period` are then handed off to the `main/show_period.rhtml` template.

Examining that template and the partial it uses (`main/_period.rhtml`), however, will be left as an exercise for you. (Like all the R4RMusic application code, those files are available on the book's Web site.) The goal of this section has been fulfilled: to look closely at the new main controller file. Although that file includes only two methods, they illustrate several useful techniques, not least of which is using custom-written methods from the model files. Facility with Ruby will stand you in good stead in your controller programming, as well as your model programming.

We'll turn next to the main event, in terms of the process of revising the R4RMusic application: the customer. We already have a customer model from chapters 14 and 15. Here, we're going to define actions and create views so that our customers can do something.

16.4   *Incorporating customer signup and login*

The first thing we want customers to be able to do is sign up for an account; the second thing we want them to be able to do is log in to the site. In the process of making these actions possible, we'll consider some issues of authorization and security as they pertain to writing controller actions.

We'll put both the login form and the signup form on the top-level welcome screen. The controller action for signing up is `customer/signup` (the `signup` method in the file `customer_controller.rb`). The login action is `customer/login`. Any new views we create will be placed in the `app/views/customer` directory.

Even though it's backward, in terms of a customer's relation to the site, let's start with the login process. Let's assume that someone has successfully signed up (or been manually created as a user), and that we need to make provisions for that person to log in.

16.4.1   *The login and signup partial templates*

The main welcome view template, shown in listing 16.9, performs a rendering of partials for login and signup forms. Those partials live in the `customer` subdirectory of `app/views`. The signup partial, `_signup.rhtml`, contains the form shown in listing 16.9.

Listing 16.9   The `customer/_signup.rhtml` partial template

```
<%= form_tag :controller => "customer",
             :action     => "signup" %>
    <p>First name:    <%= text_field "customer", "first_name"   %> </p>
    <p>Last name:     <%= text_field "customer", "last_name"    %> </p>
    <p>User name:     <%= text_field "customer", "nick"         %> </p>
    <p>Password:      <%= password_field "customer", "password" %> </p>
    <p>Email address: <%= text_field "customer", "email"        %> </p>

    <p><input type="Submit" value="Sign up"/></p>

<%= end_form_tag %>
```

The login partial, `_login.rhtml`, is shown in listing 16.10.

Listing 16.10   The customer/_login.rhtml partial template

```
<%= form_tag :controller => "customer",
             :action     => "login" %>
<p>User name: <%= text_field "customer", "nick" %></p>
<p>Password: <%= password_field "customer", "password"  %></p>
<p><input type="Submit" value="Log in"/></p>
 <%= end_form_tag %>
```

The forms defined in the partials in listings 16.9 and 16.10 appear on the welcome screen. Now let's look at what's involved in letting someone log in.

16.4.2 *Logging in and saving the session state*

From the perspective of the customer, logging in takes place once at the beginning of each session. The exact definition of *session* may vary among sites. Some terminate sessions by logging you out automatically after a certain amount of time has lapsed. Ours won't, but we'll provide a logout button.

A session has continuity in the visitor's mind. The application also has ways to perceive and maintain session boundaries. When someone requests a controller action—view details of an edition, look at all music for violin, add something to a shopping cart—either the action is performed at a point subsequent to a successful login, or it isn't. If it isn't, it may not matter; we can allow people to browse the catalogue without logging in. But it may matter a lot (for instance, if the person is trying to purchase something).

In order for the application to track a session, two things have to happen:

- When someone logs in, the fact that a login has occurred must be preserved *across multiple requests*, along with the identity of the customer (*who* has logged in, not just *that* someone has logged in).

- When a request for a controller action—any action—comes in, the application should determine two things:
  - Is someone logged in? and
  - Does it matter?

The first point can be handled easily thanks to the built-in Rails *session hash*, available via the special session method. (You can also get at the same information through the @session instance variable, but calling the session method is the preferred technique.) The session hash is maintained across actions (usually as a file in /tmp, although there are other ways to persist it). If you put data in the session hash during one action—say, the action customer/login—then other actions can pull that data out of the hash.

Here's a half-code, half-descriptive (via comments) version of the login action. This action is the target action of the login form, so when it's called, the CGI parameters are set according to what was entered in that form (nick and password):

```
class CustomerController < ApplicationController
  # other code here, then:
  def login
    # Examine the form data for "nick" and "password".
    # Retrieve the customer record for the nick, and store
    #  it in the variable 'c'.
    # If such a record exists, and its password matches the
    #  password from the form, then do this:
    session['customer'] = c.id
    redirect_to :controller => "main", :action => "welcome"
    # Otherwise, report an error.
  end
  # etc.
end
```

The key point is the saving of the customer's ID number (upon authentication of the password) in the session hash. Once that happens, the ID can be retrieved at any point by any action.

Meanwhile, the need to determine whether someone is logged in, and whether it matters, means we have to do some gate-keeping: We must be able to determine *before executing an action* what state we're in with regard to the visitor's login status and its importance.

The importance depends on the action: We don't want unauthorized access to sensitive actions. But even for harmless actions, like viewing the catalogue or the welcome screen, we still want to know whether a known person is logged in so we can greet the person by name, not bother displaying the login form, and so forth. All of this can be accomplished with the help of a "hook" or callback facility called `before_filter`.

16.4.3 *Gate-keeping the actions with before_filter*

The kind of gate-keeping called for here—examining the state of affairs with regard to the visitor after an action has been requested but before it's been executed—is accomplished with the use of special hooks, particularly a class method called `before_filter`. This method is an overseer: You give it, as arguments (in symbol form), the names of instance methods that you wish to be run before one or more actions are run.

Even though some actions aren't particularly security-sensitive (like viewing the welcome screen), you *always* want to know whether someone is logged in, and you want to know who it is. To accomplish this, you add code to the generic controller file `application.rb`. This file contains a class definition:

```
class ApplicationController < ActionController::Base
end
```

If you look at any other controller file—say, `composer_controller.rb`—you'll see that the controller class in that file inherits from `ApplicationController`:

```
class ComposerController < ApplicationController
end
```

You can put calls to `before_filter` in any controller file. But if you put them in `application.rb`, the filters you set up are called along the way to any action in any controller file.

Let's set up a filter that will always be executed whenever anyone sends in a request for any controller action at all. Listing 16.11 shows such an arrangement.

Listing 16.11 Filtering all incoming requests with `before_filter`

```
class ApplicationController < ActionController::Base
  layout("base")

  before_filter :get_customer      ⬅— ❶

  def get_customer      ⬅— ❷
    if session['customer']
      @c = Customer.find(session['customer'])
```

```
        end
      end

   end
```

We've now registered the method `get_customer` as a filter ❶. The method, meanwhile ❷, sets the instance variable `@c` to the `Customer` object drawn from the database record of the customer who's logged in, thanks to the fact that the `login` action saved that record's ID number to the `session` hash. If there's nothing in `session['customer']`, then the method is *not* assigned to `@c`, and `@c` defaults to `nil`.

For the lifespan of the current action, throughout the code that defines the action, and anywhere in the templates, we can test `@c`—and if it has a value, then someone is logged in.

You can now understand why the welcome template has this in it:

```
<% if @c %>
  <%= render :partial => "favorites" %>
<% else %>
  <h2 class="info">Log in or create an account</h2>
  #
  # display of login and signup forms handled here
  #
<% end %>
```

If a customer is logged in, then the site acts accordingly by showing that person's favorites. If not—the site also acts accordingly, by displaying login and signup forms. It all depends on whether `@c` is a customer object or `nil`, as determined by the `get_customer` filter method.

Levels of authentication concern

We now have a setup where we can always answer the question, "Who, if anyone, is logged in?" That's useful because we're now free to do things like put customer-specific greetings ("Hi, David!") on the screen—or lists of the customer's favorite composers.

But those kinds of items are cosmetic. Even visitors who aren't logged in are allowed to look at the welcome screen and the catalogues of composers and works. The real authentication issues involve placing orders. We don't want casual visitors adding to shopping carts; we only want that ability for those who are logged in. (This isn't a universal rule at all online shopping sites, but it's the way we'll do it here.) We also don't want one person prying into the shopping cart of another.

We need a filter that not only tells us whether someone is logged in but also interrupts the requested action if this is a casual visitor.

This filter goes in the Customer controller file because all the potentially sensitive operations are in that file. The relevant code looks like this:

```
before_filter :authorize, :except => ["signup","login"]

def authorize
  return true if @c
  report_error("Unauthorized access; password required")
end
```

This setup causes the authorize method to be executed before any other customer action is performed (view_cart, check_out, and so on)—except that we specifically *don't* want to check for a logged-in customer if the visitor is trying to log in or sign up. We exclude those methods by including them in a list of method names associated with the :except of the argument hash of the call to before_filter.

The way authorize works is simple: It checks for the truth of the variable @c. That variable is nil (and therefore fails the truth test) *unless* it was set to a customer object in the set_customer method in the ApplicationController class.

And what is report_error? It's a homemade, generic error-reporting method, defined as a private instance method of the ApplicationController class (which means it goes in the application.rb controller file):

```
class ApplicationController < ActionController::Base

  # prior code here, then:

  private
  def report_error(message)
    @message = message
    render("main/error")
    return false
  end
end
```

This method sets the @message instance variable to whatever the error message is and then renders a simple template residing in app/views/main/error.rhtml:

```
<% @page_title = "Error" %>
<%= @message %>
```

report_error returns false, which means that if a call to report_error is the last thing executed inside another method, such as authorize, then that method, too, will return false.

Now that people can log in, we need to back-and-fill by making it possible for them to sign up for accounts. We'll do that next.

16.4.4 *Implementing a signing-up facility*

Like logging in, signing up for an account is handled by a form on the welcome screen. You need to type your name, a nick (the username you want to log in with), your email address, and a password. When you submit the form, you trigger the `signup` action in the customer controller; this action creates a new user record based on the data you've entered:

```
def signup
  c = Customer.new(params[:customer])
  c.password = Digest::SHA1.hexdigest(c.password)
  c.save
  session['customer'] = c.id
  redirect_to :controller => "main", :action => "welcome"
end
```

This method doesn't perform any checks for the validity of the incoming data or for duplicate user entries (as measured by either nick or email address). There are a couple of ways to introduce these validity checks. ActiveRecord has a set of facilities for validating data (`ActiveRecord::Validations`) which involve defining data checks in your model files. When you try to save a new or modified record, the save fails if any of these tests fails.

Another way to perform validation in the case of incoming form data is to examine the data before you assign it to the fields of an ActiveRecord object. That's what we'll do here—using, as before, the `before_filter` technique. We'll create a filter called `new_customer` and run it as a filter only before the signup action:

```
before_filter :new_customer, :only   => ["signup"]

def new_customer
  applicant = params[:customer]    ←————❶
  if Customer.find_by_nick(applicant['nick'])    ←————❷
    report_error("Nick already in use. Please choose another.")
  elsif Customer.find_by_email(applicant['email'])
    report_error("Account already exists for that email address")
  end
end
```

The assignment to `applicant` ❶ is a hash based on the naming scheme of the input fields in the form. (We'll see the form close up shortly.) To find out whether a customer already exists with either the nick or the email address submitted on the form, we use ActiveRecord's convenient automatic `find_by_`*fieldname* ❷ method, which finds a matching record by whatever fieldname you choose (in this case, *nick* and *email*). In the event that either is found, we treat it as an error.

Next, we'll add the final link in the customer session chain: the process of logging out.

16.4.5 *Scripting customer logout*

Logging out involves setting session['customer'] to nil. When the next action, if any, is requested, filter method set_customer won't find a customer for the session, and the variable @c will be nil—as it was before the login. That's all there is to it.

It would be nice to have a Logout button on the screen all the time during a logged-in session. We can do this by adding it to app/views/layout/base.rhtml. Let's add a navigation bar at the top of the page, making sure the bar includes a logout option only if someone is already logged in. Here's the relevant part of base.rhtml:

```
<body>
<table>
  <tr>
    <td><%= link_to "Home",
                :controller => "main",
                :action     => "welcome" %></td>
    <% if @c %>    <⎯⎯❶
    <td><%= link_to "View cart",
                :controller => "customer",
                :action     => "view_cart" %></td>
    <td><%= link_to "Log out",
                :controller => "customer",
                :action     => "logout" %></td>
    <% end %>
  </tr>
</table>
```

Notice the <% if @c %> conditional clause ❶. The conditional ensures that the View Cart and Log Out options are displayed only if @c is true, which is the case only if someone is already logged in.

We now have signup, login, and logout in place. But as the innocent phrase "View cart" reminds us, we've still haven't implemented the business end of the customer controller: We must enable customers to place and complete orders. We'll do that next.

16.5 *Processing customer orders*

Logging in is a good first step; but while a customer is logged in, we need to give that customer the ability to

- Add an item to his or her shopping cart
- View the shopping cart
- Complete the order(s)

This can be accomplished easily with a bit of judicious controller and template programming.

What's notable about the shopping cart, as we're treating it here, is that it isn't a real object. There's no `ShoppingCart` class, no `shopping_cart_controller.rb` file, and so forth. *The shopping cart is essentially a view.*

The shopping cart view is the focal point of the ordering process. Every aspect of shopping leads up to the view (browsing and choosing items to buy) or tails away from it (completing orders). Because it sits in the middle of the process, logically speaking, we'll start by looking at the view and then flesh out the "how we get there" and "where we go from there" phases.

16.5.1 *The view_cart action and template*

Let's start by adding an action—an instance method—to the customer controller file, `apps/controllers/customer_controller.rb`:

```
def view_cart
end
```

(You don't *have* to write empty actions in controller files; if there's a view, it will be rendered when the same-named action is called. But the empty action is useful as a visual marker.)

As to the view: Let's start with a master template, `view_cart.rhtml`, which will mainly serve the purpose of calling up a partial containing the real business of the cart. Here's `view_cart.rhtml`:

```
<% @page_title = "Shopping cart for #{@c.nick}" %>

<%= render :partial => "cart" %>
```

(Remember that the instance variable `@c` has been set to the logged-in customer.)

The bulk of the shopping-cart view goes inside the partial template `_cart.rhtml`, which is shown in listing 16.12.

Listing 16.12 The `customer/_cart.rhtml` **partial template**

```
<table border="1">
  <tr>
    <th>Title</th>
    <th>Composer</th>
    <th>Publisher</th>
    <th>Price</th>
    <th>Copies</th>
    <th>Subtotal</th>
  </tr>

<% @c.editions_on_order.each do |edition| %>      <----●
  <% count = @c.copies_of(edition) %>
  <tr>
    <td><%= link_to_edition_title(edition) %></td>   <----②
    <td>
    <% edition.composers.each do |composer| %>      <----③
      <%= link_to_composer(composer) %>
    <% end %></td>
    <td><%= edition.publisher.name %></td>      <----④
    <td class="price"><%= two_dec(edition.price) %>   <----⑤
    <td class="count"><%= count %></td>      <----⑥
    <td class="price"><%= two_dec(edition.price * count) %></td>
  </tr>
<% end %>
  <tr><td colspan="5">TOTAL</td>
      <td class="price"><%= two_dec(@c.balance) %></td>   <----⑦
  </tr>
</table>
<p><%= link_to("Complete purchases",      <----⑧
            :controller => "customer",
            :action     => "check_out") %></p>
```

This partial is relatively long, but its logic is straightforward. It consists of one table and one link. The link, at the end, is to the `check_out` action ⑧. The table consists of headers plus one row for each edition that the customer has on order ●. The table contains various pieces of information: title ②, composer ③, publisher ④, price ⑤, and copy count ⑥. The subtotal for each edition is shown, as is the customer's total balance ⑦.

Thus the cart. Now, as promised, we'll examine the "how we got there" side of things: the process by which the customer selects an edition for inclusion in the cart.

16.5.2 *Viewing and buying an edition*

Customers will add *editions* to their carts. The logical thing to do is to modify the show template for editions so it includes a link to an action that adds the edition to the cart of the logged-in customer.

That's easily done. While we're at it, let's do a makeover of the edition show template generally. We'll break it into a master template and a partial. The master template, still called `show.rhtml`, looks like this:

```
<% @page_title = @edition.nice_title %>
<h2 class="info"><%= @page_title %></h2>
<%= render :partial => "details" %>
```

The partial, `_details.rhtml`, is shown in listing 16.13.

Listing 16.13 The `editions/_details.rhtml` **partial template**

```
<ul>
  <li>Edition: <%= @edition.description %></li>
  <li>Publisher: <%= @edition.publisher.name %></li>
  <li>Year: <%= @edition.year %></li>
  <li>Price: <%= two_dec(@edition.price) %></li>
<% if @c %>
  <li><%= link_to "Add to cart",      ◁——————❶
            :controller => "customer",
            :action     => "add_to_cart",
            :id         => @edition.id %></li>
<% end %>
</ul>
<h3>Contents:</h3>   ◁——————❷
<ul>
<% @edition.works.each do |work| %>
  <li><%= link_to_work(work) %>
    (<%= link_to_composer(work.composer) %>)
  </li>
<% end %>
</ul>
```

Note that the `_details.rhtml` partial includes a section with the heading `Con-tents` ❷. Because editions in the new version of the application can contain multiple works, it behooves us to display them all on the edition's show view.

Also, there's now a link ❶—included only if `@c` is set—that allows the logged-in customer to add the edition to his or her cart. That implies the existence of an `add_to_cart` method, which we haven't written yet but now will.

16.5.3 *Defining the add_to_cart action*

We move next back to the customer controller file, where we need to add a new action: add_to_cart. This action's job is to create a new Order object, connecting this customer with this edition. After it does this, we ask it to display the cart.

The add_to_cart method looks like this:

```
def add_to_cart
  e = Edition.find(params[:id])
  order = Order.create(:customer => @c,
                       :edition  => e)
  if order
    redirect_to :action => "view_cart"
  else
    report_error("Trouble with saving order")
  end
end
```

The method finds the Edition object corresponding to the CGI ID field and creates a new Order object linking that edition with the current customer. On success, it shows the cart with the new order included. On failure, it reports an error.

Customers can now put items in their carts and see what they've put there. To complete the cycle, we have to allow the customer to go ahead and purchase what's in the cart.

16.5.4 *Completing the order(s)*

We're only going to do a placeholder version of the purchasing process here; a real-world version would have to deal with payment, notification of the customer, and so forth. We'll print an acknowledgment to the screen on success, and do a couple of things behind the scenes to indicate that the orders in the cart have been completed.

The shopping cart partial template includes a link to a check_out action:

```
<p><%= link_to("Complete purchases",
            :controller => "customer",
            :action     => "check_out") %></p>
```

We do, however, have to write the action—once again, as an instance method in the customer controller file. This method tells the current customer object to check itself out:

```
def check_out
  @c.check_out
end
```

Here's where having written a `check_out` instance method in the customer model file (see section 15.3.3) pays off. All we have to do in the `controller` action is call that method.

We now need a view that acknowledges that the customer has checked out. (Again, we aren't doing everything we'd do if this were a full-featured application; we're just printing a message.) That view, `check_out.rhtml`, looks like this:

```
<% @page_title = "Orders complete" %>
<h2>Thanks for your order, <%= @c.first_name %>!</h2>
```

We now have customers who can log in, browse the catalog, put items in their shopping carts, and complete their purchases (in a placeholder kind of way—but still). We've made the necessary enhancements along the way to the templates and partials involved in the customer scenarios, and we've added the necessary actions to the customer controller class.

That brings us *near* the end of the development of the music store application. We'll make one more enhancement, though. In chapter 15, we wrote methods that give rankings of composers and instruments based on the customer's purchase history. Here, we'll take that process to the next step by putting a list of the customer's favorites on the welcome screen.

16.6 *Personalizing the page via dynamic code*

This is the last section where we'll add a new feature to the music store application. It will take us back to the model-coding phase, but we'll tie it into the controller/view phase through the creation of more partials.

The goal is to personalize the welcome page by displaying a list of favorite composers and instruments based on the logged-in user's ordering history. Somewhere on the page, we'll put something that says, "Your favorites!" and a list of favorite (most often ordered) composers and instruments.

This section is a bit of a cheat: It asks you to add a method to the customer model file, `customer.rb`, as well as writing template code that uses that method. The writing of that method properly belongs in chapter 15. But as this is the last of our enhancements to the application, it seems fitting to pull its various components together in one place.

16.6.1 *From rankings to favorites*

We've already written methods that rank composers and instruments according to how many works by/for each the customer has ordered. Rankings come back as an array of `Composer` objects or `Instrument` objects, with the ones the customer has ordered the most of first. When a tie occurs—for example, if the customer has ordered equal number of works for violin and works for flute—the one ordered most recently comes first, thanks to the fact that the underlying lists from which all this information is generated are lists of customer orders, and customer orders are maintained in chronological order. (See section 15.3.3 to review the details of the rankings code.)

The rankings arrays serve as the input to the methods that determine the favorites. They do most of the work for us. All we really have to do is examine a rankings array and take as many items from it as we want to display.

Except... we'll take on a coding challenge.

Instead of separate favorites methods for each of these things—a `favorite_composers` method and a `favorite_instruments` method—let's write a generic favorites method that returns *either* composers *or* instruments, depending on the argument it's called with.

So, for example, if we say

```
@c.favorites :composer
```

we'll expect the return value to be an array of `Composer` objects. And

```
@c.favorites :instruments
```

likewise, for `Instrument` objects.

The key is that (not by accident) the two rankings methods we wrote in chapter 15 have similar method names and work similarly. Consider a favorites method that works something like this:

```
def favorites(thing)                          ❶
  method_name = "#{thing}_rankings"    ⟵┘
  rankings = self.send(method_name)    ⟵┐
  # etc.                                      ❷
end
```

The strategy is to construct the correct rankings-method name ❶ (which may be `composer_rankings` or `instrument_rankings` or something else if we ever add another rankings method) and then call that method by sending the method name to `self` ❷. The `favorites` method determines the name of the correct rankings method *dynamically*, based on the argument that was passed in. As long as you name such methods with the convention `rankings_thing`, and as long as every rankings method returns a hash of IDs and their rankings, this `favorites` method (once it's completely written) will work for any and all of them.

Limiting the number of favorites listed

What about specifying how long you want the list of favorites to be? That's easy: just add another argument, a `count` argument, to `favorites`. But let's do it the Rails way: Let's have the method accept a hash of options and parse the count option out of that hash:

```
def favorites(thing,options)
  count = options[:count]      ◄———❶
  method_name = "#{thing}_rankings"
  rankings = self.send(method_name)
  return rankings[0,count].compact    ◄———❷
end
```

The value plucked out of the options hash ❶ serves to limit the number of elements returned from the whole rankings array ❷. If the requested number is greater than the size of the rankings array, the result is padded with `nil`s; but the `compact` operation removes them.

We now have a generalized way to get a customer's favorite things (composers, instruments). Let's go back and trace how the favorites mechanism figures in the application.

16.6.2 *The favorites feature in action*

In principle, the favorites list works the same way as the other lists on the welcome page (composer, instruments, and periods). The idea is to pepper the welcome screen with as many browsing opportunities as possible; showing a visitor's favorites is just another way to do this. The details of how the favorites list works are a little different from the other three (including the fact that it isn't shown if no one is logged in). But it's largely a variation on the same theme.

As you saw back in listing 16.7, the template for the main welcome view includes a reference to a favorites partial:

```
<% if @c %>
  <%= render :partial => "favorites" %>
<% else %>
  # etc.
```

The favorites partial, in the file `app/views/main/_favorites.rhtml`, is where the call to the `favorites` method goes. That partial is shown in listing 16.14.

Listing 16.14 The `main/_favorites.rhtml` partial template

```
<h2 class="info">Your favorites</h2>

<% fav_composers = @c.favorites :composer,
                         :count => 3 %>
<% fav_instruments = @c.favorites :instrument,
                            :count => 3 %>

<ul>
<% fav_composers.each do |composer| %>
  <li><%= link_to_composer(composer) %></li>
<% end %>
<% fav_instruments.each do |instrument| %>
  <li><%= link_to_instrument(instrument) %></li>
<% end %>
</ul>
```

The favorites partial uses the `:count` parameter of the `favorites` method to request a display of up to three favorite composers and up to three favorite instruments. It stores these in local variables and then iterates through them, calling the appropriate `link_to`-style helper method on each. The result is a set of links: one to each of the customer's three favorite composers and three favorite instruments.

The local variables aren't strictly necessary; you could iterate directly through the array returned by the call to favorites, like this

```
<% (@c.favorites :composer,
                :count => 3).each do |composer| %>
```

and so forth. (The variables provide nice visual encapsulation, though.) You could also extract the customer's favorites in the controller, rather than in the view, and pass them to the view in instance variables. Indeed, if more extensive model-querying were involved, it would belong in the controller; but since harvesting the favorites is just a matter of a couple of method calls on a customer object that the controller has already made available (in the instance variable `@c`), it's reasonable for the queries to take place inside the template code.

This gives us the favorites list on the welcome screen and brings us to the end of the development of the music store application. At this point, you should play with the application, add records to the database, run the application console and make changes, move things around in the views, write new controller and model methods, and generally use the music store as a practice and learning tool in any way you wish. That's what it's for.

16.7 Summary

This chapter, a companion piece to chapter 15, has taken you through the controller and view phases of the redesign and enhancement of the music store application (plus a brief foray back into the model phase, in the last section). You've seen some of the tools that Rails gives you to help you with both organizing and customizing your templates—in the form of partials and helper files—and used those tools to keep the template code readable and manageable as the application has grown. As a final enhancement, we updated the customer model file to include a mechanism for determining favorites and added template code to the main welcome view to display those favorites for the logged-in customer.

If you're left with the sense that, as of this chapter, it's become difficult to tell where Rails programming ends and Ruby programming begins, then the chapter has succeeded. *That's the goal*—to be able to bring Ruby skills to bear seamlessly on Rails tasks. Whether it's writing an action, or a method in a helper file, or a highly specialized suite of methods like the rankings and favorites facility in the music store application, the ideal situation is one in which you have a large number of programming techniques at your command and you use whichever ones help you get your application to do what you want it to do.

That, in a nutshell, is Ruby for Rails.

There's only one more area to explore: the process of becoming acquainted with the Rails source code. Chapter 17 will give you a guided tour of the basics of this process.

Techniques for exploring
the Rails source code

Exploring the Rails source code is both part of the payoff for strengthening your Ruby skills, and a great way to strengthen those skills further. The more you know about *how* Rails does *what* it does, the more deeply you can understand what your application does. Furthermore, gaining familiarity with the Rails source code opens the door to participation in discussions about Rails at a level that would otherwise be closed to you. Conceivably, it could even enable you to file intelligent bug reports and submit source-code bug fixes and enhancements. Not every Rails developer needs to, or wants to, participate in Rails culture at this level; but if you do want to, you need to know something about the source code and how to navigate it.

In this chapter, you'll learn three techniques for exploring the Rails source code: panning for info, shadowing Ruby, and consulting the documentation. You might think that the third of these techniques renders the first two unnecessary and/or undesirable. It doesn't. Rails has great documentation, and thanks to RDoc it's easy to browse and read. But reading the documentation isn't the same as exploring the source code; and the aspects of exploring the source code that are unique to that process are worthwhile and educational.

17.1 *Exploratory technique 1: panning for info*

The first exploratory technique we'll look at is the closest among the three to an informal, ad hoc technique. Nevertheless, it's extremely useful (and common), and instructive in the matter of the structure and layout of the source code.

The idea of panning for info is to go directly to the source code tree and look around.

If this sounds like a haphazard technique for studying the Rails source, try it for a while; you'll see that the layout and organization of the code imposes a certain order on your hunting. Panning for information in the source is a bit hackerly, but it's not random or undirected.

Furthermore, digging around in the Rails libraries can lead to interesting side discoveries. Looking for a specific method or class definition and, upon finding it, pulling the whole file up in a text editor is like fetching a book from a shelf on a library: There's always a possibility that something else of interest nearby will catch your eye.

And just as walking through a library without having a particular book in mind can be rewarding, so too can you learn a lot through unstructured, free-floating exploration of the Rails source code. But we'll be more structured: As a sustained case study in the info-panning technique, we'll use the ActiveRecord association method `belongs_to`. The goal is to find the method definition and see what makes the method tick.

17.1.1 *Sample info panning: belongs_to*

The first step in panning the Rails source for info is to put yourself inside the appropriate subtree within the source code. In the case of `belongs_to`, that means the ActiveRecord library—because `belongs_to` is a class method of `ActiveRecord::Base`. The first step in the search is

```
$ cd /usr/local/lib/gems/1.8/gems/activerecord-1.9.1
```

Note that the version number of ActiveRecord may be different on your system. So may some of the details of what's there. But the principles of searching, and many of the specifics of the contents, won't have changed.

You're now looking at a directory containing the following entries:

```
CHANGELOG  examples  install.rb  lib  rakefile
README  RUNNING_UNIT_TESTS  test
```

When you're panning for particular bits of source code in any of the Rails source-code areas, your best bet is the `lib` subdirectory:

```
$ cd lib
```

In the `lib` directory are two entries, one a directory and the other a Ruby program file:

```
active_record  active_record.rb
```

The file `active_record.rb`, sitting at the top of the source-code tree for ActiveRecord, consists chiefly of a sequence of `require` statements. It's the key that Rails turns to start the ActiveRecord subsystem, which is responsible for everything connected with your application's communication with the database.

To see the bulk of the ActiveRecord library code, you need to go down one more directory level:

```
$ cd active_record
```

Here you'll see a number of further Ruby program files as well as several subdirectories that contain the code for the larger subsystems of ActiveRecord—the associations subsystem being one of the largest. The Rails source code that governs the rules of associations occupies the file `associations.rb` and all the files inside the `associations` subdirectory.

At this point you can assume you're in territory where one or more files might contain what you're looking for: the file in which the `belongs_to` class method is defined. Because we're taking the panning-for-info approach, we'll reach now for the most important tool of that trade: grep. This command

```
$ grep -n "belongs_to" associations.rb
```

shows you every occurrence of the term *belongs_to* in that file, together with its line number. Clearly you don't need all of them. Because you're looking for the definition of belongs_to, you can grep more narrowly:

```
$ grep "def belongs_to" associations.rb
```

That takes you directly to line 354, where the definition of belongs_to begins. (We're going to hold off on examining the method itself until we've covered all the techniques for tracking through the source code.)

> **TIP**   INSTANT grep   If you don't have the grep utility, you can adapt the rough-and-ready grep replacement tool written in Ruby in section 6.3.2.

17.2   *Exploratory technique 2: shadowing Ruby*

The second technique for following the trail of Rails into its own source code is to shadow Ruby—to follow which program files are loaded and executed, in what order, up to and including whatever file contains the code you're trying to pin down. This technique can be a good exercise in and of itself; it's a useful way to strengthen your familiarity with the combined Ruby/Rails landscape. It can also give you a detailed understanding of mechanisms that may not be organized the way you'd expect. We'll see a concrete example of this somewhat mysterious pronouncement when we return to belongs_to later in this section.

You have to use some judgment, and make some judgments, when you shadow Ruby through the source code. You have to choose a reasonable starting point and make sensible choices at forks in the road, where the source code files you're consulting don't unambiguously pinpoint the sequence of execution without an educated guess from you. We'll expand on both of these judgment-call areas next; after that, we'll return to the belongs_to case study.

17.2.1   *Choosing a starting point*

When a request comes in to a Rails application from a Web server, certain things always happen. When you're trying to follow Ruby's footsteps through the execution process, it's reasonable to stride pretty quickly, if at all, through the preliminaries.

Here's a summary of some steps you can take for granted without digging through every file involved:

- The dispatcher (`dispatch.fcgi`, `dispatch.cgi`, or `dispatch.rb`) loads the file `config/environment.rb`.

- `environment.rb` loads the bulk of the Rails framework: `active_record`, `active_controller`, and so on.

- `dispatcher.rb`, which is located in the `rails` source tree, works with the routing (URL rewriting) facilities of ActionController to route the incoming request to the appropriate controller and action.

- `dependencies.rb` from the ActiveSupport library defines methods that support loading of model definition files (such as `edition.rb`) that match controller definition file names (such as `edition_controller.rb`) and other such automated facilities.

It's safe to assume, as a starting point, that all necessary model files are loaded courtesy of detective work on the part of Rails. In shadowing Ruby through a Rails call into the source code, we'll therefore start with the model file.

17.2.2 *Choose among forks in the road intelligently*

In numerous places in the Rails source code, master, umbrella files load in a lot of subsidiary, related files. `active_record.rb` is an example of such a file: It consists almost entirely of `require` and `include` statements.

You can't follow Ruby down every possible path and subpath when you come to a file like this. You have to make a calculation of which path or paths you need to take to get where you're going. For example, if you're interested in understanding where `belongs_to` fits in, the main lines in `active_record.rb` that will interest you are the following:

```
require 'active_record/associations'
```

and

```
ActiveRecord::Base.class_eval do
  # ...
  include ActiveRecord::Associations
  # ...
end
```

You know that `belongs_to` is an association. It's reasonable, then, to focus your attention on those `require` and `include` directives in `active_record.rb` whose targets appear to be associations-related . You don't have to look at every line of every required file; you're not a human `grep` utility. And unless there's a surprising glitch in the way the Rails source code is put together, the `requires` and `includes` that shout "Relevant!" to you when you read them probably are.

Speaking of `belongs_to`, let's use that method again as our case study to demonstrate the process of shadowing Ruby into the Rails source code.

NOTE   ACTIVESUPPORT AND NAME-BASED INFERENCE MAGIC   One area we won't go into here, but which you're encouraged to explore on your own, is *ActiveSupport*, a separate library of routines and facilities used by the other Rails libraries. ActiveSupport contains many of the routines that help those other libraries make leaps of logic involving names: If a controller field in an incoming request contains the word *edition*, then the corresponding controller file is `app/controllers/edition_controller.rb`, the corresponding model file is `app/models/edition.rb`, and so forth. This automatic, inference-based gluing of different parts of the Rails framework together means that triggering execution of a controller file can automatically trigger the loading of the correct model files; and, down the road, the correct view templates can be pinpointed automatically based on the naming conventions.

17.2.3   On the trail of belongs_to

Our starting point for tracking `belongs_to` by shadowing Ruby is the edition model file, `edition.rb`:

```
class Edition < ActiveRecord::Base
  has_and_belongs_to_many :works
  has_many    :orders
  belongs_to :publisher

  # etc.
end
```

We know that this is a class method of `ActiveRecord::Base`. At least, we know that `ActiveRecord::Base` responds to it; we don't know yet whether it's defined in the class definition body of `ActiveRecord::Base` or perhaps defined in a module and pulled into the class later—or, possibly, in a superclass of `ActiveRecord::Base`.

Back we go to

```
$ cd /usr/local/lib/ruby/gems/1.8/gems/activerecord-1.9.1/lib
```

This directory contains a subdirectory called `active_record` and a file called `active_record.rb`. This time, we'll look directly in `active_record.rb`, which we know is loaded by `environment.rb` when the application starts up.

`active_record.rb` shows the first mention of associations, in this line, about halfway through the file:

```
require 'active_record/associations'
```

As discussed in section 17.2.2, it's reasonable to make an educated guess that of the several `require` directives in `active_record.rb`, the one that mentions associations is the one we want to track. This `require` sends Ruby on a search for an `associations.rb` file (or `.so` or `.dll`—but in Rails everything is in `.rb` files). We'll follow along.

The first place to be searched is the directory we're in, the `lib.` subdirectory of the ActiveRecord installation. Starting the search in the current directory actually isn't default Ruby behavior. But at the top of `active_record.rb` is this line:

```
$:.unshift(File.dirname(__FILE__))
```

This line adds the directory containing `active_record.rb` to the loadpath of `require`. It does this in the following way:

- The variable `$:` holds the loadpath, which determines the search order used by `require`.

- `__FILE__` is a special Ruby variable that holds the name of the current file: `active_record.rb`.

- `File.dirname` returns the directory part of the full path- and filename of the file—in this case, `/usr/local/lib/ruby/gems/1.8/gems/activerecord-1.9.1/lib` or equivalent.

- The `unshift` operation adds that directory to the front of the load path.

NOTE   THE POSITION OF THE CURRENT DIRECTORY IN THE RUBY LOADPATH
By default, the Ruby loadpath includes the current directory, indicated by the single dot (`.`) at the end of the list of load directories. (You can see them all if you do `ruby -e 'p $:'`.) Also by default, the current directory is whatever directory was current when the program started executing; so if you're in directory `zero` and give the command `ruby one/two/prog.rb`, `prog.rb` will consider `zero` (not `two`) to be its runtime current directory. This means that even if two files are in the same directory, you can't necessarily just require one from the other without either modifying the loadpath (`$:`) or using a full pathname in the `require` statement. The upshot of all this is that Rails does a fair amount of directory and loadpath manipulation, so that the files that need to see each other can indeed see each other.

`require` now looks in `activerecord-1.9.1/lib` first. When it does, it sees, sure enough, a directory called `active_record`. In that directory, it sees the file `associations.rb`; and that's the file it loads.

`associations.rb` contains the definition of `belongs_to` (on line 354 in ActiveRecord 1.9.1). We've succeeded in tracking it down.

But look at where it's defined. Stripping the module and class nesting down to a shell, it's defined in this context:

```
module ActiveRecord
  module Associations
    module ClassMethods
      def belongs_to(association_id, options = {})
        # etc.
```

In other words, it's an instance method defined in a module called `ActiveRecord::Associations::ClassMethods`. But in the model file, we use it as a class method of `ActiveRecord::Base`. How does this come about?

To unravel this question, we need to go back up one directory level and into `active_record.rb`. Here, a number of lines are wrapped in a `class_eval` statement. The relevant one (plus the `class_eval`) looks like this:

```
ActiveRecord::Base.class_eval do
  include ActiveRecord::Associations
end
```

What's going on here? The `ActiveRecord::Base` class is *mixing in* `ActiveRecord::Associations`. That means *instance methods* defined in `ActiveRecord::Associations` become callable by *instances* of `ActiveRecord::Base`—and of its subclasses.

That still doesn't explain how `ActiveRecord::Base` ends up with a *class* method called `belongs_to`. Something else must be happening when `associations.rb` is loaded and `ActiveRecord::Associations` is mixed in.

Something happening when a module gets mixed in.... That sounds a lot like a hook or callback. Recall that any module has the ability to define a method called `included`, which is called with the class or module that's doing the including as the single argument whenever the module gets included. You need to know only one further thing at this point: `Module#included` used to be called `Module#append_features` and can still (as of Ruby 1.8.4) be used with that name (although `included` is preferred).

Now, if we look again inside `associations.rb`, we can spot this:

```
module ActiveRecord
  module Associations
    def self.append_features(base)
      super
      base.extend(ClassMethods)
    end
```

The code ensures that whenever a class or module *includes* the module `ActiveRecord::Associations`, *that class or module* is *extended* with the module `ActiveRecord::ClassMethods`.

If you find this convoluted, don't feel discouraged. It is—but it's convoluted for the sake of clean organization. Instead of writing `belongs_to` and the other association methods directly as class methods of `ActiveRecord::Base`, Rails puts them in a module that clearly labels them with the role they're going to play: `ActiveRecord::Associations::ClassMethods`. Then, `ActiveRecord::Base` is extended with that module, at which point things proceed *as if* that module's instance methods were class methods of `ActiveRecord::Base` the whole time. The best of both worlds is preserved: The code remains organized and labeled with meaningful class and module names, while the programmer can do things like:

```
class Edition < ActiveRecord::Base
  belongs_to :publisher
  # etc.
end
```

without having to worry about how `ActiveRecord::Base` ended up having a method called `belongs_to`.

You may find it helpful and enlightening to see a transliteration of `belongs_to` into simple terms. As you'll see, there's nothing here that isn't among the Ruby techniques you've learned already.

17.2.4 *A transliteration of belongs_to*

The real context of `belongs_to` features a lot of long names and is spread out over multiple files. But it all boils down to what's shown in listing 17.1.

Listing 17.1 A transliteration of `belongs_to` into simpler terms

```
module A            ◁——— ❶
  module M          ◁——— ❷
    module ClassMethods
      def a_sort_of_class_method    ◁——— ❸
        puts "Instance method of ClassMethods module"
        puts "So this can be made to act like a class method"
        puts "(if a Class object calls it directly)"
      end
    end

    def self.included(c)    ◁——— ❹
      c.extend(ClassMethods)
    end

  end

  class B           ◁——— ❺
    include M
  end
```

```
  end

  class C < A::B
    a_sort_of_class_method
  end
```

Module A ❶ plays the role of ActiveRecord. Module A::M ❷ is the equivalent of ActiveRecord::Associations. Like ActiveRecord::Associations, M contains a nested module called ClassMethods (whose name is preserved here to pinpoint the main action). Class A::B ❺ plays the role of ActiveRecord::Base.

The method A::M::ClassMethods#a_sort_of_class_method ❸ is the equivalent of belongs_to: It's defined as an instance method several levels deep that gets attached directly to a Class object—in this case, the object A::B—courtesy of the callback mechanism of Module#included ❹ (or append_features, in the case of the Rails code).

This transliteration shows you the essence of the mechanism whereby an instance method of a module ends up serving, from the programmer's perspective, as a separate class's class method. This brings us full circle to the mysterious claim at the beginning of section 17.2: that learning how to shadow Ruby through the Rails source can help you understand mechanisms that may not be organized the way you'd expect. From the way it's used, you might expect belongs_to to be a normal class method; but it isn't, and by tracking Ruby's actions you can both see that it isn't and also gain a complete understanding of what it *is*.

(As you'll see in the course of our consideration of the third exploratory technique—consulting the documentation—the way belongs_to and the other association methods are defined results in a documentation anomaly: Even though they look and feel and act like class methods, they're instance methods of a module—and therefore they're listed as instance methods in the Rails documentation.)

This brings us to the third and final technique for tracking through the Rails source code.

17.3 Exploratory technique 3: consulting the documentation

The third technique for tracking something through the source is to use the documentation. This will almost certainly be the technique you use most often, unless you get interested in the source and deeply involved in exploring it. (Part of the reason for presenting the other two techniques is to suggest to you that a deep level of exploration is possible.)

The components of the Rails framework are documented with the Ruby Documentation (RDoc) system, using RDoc's simple markup format to generate browsable documentation from Ruby and C source files. The files that form the Rails framework are all marked up in RDoc notation. The result is a great deal of browsable documentation for Rails. To browse it, go to http://api.rubyonrails.org. Figure 17.1 shows the top-level screen.

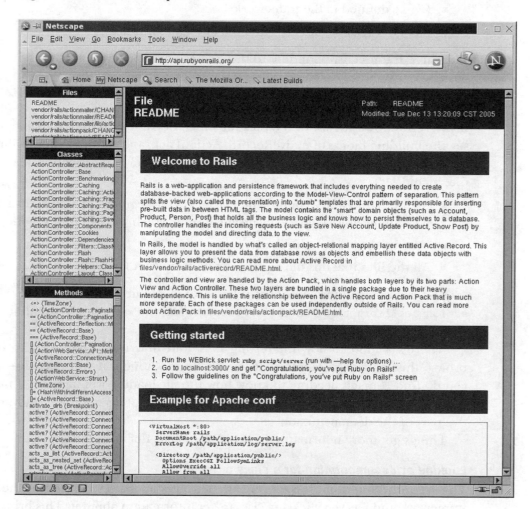

Figure 17.1   The top-level screen of `api.rubyonrails.org`

17.3.1 *A roadmap of the online Rails API documentation*

The layout of the available documentation at api.rubyonrails.org allows for several types of browsing, depending on what you're interested in. You can get directly from the top level of the site to a detailed description of the following:

- *Files* in the Rails framework
- *Classes* defined in the framework
- *Methods* (instance or class) defined anywhere in Rails

The three frames corresponding to these categories appear on the left side of the screen.

Looking at documentation for a file

If you scroll down the list of the files for which documentation is available, you'll see the building blocks of ActiveRecord, ActionPack, and various support libraries flash before your eyes. If you choose one, you're shown information about the file, including:

- Its full path (which, minus the `vendor/rails` segment, matches by name a path somewhere below your installation in which you can find the file)
- The date it was last modified
- All the files that this file *requires* (loads at runtime)

A good example (in the sense that it has a lot of required files) is `vendor/rails/actionpack/lib/action_controller/base.rb`. You can see at a glance what needs to be loaded from this file in order for it to run.

There's a limit to how interesting it is, and how useful it's likely to be, to browse this kind of meta-information. It's there, though, if you need it—and if you do find yourself needing to know how the file-loading will happen, it may be faster to look here than to plough through the files. But it's not the most informative part of the documentation.

Things get more informative in the class-by-class documentation.

Looking at documentation for a class or module

The second frame from the top, on the left, lists all classes defined in the Rails framework and lets you click any class to get information about it. This brings you to the heart of the documentation.

As an example (and because it contains `belongs_to`), click the link to `ActiveRecord::Associations::ClassMethods`. This brings up, in the right frame, a page about the class of that name. At the top of this frame is an indication of the file in which the class is defined. Keep in mind that Ruby classes and modules can be reopened and their definitions augmented across more than one file. Documentation for some of the classes and modules lists more than one file as containing the class or module's source code. However many there are, you can click them to get the information screen for each file.

You'll also see an indication at the top of this class's parent class (`Object`). This information isn't included for modules because modules don't have the same inheritance relationships as classes.

Now, the interesting material begins. In general, you'll see the following in this frame:

- Description and usage information for the class or module
- A combined list of all methods, both instance and class
- A list of all constants defined for this class or module
- A list of all classes and modules owned by (nested in) this class or module
- Detailed descriptions of class methods, alphabetically by method
- Detailed descriptions of instance methods, alphabetically by method

The latter two categories are further broken down into separate sections for public and protected methods. (Private methods aren't documented.)

Everything is hyperlinked. You can jump from the combined list of methods to a particular method's detailed description. (Note that there may be a class method and an instance method with the same name. Make sure you've jumped to the correct one.) You can click the name of a nested class or module and be taken to its descriptive page.

Most important for the focus of this chapter, you can toggle display of a method's source code. Before expanding on this, let's circle back and take stock of the third of the three frames on the left side of the screen.

Looking at documentation for a method

The third frame lists the name of every public or protected method defined in the Rails framework along with the name of the class or module where the method is defined.

You can easily find `belongs_to` in this list. When you click it, you're taken in the right frame to the page for `ActiveRecord::Associations::ClassMethods` (which you may be on anyway) and down to the description of `belongs_to`.

That brings us back to where we were a couple of paragraphs ago—about to examine the process of looking at the source code through the documentation.

When you're looking at a method's detailed description—whether you got there from clicking its name directly from the Methods list on the left or from navigating a class or module's page on the right—you'll see a Show Source hyperlink. Click it, and you'll be looking at the source code for the method together with information about what file it comes from and file-based line numbers on the left.

This is definitely the fastest way to zero in on the source code for a method. The existence of this interface to the source doesn't mean you'll never need or want to look at the source code. For example, if you ever write a patch or bug-fix for a Rails component, you need to know your way around the source.But the RDoc system is engineered to give you information, and if that's what you want, you'll find it here.

A small caveat about class vs. instance method documentation

As we've seen, Rails uses a roundabout way of defining class methods for a lot of classes. Instead of the classic class method definition style:

```
class C
  def self.meth
  # etc.
```

Rails sometimes uses the `included` hook to hand off a set of class methods (defined in a module with the name `ClassMethods`) to a given class.

If you're looking for the documentation for, say, the class methods of `ActiveRecord::Association`, you'll find them defined as *instance methods* of `ActiveRecord::Association::ClassMethods`. This is the case with `belongs_to`—if you've followed the ins and outs of that method's placement in the code and where it ends up in the documentation, you've seen one of the trickier cases. Just be aware that there may be a disconnect between the class/instance method distinction in the way we talk about the code and the way the methods are documented.

The alphabetical list of all the methods in the framework goes a long way toward making this documentation anomaly less of a problem than it might otherwise be. If you can find `belongs_to` in that list, you don't have to wrestle with its pedigree and labeling. Figure 17.2 shows the view you get if you click `belongs_to` in the method list, scroll down in the documentation, and click Show Source.

You're now in a position to use the online API documentation knowledgeably—and to use it, where appropriate for your interests and needs, both as a source of usage information and as a supplement to your understanding of the architecture of the Rails framework.

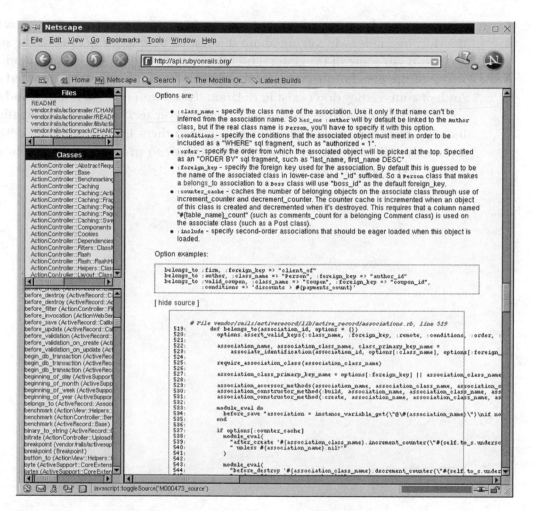

Figure 17.2 Looking at the belongs_to **source on** api.rubyonrails.org

17.4 Summary

This chapter has provided more payoff for the study of Ruby by taking you on a guided, annotated tour of techniques for exploring and studying the Rails source code. We've used the ActiveRecord association methods, particularly belongs_to, as a thread to follow as we walked through three techniques: panning for info with grep and similar tools; shadowing Ruby through the twists and turns of class, module, and method definitions (and we chose a particularly twisty example; it's likely to be easier, rather than harder, as you do more of this kind of thing on your own); and the less adventurous but extremely convenient approach of consulting the documentation. In talking about this last technique for getting at the source code, you saw some of the general usefulness of the online API documentation.

All of these techniques are useful, even the relatively scrappy, `grep`-based ones. And, of course, they don't exist in isolation. Faced with the need to find and study something in the source code, you'll use whatever technique or combination of techniques seems appropriate. But having seen them broken out and presented separately will help you think clearly about how to proceed as you explore the Rails source code further.

appendix:
Ruby and Rails
installation and resources

This appendix will help you get Ruby and Rails up and running on your system, if they aren't already.

The best possible advice in this area is to go online and get complete, up-to-date instructions. This appendix, accordingly, includes information about where to go. You'll find specific guidelines right here for common-case installation scenarios; but if you don't find what you need, have a look at the online resources.

One way or another, the goal is to install the following:

- Ruby
- Rails
- A Web server
- A database system

Discussion of Web server and database systems installation and configuration is beyond the scope of this appendix. You can always use the WEBrick server, which comes with Ruby; most sites, however, use Apache or lightTPD in production. Rails works with many database systems, including MySQL, SQLite, and PostgreSQL. You'll find more information on the Rails Web site (see the next section).

Meanwhile, what follows here are some pointers to online resources, followed by common-case instructions for installing Ruby and Rails on both Windows and *nix (i.e., Linux, BSD, Solaris, OSX, and other Unix-like systems).

A.1 *Online resources for Ruby and Rails*

The Ruby language homepage is http://www.ruby-lang.org. You'll also find the ruby-docs page (http://www.ruby-doc.org) useful. The Ruby Language FAQ can be found at http://www.rubygarden.org/faq, and Ruby Garden (the same URL, without /faq) is also a good resource. It includes a Wiki (http://www.rubygarden.org/ruby) with a lot of information.

The main English-language general-purpose Ruby mailing list is `ruby-talk`, which is also a two-way mirror of the Usenet group `comp.lang.ruby` (accessible via Google Groups). Another important mailing list, although somewhat more specialized, is `ruby-core`, where Ruby language design and development issues are discussed. You can find information about subscribing to these lists at http://www.ruby-lang.org/en/20020104.html.

A great place to get Ruby advice is the `#ruby-lang` IRC channel on irc.freenode.net (or chat.freenode.net). If you ask too many Rails-specific questions, you'll be gently steered toward the Rails channel, `#rubyonrails`.

The Rails homepage is http://www.rubyonrails.com. Here you'll find a portal to a ton of information. Of particular interest is the Wiki (http://wiki.rubyonrails.org)—and, for installation information, the installation how-to page (http://wiki.rubyonrails.org/rails/pages/HowtosInstallation). This page will probably answer any questions you have about installing Rails.

You'll find up-to-date information about mailing lists and other Rails community resources at http://www.rubyonrails.org/community.

A.2 *Common-case instructions for installing Ruby and Rails*

What follows is some quick, common-case advice about installing Ruby and Rails. It isn't a substitute for what's online, but it covers a few common installation scenarios fully enough that it may help you get started.

The procedures addressed here are these:

1. Installing both Ruby and Rails on Windows
2. Installing Ruby from the source code on *nix systems
3. Installing Ruby with a native package manager on a *nix system
4. Installing the RubyGems package manager
5. Installing Rails with the RubyGems package manager

If you're running Windows, you may need only step 1 (section A.2.1). If you're running a *nix system, you'll probably do *either* step 2 or step 3 (sections A.2.2 and A.2.3) followed by *both* steps 4 and 5 (sections A.2.4 and A.2.5).

Again, this is not, and does not claim to be, true for every case. If what's here doesn't fit your case, look at the online resources.

A.2.1 *One-Click Ruby and Instant Rails for Windows*

If you're running Microsoft Windows, you can use the One-Click Ruby Installer, by Curt Hibbs. It installs the Ruby language, dozens of popular extensions, a syntax-highlighting editor, and the free electronic first edition of the book *Programming Ruby: The Pragmatic Programmer's Guide* on your system. You can find the One-Click Installer at http://rubyforge.org/projects/rubyinstaller. Once you've done that, you can install the RubyGems package manager and Rails (see sections A.2.4 and A.2.5).

Or you can do it all in one step using another tool by Curt Hibbs: the Instant Rails package for Windows (http://instantrails.rubyforge.org/wiki/wiki.pl). Instant Rails installs Ruby, Rails, the Apache Web server, and MySQL simultaneously.

As of this writing, Instant Rails is Windows-only, but plans are afoot to port it to Linux, BSD, and OSX.

A.2.2 *Installing from the source code on *nix systems*

To install Ruby from the source code, you have to get the source code. As of this writing, the latest stable release of Ruby is 1.8.4. To get this release and compile and install it, do the following or the equivalent (for example, you can use a different FTP client):

```
$ ftp ftp.ruby-lang.org
$ cd pub/ruby
$ get ruby-1.8.4.tar.gz
$ quit
$ gzip -dc ruby-1.8.4.tar.gz | tar xf_-
$ cd ruby-1.8.4
$./configure
$ make
$ sudo make install
```

These commands install the interpreter (ruby) to /usr/local/bin and the library files to /usr/local/lib/ruby/1.8.

A.2.3 *Installing Ruby with a package manager*

If your operating system or distribution has a native package manager, you may want to use it to download and install Ruby (rather than installing from source). Exactly what you need to do depends on your system and its package manager (rpm, apt, various port utilities, and so on). Use your package manager's query facilities to find out what Ruby package or packages are available.

Some systems and distributions split Ruby into multiple packages, which can be annoying because it means you can't be sure you're getting everything that comes with the standard distribution (and whether you're getting things that don't). Many users and administrators prefer to install Ruby from the source even if packages are available.

A.2.4 *Installing the RubyGems package manager*

The best way to install Rails on a *nix system is with the RubyGems package manager. The first step in the process is to install RubyGems itself.

The RubyGems project is hosted by RubyForge. The homepage for RubyGems is http://rubyforge.org/projects/rubygems. Look for the Latest File Releases list, and download the latest version of RubyGems.

You can download it either in tar/gzip format (`.tgz` file extension) or zip format (`.zip` extension). Once you have the file, unpack it using

```
$ gzip -dc rubygems-0.8.11.tgz | tar xf -
```

or

```
$ unzip rubygems-0.8.11.zip
```

This will create a directory with the same name as the version of RubyGems you're installing; in the case shown, the directory will be called `rubygems-0.8.11`. The `README` file in the `rubygems-0.8.11` directory includes installation instructions for the version of RubyGems you've downloaded. It also includes pointers to more detailed information about installing and running RubyGems.

A.2.5 *Installing Rails with RubyGems*

Once you've installed the RubyGems package manager, all you have to do to install the entire Rails suite (the `rails` program, ActiveRecord, ActionPack, and various support libraries) is

```
$ sudo gem install -y rails
```

To learn about upgrading to future versions of Rails, see the online documentation, which is always the most up-to-date source of information.

index